SUPERDIVERSITY

Superdiversity explores processes of diversification and the complex, emergent social configurations that now supersede prior forms of diversity in societies around the world. Migration plays a key role in these processes, bringing changes not just in social, cultural, religious, and linguistic phenomena but also in the ways that these phenomena combine with others like gender, age, and legal status.

The concept of superdiversity has been adopted by scholars across the social sciences in order to address a variety of forms, modes, and outcomes of diversification. Central to this field is the relationship between social categorization and social organization, including stratification and inequality. Increasingly complex categories of social "difference" have significant impacts across scales, from entire societies to individual identities. While diversification is often met with simplifying stereotypes, threat narratives, and expressions of antagonism, super-diversity encourages a perspective on difference as comprising multiple social processes, flexible collective meanings, and overlapping personal and group identities. A superdiversity approach encourages the re-evaluation and recognition of social categories as multidimensional, unfixed, and porous as opposed to views based on hardened, one-dimensional thinking about groups. Diversification and increasing social complexity are bound to continue, if not intensify, in light of climate change. This will have profound impacts on the nature of global migration, social relations, and inequalities.

Superdiversity presents a convincing case for recognizing new social formations created by changing migration patterns and calls for a rethinking of public policy and social scientific approaches to social difference. This introduction to the multi-disciplinary concept of superdiversity will be of considerable interest to students and researchers in a range of fields in the humanities and social sciences.

Steven Vertovec is Founding Director at the Max Planck Institute for the Study of Religious and Ethnic Diversity, Göttingen, Germany. Previously, he was Professor of Transnational Anthropology at the University of Oxford and Director of the British Economic and Social Research Council's Centre on Migration, Policy and Society (COMPAS). He is the author of *Transnationalism* (Routledge, 2009), *The Hindu Diaspora: Comparative Patterns* (Routledge, 2000), and *Hindu Trinidad: Religion, Ethnicity and Socio-economic Change* (Palgrave, 1992) and co-author of *Diversity and Contact: Immigration and Social Interaction in German Cities* (Palgrave, 2016). He is also editor/co-editor of numerous volumes, including *Conceiving Cosmopolitanism* (Oxford University Press, 2003), *The Multiculturalism Backlash* (Routledge, 2010), *Routledge International Handbook of Diversity Studies* (Routledge, 2015), *Diversities Old and New* (Palgrave, 2015), and *The Oxford Handbook of Superdiversity* (Oxford University Press, 2022).

SUPERDIVERSITY

Migration and Social Complexity

Steven Vertovec

Routledge
Taylor & Francis Group

LONDON AND NEW YORK

Designed cover image: Flickr (Chris Yates Studios)

First published 2023
by Routledge
4 Park Square, Milton Park, Abingdon, Oxon OX14 4RN

and by Routledge
605 Third Avenue, New York, NY 10158

Routledge is an imprint of the Taylor & Francis Group, an informa business

British Library Cataloguing-in-Publication Data
A catalogue record for this book is available from the British Library

ISBN: 978-0-415-83462-9 (hbk)
ISBN: 978-0-415-83463-6 (pbk)
ISBN: 978-0-203-50357-7 (ebk)

DOI: 10.4324/9780203503577

Typeset in Bembo
by KnowledgeWorks Global Ltd.

To Lia

CONTENTS

ILLUSTRATIONS

Figures

Tables

ACKNOWLEDGEMENTS

This book is long overdue, literally and figuratively. I was originally supposed to deliver the book manuscript to Routledge in 2015 but was unable to accomplish this due to a family tragedy. This knocked me off my feet for a long while. By the time I was able to pick up the book project once more, managerial duties and a barrage of other responsibilities and commitments always kept research and writing slow. Only with the Covid pandemic, it seems, did some space/time open up and allow me to get back to writing this. In the meantime, as the intervening years passed, my own thoughts on superdiversity, migration, and social complexity developed – not least stimulated by the discussions and work carried on at our Max Planck Institute. In this way, the book is overdue in terms of a device to express the development of my own thoughts on the topic as well as the development of the concept in the public and academic spheres where it has taken on a life of its own.

Across more than 15 years, from when I first cooked up the concept till now as I seek to embellish it, I have received help, feedback, criticism, and advice from a very wide set of people. Concerning the original work leading to the 2007 article in *Ethnic and Racial Studies* which really launched the concept into the academic sphere, I gained from important comments particularly from Robin Cohen, Alisdair Rogers, Susanne Wessendorf, Andreas Wimmer, Gerd Baumann, Danny Sriskandarajah, Sarah Kyambi, Dan Hiebert, David Ley, and the staff and students of the ESRC Centre on Migration, Policy and Society (COMPAS) at the University of Oxford. There, Alessio Cangiano also gave me special help with data. A joint fellowship from the Economic and Social Research Council (UK) and Social Science Research Council (USA) also importantly supported this work. I also gained much from discussions with participants in seminars at Harvard University and the University of British Columbia, and at conferences of the Swedish Anthropological Association and European Association of Social Anthropologists.

Since then, work leading up to this book has been bolstered by the help of excellent research assistants at the Max Planck Institute, especially Wiebke Unger, Margherita Cusmano, Zeynep Bozkurt, and Carolina Reiners. As with practically everything around my directorship and work, Jutta Esser has been at the centre, keeping it all together. Chris Kofri has undertaken an essential set of support tasks necessary to make the publication happen. Other Institute colleagues who have played important roles in helping me with research are Simone Dietrich, Renate Hägele, Ulrike Koecher, Norbert Winnige, Birgitt Sippel, Rami Higazi, and Alexei Matveev. A changing, but ever-intellectually dynamic and extremely interesting team of PhD students and postdocs at the Institute – who have gladly never been shy to criticize their boss! – have continuously stimulated my thoughts and kept me on my argumentative toes.

While of course I am solely responsible for the ideas, analyses, interpretations, and their possible flaws throughout this work, I have been fortunate to be enormously influenced by large number of outstanding thinkers. This commenced while I was a student at various stages, with inspiration and guidance by my mentors David Carrasco, Ninian Smart, and J. Clyde Mitchell. As a young scholar and through the present, I have especially valued the feedback, ideas, and views of my friend and occasional co-author Robin Cohen. During my Oxford years when the superdiversity concept was taking shape, I was fortunate to be surrounded by extremely knowledgeable experts who greatly influenced my thought, particularly Stephen Castles, Bridget Anderson, Nick Van Hear, and Sarah Spencer. Since commencing my position at the Max Planck Institute, I have benefitted enormously from a special set of scholarly friends to whom I have regularly and happily returned (in idyllic gatherings at Harnack House Berlin and Schloss Ringberg, Bavaria) to gather their views. This includes Ralph Grillo, Mary Waters, Phil Kasinitz, Nancy Foner, Dan Hiebert, Brenda Yeoh, Karen Schoenwaelder, Loren Landau, Thomas Hylland Eriksen, Marco Martiniello, and the late, great Jan Blommaert. Other close colleagues who have helped me shape ideas include Nando Sigona, Jenny Phillimore, Peter Scholten, Miles Hewstone, Ewa Morawska, Douglas Massey, Rogers Brubaker, Andreas Wimmer, Michèle Lamont, Paul Spoonley, Boris Nieswand, Matthias Koenig, Rainer Bauböck, Thomas Faist, Virginie Guiraudon, Ajay Gandhi, Phil Gorski, John Solomos, Jeremy Walton, Lucas Drouhot, Maria Schiller, Georg Diez, and Van Tran. Just as importantly, I have greatly benefitted from the ongoing work and thoughts of outstanding former students, especially Fran Meissner, Alan Gamlen, Susanne Wessendorf, Tilmann Heil, and Sakura Yamamura. At Routledge, Chris Parry, Rebecca Brennan, Diana Ciobotea, and Alyson Claffey have importantly helped bring this publication to fruition.

Part of the work that went into this book was supported by an Advanced Investigator Grant (269784) from the European Research Council. Supportive work environments and stimulating discussions with students and colleagues on relevant themes took place in seminars at the Max Planck Institute, Autonomous

University Barcelona, University of Tübingen, University of Göttingen, and during my visiting professorships in recent years at Erasmus University Rotterdam and Monash University.

Materials have been reproduced or drawn from a number of my previous publications, especially: Chapter 2 – Vertovec (2007); Chapter 3 – Vertovec (2019); Chapter 4 – Vertovec (2012, 2017, 2018, 2020a); Chapter 5 – Vertovec (2019); Chapter 6 – Vertovec (2021); and Chapter 7 – Vertovec (2020a, 2020b).

References

Vertovec, S. 2007. "Super-diversity and its implications," *Ethnic and Racial Studies* 30(6): 1024–54 https://doi.org/10.1080/01419870701599465

Vertovec, S. 2012. "'Diversity' and the social imaginary," *Archives Européennes de Sociologie/ European Journal of Sociology* 53(3): 287–312 https://doi.org/10.1017/s000397561200015x

Vertovec, S. 2017. "Mooring, migration milieus and complex explanation," *Ethnic and Racial Studies* 40(9): 1574–81 https://doi.org/10.1080/01419870.2017.1308534

Vertovec, S. 2018. "What's the matter with Rotterdam?" in *Coming to Terms with Superdiversity*, P. Scholten and M. Crul (eds.), Cham: Springer, pp. 337–44 https://doi. org/10.1007/978-3-319-96041-8_13

Vertovec, S. 2019. "Talking around super-diversity," *Ethnic and Racial Studies* 42: 125–39 https://doi.org/10.1080/01419870.2017.1406128

Vertovec, S. 2020a. "Afterword: "The work of 'integration'," in *Digesting Difference*, K. McKowen and J. Borneman (eds.), Cham: Palgrave Macmillan, pp. 251–66 https:// doi.org/10.1007/978-3-030-49598-5_12

Vertovec, S. 2020b. "Low-skilled migrants after Covid19: Singapore futures?" COMPAS Coronavirus and Mobility Forum blog, https://www.compas.ox.ac.uk/2020/low-skilled-migrants-after-covid-19-singapore-futures/

Vertovec, S. 2021. "The social organization of difference," *Ethnic and Racial Studies* 44(8): 1273–95 https://doi.org/10.1080/01419870.2021.1884733

1

INTRODUCTION

In 1985, the influential American anthropologist Clifford Geertz delivered one of the prestigious Tanner Lectures on Human Values. The purpose of his lecture, entitled "The Uses of Diversity," was to address not just certain globally changing empirical conditions, but also the ways that those conditions are conceived. The set of changes that Geertz described was that the world was increasingly becoming more connected and more mobile (still a rather novel notion in the 1980s), and hence "cultures" could not be situated in specific places (if they ever could be). Another, related point of his lecture was that any idea of social difference that was based on fixed and bounded identity categories was changing too. Geertz emphasized that these trends do not stop people from ill-treating others based on ethnocentrism and crude stereotypes. What's needed in light of these matters, he urged, is a conceptual re-orientation to social difference that might, quite literally and thoroughly, change our minds. "It is in this," Geertz (1986: 274) said, "strengthening the power of our imaginations to grasp what is in front of us, that the uses of diversity, and of the study of diversity, lie."

The global trends that Geertz spoke of in the 1980s have continued through the present day, albeit with different speeds, shapes, factors and outcomes from place to place. Societies around the world are diversifying profoundly. This takes many forms, manners, and courses – indeed, we might best talk of many overlapping, entangled and mutually determining diversifications – from the skewed globalization of neoliberal practices and spread of consumer goods, popular media, and modes of communication, through the diffusion of ideas, policies and social movements, to the multiplication of lifestyles, family structures, identities, moral codes, and social practices. Global migration is a key component of diversification processes. Most obviously, this is because migrants tend to bring newness to their societies of arrival, influencing the nature of social categories such as race, ethnicity and nationality, contributing to the corpus of cultural forms including

DOI: 10.4324/9780203503577-1

styles, cuisines, and artistic expressions, expanding sets of linguistic and semiotic practices, enlarging the array and expressions of religious traditions, and extending or initiating social and political initiatives. Diversification is also inherently bound up with many kinds of inequalities, too. Who or what changes by way of diversification is both determined by and a determinant of patterns of social stratification. Diversification is thus one of the foremost social processes of our age. As we consider the future, impacted profoundly by climate change, it is clear that diversification will continue to shape societies the world over – again in uneven and unfair ways as some people, depending on their combination of characteristics, will suffer climate impacts far more than others.

Superdiversity is a concept coined to convey the multidimensional nature of diversification processes and how these condition social patterns and stratification. It was conceived by me, and is still largely invoked by others, as a way to think about and approach research concerning contemporary migration processes and outcomes. The concept of superdiversity also offers a way to consider other concurrent modes of diversification. Superdiversity and diversification are notions pointing to the ongoing creation of ever more complex societies. What is considered in the idea of superdiversity, what is entailed in processes of diversification, and how can we understand the rise of new forms of social complexity? These are among the main questions engaged by this book.

What's at stake?

Diversification entails a fundamental mode of social transformation. With this statement, I draw upon important academic works on the idea of social transformation to indicate a kind and degree of change that cuts across economic, political, social and cultural terrains as well as macro- to micro-scales (see Smelser 1998; Wiltshire 2001; Castles 2001, 2010; Rosenau 2003). When we speak of social transformation, we are talking about extensive shifts in the ways societies are organized and in the ways we think about them. As societies diversify across a range of scales, from the national, urban, and neighbourhood to the classroom, workplace and local park, inherent features of the social are subject to change. This includes the ways we conceptually categorize one another, the attitudes we have towards those deemed however "different," the interactions and practices that arise or are reproduced by encounters with others, and the social positions or statuses that both underpin and develop out of all of these. Diversification and evolving dynamics of diversity affect changes at the core of social structure and social relations. For these reasons, following Geertz, the study of diversification and diversity must be one of the most fundamental areas of social science inquiry. It involves the attempt to understand how we live, how we can live and how we are going to live together as intrinsically distinctive people.

The study of diversification and diversity itself is certainly not new, nor of course is the phenomenon of highly diverse societies. Since ancient times, most societies and certainly empires in the past were highly diverse linguistically, religiously, and in terms of what we now describe as ethnicity (see among others, Grillo 1998, Greatrex and Mitchell 2000; Hoerder 2002; Heather 2010; McInerney 2014; Blanton 2015; Vertovec 2015). The distinguished historian William McNeill (1986) famously asserted that "polyethnicity" was the condition describing practically all societies throughout history. Further, he noted, the idea of societies being actually or ideally "homogeneous" (ethnically and racially, linguistically and religiously) was something that arose as a kind of historical aberration, based on modernist nation-building pursuits especially in Western Europe since about 1750. However, such a presumption of homogeneity-as-norm and diversity-as-exception has long shaped not only national narratives and policies, but social scientific paradigms as well (coinciding with the "container model" of nation states upon which "methodological nationalism" is based; cf. Beck 2000, 2002, 2004; Wimmer and Glick Schiller 2002). Accordingly, we have had numerous sociological studies of what diversity, arguably seen as a deviation from an ideal state, "does" to societies. This includes well known (and criticized) studies of diversity as: a threat to social cohesion (Putnam 2007), a hindrance to political and economic development (Alesina and Ferrara 2005), or a significant if not problematic factor in the redistribution of public goods (Singh and Vom Hau 2016). This is countered by more positive views, still based on a kind of diversity-as-exception premise, such as that the introduction of diversity is a key to stimulating creativity and innovation in urban settings (Florida 2002) and similarly to building more effective, problem-solving management teams (Page 2007). For a long time – but seemingly exacerbated more recently – the belief that diversification is a threat to homogeneous nation-states underlays much right-wing nationalism as well.

While few societies have actually ever been "homogeneous," the idea of the homogeneous nation has without a doubt played a central role in creating hierarchical social structures and systems of inequality, greatly affecting those who have been categorized as outside the homogenous norm. Thus, it also provides the basis of most national discourses and policies concerning social "integration" (Favell 2022). This is a key reason why it is essential to consider dynamics of social categorization when seeking to understand how societies (again, right down to micro-scales) are organized and reproduced. It is particularly essential during times, such as the present, when diversifications of many kinds are proceeding, if not increasing, apace.

For some years at the University of Oxford, I taught a postgraduate course on the Anthropology of Cultural Complexity. This included critical reviews of thinking about historical and cross-cultural forms of social organization, through to considering what phenomena and processes are at play in so-called plural societies, border cultures, syncretism and creolization, global-local relations, diasporas and transnationalism. As my students and I examined a wide assortment of relevant literature, it became clearer each term that whatever we consider to be social and cultural complexity entails not just structures of power and sets of social relations, but inherently the ways people construct and implement conceptions about the nature of groups and identities. It is both social organization and social categories that combine to produce ever more complex social dynamics, as well as modes of stratification. This view runs through the book and is the focus of theoretical development in the last chapters.

Once again, now is a vital time to study diversification and forms of diversity. In the 21st century, "The world is much more diverse on multiple dimensions and at many levels, typified by the salience of differences and their dynamic intersections" (Jones and Dovidio 2018: 45). The reasons for this are numerous, including the facts that:

- worldwide, societies are diversifying – ethnically/racially, linguistically, religiously, and along several other characteristics – considerably through migration;
- in many countries, even apart from migration, populations are also diversifying through natural demographic growth within a range of existing categories, along with a marked rise in the number of people identifying with "mixed" backgrounds;
- there is more evidence and public concern about growing social and economic inequalities – disparities surrounding resources, opportunities, material outcomes, representation and relative social status – and the ways in which these are disproportionately distributed in relation to categories of social "difference";
- rapid diversification is known to stimulate support for populist right-wing parties, while significantly at the same time, as measured in academic studies and public opinion surveys, pro-diversity attitudes remain high and stable. Such divergent trends and patterns of attitudes contribute to growing social and political fragmentation of societies; and
- while an escalating number of cities around the world are becoming what some, correctly or incorrectly, term "majority-minority," everyday urban exposure to complex forms of diversity is now often considered commonplace or "normal."

Superdiversity is a concept offered to stimulate an understanding of the intersection of multiple characteristics that comprise contemporary processes of diversification. With new modalities, permutations and effects of diversification, new concepts can serve to help academics, policymakers, practitioners and the general public gain better and more productive grasps of what's happening around them. In this way, the concept arose as a proposed corrective to existing concepts, and one more fitting to a changing reality.

The superdiversity concept

Multiculturalism, interculturalism, and "diversity" itself, as a normative concept and policy term, have been notions in play across the public sphere for many years. They have done much work, not least by way of providing a view onto the representation of "difference" in society. Further, these terms have been operationalized in social policies and institutional practices to variable effect. Inherent to each – or at least within prominent interpretations of each – is a kind of premise that social difference is something that can or should be "managed," usually from the top down (i.e., arranged by a state agency or public organization). A common critique follows, namely that each of these terms tends to be based on, or at least replicate, a rather flat, homogenizing or unidimensional view of difference: that is, that every person belongs to one or another group that can be represented by the presence of a single individual in an organization or activity. This is well encapsulated in the critical words of one British civil servant, who said: "If you think that adding me to your Board creates diversity, you'd be wrong. I am middle aged, in senior management and Oxbridge educated. The fact that I am Asian does not make any difference. On a charity Board I am just more of the same" (in Fanshawe and Sriskandarajah 2010: 25). Such approaches to difference may tend to equalize categories: race is treated as equivalent to gender which is equivalent to sexuality or disability, etc. Questions of dissimilar social positions and power relations might also often be sidelined in these approaches to difference as well. Debates over the pros and cons of multiculturalism, interculturalism, and "diversity" very much continue in both academic and institutional domains (see for instance, Vertovec 2012; Meer et al. 2016; Grillo 2018; Carlsson and Pijpers 2021; Loh 2022).

In fundamental ways, the concept of superdiversity arose as a critique of British multiculturalism specifically. For many years before I developed the superdiversity concept, I had written about a range of problems associated with notions of multiculturalism (including Vertovec 1996, 1998). These critiques resonated with those of many colleagues at the time, who also thought that multiculturalist frameworks tended to foster rather staid, essentialist and bounded ideas of ethnic groups and cultures, created a kind of internal colonialism if not system inter-ethnic competition, and didn't adequately address inequality. Moreover, multiculturalist views of British society completely ignored real changes that were taking place regarding new, non-British populations. That is, British public discussions of multiculturalism centred almost entirely on Asian (here, Indian, Pakistani and Bangladeshi) and West Indian (largely Jamaican but also Trinidadian, Barbadian, Guyanese and other small Caribbean) categories. For decades these categories certainly pertained to the largest segments of post-migration populations. However, by the early 2000s, significant changes to migration and population were underway.

An important stimulus for developing the superdiversity concept came when I saw a small graphic in *The Economist* in the early 2000s. This depicted migrant inflows to the UK between 1993 and 2002 by way of the broad country of origin categories of: UK (for return migrants), EU (essentially free movement of workers), Old Commonwealth (particularly Canada, Australia and New Zealand), New Commonwealth (countries that became independent after WWII, especially India, Pakistan and several Caribbean nations), and "Other" (residually relating to the rest of the world). From the 1950s to 1970s, immigration to

Britain was dominated by New Commonwealth origin; thereafter, most immigration in this category has been by way of family reunification channels. The *Economist* graphic depicted relatively stable and equivalent numbers in the early to mid-1990s, specifically 20–30,000 people per year arriving in each category. But from around 1997, the "Other" category grew massively, amounting to some 200,000 immigrants by 2002. It was clear to me that the conventional understanding of British social diversity needed to be re-addressed. I was intrigued, and sought to research the questions: who are these "Other," what is shaping their migration, what are their characteristics, what are the effects of this migration shift on British society, and how might it challenge the way that migrants and ethnicity are conceived? This research entailed the data presented in a Working Paper (Vertovec 2006), which led eventually to a journal article (Vertovec 2007, reproduced here as Chapter 2).

Boiled down to its basics, the concept of superdiversity provides a way to think about multidimensionality or intersectionality with regard to new patterns of migration. Firstly, I point to increasing movements of people from more varied backgrounds represented by more differentiated categories. Not only are there more, smaller cohorts of people from a wider range of origin countries, but I point to shifting flows of people with wide-ranging nationalities, ethnicities, languages, religions, gender balances, age ratios, human capital, transnational practices and, especially, migration channels and legal statuses. Secondly, I emphasize the shifting combinations of these backgrounds and categories, such that entire cohorts of migrants become characterized by particular intersections. Examples include the fact that (at the time of writing the 2007 article) 71% of Filipinos in the UK were young women with visas to work in the health service, while 71% of Algerians were older males who were mostly asylum-seekers prohibited from working. The inadequacy of thinking of multiculturalism and diversity solely in terms of ethnic groups seemed clear. One of the main reasons for stressing a multidimensional approach has been to stress that difference and diversity needs to be understood via "a dynamic interplay of variables among an increased number of new, small and scattered, multiple-origin, transnationally connected, socio-economically differentiated and legally stratified immigrants" (Vertovec 2007: 1024)

The concept of superdiversity was created for purposes of denoting these kinds of important shifts in migration patterns and social outcomes. In itself it does not offer explanations for why these have occurred, but rather prompts the quest for explanations (see Chapter 3). As I have written elsewhere:

> I must first stress that super-diversity is not a theory. I regard theory as providing an account of how-things-work (inherent relations or causalities). Nor is it a hypothesis (or to-be-tested theory). As its author (Vertovec 2007), I always intended super-diversity to be first and foremost a descriptive concept, constructed for a special purpose in order to tie together a set of observed, co-occurring phenomena that supersede phenomena that

were previously evident (hence the "super–" prefix). For this purpose, super-diversity was coined to draw attention to complex – and arguably new – patterns in migration phenomena over the past three decades or so.

Vertovec (2017: 1575)

The multidimensional aspect is crucial, not least to avoid a misunderstanding that has often subsequently arisen. That is, superdiversity does not suggest a kind of threshold. I have often been asked, "At what point does diversity become superdiversity?" As I describe in Chapter 3, many people have simply assumed that superdiversity merely means "more ethnicity" within a national or urban population. This misconstrual is what Ralph Grillo (2015) calls "Superdiversity Lite." It is in contrast to "Superdiversity Heavy," which is the original meaning relating to new, complex configurations of multiple categories concerning migrants. So the diversity-superdiversity distinction is not a matter of quantity, but of the co-occurrence and mutual influence of a number of classifications.

Following the growing interest in superdiversity, at least one similar notion has been proposed by scholars, that is "hyperdiversity." This was the central organizing concept for the EU-funded DiverCities project, initiated by the late Ronald van Kempen, which explored ways that urban diversity can be harnessed as an asset to foster social cohesion and economic development. The project team engaged the concept of superdiversity and used it as a springboard for their work (Oosterlynck et al. 2019). In order to shift attention from superdiversity's concern with migration-driven diversification, they proposed the term "hyper-diversity" to describe urban developments not just with respect to ethnicity, but also in terms of general social lifestyles, attitudes and activities (Taşan-Kok et al. 2017). The project was certainly interesting and produced many valuable findings. However, I remain sceptical of their central concept. This scepticism (not solely of the DiverCities project, but also towards others who have talked of "hyperdiversity") was voiced by Fran Meissner and me in this way:

In some spheres, commentators speak of the growth of "hyperdiversity" (or use this term interchangeably with super-diversity). We suggest that this is not helpful for two reasons. The first is that hyperdiversity tends to convey the idea that we are merely faced with "more diversity" in terms of ethnicity. This is a unidimensional model that misses the main point argued by super-diversity (again, that several dimensions of migration flows have been changing at once). The second reason why hyperdiversity is an unfortunate term is that "hyper–" can inherently suggest that something is overexcited, out of control and therefore generally negative or undesirable (like hyperactivity or hyperinflation). Again, "super–" is our preferred modifier in order to emphasize the sense of superseding, or addressing what is "above and beyond" what was previously there.

Meissner and Vertovec (2015: 5)

Thus, while I continue to somewhat distance myself from "hyperdiversity" and remain grounded in superdiversity as a core concept and approach, I do share with the DiverCities team a common concern. That is, we need to recognize that all people do not have a single identity but belong to diverse categories such as gender, race, class, ability, sexual orientation, and other axes of identity, all of which intersect and interact in a variety of ways and with various effects. Such a common perspective is part of what we might call the "long arm of anti-essentialism."

Having spent my post-doctoral and early career in the UK during the 1990s and early 2000s, I was steeped in an intellectual environment dominated by numerous concepts and approaches to migration and social difference that – especially looking back – all inherently shared a methodology based in anti-essentialism. Essentialism was the term (which sometimes turned into a kind of swearword or internecine accusation; see Grillo 1998: 195–200) with reference to depictions of any social category as having hard boundaries and an unchanging, ontological quality or trait – an essence – shared by all deemed to be within it (see Sayer 1997). Critiques of essentialist notions, particularly gender-based, were central in much feminist theory at the time (e.g., Witt 1995; Grillo 1995; also see Mikkola 2017). Anti-essentialism, as a stance against simplistic and unidimensional views of social categories, is inherent to numerous other key concepts that have been developed since the 1990s, including: intersectionality (Crenshaw 1991); segmented assimilation (Portes and Zhou 1993); ethnic options (Waters 1990); postethnicity (Hollinger 1995); hyphenated identities (e.g., Verkuyten 2004); creolization (e.g., Hannerz 1987); hybridity (e.g., Werbner and Modood 1997); Third Space (Bhabha 1994); between two cultures (e.g., Watson 1997); biculturalism or dual identity (e.g., Yamada and Singelis 1999); multiculture (e.g., Gilroy 1993); bright versus blurred social boundaries (Alba 2005); transnationalism (e.g., Glick Schiller et al. 1992); diasporas (e.g., Cohen 1997); and cosmopolitanism (e.g., Vertovec and Cohen 2002). All of these are important forerunners, if not direct stimuli, of the concept of superdiversity. That is, like these coevolving concepts, superdiversity is also built on the perspective that no single category is so bounded and ontological, and that it is not one, but a confluence of several open and ever-changing categories that matters most to people's lives, their social positions and the social structures around them.

These antecedent, anti-essential concepts helped me in thinking through the changes to global migration flows mentioned earlier. Yet somehow none of them was describing exactly what I wanted to put my finger on. I wanted to acknowledge their insights, but still point to the kinds of transformations that I was seeing in and through the British migration data. I wanted to capture, especially, both an intersectionality of categories (specifically concerning migration, not solely the categories of gender-race-class with which much of the existing literature dealt) and new configurations of features surrounding migrant populations. Superdiversity was coined as a way to capture these processes and phenomena in an attempt to contribute to the corpus of social scientific concepts and literature.

The substantial social scientific interest in the concept has not been entirely surprising (while some of its interpretations certainly have been; see Chapter 3). The more we have moved into the 21st Century, the more have scholars observed complexifying trends and searched for ways to describe and theorize them. This was meaningfully pointed out by the late, prominent German sociologist Ulrich Beck. He (2011: 53) saw "the superdiversity of cities and societies of the 21st century" and suggested that their rise is "both inevitable (because of global flows of migration, flows of information, capital, risks, etc.) and politically challenging." However, he added,

> It is in this sense that over the last decades the cultural, social and political landscapes of diversity are changing radically, but we still use old maps to orientate ourselves. In other words, my main thesis is: *we do not even have the language through which contemporary superdiversity in the world can be described, conceptualized, understood, explained and researched.*
>
> *(Ibid., italics in original)*

In this way, superdiversity has been a generative concept, stimulating works in a tremendous variety of fields. In June 2022, Google Scholar indicates that the original *Ethnic and Racial Studies* journal article (Vertovec 2007) has been cited over 7,200 times, while the COMPAS Working Paper on superdiversity (Vertovec 2006), on which the 2007 article is based, has been cited over 850 times. These academic citations are found in journals across a span of disciplines including Sociology, Anthropology, Geography, Political Science, Sociolinguistics and History, and particularly in the research fields of Migration Studies and Social Policy. Beyond articles, at least a dozen books on superdiversity have been published, too. These include titles such as *On Superdiversity* (Ramadan 2011), *Superdiversity in the Heart of Europe* (Geldof 2016), *Diversity and Super-diversity* (De Fina et al. 2017) and *The Routledge Handbook of Language and Superdiversity* (Creese and Blackledge 2018a).

Following Beck, much of this profuse scholarly interest and endeavour triggered by the superdiversity concept has represented a kind of search for language and lines of thought to describe ever better various, often interdependent, contemporary and emergent modes and forms of social complexity. As stated by Angela Creese and Adrian Blackledge (2018b: xxiii), "More than merely describing the diversification of diversity as a result of recent migration, superdiversity has the potential to offer an interdisciplinary perspective on change and complexity in changing social and cultural worlds." That's why, as a way of developing the approach and insights offered by the superdiversity concept, this book moves from discussions of the concept and it uses to related forms of diversification, to responses to processes of diversification and superdiversity, to an explicit concern with emergent features of social complexity more broadly. Running through all of these topics are concerns with diversification, categorization and the shaping of multiple categories, mutually conditioning processes, social stratification and inequality. In these ways, each chapter is intended to add something to our broader understanding of complexification processes within the co-dependent realms of social categorizations and social formations.

Chapter synopses

The material compiled for this book is wide-ranging, entailing an enterprise conjoining many approaches and disciplines. This kind of synthesis draws on many years of experience, initially by early training in both Anthropology and the multidisciplinary field of Religious Studies. This was followed by successive postdoctoral fellowships and jobs in university departments of Anthropology, Geography and Sociology. I have also had a career with positions traversing American, British and German intellectual environments. Finally, I believe that I learned much about academic cross-fertilization while serving as Founding Director of three major interdisciplinary institutions: namely, the British Economic and Social Research Council (ESRC) Transnational Communities Programme, ESRC Centre on Migration, Policy and Society (COMPAS), and the Max Planck Institute for the Study of Religious and Ethnic Diversity. Although I would still hold that there is no single or even ideal way to "do inter-disciplinarity," I believe these experiences helped me to be able to make connections, "translate" and develop common conceptual frameworks spanning several social sciences. Disciplinary purists may not like the ways that I draw from otherwise distinct methods and bodies of terminology and theory, but I believe this is absolutely necessary if we are to gain better purchase on our attempts to grasp complex social processes, forms and dynamics.

Although I have done a certain amount of research in places like Trinidad, Singapore and South Africa, I am fully aware that most examples in this book draw from European and North American contexts. This reliance on the Global North certainly has serious limitations if not drawbacks. However, I have to write with confidence about contexts I know best. I try to indicate literature from contexts in the Global South as and where I can, since most of the processes and phenomena I discuss are certainly to be found in these parts of the world too. In any case, it is not for me to decide or impose my conceptual frameworks on these locations, but for local voices to draw upon or critique these ideas in light of the contexts that they themselves know best. This has certainly been the case with the concept of superdiversity, which has indeed been taken up extensively in and by scholars of the Global South.

And so to the Chapter summaries. Given that I can by no means assume that the reader is familiar with the original *Ethnic and Racial Studies* article which has made an impact on the field, this is reproduced in its entirely as Chapter 2. Much of the rest of the book refers to this primary publication, so it is useful to have it incorporated. This piece is where I introduce the concept as a way to make sense of changes in the nature of diversity – both its forms and its representation. I draw on a range of data in the UK to indicate shifts in migrant populations across key categories such as county of origin, gender, age, language, religion and legal status. Significantly, the fluctuating combinations of these categories across sets of migrant newcomers were seen to change the social configuration of London and Britain. The emergent nature of migrant-driven diversification *superseded* the configurations of diversity in Britain that preceded them – hence I called it *super*diversity. Beyond showing these changes, the article draws attention to some of the challenges this changing reality poses to certain areas of research and to social policy.

As mentioned previously, this 2007 *Ethnic and Racial Studies* article and its concept of superdiversity quickly gained traction across the social sciences, particularly in Europe. In a handful of years, it became and remains the most cited article in the leading journal's history. However, the ways in which the concept has been understood, used, abused, criticized and utilized as a springboard for theoretical and methodological development are many. Chapter 3 reviews the multiple meanings of superdiversity as they appear in a now considerable literature across the social sciences. This includes a typology of eight ways in which superdiversity has been invoked. That is, as: a marker of very much diversity; a context or backdrop to for research studies; a description of "more ethnicity"; a call to move beyond ethnicity in social analysis; a multidimensional reconfiguration of social categories; the grounds for a methodological reassessment of a field or discipline; a way of addressing emergent social complexities (around globalization and migration, ethnic categories, and new social formations); and the basis for addressing a field of political policy and governance. Special attention is given to Sociolinguistics, within which an entire new field of "sociolinguistic superdiversity" has arisen, and History, in which experts have debated superdiversity's "newness" and effects. I also address some important criticisms that have been made around the concept, especially with regard to notions of race and racism, power, colonialism, and the academic endeavour itself. Even if sometimes based on misnomers, these are healthy and useful conversations to have. If it has achieved nothing else, it seems that the concept of superdiversity, "with all the semantic breath and defining ramifications that characterize it, has opened an interpretive door, and made possible an analytical framework that differs from the rest" (López Peláez et al. 2022: 161).

Some scholars, including myself and my colleague Fran Meissner, suggested that superdiversity addresses not just an emergent social condition but a variety of interconnected processes of diversification that lead to it, sustain it and stem from it. Chapter 4 describes a number of these processes, especially around migration-driven and demographically arising modalities. Migration-driven diversification entails major transformations of international migration flows over the past thirty years or so. People are increasingly moving for more complex reasons in terms of various, mixed and compounded causes spanning political, social, economic, demographic and environmental spheres. This is linked to the fact that more people are moving across borders from more countries. At the same time, migration categories and legal statuses have become ever more perplex — that is, complicated, confounding and designed to hamper, sort and stratify migrants in their countries of destination. These, in themselves, are a source of much inequality. Yet even without migration-driven diversifications, many countries are diversifying demographically or in terms of official state categories such as race and ethnicity. The demographic makeup of cities (especially in the Global North, but also in the South) is diversifying in several ways while economic hierarchies largely remain. Other significant features of demographic change include: the differential ethnoracial profiles of contrasting age cohorts; the marked rise in the number of people identifying as "mixed," a development calling into question the nature of official categories themselves; and the proliferation of languages and innovative language practices in given localities, leading to both new modes of discrimination and to intriguing if not exciting new forms of communication.

How do people react to these kinds of diversification and superdiversity appearing around them? Chapter 5 examines some of the main public responses to diversification. This includes a look at the seeming paradox that, according to surveys, many people generally accept if not value the *current* levels of difference and diversity in their country or immediate living environment, but express anxiety about *increasing* levels. In order to address this paradox, the chapter approaches the topic by asking: what do people actually know, think, and understand about the diversification of their societies, and how do they react perceptually, socially and politically? What is it about increasing diversification that especially prompts negative reactions? A key to assessing these matters lies in the nature of social categorization, or how people construct categories to make sense of the social world, and how they place others in them. At the core of the ways such categories are often made and maintained in much public understanding are a set of important conceptual premises or outlooks: groupism (an assumption that society is comprised of numerous bounded, fixed, internally homogeneous groups), singular affiliation (a belief that everyone pre-eminently belongs to one or another significant group), culturalism (a view that cultures are neat, discrete packages of immutable traits), and racialization (the idea that culture and group belonging are natural or genetic). These premises tend to support the presumption that there must be some kind of threshold beyond which "too much" diversity will have unwanted consequences. This is a central reason for anxieties around diversification. Yet the chapter also includes a look at several prominent theories concerning negative public responses to diversification. Features of such negative responses are often stoked and played upon by right-wing politicians. Conversely, the emergence of positive attitudes stemming from diversification are examined, as well, especially with regard to longstanding ideas around contact theory. That is, research shows how even in cases where diversification is at first reacted to negatively, over time and with increasing contact between people, attitudes toward difference considerably improve. Indeed, important findings across 46 countries shows that the perception of diversification itself serves to break down crude conceptualizations and stereotypes, leading to more positive social relations over time.

All of these topics signalled by superdiversity – changing migration configurations, varieties of diversification, modes of social categorization and contrasting responses to them – together entail features of social complexification. In order to better help meet the challenge, expounded earlier by Beck (2011: 53), of finding "the language through which contemporary superdiversity in the world can be described, conceptualized, understood, explained and researched," Chapter 6 explores the ways we might consider social complexity. Within Anthropology, complexity has long been regarded as an evolutionary feature of social organization, with societies incrementally becoming more complex (especially stratified and role differentiated) over time. Yet some anthropologists, namely Fredrik Barth, Ulf Hannerz and Thomas Hylland Eriksen, have also crucially stressed the complexity of human meanings – grounded in differential social positions – as fundamental components of social complexity as well. While bearing these insights in mind, the chapter draws on some central notions from complexity science (such as multiple causation, non-linearity and emergence) before returning to the realm of meanings, in this case the idea of social differences and social categorization as discussed in Chapter 5. Especially with regard to examples around race and ethnicity, gender and sexuality, religion, and language, we can observe how many basic social categories are being unmade, made, mixed and multiplied in ways that serve not only to make societies more complex, but to create and sustain structures of what has been called complex inequality. These are processes that occur across online and offline practices, too. These multiplicities of categorization and identification are not just evident across society, but within individuals. Therefore, the chapter rounds off with an exposition of Social Identity Complexity theory in contemporary Social Psychology. This entails the ways and degrees to which individuals are aware of their own distinct multiple identity categories. Extensive research in this field shows that when individuals rely less on singular, essentialized categories of identification and have more awareness of their own identity complexity, the more likely they are to develop positive attitudes and interactions with others. In conditions of increasing superdiversity, this finding holds much potential for mitigating negative responses to diversification and improving social relationships more broadly. Perhaps this is in line with the hopes of author Suketu Mehta, who writes:

> We classify people in huge categories: blacks, whites, migrants, trans, feminists, police, Democrats, Republicans. And then each member of that category has to walk around with the heavy weight of this classification on their head. Within each group, we are assumed to be fungible. The individual human being is complex... Diversity, or heterogeneity, will save us.
>
> *2021*

The concluding Chapter 7 recaps central discussions and points made throughout the book. These are important, it is argued, as superdiversity, diversification, and their relations to social stratification are bound to continue if not magnify in a future conditioned by climate change and its effects on global migration.

Enhanced understandings of social complexity will be critical for the future of social science. A significant base for such understandings is the recognition of social categories as multiple, unfixed and porous as opposed to views of social categories based on groupism, singular affiliation, culturalism, racialization and linguistic boundedness. Such a perspective can be enhanced not just within academia, but in public life as well. In this chapter, it is suggested that interventions in policy, political representation and information campaigns might support the shift to more widespread rethinking of social categories. One of the main points of this chapter is that, in ever-complexifying contexts of superdiversity, in order to promote more complex understanding of social categories, we should not to do away altogether with group categories but foster awareness of *category plus* – that is, the recognition that individuals are always part of more than one category, and any category involves people with more that than identity.

Superdiversity is a concept intended primarily to help an observer gain a perspective to interpret what is going on by way of the diversification of societies. The trends are of utmost significance to how societies do and can work, how social structures do and can function, and how people do and can treat one another. To echo Geertz: how we conceive and think about difference does and can have considerable impacts outside of the conceptual realm. It is hoped that the concept of superdiversity, along with other ideas offered in this book, might have such positive bearing.

References

Alba, R. 2005. "Bright vs. blurred boundaries: Second-generation assimilation and exclusion in France, Germany, and the United States," *Ethnic and Racial Studies* 28: 20–49 https://doi.org/10.1080/0141987042000280003

Alesina, A. and E. L. Ferrara 2005. "Ethnic diversity and economic performance," *Journal of Economic Literature* 43(3): 762–800 https://doi.org/10.1257/002205105774431243

Beck, U. 2000. *What Is Globalization?* Cambridge: Polity Press.

Beck, U. 2002. "The terrorist threat: World risk society revisited," *Theory, Culture & Society* 19(4): 39–55 https://doi.org/10.1177/0263276402019004003

Beck, U. 2004. "Cosmopolitan realism: On the distinction between cosmopolitanism in philosophy and the social sciences," *Global Networks* 4(2): 131–56 https://doi.org/10.1111/j.1471-0374.2004.00084.x

Beck, U. 2011. "Multiculturalism or cosmopolitanism: How can we describe and understand the diversity of the world?" *Social Sciences in China* 32(4): 52–58 https://doi.org/10.1080/02529203.2011.625169

Bhabha, H. 1994. *The Location of Culture*, Abingdon: Routledge

Blanton, R. E. 2015. "Theories of ethnicity and the dynamics of ethnic change in multiethnic societies," *Proceedings of the National Academy of Sciences* 112(30): 9176–81 https://doi.org/10.1073/pnas.1421406112

Carlsson, H. and R. Pijpers 2021. "Diversity-mainstreaming in times of ageing and migration: Implementation paradoxes in municipal aged care provision," *Journal of Ethnic and Migration Studies* 47(11): 2396–2416 https://doi.org/10.1080/1369183X.2020.1857231

Castles, S. 2001. "Studying social transformation," *International Political Science Review* 22: 13–32 https://doi.org/10.1177/0192512101221002

Castles, S. 2010. "Understanding global migration: A social transformation perspective," *Journal of Ethnic and Migration Studies* 36: 1565–86 https://doi.org/10.1080/1369183x. 2010.489381

Cohen, R. 1997. *Global Diasporas: An Introduction*, London: University College London Press

Creese, A. and A. Blackledge (eds.) 2018a. *The Routledge Handbook of Language and Superdiversity*, London: Routledge https://doi.org/10.4324/9781315696010

Creese, A. and A. Blackledge 2018b. "Language and superdiversity: An interdisciplinary perspective," in *The Routledge Handbook of Language and Superdiversity*, A. Creese and A. Blackledge (eds.), London: Routledge, pp. xxi–xiv https://doi.org/10.4324/9781315696010

Crenshaw, K. 1991. "Mapping the margins: Identity politics, intersectionality, and violence against women," *Stanford Law Review* 43(6): 1241–99 https://doi.org/10.2307/1229039

De Fina, A., D. Ikizoglu and J. Wegner (eds.) 2017. *Diversity and Super-Diversity: Sociocultural Linguistic Perspectives*, Washington, D.C.: Georgetown University Press

Fanshawe, S. and D. Sriskandarajah 2010. *You Can't Put Me in a Box: Super-Diversity and the End of Identity Politics in Britain*, London: Institute for Public Policy Research

Favell, A. 2022. *The Integration Nation: Immigration and Colonial Power in Liberal Democracies*, Cambridge: Polity

Florida, R. 2002. *The Rise of the Creative Class*, New York: Basic Books

Geertz, C. 1986. "The uses of diversity," *Michigan Quarterly Review* 25(1): 105–23

Geldof, D. 2016. *Superdiversity in the Heart of Europe: How Migration Changes Our Society*, The Hague: Acco

Gilroy, P. 1993. *The Black Atlantic: Modernity and Double Consciousness*, Cambridge, MA: Harvard University Press

Glick-Schiller, N., L. Basch and C. Blanc-Szanton 1992. "Transnationalism: A new analytic framework for understanding migration," *Annals of the New York Academy of Sciences* 645(1): 1–24 https://doi.org/10.1111/j.1749-6632.1992.tb33484.x

Greatrex, G. and S. Mitchell (eds.) 2000. *Ethnicity and Culture in Late Antiquity*, Swansea: Classical Press of Wales

Grillo, R. D. 2015. "Reflections on super-diversity by an urban anthropologist, or 'Superdiversity so what?'" Paper presented at the Academy of Urban Super-Diversity, Berlin

Grillo, R. D. 1998. *Pluralism and the Politics of Difference: State, Culture, and Ethnicity in Comparative Perspective*, Oxford: Clarendon Press.

Grillo, R. D. 2018. *Interculturalism and the Politics of Dialogue*, Lewes: B and RG Books of Lewes

Grillo, T. 1995. "Anti-essentialism and intersectionality: Tools to dismantle the master's house," *Berkeley Women's Law Journal* 10: 16–30

Hannerz, U. 1987. "The world in creolization," *Africa* 57(4): 546–59 https://doi.org/10.2307/1159899

Heather, P. 2010. *Empires and Barbarians: The Fall of Rome and the Birth of Europe*, Oxford: Oxford University Press

Hoerder, D. 2002. *Cultures in Contact: World Migrations in the Second Millennium*, Durham: Duke University Press

Hollinger, D. 1995. *Postethnic America: Beyond Multiculturalism*, New York: Basic Books

Jones, J. M. and J. F. Dovidio 2018. "Change, challenge, and prospects for a diversity paradigm in social psychology," *Social Issues and Policy Review* 12(1): 7–56 https://doi.org/10.1111/sipr.12039

Loh, S. H. 2022. "The continued relevance of multiculturalism: Dissecting interculturalism and transculturalism," *Ethnic and Racial Studies* 45(3): 385–406 https://doi.org/10.1080/01419870.2021.1963459

López Peláez, A., M. V. Aguilar-Tablada, A. Erro-Garcés and R. M. Pérez-García 2022. "Superdiversity and social policies in a complex society: Social challenges in the 21st century," *Current Sociology* 70(2): 166–92 https://doi.org/10.1177/0011392120983344

McInerney, J. (Ed.) 2014. *A Companion to Ethnicity in the Ancient Mediterranean*, Chichester: John Wiley & Sons

McNeill, W. H. 1986. *Polyethnicity and National Unity in World History*, Toronto: University of Toronto Press

Meer, N., T. Modood and R. Zapata-Barrero (eds.) 2016. *Multiculturalism and Interculturalism: Debating the Dividing Lines*, Edinburgh: Edinburgh University Press

Mehta, S. 2021. "'We need a new commons': How city life can offer us the vital power of connection," *The Guardian* 23 December

Meissner, F. and S. Vertovec 2015. "Comparing super-diversity," *Ethnic and Racial Studies* 38(4): 541–55 https://doi.org/10.1080/01419870.2015.980295

Mikkola, M. 2017. "Gender essentialism and anti-essentialism," in *The Routledge Companion to Feminist Philosophy*, A. Garry et al. (eds.), pp. 168–179, London: Routledge

Oosterlynck, S., G. Verschraegen and R. van Kempen (eds.) 2019. *Divercities: Understanding Super-Diversity in Deprived and Mixed Neighbourhoods*, Bristol: Policy Press

Page, S. E. 2007. *The Difference: How the Power of Diversity Creates Better Groups, Firms, Schools, and Societies*, Princeton: Princeton University Press

Portes, A. and M. Zhou 1993. "The new second generation: Segmented assimilation and its variants," *The Annals of the American Academy of Political and Social Science* 530(1): 74–96 https://doi.org/10.1177/0002716293530001006

Putnam, R. 2007. "E pluribus unum: Diversity and community in the twenty-first century - the 2006 Johan Skytte Prize," *Scandinavian Political Studies* 30(2): 137–74 https://doi.org/10.1111/j.1467-9477.2007.00176.x

Ramadan, T. 2011. *On Superdiversity*, Berlin: Sternberg Press

Rosenau, J. N. 2003. *Distant Proximities: Dynamics beyond Globalization*, Princeton: Princeton University Press

Sayer, A. 1997. "Essentialism, social constructionism, and beyond," *The Sociological Review* 45(3): 453–87 https://doi.org/10.1111/1467-954x.00073

Singh, P. and M. Vom Hau 2016. "Ethnicity in time: Politics, history, and the relationship between ethnic diversity and public goods provision," *Comparative Political Studies* 49(10): 1303–40 https://doi.org/10.1177/0010414016633231

Smelser, N. J. 1998. "Social transformations and social change," *International Social Science Journal* 156: 173–8 https://doi.org/10.1111/1468-2451.00121

Taşan-Kok, T., G. Bolt, L. Plüss and W. Schenkel 2017. *A Handbook for Governing Hyper-Diverse Cities*, Utrecht: Utrecht University, Faculty of Geosciences

Verkuyten, M. 2004. *The Social Psychology of Ethnic Identity*, London: Psychology Press https://doi.org/10.4324/9780203338704

Vertovec, S. 1996. "Multiculturalism, culturalism and public incorporation," *Ethnic and Racial Studies* 19(1): 49–69 https://doi.org/10.1080/01419870.1996.9993898

Vertovec, S. 1998. "Multi-multiculturalisms," in *Multicultural Policies and the State*, M. Martiniello (ed.), Utrecht: ERCOMER, pp. 25–38

Vertovec, S. 2006. "The emergence of super-diversity in Britain," ESRC Centre on Migration, Policy and Society *Working Paper* WP-06-25

Vertovec, S. 2007. "Super-diversity and its implications", *Ethnic and Racial Studies* 30(6): 1024–54 https://doi.org/10.1080/01419870701599465

Vertovec, S. 2012. "'Diversity' and the social imaginary," *Archives Européennes de Sociologie/ European Journal of Sociology* 53(3): 287–312 https://doi.org/10.1017/s000397561200015x

Vertovec, S. 2015. "Introduction: Formulating diversity studies," in *Routledge International Handbook of Diversity Studies*, S. Vertovec (ed.), London: Routledge, pp. 1–20 https://doi.org/10.4324/9781315747224

Vertovec, S. 2017. "Mooring, migration milieus and complex explanation," *Ethnic and Racial Studies* 40(9): 1574–81 https://doi.org/10.1080/01419870.2017.1308534

Vertovec, S. and R. Cohen 2002. "Introduction: Conceiving cosmopolitanism," in *Conceiving Cosmopolitanism*, S. Vertovec and R. Cohen (eds.), Oxford: Oxford University Press, pp. 1–22

Waters, M. C. 1990. *Ethnic Options: Choosing Identities in America*, Berkeley: University of California Press

Watson, L. (ed.) 1997. *Between Two Cultures: Migrants and Minorities in Britain*, Oxford: Blackwell

Werbner, P. and T. Modood (eds.) 1997. *Debating Cultural Hybridity: Multi-Cultural Identities and the Politics of Anti-Racism*, London: Zed

Wiltshire, K. 2001. "Management of social transformations: Introduction," *International Political Science Review* 22(1): 5–11 https://doi.org/10.1177/0192512101221001

Wimmer, A. and N. Glick Schiller 2002. "Methodological nationalism and beyond: Nation-state building, migration and the social sciences," *Global Networks* 2(4): 301–34 https://doi.org/10.1111/1471-0374.00043

Witt, C. 1995. "Anti-essentialism in feminist theory," *Philosophical Topics* 23(2): 321–44 https://doi.org/10.5840/philtopics19952327

Yamada, A. M. and T. M. Singelis 1999. "Biculturalism and self-construal," *International Journal of Intercultural Relations* 23(5): 697–709 https://doi.org/10.1016/s0147-1767(99)00016-4

2

SUPER-DIVERSITY AND ITS IMPLICATIONS (2007)

[This chapter reproduces the original article from 2007 in which the concept of super-diversity was introduced.]

At a Trafalgar Square vigil for the victims of the 7 July 2005 terrorist attacks – in which victims included migrants from more than twenty countries and alleged perpetrators from a further six – Mayor Ken Livingstone stated that in London "you see the world gathered in one city, living in harmony, as an example to all" (in Freedland 2005). The "world in one city" idea was also the title of a special section in *The Guardian* newspaper celebrating "the most cosmopolitan place on earth" where "Never have so many different kinds of people tried living together in the same place before" (Benedictus and Godwin 2005, p. 2). The "world in one city" was the title of the Greater London Authority's analysis of the 2001 Census (GLA 2005a), too, which examined the presence of people from 179 nations within the capital. The successful London bid to host the 2012 Olympics also used the "world in one city" slogan, suggesting that "In 2012, our multicultural diversity will mean every competing nation in the Games will find local supporters as enthusiastic as back home" (www.london2012.org/en/city/onecity).

To be sure, the ethnic and country of origin diversity of London is remarkable. Such diversity is manifesting in other parts of the country as well. However, observing ethnicity or country of origin (the two often, and confusingly, being used interchangeably) provides a misleading, one-dimensional appreciation of contemporary diversity. Over the past ten years, the nature of immigration to Britain has brought with it a transformative "diversification of diversity" (cf. Hollinger 1995, Martiniello 2004) not just in terms of bringing more ethnicities and countries of origin, but also with respect to a multiplication of significant variables that affect where, how and with whom people live.

In the last decade the proliferation and mutually conditioning effects of additional variables shows that it is not enough to see diversity only in terms

DOI: 10.4324/9780203503577-2

of ethnicity, as is regularly the case both in social science and the wider public sphere. Such additional variables include differential immigration statuses and their concomitant entitlements and restrictions of rights, divergent labour market experiences, discrete gender and age profiles, patterns of spatial distribution, and mixed local area responses by service providers and residents. Rarely are these factors described side by side. The interplay of these factors is what is meant here, in summary fashion, by the notion of "super-diversity".

By invoking "super-diversity" I wish, firstly, to underscore the fact that in addition to more people now migrating from more places, significant new conjunctions and interactions of variables have arisen through patterns of immigration to the UK over the past decade; their outcomes surpass the ways – in public discourse, policy debates and academic literature – that we usually understand diversity in Britain. Secondly, then, the article serves as a call – or at least reminder – to social scientists and policy-makers to take more sufficient account of the conjunction of ethnicity with a range of other variables when considering the nature of various "communities", their composition, trajectories, interactions and public service needs.

Much of the material and data in this article is certainly not new or unknown to specialists in the field; what is hopefully of value, however, is its assemblage and juxtaposition by way of re-assessing how diversity is conventionally conceived. My view draws upon several previous approaches to diversity, particularly concerning: multi-ethnic arenas of interaction (importantly Lamphere 1992 and Sanjek 1998), hypersegregation or the simultaneous impact of numerous dimensions of ethnic residential concentration (Massey and Denton 1989), minorities' "multilayered experience" within unequal power structures and social locations (Harzig and Juteau 2003), and notions of pluralism that take into account differential rights and modes of incorporation among ethnic groups (Kuper and Smith 1969). I have also been particularly influenced by ideas around cultural complexity as considered by Fredrik Barth (1989, 1993) and Ulf Hannerz (1992), particularly their thinking about modes of cultural confluence, the coexistence of multiple historical streams and the ways individuals in complex settings relate to each other from different vantage points.

Again, the variables of super-diversity themselves are not new, nor are many of their correlations. But, as described in this article, it is the emergence of their scale, historical and policy-produced multiple configuration and mutual conditioning that now calls for conceptual distinction. "Super-diversity" is proposed as a summary term. Whatever we choose to call it, there is much to be gained by a multi-dimensional perspective on diversity, both in terms of moving beyond "the ethnic group as either the unit of analysis or sole object of study" (Glick Schiller et al. 2006, p. 613) and by appreciating the coalescence of factors which condition people's lives.

Noting similar changes concerning urban social, geographic and economic conditions in North American cities and patterns of diversification among ethnic groups themselves, Eric Fong and Kumiko Shibuya (2005, p. 286) suggest that "theories developed in the past may have only limited application in the study of multigroup relations today." The present article follows a similar line. In the first part a variety of data is presented indicating the emergence of super-diversity (especially pointing to developments in London, but emphasizing that these variables, dimensions and dynamics hold proportionately in many other parts of the UK too); this is followed by sections suggesting some implications that super-diversity may have for social scientific theory and method alongside challenges it poses for particular areas of public policy formation and delivery.

Diversity in Britain

Diversity is endemic to Britain, of course. Peter Ackroyd's (2000) monumental *London: The Biography* describes the long history of a city of assorted immigrants. Roman Londinium was full of administrators, traders, soldiers and slaves from Gaul, Greece, Germany, Italy and North Africa. "By the tenth century," Ackroyd (Ibid., p. 702) writes, "the city was populated by Cymric Brythons and Belgae, by remnants of the Gaulish legions, by East Saxons and Mercians, by Danes, Norwegians and Swedes, by Franks and Jutes and Angles, all mingled and mingling together to form a distinct tribe of 'Londoners'."

In the late twelfth century locals throughout Britain complained that all sorts of foreigners were practicing their own customs, and by the early sixteenth century such intolerance saw riots in which shops and homes of foreigners were burnt. In the middle of the eighteenth century diversity fuelled a struggle between people with "culturally cosmopolitan" outlooks and those with populist xenophobic attitudes (Statt 1995). Nineteenth-century poets like Wordsworth described London's heterogeneity of peoples, while in an 1880 book *The Huguenots*, Samuel Smiles called London "one of the most composite populations to be found in the world" (in Holmes 1997, p. 10). Indeed, as Michael Keith (2005, pp. 49–50) notes, "There is not a point in the history of London when cultural differences have not played a significant role in shaping the life of the city."

Irish in the nineteenth and twentieth centuries and Jews from throughout eastern Europe in the late nineteenth and early twentieth centuries comprised significant immigrant influxes. Yet it was the post-war large-scale immigration of African-Caribbean and South Asian (i.e. non-White) peoples which particularly prompted a set of changes in public policy. British policy-makers responded with various strategies for a kind of diversity management strategy that came to be called multiculturalism.

In this way most of the discourse, policy and public understanding of migration and multiculturalism evident in Britain over the past thirty years has been based on the experience of people who arrived between the 1950s and 1970s from Jamaica, Trinidad, Guyana and other places in the West Indies alongside those from India, Pakistan and what is now Bangladesh. These were major inflows from former British colonies, with people subject to initial rights of entry that were gradually restricted during the 1960s and early 1970s until only families of settled migrants could enter. Citizenship and all the civil, political and social rights associated with it were gained by most under post-colonial arrangements (Hansen and Weil 2001). Large and eventually well-organized communities were formed, particularly through the establishment of community associations and places of worship.

Multicultural policies have had as their overall goal the promotion of tolerance and respect for collective identities. This has been undertaken through supporting community associations and their cultural activities, monitoring diversity in the workplace, encouraging positive images in the media and other public spaces, and modifying public services (including education, health, policing and courts) in order to accommodate culture-based differences of value, language and social practice. While developed from the 1960s onwards, most of these policies and goals still obtain today. Meanwhile, multiculturalism continues to be conceived of mainly in terms of the African-Caribbean and South Asian communities of British citizens.

New, smaller, less organized, legally differentiated and non-citizen immigrant groups have hardly gained attention or a place on the public agenda (cf. Kofman 1998). Yet it is the growth of exactly these sorts of groups that has in recent years radically transformed the social landscape in Britain. The time has come to re-evaluate – in social scientific study as well as policy – the nature of diversity in Britain today.

New immigrants and the emergence of super-diversity

Over the past ten to fifteen years, immigration – and consequently the nature of diversity – in the UK has changed dramatically. Since the early 1990s there has been a marked rise in net immigration and a diversification of countries of origin. This shift has coincided with no less than six Parliamentary measures: the Asylum and Immigration Acts of 1993, 1996, 1999, the Nationality, Immigration and Asylum Act 2002, the Asylum and Immigration Act 2004 and the Immigration, Asylum and Nationality Bill 2005. Throughout this time there has been a proliferation of migration channels and immigrant legal statuses. In addition, this decade was a time when numerous conflicts were taking place around the world leading to a significant expansion in the numbers of those seeking asylum. The various flows and channels have been characterised as "the new migration" and the people involved as "the new immigrants" (see Robinson and Reeve 2005, Berkeley et al. 2005, Kyambi 2005). Multiple dimensions of differentiation characterize the emergent social patterns and conditions.

Net inflows

Prior to the early 1990s, the UK was characterized by net outflows of people; since 1994 it has been marked by net inflows. Annual net inflows of immigrants to Britain peaked at 171,000 in 2000, declined to 151,000 by 2003 then rose markedly to 222,600 in 2004 (Office for National Statistics, www.statisics.gov.uk). In 2004 there were an estimated 2,857,000 foreigners (foreign-born and without UK citizenship) living in the UK, comprising some 4.9% of the total population of 58,233,000 (Salt 2004). This number represented an increase of some 857,000 or over 40% since 1993. There have been substantial further increases since eight new states acceded to the European Union in 2004 (see below).

There are many simultaneous reasons for the increased net inflows. One set of reasons surround Britain's high economic performance (including low unemployment and job shortages in some sectors) coupled with growing inequalities in many developing and middle-income countries (Hatton 2003). Much of the increase during the 1990s was within the category of asylum seekers: while there have been many accusations that a high proportion of these are "bogus" or "really economic migrants", the increase in asylum-seekers over the past ten years has been demonstrated to be directly linked with forced migration factors and conflict situations in source countries during this time (Castles et al. 2003). Even before EU accession, migration flows from Eastern Europe also increased since the opening of borders following the fall of the Berlin Wall in 1989 (see Kaczmarczyk and Okólski 2005).

Countries of origin

One of the most noteworthy features of "the new migration" is the multiplicity of immigrants' countries of origin. Moreover, most of this new and diverse range of origins relates to places which have no specific historical – particularly, colonial – links with Britain.

In the 1950s and 1960s almost all immigrants came from colonies or Commonwealth countries (again, mostly in the Caribbean and South Asia). By the early 1970s most newcomers were arriving as dependants of the newly settled migrants. The decades since then have seen fairly dramatic change. Alongside relatively constant inflows of returning British people, in 1971 people from "Old" and "New" Commonwealth countries accounted for 30% and 32% of inflow; by 2002 these proportions were 17% and 20% respectively. EU citizens represented 10% of newcomers in 1971, rising to 17% in 2002; however, those in a broad "Middle East and Other" category have gone from 16% in 1971 to 40% in 2002 (National Statistics Online). Since the beginning of the 1990s alone, the diversity of immigrants' places of origin has been growing considerably (see Figure 2.1).

Britain is now home – temporary, permanent or one among many – to people from practically every country in the world. As Table 2.1 suggests, various waves of immigrants from rich, middle income and poor countries have accumulated. All the groups, as well as many individuals within these, have diverse migration experiences in the UK – some over the last decade, others over generations, still others over more than a century. With regard to this dimension of super-diversity, we should consider how the assorted origins and experiences of migrants condition social relations with non-migrant Britons and with each other.

In London alone there are people from some 179 countries. Many represent just a handful of people, but there are populations numbering over 10,000 respectively

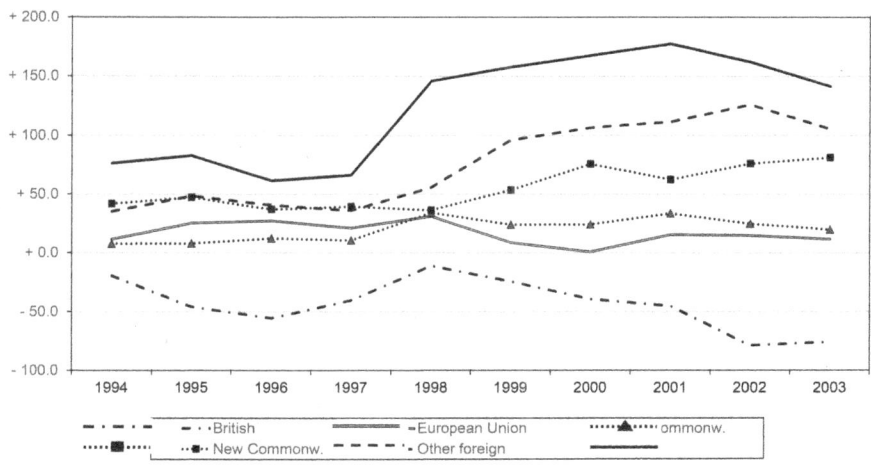

FIGURE 2.1   Net international migration to Britain by citizenship

Source: statistics.gov.uk

TABLE 2.1   Foreign nationals living in the UK, largest twenty-fivegroups, 2004

Rank	Nationality	Number in UK	Percent
1	Ireland	368000	12.9
2	India	171000	6.0
3	USA	133000	4.7
4	Italy	121000	4.2
5	Germany	96000	3.4
6	France	95000	3.3
7	South Africa	92000	3.2
8	Pakistan	86000	3.0
9	Portugal	83000	2.9
10	Australia	80000	2.8
11	Zimbabwe	73000	2.5
12	Bangladesh	69000	2.4
13	Somalia	60000	2.1
14	Former Yugoslavia	54000	1.9
15	Philippines	52000	1.8
16	Turkey	51000	1.8
17	Netherlands	48000	1.7
18	Poland	48000	1.7
19	Jamaica	45000	1.6
20	Former USSR	44000	1.5
21	Nigeria	43000	1.5
22	Spain	40000	1.4
23	Greece	37000	1.3
24	Canada	37000	1.3
25	Iran	36000	1.3
	All foreign nationals	**2,857,000**	**100**

Source: Salt (2004).

TABLE 2.2 Number of people living in London by Country of Birth outside the UK, largest twenty-five groups, 2001

Rank	Country of birth	Number
1	India	172,162
2	Republic of Ireland	157,285
3	Bangladesh	84,565
4	Jamaica	80,319
5	Nigeria	68,907
6	Pakistan	66,658
7	Kenya	66,311
8	Sri Lanka	49,932
9	Ghana	46,513
10	Cyprus	45,888
11	South Africa	45,506
12	U.S.A.	44,622
13	Australia	41,488
14	Germany	39,818
15	Turkey	39,128
16	Italy	38,694
17	France	38,130
18	Somalia	33,831
19	Uganda	32,082
20	New Zealand	27,494
21	Hong Kong	23,328
22	Spain	22,473
23	Poland	22,224
24	Portugal	21,720
25	Iran	20,398

Source: GLA (2005a).

from each of no less than 42 countries; there are populations of over 5,000 from a further 12 countries (GLA 2005a). Reflecting trends in Britain as a whole, 23 per cent of foreign-born people came to London before 1970, 32 per cent between 1970 and 1990 and 45 per cent since 1990. The 25 largest such populations reflect a wide range of countries, from rich to poor, peaceful to conflict-ridden, European to African and Asian (Table 2.2). Overall 30% of London's migrants are from high income countries and 70% are from developing countries (GLA 2005b)

Once more, the above figures for both the UK and London will by now have changed considerably, not least due to the influx of eastern Europeans both before and after EU accession in May 2004.

Foreign-origin populations in London are widespread and unevenly distributed (see Kyambi 2005). The borough of Brent has the highest percentage of its 2001 population born outside the EU, with 38.2% (100,543 people), followed by Newham with 35.6% (86,858 people), Westminster with 32.4% (58,770 people) and Ealing with 31% (93,169 people) (see www.statistics.gov.uk). Within each such area, the diversity of origins is staggering, as depicted by way of example in Figure 2.2 with reference to Newham.

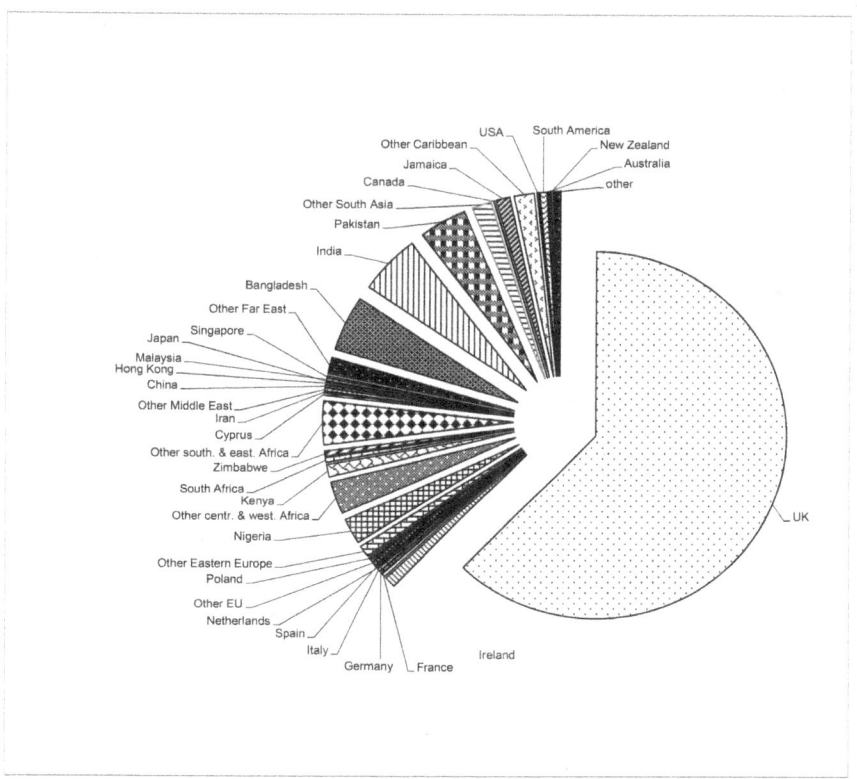

FIGURE 2.2 Newham (total; population 243,898) by country/region of birth

Source: 2001 census

Such a relatively new and high proportion of immigrants characterizes many places in the UK, but London most. Of the local authorities with the highest percentage of population who are non-UK born, the top twenty-two are all London boroughs, from the first, Brent with 46.5% of its 263,463 population, to the twenty-second, Redbridge with 24.2% of its 238,634 population.

However, high proportions of foreign-born – with all the accompanying dimensions of diversity that go with them – are found throughout the UK (see especially Kyambi 2005). In these terms, outside of London it is Slough that has the highest proportion, nationally ranked as twenty-third among local authorities, with 22.3% of its 119,072 population counted as foreign-born. Leicester and Forest Heath are ranked twenty-fourth and twenty-fifth (each with 23% of their respective populations of 279,925 and 55,523), Luton twenty-seventh (19.6% of 184,369) and Oxford twenty-ninth (19.3% of 134,250); intervening ranks are again London local authorities (2001 census). Among the foreign-born, regions of origin are quite varyingly distributed. By way of example, Figure 2.3 indicates such differential patterns of distribution in four cities of Britain.

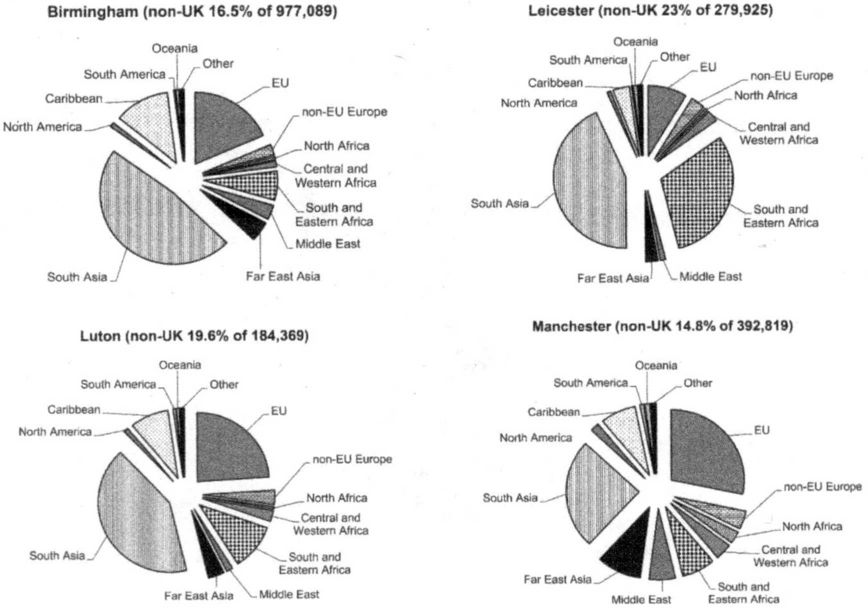

Birmingham (non-UK 16.5% of 977,089)

Leicester (non-UK 23% of 279,925)

Luton (non-UK 19.6% of 184,369)

Manchester (non-UK 14.8% of 392,819)

FIGURE 2.3   Local authorities by non–UK region of birth (with total foreign-born percent of local population)

Source: 2001 census

While pointing to important indicators of diversity, country of origin data itself, however, may mask more significant forms of differentiation than it reveals. Within any particular population from a given country, there will be important distinctions with reference to ethnicity, religious affiliation and practice, regional and local identities in places of origin, kinship, clan or tribal affiliation, political parties and movements, and other criteria of collective belonging. Linguistic differentiation, for instance, represents one such important social marker which may lie within one or more country of origin categories.

Languages

The growth of multilingualism has been recognized and engaged in various ways by both social scientists and policymakers, although the latter have often arguably failed to respond in positive or adequate ways (Rampton et al. 1997). Still, it is now often proclaimed with pride (for instance in the city's successful 2012 Olympic bid) that 300 languages are spoken in London. This figure is based on a survey of no less than 896,743 London schoolchildren concerning which language(s) they speak at home (Baker and Mohieldeen 2000). Despite some methodological flaws, this remarkable data source provides an important look into a much under-studied field of diversity in the UK. The study does

TABLE 2.3 Estimated number of speakers of top
20 languages in London, 2000

Rank	Language name	Number
1	English	5,636,500
2	Panjabi	155,700
3	Gujarati	149,600
4	Hindi/Urdu	136,500
5	Bengali & Sylheti	136,300
6	Turkish	73,900
7	Arabic	53,900
8	English Creole	50,700
9	Cantonese	47,900
10	Yoruba	47,600
11	Greek	31,100
12	Portuguese	29,400
13	French	27,600
14	Akan (Twi & Fante)	27,500
15	Spanish	26,700
16	Somali	22,343
17	Tamil	19,200
18	Vietnamese	16,800
19	Farsi	16,200
20	Italian	12,300

Source: Storkey (2000).

not take account of languages among groups with few children in schools (for instance because of a high number of young, single migrants in a particular group), which would represent ones like Polish, Czech, Hungarian and other east European languages. Nevertheless, findings like those in Table 2.3 indicate sometimes surprisingly sizeable numbers speaking particular languages within a divergent range.

The data also show some interesting local configurations. There are predictable groupings of South Asian languages in places of renowned Asian settlement like Harrow, where the top three non-English languages are Gujarati, Hindi/Urdu and Punjabi. Other places show fascinating conjunctions, such as in Haringey where Turkish is commonly spoken alongside Akan and Somali, in Lambeth where Yoruba speakers mingle with speakers of Portuguese and Spanish, and in Merton where English Creole is common next to Cantonese and French (Baker and Mohieldeen 2000). In Tower Hamlets, where British Bangladeshis are highly concentrated, "the demand for Eastern European language services collectively now exceeds that for Sylheti translation" (Keith 2005, p. 177).

School districts, health services and local authorities are among those institutions which have to meet the challenges of growing linguistic complexity. Many new initiatives have arisen for this purpose. For example, the Language Shop provides a comprehensive translation and interpretation service in more than 100 languages to Newham Council and its partners, such as community groups and neighbouring councils, while Language Line provides telephone or in-person translations in 150 languages to health authorities and other public sector clients.

Religions

The religious diversity that migrants have brought to Britain is well documented and is not possible to detail here (see for instance Parsons 1994, Peach 2005 as well as National Statistics Online). On the whole we can say that among immigrants to Britain, Christianity is the main religion for people born in all continents except Asia; Asia-born people in the UK are more likely to be Muslim than any other religion, although of course Indians include a majority of Hindus and a significant number of Sikhs. For many, religions tend to be broadly equitable with countries of origin – Irish and Jamaicans are mostly Christian, Bangladeshis mostly Muslim and so forth – but even so these categories often miss important variations in devotional traditions within each of the world religions.

Taking Islam as example, it is often pointed out that there are several traditions within the faith as practiced by South Asians in the UK (Deobandi, Tablighi, Barelvi, Sufi orders and more; see Lewis 2002). Such variations are multiplied many times when we consider the breadth of origins among Muslims from around the world who now live in Britain (such as Nigerians, Somalis, Bosnians, Afghans, Iraqis and Malaysians). In London Muslims are the most heterogeneous body of believers in terms of ethnicity and country of origin, with the largest group (Bangladeshis) making up only 23.5%. "London's Muslim population of 607,083 people is probably the most diverse anywhere in the world, besides Mecca" (*The Guardian* 21 January 2005).

Socio-cultural axes of differentiation such as country of origin, ethnicity, language and religion are of course significant in conditioning immigrants' identities, patterns of interaction and – often through social networks determined by such axes – their access to jobs, housing, services and more. However, immigrants' channels of migration and the myriad legal statuses which arise from them are often just as, or even more, crucial to: how people group themselves and where people live, how long they can stay, how much autonomy they have (versus control by an employer, for instance), whether their families can join them, what kind of livelihood they can undertake and maintain, and to what extent they can make use of public services and resources (including schools, health, training, benefits and other "recourse to public funds"). Therefore such channels and statuses, along with the rights and restrictions attached to them (Morris 2002), comprise an additional – indeed, fundamental – dimension of today's patterns and dynamics of super-diversity.

Migration channels and immigration statuses

Coinciding with the increasing influx of immigrants to the UK in the 1990s, there has been an expansion in the number and kind of migration channels and immigration statuses. Each carries quite specific and legally enforceable entitlements, controls, conditions and limitations (see JCWI 2004). The following section outlines many of the key channels and statuses, particularly with regard to how they have shaped current patterns of super-diversity in the UK.

Workers

Between 1993 and 2003 the number of foreign workers in the UK rose no less than 62% to 1,396,000 (Sriskandarajah et al. 2004). This large-scale increase in workers includes people who have come under numerous categories and quota systems (see Clarke and Salt 2003, Salt 2004, Kofman et al. 2005). These have included: foreign nationals who do not need a visa or permit to work in the UK (mainly members of the European Economic Area, including members of the eight new EU accession states who can travel to the UK freely, but should register with government offices if they find employment; by mid-2006 there were some 427,000 applications under this Worker Registration Scheme); work permit holders (whose employers obtained the permits); workers on special schemes (especially the Seasonal Agricultural Workers' Scheme and the Sector Based Scheme directed mainly at hotels, catering and food processing industries); highly skilled migrants (from over 50 countries, working in finance, business management, information technology and medical services); working holiday-makers (from more than 90% from "Old Commonwealth" countries such as New Zealand and Australia); and special visa holders (importantly including domestic workers, au pairs, volunteers and religious instructors).

Students

The number of foreign students entering the UK recently peaked at 369,000 in 2002 before reducing to 319,000 in 2003. Non-EU students accounted for some 38% of all full-time higher degree students in 2003 (Kofman et al. 2005, p. 20); they numbered over 210,000 in 2004. In this year 47,700 Chinese students came to Britain, marking a seventeen-fold increase from the 2,800 Chinese students in the UK in 1998. The number of Indian students has grown from under 3,000 in 1998 to nearly 15,000 in 2004. The third largest sender is the USA with over 13,000 students in 2004.

Spouses and family members

This is an extremely important immigration category, not least since "family migration has emerged as the single most enduring, though also restricted, basis for entry of migrants to the UK" (Kofman et al. 2005, p. 22). The number of migrating spouses and family members coming to the UK more than doubled between 1993-2003. Furthermore this is a particularly feminised channel of migration compared with others; for instance, of the 95,000 grants of settlement to spouses and dependents in 2004, 20.6% were made for husbands, 40% for wives and 28.8% children. Their geographical provenance varied significantly, however: the Indian sub-continent was origin to 36% of husbands, 28% of wives and 15% of children; the rest of Asia brought 8% of husbands, 21% of wives and 18% of children, while from Africa there came 24% of husbands, 17% of wives and 42% of children (Salt 2004). Not all have come under the same conditions: within the spouses and family migrant category Kofman (2004) distinguishes a number of types, including family reunification migration (bringing members of immediate family), family formation migration (bringing marriage partners from country of origin), marriage migration (bringing partners met while abroad) and family migration (when all members migrate simultaneously).

Asylum-seekers and Refugees

Throughout the 1990s the number of asylum applications rose considerably in the UK and indeed throughout Europe. Applications (including dependents) in Britain rose from 28,000 in 1993 to a peak of 103,100 in 2002; these amounted respectively to 15.6% and 26.5% of all non-British immigration (179,200 in 1993 and 418,200 in 2002). Applications have since declined significantly: in 2003 the number of asylum applications declined to 60,045 (which is 14.7% of 406,800 total non-British immigrants; Salt 2004, p. 71). This too is a highly gendered channel of migration: in 2003 some 69% were male. The provenance of asylum-seekers represents a broad range: again in 2003 applications were received from persons spanning over 50 nationalities, including 10% Somali, 8% Iraqi, 7% Chinese, 7% Zimbabwean, and 6% Iranian. However, numbers of asylum-seekers from various countries have fluctuated much over the years (see Table 2.4).

Many asylum-seekers wait long periods for decisions, many are rejected and leave the country, others are rejected and stay as irregular migrants. It is estimated that some 28% of asylum applicants are granted asylum, extended leave to remain, humanitarian protection or some other category allowing them to stay

TABLE 2.4 Applications received for asylum in the United Kingdom 1994–2003, selected nationalities

Nationality	1994	1995	1996	1997	1998	1999	2000	2001	2002	2003
Serbia-Montenegro	n/a	n/a	400	1865	7395	11465	6070	3230	2265	815
Turkey	2045	1820	1495	1445	2015	2850	3990	3695	2835	2390
Nigeria	4340	5825	2900	1480	1380	945	835	810	1125	1010
Somalia	1840	3465	1780	2730	4685	7495	5020	6420	6540	5090
Zimbabwe	55	105	130	60	80	230	1010	2140	7655	3295
Iran	520	615	585	585	745	1320	5610	3420	2630	2875
Iraq	550	930	965	1075	1295	1800	7475	6680	14570	4015
Afghanistan	325	580	675	1085	2395	3975	5555	8920	7205	2280
Sri Lanka	2350	2070	1340	1830	3505	5130	6395	5510	3130	705
All nationalities	**32830**	**43965**	**29640**	**32500**	**46015**	**71160**	**80315**	**71025**	**84130**	**49405**

Source: Salt (2004).

in the UK (Salt 2004). Cumulatively there were some 289,100 refugees in UK by the end of 2004 (UNHCR 2005).

Irregular, illegal or undocumented migrants

This category, variously termed, pertains to people whose presence is marked by clandestine entry, entry by deceit, overstaying or breaking the terms of a visa. It is not a black-and-white classification, however: Anderson and Ruhs (2005) discuss grey areas of "semi-compliance" under which only some, sometimes minor, conditions are violated.

As Pinkerton et al. (2004) describe, it is very difficult to reliably estimate numbers within this category. In 2005 the Home Office offered a "best guess" number between 310,000 and 570,000 irregular migrants in the UK. Without a regularisation exercise, learning the breadth of undocumented migrants places of origin would be even more difficult. In any case, their social and legal position is one of almost total exclusion from rights and entitlements.

New citizens

A great many migrants become full citizens. During the 1990s around 40,000 people became citizens each year. This number has risen dramatically since 2000, with 2004 seeing a record number of 140,795 granted British citizenship (*The Guardian* 18 May 2005). According to Home Office estimates, 59% of the foreign-born population who have been in the UK more than five years – the minimal stay to become eligible – have indeed become citizens.

In attempting to understand the nature and dynamics of diversity in Britain, close attention must be paid to the stratified system of rights, opportunities, constraints and partial-to-full memberships that coincide with these and other immigrant categories (Morris 2002, 2004). And as pointed out by Lisa Arai (2006, p. 10),

> There is a complex range of different entitlements, even within one migrant status category (e.g. overseas students), and a lack of coherence or rationale to a system developed *ad hoc* over many years, and which reflects competing pressures, such as whether to provide access to a service because the individual needs it, or because it is good for society (e.g. pubic health). Or whether to deny a service in order to protect public funds, ensure that access does not prove an attraction for unwanted migrants or to appease public opinion. This means that neither service providers, advice-givers nor migrants themselves are clear as to what services they might be entitled.

Moreover – denoting a key feature of super-diversity – there may be widely differing statuses *within* groups of the same ethnic or national origin. For example, among Somalis in the UK – and in any single locality – we will find British citizens, refugees, asylum-seekers, persons granted exceptional leave to remain, undocumented migrants, and people granted refugee status in another European country but who subsequently moved to Britain. This fact underscores the point that simple ethnicity-focused approaches to understanding and engaging various minority "communities" in Britain, as taken in many models and policies within conventional multiculturalism, is inadequate and often inappropriate for dealing with individual immigrants' needs or understanding their dynamics of inclusion or exclusion.

Immigration status is not just a crucial factor in determining an individual's relation to the state, its resources and legal system, the labour market and other structures. It is an important catalyst in the formation of social capital and a potential barrier to the formation of cross-cutting socio-economic and ethnic ties.

Many immigration statuses set specific time limits on people's stay in Britain. Most integration policies and programmes, in turn, do not apply to people with temporary status. Temporary workers, undocumented migrants and asylum-seekers often only spend short periods of time in given locations, either due to the search for work or relocation by employers or authorities such as the National Asylum Support Service. Short periods of duration may pose difficulties not jus for them, but for local institutions, such as schools (Ofsted 2003), to provide services.

In order to understand the nature and complexity of contemporary super-diversity, we must examine how such a system of stratified rights and conditions created by immigration channels and legal statuses cross-cuts socio-cultural and socio-economic dimensions.

Gender

Over the past thirty years, more females than males migrated to the UK; since about 1998, males have come to predominate in new flows. The reason for this, Kyambi (2005) suggests, may be due to a general shift away from more female oriented family migration to more male dominated work-based migration schemes since 1995. It is likely also related to the inflow of asylum-seekers, most of whom have been male.

There is considerable variation of gender structures among different groups, and this mostly relates to channels of migration and the evolution of migration systems from particular countries of origin. For instance, 80% of Slovakians, 72% of Czechs, 71% of Filipinos, 70% of Slovenes, 68% of Thais and 67% of Madagascars are women (GLA 2005a, p. 89). They are mostly to be found in domestic or health services. Meanwhile, 71% of Algerians, 63% of Nepalese, 61% of Kosovars, 61% of Afghans, 60% of Yemenis and 60% of Albanians are males, almost all of whom are asylum-seekers (Ibid., p. 90).

Among migrants in London generally, women migrants have a far lower employment rate (56%) than men (75%). Employment rates are especially low for women born in South Asia (37%) and the Middle East and North Africa (39%) (GLA 2005b, p. 2). Indeed many basic features of super-diversity – especially the inter-related patterns surrounding immigrants' country of origin, channels of migration, employment, legal status and rights – tend to have highly gendered patterns (cf. Kofman et al. 2005).

Age

The new immigrant population has a higher concentration of 25-44 year olds and a lower proportion of under-16s than a decade ago, also perhaps reflecting a shift away from family migration (Kyambi 2005). Variance in age structure among various ethnic groups reflects different patterns of fertility and mortality as well as migration (GLA 2005a, p. 6). The mean age of new immigrants is 28 – averaging eleven years younger than the mean age of 39 for the British Isles born population.

> There is a considerable amount of diversity in the proportion of the new immigrant population being in the age group 25-44, which we have considered to be a primary working age. While Cyprus (31.03%), Hong Kong (32.65%), Somalia (37.26%), Germany (37.85%), Norway (38.18%) and Albania (38.56%) have the smallest fraction of their population falling within this age group, they are counterbalanced by Algeria (78.24%), Philippines (74.49%), New Zealand (73.92%), and Italy (70.24%) with the greatest proportions being 25-44 years old.
>
> *(Kyambi 2005, p. 133)*

Space/place

New immigrants often settle in areas with established immigrant communities from the same country of birth. Pointing to this fact, and by way of recognising the boom in migrant-derived diversity, in 2005 *The Guardian* newspaper published a special section called "London: the world in one city" which described and mapped one hundred places and specific groups within "the most diverse city ever" (Benedictus and Godwin 2005). Another was published in January 2006 called "The world in one country", repeating the exercise on a national scale. These special sections were revealing and celebratory, but were in many ways misleading.

The Greater London Authority's analysis of the 2001 Census shows that there are only a few common country of origin populations that are highly concentrated in the capital – namely Bangladeshis in Tower Hamlets (where 42% of the capital's 35,820 Bangladeshis live), people from Sierra Leone living in Southwark (26% of 3,647), Cypriots in Enfield (26% of 11,802), Afghanis in Ealing (23% of 2,459) and Turks in Haringey (22% of 8,589). The report points out that "although there are areas which have come to be associated with particular migrants, nearly all migrant groups tend to live in a number of different boroughs" (GLA 2005a, p. 88).

Therefore, while *The Guardian* wished to highlight the cosmopolitan nature of contemporary London and Britain, it made a mistake in suggesting certain groups are fixed to certain places. Instead, as implied by the GLA analysis and stressed by Geraldine Pratt (1998, p. 27),

> there is deep suspicion about mapping cultures onto places, because multiple cultures and identities inevitably inhabit a single place (think of multiple identities performed under the roof of a family house) and a single cultural identity is often situated in multiple, interconnected spaces.

London is the predominant locus of immigration and it is where super-diversity is at its most marked. But, following Kyambi (2005), we should note that increased diversification (of countries of origin, immigrant categories, etc.) are not a matter of increased numbers but relative change in a given locality. A city or neighbourhood may have small numbers of new migrants but relatively high indices of diversity (cf. Allen and Turner 1989). In terms of numbers of new migrants London still shows the highest degree of relative change, but significant trends are also to be found in the South East, West Midlands, East of England, North West, and Yorkshire and Humberside (Kyambi 2005). A "diversity index" recently created by the Office for National Statistics – based on the probability of two persons selected at random belonging to different ethnic groups – also shows a high ethnic mix outside as well as within London (Large and Ghosh 2006).

One major avenue by which newcomers have come to places of previously low immigrant density has been through government dispersal. In order to relieve pressure on councils in London and the south-east of England, since 2000 the National Asylum Support Service (NASS) has made considerable effort to disperse people seeking asylum. By its peak in 2003 the dispersal system had spread 54,000 asylum-seekers to 77 local authorities across Britain, including several in Yorkshire (18%), the West Midlands (18%), the north-west (18%) and Scotland (11%).

New immigrants with less established networks and patterns of settlement are currently being drawn to locations with a wider range of employment opportunities – principally to London but also to small towns and mid-sized cities (for instance to work in construction), coastal and other leisure-centred localities (where they might engage in hospitality and catering services) and rural areas (usually for short-term jobs in agriculture and food processing).

Transnationalism

Perhaps throughout history, and certainly over the last hundred years or more, immigrants have stayed in contact with families, organizations and communities in their places of origin and elsewhere in the diaspora (Foner 1997, Morawska 1999, Glick Schiller 1999). In recent years, the extent and degree of transnational engagement has intensified due in large part to changing technologies and reduced telecommunication and travel costs. Enhanced transnationalism is substantially transforming several social, political and economic structures and practices among migrant communities worldwide (Vertovec 2004a).

The "new immigrants" who have come to live in Britain over the past ten years have done so during a period of increasingly normative transnationalism (cf. Portes et al. 1999). Today in Britain, cross-border or indeed global patterns of sustained communication, institutional linkage and exchange of resources among migrants, homelands and wider diasporas are commonplace (see for example Anderson 2001, Al-Ali et al. 2001, Spellman 2004, Zontini 2004). This can be observed in the increasing value of remittances sent from Britain (now estimated at up to £3.5 billion per year; Blackwell and Seddon 2004), the growing volume of international phone calls between the UK and various places of migrant origin (Vertovec 2004b), the frequency of transnational marriage practices and the extent of engagement by various UK-based diasporas in the development of their respective homelands (Van Hear et al. 2004).

The degrees to and ways in which today's migrants maintain identities, activities and connections linking them with communities outside Britain are unprecedented. Of course, not all migrants maintain the same level of kinds of transnational engagement: much of this will be largely conditioned by a range of factors including migration channel and legal status (e.g. refugees or undocumented persons may find it harder to maintain certain ties abroad), migration and settlement history, community structure and gendered patterns of contact, political circumstances in the homeland, economic means and more. That is, transnational practices among immigrants in Britain are highly diverse between and within groups (whether defined by country of origin, ethnicity, immigration category or any other criteria), adding yet another significant layer of complexity to all those outlined above.

The "new immigration" and its outcomes in Britain have entailed the arrival and interplay of multifaceted characteristics and conditions among migrants. This has resulted in a contemporary situation of "super-diversity". Compared to the large-scale immigration of the 1950s-early 1970s, the 1990s-early 2000s have seen more migrants from more places entailing more socio-cultural differences going through more migration channels leading to more, as well as more significantly stratified, legal categories (which themselves have acted to internally diversify various groups), and who maintain more intensely an array of links with places of origin and diasporas elsewhere. Super-diversity is now all around the UK, and particularly in London. It has not brought with it particular problems or conflicts, but it certainly presents some challenges to policy-makers and social scientists alike.

Super-diversity: Social scientific challenges

The theories and methods that social scientists use to study immigrants still owe much to the Chicago school of urban studies set out in the early and mid-part of the last century (Waters and Jiménez 2005). This primarily entails looking comparatively at processes of assimilation among particular, ethnically-defined groups measured in terms of changing socio-economic status, spatial concentration/segregation, linguistic change and intermarriage.

In many places and times, specific immigrant or ethnic minorities have largely shared such sets of traits, so that analyzing a group at large has indeed demonstrated many significant trends. Elsewhere, however, the array of traits akin to super-diversity has obfuscated attempts discern a clear comparison or relation between groups. For instance, Janet Abu-Lughod (1999, p. 417) describes how,

> In New York, a city long accustomed to an ethnic "poker game" in which no single group commands most of the chips and where the politically federated system provides numerous entry points, albeit not equally advantageous, the sheer diversity of subgroups – both old-timers and new immigrants, and the criss-crossing of pigmentation, immigrant/citizen status, and religious identities by class and residence – has tended to mute the polarities found along language-descent lines in Los Angeles and along the color line in Chicago.

John Mollenkopf and Manuel Castells (1991, p. 402), too, have highlighted in New York City the existence of social dynamics marked by "an articulate core and a disarticulated plurality of peripheries" differentiated by variable conglomerations of race, immigration status, gender, economic activity and neighbourhood. Such observations point towards the need to go beyond studies of socio-economic mobility, segregation and such based on ethnic or immigrant classification alone.

There have indeed been inquiries into how best to gauge diversity in ethnic terms, but also with respect to variables such as age, income and occupational types (e.g., Allen and Turner 1989) or how adequately to derive and evaluate measures of multi-group segregation (e.g., Reardon and Firebaugh 2002). The development of quantitative techniques for multivariate analysis surely have much to offer the study of super-diversity, particularly by way of the understanding the interaction of variables such as country of origin, ethnicity, language, immigration status (and its concomitant rights, benefits and restrictions), age, gender, education, occupation and locality.

Yet there is also much need for more and better qualitative studies of super-diversity. Not least, such a need arises from the Cantle Report into the 2001 riots in Oldham (Home Office 2001; also see Home Office 2004). The Report painted a now infamous picture of groups living "parallel lives" that do not touch or overlap by way of meaningful interchanges. But social scientists – to say nothing of civil servants – have few accounts of what meaningful interchanges look like, how they are formed, maintained or broken, and how the state or other agencies might promote them.

"There are plenty of neighbourhoods," writes Ash Amin (2002, p. 960), "in which multiethnicity has not resulted in social breakdown, so ethnic mixture itself does not offer a compelling explanation for failure." In order to foster a better understanding of dynamics and potentials, Amin calls for an anthropology of "local micropolitics of everyday interaction" akin to what Leonie Sandercock (2003, p. 89) sees as "daily habits of perhaps quite banal intercultural interaction." Such interaction, again, should be looked at in terms of the multiple variables mentioned above, not just in basic ethnic categories.

Social scientific investigation of the conditions and challenges of super-diversity will throw up a wide variety of material and insights with theoretical bearing. For example, these could include contributions toward a better understanding of some of the following areas.

New patterns of inequality and prejudice

The "new immigration" since the early 1990s has brought with it emergent forms of racism: (a) among resident British targeted against newcomers – who may be specifically seen as East Europeans, Gypsies, Somalis, Kosovans, "bogus asylum-seekers", or other constructed categories of otherness; (b) among longstanding ethnic minorities against immigrants; and (c) among newcomers themselves, directed against British ethnic minorities. The new immigration and super-diversity have also stimulated new definitions of "whiteness" surrounding certain groups of newcomers (cf. Keith 2005, p. 177).

New patterns of segregation

Several new immigrants have, as in waves before them, clustered in specific urban areas; others are far more dispersed by choice, by employers or by the NASS dispersal system. While some statistical mapping of new immigrant distribution and concentration has been done (e.g. Kyambi 2005), much remains to be studied in terms of detailed patterns of segregation, housing experiences and residential opportunities.

New experiences of space and "contact"

There is a school of thought in social psychology that suggests regular contact between groups may mutually reduce prejudice and increase respect (cf. Hewstone and Brown 1986). Yet "Habitual contact in itself is no guarantor of cultural exchange" (Amin 2002, p. 969). Indeed, regular contact can entrench group animosities, fears and competition. More research is needed here to test these hypotheses and to identify key forms of space and contact that might yield positive benefits. Further, as Jane Jacobs and Ruth Fincher (1998) advocate, in many cases we need to consider the local development of "a complex entanglement between identity, power and place" which they call a "located politics of difference". This entails examining how people define their differences in relationship to uneven material and spatial conditions.

New forms of cosmopolitanism and creolisation

The enlarged presence and everyday interaction of people from all over the world provides opportunities for the development of research and theory surrounding multiple cultural competences (Vertovec and Rogers 1995), new cosmopolitan orientations and attitudes (Vertovec and Cohen 2002), creole languages (Harris and Rampton 2002), practices of "crossing" or code-switching, particularly among young people (Rampton 2005) and the emergence of new ethnicities characterised by multi-lingualism (Harris 2003).

New "bridgeheads" of migration

As noted earlier, many of the groups which have come to Britain in the past decade originate from places with few prior links to this country. For example, how did French-speaking Algerians or Congolese start coming to the UK (Collyer 2003)? We could learn much about contemporary global migration processes by looking at how migration channels and networks have been newly formed and developed.

Secondary migration patterns

It is now commonplace for migrants to arrive in the UK after spending periods in other, usually EU, countries; this is particularly the case with people granted refugee status such as Somalis from the Netherlands or Denmark. Again, research on such migration systems can tell us much about the current transformation of migration systems.

Transnationalism and integration

While much academic work has been devoted to these two topics over the past decade, there has been much less attention on their relationship. Many policy-makers and members of the public assume a zero-sum game: that is, it is presumed the "more transnational" migrants are, the "less integrated" they must be. Such an assumption is likely false, but needs to be contested with more research evidence (akin to Snel et al. 2006) as well as theoretical reflection (like that undertaken by Kivisto 2005).

Methodological innovation

Research on super-diversity could encourage new techniques in quantitatively testing the relation between multiple variables and in qualitatively undertaking ethnographic exercises that are multi-sited (considering different localities and spaces within a given locality) and multi-group (defined in terms of the variable convergence of ethnicity, status, gender and other criteria of super-diversity). Much value would also doubtless come from the application of a revitalized situational approach – pioneered by Max Gluckman (1958) and J. Clyde Mitchell (1956) – in which a set of interactions are observed and an analysis "works outward" to take account of not only of the meaning of interactions to participants themselves, but also the encompassing criteria and structures impacting upon the positions, perceptions and practices of these actors (cf. Rogers and Vertovec 1995).

Research-policy nexus

Social scientists are not very good at translating data and analysis of complexities into forms that can have impact on policies and public practices. Research on super-diversity will provide this opportunity, especially at a time when policy-makers are eager to gain a better understanding of "integration" and "social cohesion". Indeed, as outlined below, there is a range of policy issues raised or addressed by conditions of super-diversity.

Super-diversity: Policy challenges

At both national and local levels, policy-makers and public service practitioners continuously face the task of refashioning their tools in order to be most effective in light of changing circumstances (whether these are socio-economic, budgetary, or set by government strategy). This is equally the case surrounding policies for community cohesion, integration, managed migration and "managed settlement" (Home Office 2004). The following section points to just a handful of possible issues in which super-diversity impacts on the current development of public policies and practices.

Community organizations

Structures and modes of government support for, and liaison with, ethnic minority organizations have for decades formed the backbone of the British model of multiculturalism. Especially on local levels, these have indeed often provided important forums for sharing experiences and needs, establishing good practices and providing access to services. However, in light of the numerous dimensions of super-diversity, such structures and modes are inadequate for effective representation. Most local authorities have been used to liaising with a limited number of large and well-organized associations; now there are far more numbers in smaller, less (or not at all) organized groups. In any case, just how many groups could such structures support? And how should local authorities account for the internal diversity of various groups, not least in terms of legal status? Already, existing minority ethnic agencies often cannot respond to the needs of the various newcomers.

It can take years to develop effective community organizations which can deliver services and impact on local decision-making. "Meanwhile, new immigrant populations are effectively "squeezed out" of local representative structures and consequently wield little power or influence" (Robinson and Reeve 2005, p. 35). Also, as Roger Zetter and colleagues (2005, p. 14) point out, "In the present climate of immigration policy, there are good reasons why minorities may wish to remain invisible to outsiders and resist forming themselves into explicit organisational structures." None of this is to say that community organizations no longer have a place in bridging migrant groups and local authorities or service providers. Such bodies remain crucial to the process, but should be recognized as only partially relevant with regard to their representativeness and scope.

Public service delivery

The growing size and complexity of the immigrant population carries with it a range of significant public service implications. Executives in local authorities around Britain have voiced concerns about the ability of transport systems, schools and health services to manage new needs (Johnston 2006), while a leaked Home Office document reveals that government departments have been ordered to draw up emergency plans to deal with potential increased demands on public services (Tempest 2006). Such concerns flag up a substantial shift in strategies across a range of service sectors concerning the assessment of needs, planning, budgeting, commissioning of services, identification of partners for collaboration and gaining a broader appreciation of diverse experiences in order generally to inform debate.

Such a shift must begin with gathering basic information on the new diversity, since "being able to identify new minority ethnic groups is a key factor in distributing resources" (Mennell 2000, p. 82). Existing measures are inadequate and may even impair service delivery. As one health expert puts it, "the ten census categories for ethnicity do not reflect the diversity of communities in this country, and mask the differences of their health needs" (Pui-Ling 2000, p. 83).

A comprehensive examination of super-diversity's impacts on public services is well beyond the scope of this paper and capability of this author. It seems evident, however, that most areas of service provision have not caught up with the transformations brought about by the new immigration of the last decade. In one well-informed overview of current institutions, for instance, Anja Rudiger (2006, p. 8) concludes that "Despite statutory provisions, there is little evidence to date that local authorities are in a position to identify how targets relating to service delivery and economic development intersect with the dynamics of diverse community relationships and networks."

In order to avoid the conventional trap of addressing newcomers just in terms of some presumably fixed ethnic identity, an awareness of the new super-diversity suggests that policy-makers and practitioners should take account of new immigrants' "plurality of affiliations" (recognizing multiple identifications and axes of differentiation, only some of which concern ethnicity), "the coexistence of cohesion and separateness" (especially when one bears in mind a stratification of rights and benefits around immigrant categories), and – in light of enhanced transnational practices – the fact that "migrant communities, just as the settled population, can "cohere" to different social worlds and communities simultane-ously" (Zetter et al. 2005, pp. 14, 19).

Conclusion

Described here as "super-diversity", features of Britain's contemporary social con-dition arise from the differential convergence of factors surrounding patterns of immigration since the early 1990s. The experiences, opportunities, constraints and trajectories facing newcomers – and the wider set of social and economic relations within the places where they reside – are shaped by complex interplays.

To recap, these factors include: *country of origin* (comprising a variety of possible subset traits such as ethnicity, language[s], religious tradition, regional and local identities, cultural values and practices), *migration channel* (often related to highly gendered flows and specific social networks), *legal status* (determining entitlement to rights), *migrants' human capital* (particularly educational background), *access to employment* (which may or may not be in immigrants' hands), *locality* (related espe-cially to material conditions, but also the nature and extent of other immigrant and ethnic minority presence), *transnationalism* (emphasizing how migrants' lives are lived with significant reference to places and peoples elsewhere) and the usu-ally chequered *responses by local authorities, services providers and local residents* (which often tend to function by way of assumptions based on previous experiences with migrants and ethnic minorities). Fresh and novel ways of understanding and responding to such complex interplays must be fashioned if we are to move beyond the frameworks derived from an earlier, significantly different, social formation.

A range of existing frameworks, including those which focus on ethnicity as the predominant or even sole criterion marking social processes, should be reshaped and extended. The conventional focus on ethnicity shapes, and may obscure, understanding of "the diversity of migrants' relationships to their place of set-tlement and to other localities around the world" (Glick Schiller et al. 2006, p. 613). A similar conclusion was recently made by Fong and Shibuya (2005, p. 299), who stress that contemporary configurations "require social scientists to go beyond existing theoretical frameworks and methodology to explore the complexity of the multiethic group context." Methodologically addressing and theoretically ana-lyzing processes and effects of super-diversity should stimulate social scientists to creatively consider the interaction of multiple axes of differentiation. This will also help us, thereby, to answer the critical questions posed by Jacobs and Fincher (1998, p. 9), namely: "How does one speak (and write) about such multiply constituted and locationally contingent notions of difference? What are the pertinent dimen-sions along which different identities are expressed or represented?"

For policy-makers and practitioners in local government, NGOs and social service departments, appreciating dimensions and dynamics of super-diversity has profound implications for how they might understand and deal with modes of difference and their interactions within the socio-economic and legal circum-stances affecting members of the population. Discovering and acknowledging the nature and extent of diversity is a crucial first step in the development of adequate policies on both national and local levels. Here social scientific research and analysis can provide many of the key points of information and insight.

Ultimately, however, policy responses to diversification rest on political will and vision. As Leonie Sandercock (2003, p. 104) suggests, "the good society does not commit itself to a particular vision of the good life and then ask how much diversity it can tolerate within the limits set by this vision. To do so would be to foreclose future societal development." The future, immediate and long-term, will inherently be typified by diversity issues: indeed, Keith (2005, p. 1) emphasizes, "the cities of the 21st century will increasingly be characterized by the challenges of multiculturalism." It is here further suggested that such challenges will be marked and conditioned by the kind of factors and issues encapsulated in this article by the notion of "super-diversity".

Although perhaps rather glib, the concept of super-diversity points to the necessity of considering multi-dimensional conditions and processes affecting immigrants in contemporary society. Its recognition will hopefully lead to public policies better suited to the needs and conditions of immigrants, ethnic minorities and the wider population of which they are inherently part.

References

Abu-Lughod, J. L. 1999. *New York, Chicago, Los Angeles: America's Global Cities*, Minneapolis: University of Minnesota Press

Ackroyd, P. 2000. *London: The Biography*, London: Vintage

Al-Ali, N., R. Black and K. Koser 2001 "Refugees and transnationalism: the experience of Bosnians and Eritreans in Europe", *Journal of Ethnic and Migration Studies* 27(4): 615–34 https://doi.org/10.1080/13691830120090412

Allen, J. P. and E. Turner 1989. "The most ethnically diverse urban places in the United States," *Urban Geography* 10(6): 523–39 https://doi.org/10.2747/0272-3638.10.6.523

Amin, A. 2002. "Ethnicity and the multicultural city: Living with diversity," *Environment and Planning A* 34: 959–80 https://doi.org/10.1068/a3537

Anderson, B. 2001. "Different roots in common ground: Transnationalism and migrant domestic workers in London," *Journal of Ethnic and Migration Studies* 27(4): 673–683 https://doi.org/10.1080/13691830120090449

Anderson, B. and M. Ruhs 2005. "What's in a name? Exploring immigration status and compliance," paper given at COMPAS Annual Conference, Oxford

Arai, L. 2006. "Migrants and public services in the UK: A review of the recent literature," Oxford: ESRC Centre on Migration, Policy and Society

Baker, P. and Y. Mohieldeen 2000. "The languages of London's schoolchildren," in *Multilingual Capital*, P. Baker and J. Eversley (eds.), London: Battlebridge, pp. 5–60

Barth, F. 1989. "The analysis of culture in complex societies," *Ethnos* 54: 120–42 https://doi.org/10.1080/00141844.1989.9981389

Barth, F. 1993. *Balinese Worlds*, Chicago: University of Chicago Press.

Baumann, G. 1996. *Contesting Culture: Discourses of Identity in Multi-Ethnic London*, Cambridge: Cambridge University Press

Baumann, G. 1999. *The Multicultural Riddle: Rethinking National, Ethnic and Religious Identities*, London: Routledge https://doi.org/10.4324/9780203906637

Benedictus, L. and M. Godwin 2005. "Every race, colour, nation and religion on earth," *The Guardian* 21 January

Berkeley, R., O. Khan and M. Ambikaipaker 2005. "What is new about the new immigrants in 21ˢᵗ Century Britain?," York: Joseph Rowntree Foundation

Blackwell, M. and D. Seddon 2004. *Informal remittances from the UK: Values, flows and mechanisms*, Norwich: Overseas Development Group Report to the Department for International Development

Castles, S. H. Crawley and S. Loughna 2003. *States of Conflict*, London: Institute for Public Policy Research

Clarke, J. and J. Salt 2003. "Work permits and foreign labour in the UK: A statistical review," *Labour Market Trends* 111(11): 563–74, London: HMSO

Cole, I. and D. Robinson 2003. *Somali Housing Experiences in England*, Sheffield: Centre for Regional Economic and Social Research, Sheffield Hallam University

Collyer, M. 2003. "Explaining change in established migration systems: The movement of Algerians to France and the UK," Brighton: Sussex Migration

Foner, N. 1997. "What's new about transnationalism? New York immigrants today and at the turn of the century", *Diaspora* 6(3): 355–75 https://doi.org/10.3138/diaspora.6.3.355

Fong, E. and K. Shibuya 2005. "Multiethnic cities in North America," *Annual Review of Sociology* 31: 285–304 https://doi.org/10.1146/annurev.soc.31.041304.122246

Freedland, J. 2005. "The world in one city," *The Guardian* 15 July

GLA [Greater London Authority] 2005a. *London – The World in a City: An analysis of the 2001 Census results*, London: Greater London Authority Data Management and Analysis Group Briefing 2005/6

GLA [Greater London Authority] 2005b. *Country of Birth and Labour Market Outcomes in London: An analysis of Labour Force Survey and Census data*, London: Greater London Authority Data Management and Analysis Group Briefing 2005/1

Glick Schiller, N. 1999. "Transmigrants and nation-states: Something old and something new in U.S. immigrant experience", in *Handbook of International Migration: The American Experience*, C. Hirschman, J. DeWind and P. Kasinitz (eds.), New York: Russell Sage, pp. 94–119

Glick Schiller, N., A. Caglar and T. C. Guldbrandsen 2006. "Beyond the ethnic lens: Locality, globality, and born-again incorporation," *American Ethnologist* 33(4): 612–33

Gluckman, M. 1958. "Analysis of a social situation in modern Zululand," *Rhodes-Livingston Papers No. 28*, Manchester: Manchester University Press

Goździak, E.M. and M.J. Melia 2005. "Promising practices for immigrant integration," in *Beyond the Gateway*, E.M. Goździak and S.F. Martin (eds.), Lanham: Lexington, pp. 241–74

Hannerz, U. 1992. *Cultural Complexity: Studies in the Social Organization of Meaning*, New York: Columbia University Press

Hansen, R. and P. Weil 2001. *Towards a European Nationality: Citizenship, Immigration and Nationality Law in the EU*, New York: Palgrave

Harris, R. 2003. "Language and new ethnicities: Multilingual youth and diaspora," London: King's College Working Papers in Urban Language & Literacies no. 22

Harris, R. and B. Rampton 2002. "Creole metaphors in cultural analysis: On the limits and possibilities of (socio-)linguistics," *Critique of Anthropology* 22: 31–51 https://doi.org/10.1177/0308275x020220010101

Harzig, C. and D. Juteau 2003. "Introduction: Recasting Canadian and European history in a pluralist perspective," in *The Social Construction of Diversity*, C. Harzig and D. Juteau (eds), Oxford: Berghahn, pp. 1–12

Hatton, T. 2003. "Explaining trends in UK Immigration," London: Centre for Economic Policy Research, CEPR Discussion Papers 4019

Hewstone, M. and R. Brown (eds) 1986. *Contact and Conflict in Intergroup Encounters*, Oxford: Blackwell

Hollinger, D. 1995. *Postethnic America: Beyond Multiculturalism*, New York: Basic Books

Holmes, C. 1997. "Cosmopolitan London," in *London: The Promised Land?*, A.J. Kershen (Ed.), Aldershot: Avebury, pp. 10–37

Home Office 2001. *Community Cohesion: A Report of the Independent Review Team* (aka the Cantle Report), London: Home Office

Home Office 2002a. *Control of Immigration: Statistics United Kingdom 2001*, London: HMSO

Home Office 2002b. *Migrants in the UK: Their characteristics and labour market outcomes and impacts*, London: Home Office, Research Development and Statistics Occasional Paper No. 82

Home Office 2003. *Building a Picture of Community Cohesion: A guide for local authorities and their partners*, London: Home Office

Home Office 2004. *The End of Parallel Lives? The Report of the Community Cohesion Panel*, London: Home Office

Home Office 2005. "An exploration of factors affecting the successful dispersal of asylum seekers," London: Home Office, Research Development and Statistics Online Report 50/05

Jacobs, J.M. and R. Fincher 1998. "Introduction," in *Cities of Difference*, R. Fincher and J.M. Jacobs (eds.), New York: The Guilford Press, pp. 1–25

JCWI (Joint Council for the Welfare of Immigrants) 2004. *Immigration, Nationality and Refugee Law Handbook*, London: Joint Council for the Welfare of Immigrants.

Johnston, P. 2006. "Immigrants 'swamping' council services," *Daily Telegraph* 26 June

Jordan, B. and F. Düvell 2002. *Irregular Migration: The Dilemmas of Transnational Mobility*, Cheltenham: Edward Elgar https://doi.org/10.4337/9781781950456

Kaczmarczyk, P. and M. Okólski 2005. *International Migration in Central and Eastern Europe: Current and Future Trends*, New York: United Nations Population Division UN/POP/MIG/2005/12

Kai, J. 2003. "Toward quality in health care for a diverse society," in *Ethnicity, Health and Primary Care*, J. Kai (Ed.), Oxford University Press, pp. 27–37

Keith, M. 2005. *After the Cosmopolitan? Multicultural Cities and the Future of Racism*, London: Routledge

Kivisto, P. 2005. "Social spaces, transnational immigrant communities, and the politics of incorporation," in *Incorporating Diversity*, P. Kivisto (ed.), Boulder: Paradigm, pp. 299–319

Kofman, E. 1998. "Whose city? Gender, class, and immigrants in globalizing European cities," in *Cities of Difference*, R. Fincher and J.M. Jacobs (eds.), New York: The Guilford Press, pp. 279–300

Kofman, E. 2004. "Family-related migration: A critical review of European studies," *Journal of Ethnic and Migration Studies* 30(2): 243–62 https://doi.org/10.1080/1369183042000200687

Kofman, E., P. Taghuram and M. Merefield 2005. "Gendered migrations: Towards gender sensitive policies in the UK," London: Institute for Public Policy Research, Asylum and Migration Working Paper 6

Kuper, L. and M. G. Smith (eds) 1969. *Pluralism in Africa*, Berkeley: University of California Press

Kyambi, S. 2005. *New Immigrant Communities: New Integration Challenges?* London: Institute for Public Policy Research

Lamphere, L. (ed.) 1992. *Structuring Diversity: Ethnographic Perspectives on the New Immigration*, Chicago: University of Chicago Press

Large, P. and K. Ghosh 2006. "Estimates of the population by ethnic group for areas within England," Office for National Statistics Population Trends 124

Lewis, P. 2002. *Islamic Britain: Religion, Politics and Identity among British Muslims* London: I.B. Tauris, 2nd edn.

Martiniello, M. 2004. "How to combine integration and diversities: The challenge of an EU multicultural citizenship," Vienna: European Monitoring Centre on Racism and Xenophobia, Discussion Paper

Massey, D. S. and N. A., Denton 1989. "Hypersegregation in U.S. metropolitan areas: Black and Hispanic segregation along five dimensions," *Demography* 26(3): 373–91

Mennell, J. 2000. "Ethnic and linguistic diversity: The impact on local authority expenditure," in *Multilingual Capital*, P. Baker and J. Eversley (eds.), London: Battlebridge, pp. 81–82

Mitchell, J. C. 1956. "The Kalela dance," Rhodes-Livingston Papers No. 27, Manchester: Manchester University Press

Mollenkopf, J. and M. Castells 1991. "Conclusion: Is New York a dual city?," in *Dual City: Restructuring New York*, J. Mollenkopf and M. Castells (eds.), New York: Russell Sage Foundation, pp. 399–418

Morawska, E. 1999. "The new-old transmigrants, their transnational lives, and ethnicization: A comparison of 19th/20th and 20th/21st C situations," Florence: European University Institute Working Papers EUF No. 99/2

Morris, L. 2002. *Managing Migration: Civic Stratification and Rights*, London: Routledge https://doi.org/10.4324/9780203447499

Morris, L. 2004. "The control of rights: The rights of workers and asylum seekers under managed migration," London: Joint Council for the Welfare of Immigrants, Discussion Paper

OFSTED (Office for Standards in Education) 2003. *The education of asylum-seeker pupils*, Report HMI 453

Parsons, G. 1994. *The Growth of Religious Diversity: Britain from 1945*, London: Routledge, 2 vols.

Peach, C. 2005. "The United Kingdom: A major transformation of the religious landscape," in *The Religious Landscape of Europe*, H. Knippenberg (Ed.), Amsterdam: Het Spinhuis, pp. 44–58

Pinkerton, C., G. Mclaughlan and J. Salt 2004. *Sizing the illegally resident population in the UK*, London: Home Office Online Report 58/04

Portes, A., L. E. Guarnizo and P. Landolt 1999. "The study of transnationalism: pitfalls and promise of an emergent research field", *Ethnic and Racial Studies* 22(2): 217–237 https://doi.org/10.1080/014198799329468

Pratt, G. 1998. "Grids of difference: Place and identity formation," in *Cities of Difference*, R. Fincher and J. M. Jacobs (eds.), New York: The Guilford Press, pp. 26–48

Pui-ling Li 2000. "An indicator for health needs of minority ethnic communities in the capital," in *Multilingual Capital*, P. Baker and J. Eversley (eds.), London: Battlebridge, p. 83

Rampton, B. 2005. *Crossing: Language & Ethnicity among Adolescents*, Manchester: St Jerome Press, 2nd edn.

Rampton, B., R. Harris and C. Leung 1997. "Multilingualism in England," *Annual Review of Applied Linguistics* 17: 224–41 https://doi.org/10.1017/s0267190500003366

Reardon, S.F. and G. Firebaugh 2002. "Measures of multigroup segregation," *Sociological Methodology* 23: 33–67 https://doi.org/10.1111/1467-9531.00110

Robinson, D. and K. Reeve 2005. *The Experiences and Consequences of New Immigration at the Neighbourhood Level: Reflections from the evidence base*, Project Report, York: Joseph Rowntree Foundation

Rudiger, A. 2006. "Integration of new migrants: Community relations," in *New Migrants and Refugees*, S. Spencer (Ed.), Oxford: ESRC Centre on Migration, Policy and Society (COMPAS), Report prepared for Home Office

Salt, J. 2004. *International Migration and the United Kingdom: Report of the United Kingdom SOPEMI Correspondent to the OECD 2004*, London: Migration Research Unit, University College London

Sandercock, L. 2003. *Cosmopolis II: Mongrel Cities of the 21st Century*, London: Continuum

Sanjek, R. 1998. *The Future of Us All: Race and Neighborhood Politics in New York City*, Ithaca: Cornell University Press

Shashahani, S. 2002. "To cross or not to cross the boundaries in a small multi-ethnic area of the city of Tehran," in *Urban Ethnic Encounters*, A. Erdentug and F. Colombijn (eds.), London: Routledge, pp. 160–73 https://doi.org/10.4324/9780203218778

Snel, E., G. Engbersen and A. Leekres 2006. "Transnational involvement and social integration," *Global Networks* 6(3): 285–308

Spellman, K. 2004. *Religion and Nation: Iranian Local and Transnational Networks in Britain*, Oxford: Berghahn

Sriskadarajah, D. 2004. *Labour Migration to the UK: An ippr factfile*, London: Institute for Public Policy Research

Statt, D. 1995. *Foreigners and Englishmen: The Controversy over Immigration and Population, 1660–1760*, Newark: University of Delaware Press

Tempest, M. 2006. "New EU migrants may put pressure on public services, says report," *The Guardian* 31 July

UNHCR (United Nations High Commissioner for Refugees) 2005. *2004 Global Refugee Trends*, Geneva: UNHCR

Urry, J. 2005. "The complexity turn," *Theory, Culture & Society* 22(5): 1–14 https://doi.org/10.1177/0263276405057188

Van Hear, N., F. Pieke and S. Vertovec 2004. *The Contribution of UK-based Diasporas to Development and Poverty Reduction*, Oxford: ESRC Centre on Migration, Policy and Society (COMPAS) Report to the Department for International Development

Vertovec, S. 2004a. "Migrant transnationalism and modes of transformation," *International Migration Review* 38(3): 970–1001 https://doi.org/10.1111/j.1747-7379.2004.tb00226.x

Vertovec, S. 2004b. "Cheap Calls: the social glue of migrant transnationalism", *Global Networks* 4(2): 219–24 https://doi.org/10.1111/j.1471-0374.2004.00088.x

Vertovec, S. 2005. "Religion and diaspora," in *New Approaches to the Study of Religion*, P. Antes, A. W. Geertz and R. Warne (eds.), Berlin & New York: Verlag de Gruyter, pp. 275–304

Vertovec, S. and R. Cohen 2002. "Introduction: Conceiving cosmopolitanism," in *Conceiving Cosmopolitanism*, S. Vertovec and R. Cohen (eds.), Oxford: Oxford University Press, pp. 1–22

Vertovec, S. and A. Rogers 1995. "Introduction," in *Muslim European Youth*, S. Vertovec and A. Rogers (eds.), Aldershot: Ashgate, pp. 1–24

Waldinger, R. and M. Bozorgmehr 1996. "The making of a multicultural metropolis," in *Ethnic Los Angeles*, R. Waldinger and M. Bozorgmehr (eds.), New York: Russell Sage Foundation, pp. 3–37

Waters, M. C. and T. R. Jiménez 2005. "Assessing immigrant assimilation: New empirical and theoretical challenges," *Annual Review of Sociology* 31: 105–25 https://doi.org/10.1146/annurev.soc.29.010202.100026

Winder, R. 2004. *Bloody Foreigners: The Story of Immigration to Britain*, London: Abacus

Zetter, R., D. Griffiths, N. Sigona, D. Flynn, T. Pasha and R. Beynon 2005. "Immigration, social cohesion and social capital: What are the links?," *Concepts Paper*, York: Joseph Rowntree Foundation

Zontini, E. 2004. "Italian families and social capital: Rituals and the provision of care in British-Italian transnational families," London: ESRC Research Group on Families & Social Capital Working Paper no. 6

3

THE MANY MEANINGS OF SUPERDIVERSITY

The concept of superdiversity was surprisingly quick to gain attention after the publication of the original article "Super-diversity and its implications" (Vertovec 2007a), its earlier incarnation (Vertovec 2006), and a commissioned report that was written for the UK's national Commission on Integration and Cohesion (Vertovec 2007b). In policy circles, superdiversity was soon invoked in relation to health, social services, and education. In public debates among local governments, non-government organizations (NGOs) and think tanks, media outlets, and internet forums, superdiversity was drawn upon especially concerning issues such as immigration, diversity, and urban development.

Already in the early years after the concept began to circulate, public and policy attention included: a 2010 public discussion on super-diversity in the visual arts conducted at London's Institute of International Visual Arts; a conference in 2011 on "Linguistic super-diversity in urban areas" convened by the European Educational Research Association; a series of public debates in 2012 on "Religious identity in 'superdiverse' societies" organized by the Religion and Society programme of the joint UK research councils; a 2011 Symposium on Super-Diversity in Dynamic Cities organized by Kosmopolis Rotterdam, The Hague and Utrecht; a public discussion in 2012 at the Witte de With Center for Contemporary Art in Rotterdam to mark the launch Tariq Ramadan's (2011) book, *On Super-diversity*. Public policy publications included: the Institute of Public Policy Research *You can't put me in a box: Super-diversity and the end of identity politics in Britain* (Fanshawe and Sriskandarajah 2010); the University of Birmingham and the Department of Health West Midlands review of maternity services *Delivering in an age of super-diversity* (Phillimore et al. 2011); a report in 2011 on *Super Diversity in Canada* published by the Policy Horizons unit of the Government of Canada (Gaye 2011); and a 2012 Green Paper by Birmingham City Council grounding their approach to social inclusion on the concept of super-diversity (Birmingham City Council 2012).

DOI: 10.4324/9780203503577-3

Despite such interest across a number of public sectors, Michael Silverstein (2015) believes that state institutions remain unprepared for the multidimensional fluidity described by the concept of superdiversity, while Mette Berg and Nando Sigona (2013) observe how British local authorities are largely still trying to work out the implications of emergent superdiversity.

The concept of superdiversity has also been variously invoked in a wide range of print media, as well, mainly to address issues of migration, race or ethnicity, and language. The geographical breadth demonstrates the travels of the superdiversity term (although perhaps not truly the concept) not just beyond its British origins but beyond academia. Searching with LexisNexis, newspapers and magazines that in one way or another invoke superdiversity since 2010 include: *The Economist, The Guardian, Daily Mail* and *Evening Standard* (all UK); *New Zealand Herald, Waikato Times* and *Dominion Post* (all New Zealand); *The Australian* (Australia); *The Straights Times* and *Today* (both Singapore); *The Bangkok Post* (Thailand); *The New Age* and *Pretoria News* (both South Africa); *Irish Daily Mail* (Ireland); *Frankfurter Rundschau, Der Tagesspiegel, Frankfurter Allgemeine Zeitung* and *Süddeutsche Zeitung* (all Germany); *La Verdad* (Spain); *Toronto Star, Vancouver Sun, Edmonton Journal* and *The Gazette* (all Canada); and *The American Prospect* and *Cosmopolitan* (both USA). In most cases, these media references to the concept are made in order to signal brief and broad reference to increasing diversities, mainly resulting from international migration.

This chapter, however, reviews and assesses many of the ways the concept of superdiversity has been used and drawn upon (and at times misunderstood) among academics. After the *Ethnic and Racial Studies* article appeared in 2007, I started to see references made to the term by other scholars already commencing in 2008. At first, of course it was gratifying to see such references, however, intended. However, as the years passed and I read more published works referring to super-diversity, I realized that readings of the term were taking many forms. Sometimes I would read a social scientific article referring to super-diversity and think, "ah yes, that's good, the author has 'got it'." With other articles I'd think, "how could the author have gotten it so wrong?" Occasionally I'd read a piece and think "well, it's nice that he or she cited it – but it really has nothing to do with the topic they're really writing about or the point they're trying to make." And – certainly the best reaction – sometimes I'd read a work using the notion of super-diversity in an unconventional or highly innovative way to discuss a cutting-edge issue, and think to myself "I never envisioned this use of the concept or approach – but this author is doing something new and exciting with it."

Across a range of social scientific terrains, the concept of superdiversity has been variably – often highly differentially – invoked, referenced, concocted, or criticized as an idea, setting, condition, theory, or approach. Sometimes scholars have really engaged the concept; that is, they engage empirical data or juxtapose theories with reference to its original meaning or intention. Other times, superdiversity is merely a prompt enabling scholars to discuss something else – a springboard to present a set of related research findings, a segue to another topic, or indeed a false starting point, misnomer, or sheer strawman. Such divergence is surely OK – indeed, that's what happens to many scholarly ideas, concepts, and theories. Once a notion is "out there," its development takes on a life of its own. Multiple understandings, misunderstandings, and misuses arise – and such conceptual evolution (including mutation) mostly moves social science forward.

I have always advocated superdiversity as a concept and approach about new migration patterns. It is not a theory (which, for me, would need to entail an explanation of how and why these changing patterns arose, how they are inter-linked, and what their combined effects causally or necessarily lead to). However, for all sorts of reasons, since 2007 superdiversity has been taken up by a wide variety of scholars from an array of disciplines and fields, in myriad (sometimes helpful, sometimes obfuscating, sometimes brilliant) ways and for multiple (sometimes poignant, sometimes curious) purposes. The same can be said of the various ways superdiversity has been used in policy circles – in relation to integration, health, social services, and education – and in public debates among NGOs and think tanks, media outlets, and internet forums – concerning issues such as immigration, diversity, and urban development. (For a fuller discussion of the many understandings of super-diversity, see the online lecture "Super-diversity as concept and approach" at www.mmg.mpg.de.)

Since the publication of the *Ethnic and Racial Studies* article "Super-diversity and its implications" in 2007, the concept has been picked up across a surprising range of disciplines and fields. Its meanings have interestingly multiplied in the process.

Meanings of superdiversity: A typology

As in policy and media, there is certainly no consensus on the meaning of super-diversity "out there" in academia. The multiple meanings of superdiversity are evident in a limited exercise that traced ways that the term has been invoked or employed in academic literature at least in the first years after publication. (The trends identified here have certainly continued in the years since this initial review.) Together with a research assistant, Wiebke Unger, I acquired 325 publications between 2008 and 2014 through broad online searches for the term. The results of the review were interesting and telling.

One immediate observation is the variable use of the specific terms "super-diversity" or "superdiversity." The hyphen-less term is preferred in this book. Fran Meissner and I wrote:

> [I]n a variety of publications, there has been divergence on whether the word super-diversity is spelled with a hyphen or without. For very many writers, this does not matter; for others, this punctuation mark can bear meaning. While not wanting to be pedantic or to over-theorize the writing of the word, it might be useful to recall the debate in postcolonial studies: for many scholars in that field, the hyphen's removal from 'post-colonial' implies displacing emphasis from the 'post-' in order to create a new sense of a historical condition. A parallel intention surrounds 'superdiversity':

that is, some scholars suggest that the hyphen may tend to promote the skewed or limited understanding of the term as 'more' (ethnic) diversity. Instead, some advocate the removal of the hyphen – hence 'superdiversity' – in order to emphasize the multidimensionality of the notion.

Meissner and Vertovec (2015: 545)

Next, the review shows considerable disciplinary spread of articles referring to superdiversity. These go well beyond the expected ones – Sociology, Anthropology, Geography and Political Science as well as the multidisciplinary fields of Migration and Ethnic Studies – to include Linguistics and SocioLinguistics, History, Education, Law, Business Studies, Management, Literature, Media Studies, Public Health, Social Work, Urban Planning and Landscape Studies.

Further, while the original article described phenomena in London and the UK, the term has been used subsequently to describe social, cultural, and linguistic dynamics in such widespread contexts as Brussels, Venice, New York, Jerusalem, the Baltic states, Italy, Cyprus, Egypt, Nigeria, French Guiana, Zimbabwe, Hong Kong, Hokkaido, Oaxaca, villages of south-west Slovakia, the German state of Brandenburg, the border province of Limburg, Manenberg township in Cape Town, and Enshi in China.

Across all of these disciplines and research contexts, we can see a number of ways that the concept of superdiversity has been used (so far). This typology is certainly not intended as particularly scientific: it is based on my reading of the ways that various authors have used the concept of superdiversity. The authors themselves may well contend my reading.

A marker of very much diversity

Some social scientists have understood superdiversity as a term that is basically synonymous with "diversity" or perhaps simply meaning *very much diversity*. This has included attention to more pronounced kinds and dimensions of social differentiation – particularly cultural identities. For instance, van Ewijk (2011: 1) has invoked superdiversity to stress the fact that "European countries have become more diverse and this diversity is more and more salient." Other examples or this reading of the concept are works that refer to superdiversity in terms of ways of thinking about difference (Mavroudi 2010; Baycan and Nijkamp 2012), "diversity, or what recently has been called 'superdiversity'" (Hüwelmeier 2011: 450), "emerging cultural and demographic diversity" (Svenberg et al. 2011: 2), "multiple dimensions of differentiation" (Kandylis et al. 2012: 268), "significant demographic change and diversification" (Aspinall and Song 2013: 548), and "classification encompassing dozens of different cultures and nationalities" (Aspinall 2009: 1425). Obviously, if diversity and superdiversity were referring to exactly the same phenomena, with the latter merely meaning "a bit more," then the concept would have very little purpose or use. Further, "Diversity" also has very many meanings in both academic and public uses (see Vertovec 2011, 2015a).

As discussed in the original article, many works since, and this book, "superdiversity" does have a core meaning and intention as a descriptive concept of new social patterns – a meaning that has transmogrified as it has been variously adopted.

A context or backdrop

Another common way that superdiversity has been used in many academic articles is to signal increasing social if not ethnic differentiation as a contextual *backdrop to a specific study*. That is, scholars invoke superdiversity as an emergent condition or setting that helps them make sense of whatever set of research findings or theoretical contribution they wish to present (in many if not most cases, these don't actually have much directly to do with superdiversity itself). Such stage-setting use of superdiversity sometimes entails a deeper probe into methodologies for examining emergent modes of social, cultural, and geographic change, such as Suzanne Hall's (2015) description of "super-diverse streets" and Jan Blommaert's (2013a) exploration of the sociolinguistics of superdiversity through his attention to linguistic landscapes.

In this way, we have seen ubiquitous, scene-setting statements about: "'super-diverse' places" (Osipovič 2010: 212), "a super-diverse social space" (Leppänen and Häkkinen 2012: 18), "superdiverse circumstances" (Jørgensen 2012: 57), "the super-diversity of today's cities" (Ros i Solé 2013: 336), superdiverse cities with no ethnic group majorities (Parker and Freathy 2011), Leicester as "the first super-diverse city" in the UK (Hill 2007), "superdiverse London" (Poppleton et al. 2013), and an observation that "America is well on its way to becoming the great super-diverse nation" (Bobo 2013). In more sweeping or macro-sociological terms, some social scientists have set their work in a perspective of encompassing "super-diverse realities" (Juffermans 2012: 33), "life world super-diversity" (Dietz 2013: 27), "super-diverse society" (Hawkey 2012: 175), "the superdiverse condition" (Neal et al. 2013: 309), "a stage of 'super-diversity'" (Colic-Peisker and Farquharson 2011: 583), "a 'super-diverse' world" (Jacquemet 2011: 494), "this time of 'super-diversity'" (Catney et al. 2011: 109), and an "era of super-diversity" (Burdsey 2013). The concept of superdiversity has also been broadly utilized "to signal the scale and multi-dimensional phenomena of mobilities of socio-cultural, spatial, technological, material and metaphysical conditions of human existence in the 21st century" (Heugh 2013: 7). To be sure, across a miscellaneous array, numerous academics have adopted a "superdiversity lens" that has seemingly brought about "a superdiversity turn" in the study of contemporary societies (nandosigona.worldpress.com).

A description of more ethnicity

There are many writers who invoke superdiversity merely to mean *more ethnicity* – meaning that new migration processes have brought more ethnic groups to a nation or city than in the past. While often true (and forming the point of some studies), this is certainly not the intention of the superdiversity concept. However, such a reading is prevalent among scholars who draw upon superdiversity to call attention to: additional ethnicities (Hogg 2011; Salway et al. 2011), ever wider ranges of new migrant groups (Nathan and Lee 2013), people arriving from more countries (Syrett and Lyons 2008), migration from more remote corners of the world (Drinkwater 2010), a new diversity of migrant origins (Antonsich 2012), the growth in the percentage of population born abroad (Hollingworth and Williams 2010), the presence of polyethnic minorities (Aspinall and Hashem 2011), the shift from Commonwealth to non-Commonwealth and Eastern European migration flows (Coleman and Dubuc 2010), immigrant arrivals from different countries and the proliferation of smaller groups of migrants (Phillimore 2010), the increasing spread of new communities, languages, religious practices and people flows (Nathan 2011) or the sheer plurality of minorities (Hill 2007) or polyethnic minorities (Aspinall and Hashem 2011). This understanding of super-diversity was also evident in a 2013 conference at the Kazan Federal University in Russia, entitled "Issues of super-diversity: Migration in Russia and EU." Here, the organizers invoked superdiversity to describe the ever-increasing heterogeneity of urban communities, with some cities hosting in excess of 100 different nationalities. Similarly, a 2013 conference at the University of California – Los Angeles (UCLA) entitled "Superdiversity California Style" looked at dramatically increased ethnic, racial, linguistic, and religious diversity in the USA generally and Los Angeles specifically. Most of these studies do not take into account the multidimensional nature of categories, shifting configurations and new social structures that these entail. Hence, the "more ethnicities" understanding of superdiversity is, unfortunately, rather misplaced. It is what Ralph Grillo (2015) has called the "Super-Diversity Lite" understanding.

A call to move beyond ethnicity

Many scholars indeed draw upon the multidimensionality of characteristics highlighted by the concept of superdiversity to augment their desire to move *beyond a focus on ethnicity* as the sole or optimal category of analysis surrounding migrants. This follows a well-known call by Nina Glick Schiller, Ayşe Çağlar and Thaddeus Guldbrandsen (2006) for scholars to move "beyond the ethnic lens" in assessing migration dynamics – that is, to resist analyses focused on the ethnic dimension alone when considering migration processes and outcomes. Subsequently, social scientists have used the concept of superdiversity in this way to emphasize that: ethnic groups are not the optimal units of analysis (Cooney 2009); an overly ethnic focus may actually mask more significant forms of differentiation (Fomina 2006); social scientists need to move beyond simplified conceptualizations of ethnic and racial groups (Piekut and Rees 2011; Bradby 2012); ethnic boundaries are increasingly blurred (Lobo 2010; Pecoud 2010); there are internal divisions within ethnic groups (Schiller and Çağlar 2009); there are other "strands of identity" that people experience are equally or more important than their identity (Reid and Sriprakash 2012; Schmidt 2012); ethnicity must be cross-tabulated with other categories to get truer picture of contemporary diversity (Aspinall 2011); multiple "modes of differentiation" come into play from context to context (van Ewijk 2011); and ethnicity-only approaches in social policy are inadequate for addressing needs (Bauböck 2008; Crawley 2010). Overall, superdiversity has been used to emphasize the inherent complications of classifying people (Aspinall 2009; Song 2009; Wimmer 2009) and a need to break from a conceptually bounded approach like a focus on ethnicity, since given the contemporary dynamics of migration and diversity, "the result is not communities, but a churning mass of languages, ethnicities and religions, all cutting across each other" (Modood 2008), 85). As a corrective, superdiversity has been used to place stress on the intersectionality between ethnicity and other categories (Christensen and Jensen 2011).

The move away from bounded categories advocated by superdiversity also effects the ways complex social environments should be studied. As Jan Blommaert and Ad Backus (2013: 13) suggest:

> The impact of superdiversity is therefore paradigmatic: it forces us to see the new social environments in which we live as characterized by an *extremely low degree of presupposability* in terms of identities, patterns of social and cultural behavior, social and cultural structure, norms and expectations. People can no longer be straightforwardly associated with particular (national, ethnic, sociocultural) groups and identities; their meaning-making practices can no longer be presumed to 'belong' to particular languages and cultures – the empirical field has become extremely complex, and descriptive adequacy has become a challenge for the social sciences as we know them.
>
> *(italics in original)*

A multidimensional reconfiguration

In this spirit of utilizing the concept of superdiversity to call more attention to multiple, intersecting categories in social scientific research and analysis, several works elaborate descriptions and analyses of superdiversity as *a multidimensional reconfiguration* of various social forms. One such piece is by Janine Dahinden (2009) concerning the emergence of superdiversity, coupled with heightened transnationalism, as it fundamentally affects social networks and cognitive classifications among migrants. Other publications note how new superdiverse configurations raise the need to take multiple variables into account when trying to measure diversity (Longhi 2013) or call attention to how a combination of variables and attributes are variously combined and used by migrants as different forms of capital (Vershinina et al. 2009). Similarly, the superdiversity concept has been employed in order to recognize how a confluence of factors shape the life chances of ethnic minorities (Stubbs 2008) or to critique the ways older categories may be getting in the way of understanding minority communities' achievements as well as needs (Hollingworth and Mansaray 2012). Approaches calling on the concept have also been used to examine multiple variables as they relate to media uses (Dhoest et al. 2012) and to construct narratives of migration and work among low-paid migrant men (Datta et al. 2009). The multiple variable understanding is what Grillo (2015) has called "Super-Diversity Heavy (à la Vertovec)."

A methodological reassessment

The kinds of changing multidimensional patterns referred to as superdiversity, and the intersectional approach it calls for, have also been underlined by scholars in order to urge a *methodological reassessment* of their respective field or discipline. Here, for example, Jan Blommaert (2013a: 6) has stressed "the paradigmatic impact of super-diversity: it questions the foundations of our knowledge and assumptions about societies, how they operate and function at all levels, from the lowest level of human face-to-face communication all the way up to the highest levels of structure in the world system." Massimo Leone (2012: 189) suggests that in key migrant-receiving societies, "it is increasingly found that the conceptual framework of 'cultural integration', predominant thus far in social research and policy making about social cohesion and harmony, is largely unsatisfactory in dealing with the challenges of the so-called super-diverse cities."

Charlotte Williams and Mark R.D. Johnson (2010) argue that new complexities and mixtures brought about by contemporary migration create conditions that policymakers and practitioners of all kinds – particularly in welfare services – must grapple with. Appeals for conceptual and methodological retooling have been strong in fields of practice such as education (e.g., Guo 2010; Gogolin 2011; Gross 2020; Li et al. 2021), medical sociology (Bradby et al. 2017), health (Phillimore 2010) and health workers (Ní Shé and Joye 2018), mental illness (Kirwan 2022), child protection services (Leitão Ferreira 2021), technical communication (Cardinal 2022), social work (van Ewijk 2018), and social policy more broadly (Phillimore in press). Regarding the latter, the conditions of superdiversity have prompted assessments that "policies and discourses need updating in order to match and facilitate new multicultural realities" (Colic-Peisker and Farquharson 2011: 583). Can Yildiz and Annie Bartlett (2011) make a similar case regarding superdiversity and public services especially surrounding health, just as Jenny Phillimore (2013) does for housing. Dave Newall, Jenny Phillimore and Hilary Sharpe (2012, 22) argue that "The complexity associated with superdiverse populations, combined with lack of funds or political will to develop specialist services, means it will not be easy to improve migrant women's experiences of maternity in the UK unless universal maternity services are better equipped to meet the needs of all women." Elsewhere, it has been argued that taking account of superdiversity may affect strategies for recruitment in social and advocacy services (Richardson and Fulton 2010).

Across these fields, Antonio López Paláez and his colleagues (2022) conducted a bibliometric and meta-analysis of 76 publications on superdiversity in English and Spanish from 2007 to 2019 with an eye to social policy. "The methodological lens of superdiversity can aid in improving the implementation of social policies in disadvantaged groups. New research approaches must take into account the practical utility of superdiversity. In this regard, this analysis has detected the inclusion of superdiversity-based policies to improve access to welfare state services" (Ibid.: 176).

With regard to social scientific purposes, Blommaert (2013a: 131) adds to this methodological call by writing that:

> Now that we begin to get a glimpse of what the order of superdiversity consists of, our theoretical, conceptual and methodological toolkit must be adjusted so as to capture what we believe we need to capture: the logic of change instead of the 'laws' of the system, the 'deep' immutable, timeless and static features that make the system into what it is, its generative grammar so to speak. We have to look for structures, indeed – the same targets remain in place – but structure understood in an entirely different sense now.

Perhaps no other field or discipline has employed superdiversity for methodological reassessment more than sociolinguistics. This is also illustrated by Blommaert (2013a: 8) who states that:

> Superdiversity, thus, seems to add layer upon layer of complexity to sociolinguistic issues. Not much of what we were accustomed to methodologically and theoretically seems to fit the dense and highly unstable forms of hybridity and multimodality we encounter in fieldwork data nowadays. Patching up will not solve the problem; fundamental rethinking is required.

The substantial methodological impacts of superdiversity in sociolinguistics are described further below.

A way of addressing emergent social complexities

Finally, there are numerous academics who, although invoking the concept of superdiversity, actually draw attention to something rather different (though often not wholly unrelated) to what was originally intended: *emergent social complexities*. Within this type of usage, scholars have referred to superdiversity with regard to at least three fields of such complexity. (Social complexity as a concept and approach will be addressed in Chapter 6.)

(a) One field of complexity concerns *globalization and migration*. Regarding the latter, a variety of writers discuss superdiversity with regard to issues like: "the complexity of new migration and non-linear trajectories of migrants" (McCabe et al. 2010: 19); "the arrival of new streams of migrants" (Phillips 2007: 1151);

"streams of migrants with different legal statuses" (Walton-Roberts 2011: 464); migrants' mixed motivations for migrating (Perrons et al. 2010); how "migrants have become more transitory and more diverse not only in terms of their origins, but also in their motives, intentions and statues within destination countries" (McDowell 2013: 19); how "International migration has become 'liquid'" (Engbersen et al. 2010: 117). The superdiversity of particular streams or groups of migrants has been described too, such as among international footballers (Storey 2011), British expatriates (Hampshire 2013), and the African (Hiruy and Hutton 2020), Roma (Tremlett 2014), Tamil (Jones 2019), and Indonesian (Goebel 2015) diasporas. Regarding the former field, globalization, superdiversity has been used to highlight how "there are now many sources for ideas and commodities, not simply from Europe or the US or from East to West" (Nolan et al. 2010: 11). In discussing the emergence of "complex diversity," Peter Kraus (2012: 12) draws attention to:

> a cycle of transformations – tentatively captured by such labels as 'globalization' or 'transnationalism' – that have important consequences for how we experience our identities as individuals and citizens all over the world. In this regard, we seem to have moved toward more fluid and complex forms of diversity in Europe, to forms that are leading to manifold new categories for grasping the phenomena in question, such as 'postnationalism' or, at a somewhat different level, 'cosmopolitanism' and 'super-diversity'.

(b) Another field of complexity concerns *ethnic categories and social identities*. Here, superdiversity has prompted renewed interest in: "the origins of people, their presumed motives for migration, their "career" as migrants (sedentary versus short-term and transitory), or their sociocultural and linguistic features [that] cannot be presupposed" (Jacquemet 2011: 494); "individuals and groups who themselves are superdiverse … across a wide range of variables" (Leppänen and Häkkinen 2012: 18); "socially and culturally complex individuals who cannot be pigeonholed in particular ways and are not necessarily segregated into closed-off communities" (Ros i Solé 2013: 327); "a new, 'super-diverse' terrain in which 'old' structural indicators are less salient to social identities" (Francis et al. 2013: 2).

With regard to a topic that is increasingly significant in the social sciences at present, superdiversity has also been invoked to address the "blurring of distinctions" between social categories (Newton and Kusmierczyk 2011: 76), to "the discourse of ambiguity, complexity, and multiplicity that permeates debates on 'race' [and] 'ethnicity'" (Ram et al. 2012: 507) or situations in which "clear-cut categories of difference (race, ethnicity, culture, religion) are no more: notions of Whiteness and Blackness, and minority categories as constructed in the postcolonial context and in the premises of multiculturalism, are blurred" (Hatziprokopiou 2008: 24). This includes uses of superdiversity to call attention to "encounters which undermine held stereotypes" (Osipovič 2010: 171); the ways "cultural traditions become manifold or hazy" (Koch 2009); how "it is descriptively inadequate to assume fixed relations between ethnicity, citizenship, residence, origin, language, profession, etc. or to assume the countability of cultures, languages, or identities" (Juffermans 2012: 33); the "complexity of multiple, fluid, intersectional identifications" (Dhoest et al. 2013: 13). Accordingly, David Parkin (2012: 79) advocates that we turn our attention to the rise of "a form of identity-making which transcends, through its superdiversity, that of conventional contours of ethnicity."

Pulling together various takes on the term, Blommaert and Backus write:

> The impact of superdiversity is therefore paradigmatic: it forces us to see the new social environments in which we live as characterized by an extremely low degree of presupposability in terms of identities, patterns of social and cultural behavior, social and cultural structure, norms and expectations. People can no longer be straightforwardly associated with particular (national, ethnic, sociocultural) groups and identities; their meaning-making practices can no longer be presumed to 'belong' to particular languages and cultures – the empirical field has become extremely complex, and descriptive adequacy has become a challenge for the social sciences as we know them.
>
> *2013: 13*

(c) A third take on complexity for which scholars draw from the concept of superdiversity concerns *new social formations*. Here, a variety of articles invoke the term to address issues such as: processes leading to "a churning mass of languages, ethnicities, and religions, all cutting across each other" (Palaiologou and Faas 2012: 570); "new dimensions of sociocultural and linguistic diversity, which emphasise the variability, fluidity, and complexity of today's global contexts and especially urban settings" (Cogo 2012: 289); sites of research that are "more varied and fluid" (Hawkey 2012: 166); "trends [that] have diversified the varied forms of contestation of belonging, including new dynamics of spatial segregation and cross-cultural contacts" (Matejskova 2013: 46); the fact that "superdiverse social environments are intensely polycentric" (Blommaert 2013b: 3); "complex links" (Hambye and Richards 2012: 170) and "complex new 'meaningful exchanges'" (Butcher 2010: 510) that can lead to "greater interaction, to the evolution of culture, and to the development of convivial and cosmopolitan identities" (Taylor-Gooby and Waite 2014, 272); how "daily life worlds are increasingly diverse, a process which affects both native and migrant populations .... Institutional monoculturalism and life world superdiversity thus end up coexisting" (Dietz 2013: 27); and the ways that "superdiversity, and its superimposition of diverse networks, brings groups together with very different frames of reference" (Bailey 2013: 203). Underlining social change in Belgium and the Netherlands, Dirk Geldof (2016: 35) points to "a new superdiverse reality, which is characterized by a greater complexity in the composition of local populations and an equally greater complexity and ambiguity in the interaction between the different elements of those populations." This ever-emerging reality entails "diversity *between* groups and communities," Geldof (Ibid.: 38) suggests, "as well as *among* those groups and communities. The 'complexity axis' and the interactions between all these different factors form the core of superdiversity."

Jorge Manuel Leitão Ferreira (2021: 4) elaborates his understanding of the concept of superdiversity, particularly centring on:

> the prefix 'super' – which in my conception means the interface between different elements including: groups, policies, contexts, cultures, values, and enables better cooperation among differentiated actors who cross interests, knowledge and experiences that enhance society's innovation and social and human development.

> Several of these matters are brought together in a perspective on the observation of phenomena of globally expanded mobility, which entail new and increasingly complex social formations and networking practices beyond traditional affiliations. Although one could formerly assume the existence over a longer span of time of relatively stable communities of practice, these have become more temporary given the conditions of super-diversity.
>
> *Busch (2012: 505)*

The breakdown of these articles into seven usages of superdiversity by discipline or multidisciplinary field is represented in Figure 3.1. It is immediately interesting to see that no discipline or field is wholly associated with a particular usage.

A field of political policy and governance

More recently, after the above exercise in typology was undertaken, another body of literature has emerged that specifically entails political implications of superdiversity in terms of governance and policy development. Jenny Phillimore, Nando Sigona, and Katherine Tonkiss discern that "while some studies have examined the impact of superdiversity in specific fields of social policy, little is as yet known about the processes and practices of policymaking and governance" (Phillimore et al. 2017: 489). Therefore, a number of social scientists from across disciplines have come to examine how governments at various scales can understand and create appropriate policy tools for an ever more complex populace. In this body of literature, superdiversity is used as a conceptual platform on which to build work on policy and governance (also see Phillimore et al. 2020). Studies have subsequently examined superdiversity in relation to: urban design and planning (Pemberton 2016; Rishbeth 2016), governance models (Raco and

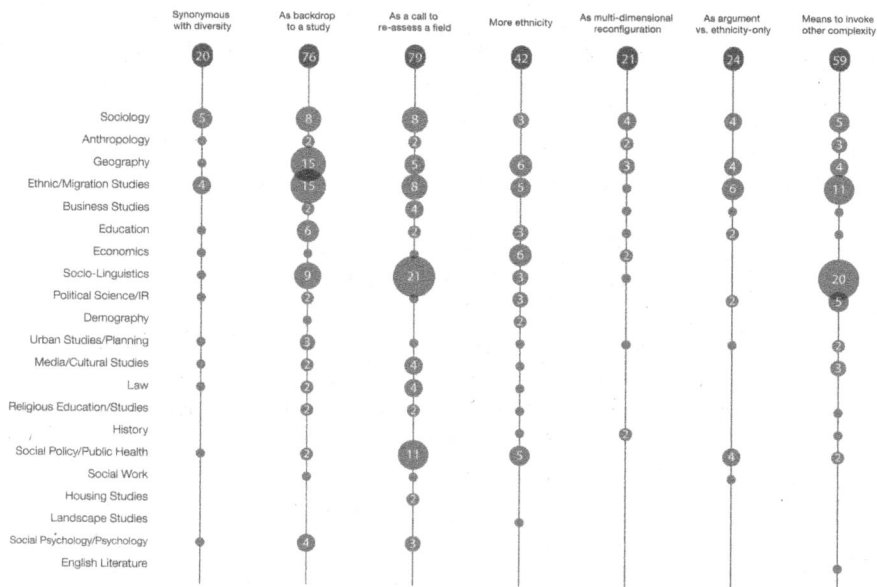

FIGURE 3.1 A typology of articles referring to superdiversity, 2008–2014: number of articles by discipline/field and type

Taşan-Kok 2020), migrant integration policies (Meissner 2018) and diversity management policies (Magazzini 2017), local migration strategies (Geldof et al. 2017), municipal involvement with civil society organizations (Ambrosini 2016), place marketing and city branding (Oliviera and Padilla 2017), and European intercultural policies (Hadj Abdou and Geddes 2017).

Here, too, Peter Scholten (2020) has engaged in a wide-ranging look at government policy challenges wrought by multiple kinds of complexification, a key one of which is superdiversity. These challenges arise because, Scholten says:

> Faced with complexity and contestation, it becomes more difficult to institutionalize specific policy approaches and to identify clear target groups of policies. In complex social settings, characterized by mobility and superdiversity, it becomes hard to define specific groups as targets of policies, not only as there can be many groups involved … but also as the 'boundaries' between groups fade as part of processes of cultural hybridization.
>
> *Ibid.: 12*

Some of the responses he describes include trends towards both "alienation" or discrepancies of policy and emergent social realities, as well as policy mainstreaming of non-group-specific approaches. Scholten advocates mainstreaming as a generic approach across policy areas and levels, adopting a whole-society approach to diversity rather than a set of policies targeting specific migrant or minority groups (also see van Breugel and Scholten 2017; Scholten and van Breugel 2018).

The spread of meanings, uses, and understandings of superdiversity are ever broadening and proliferating. In June 2022, Google Scholar indicates that the original *Ethnic and Racial Studies* journal article of 2007 has been cited over 7,200 times, while the 2006 COMPAS Working Paper on superdiversity, on which the 2007 article is based, has been cited over 850 times. Beyond separate articles, a dozen monographs centring on – or at least springing from – the concept have been published. In particular, we have seen *On Superdiversity* by Tariq Ramadan (2011), *Superdiversity* by Maurice Crul, Jens Schneider, and Frans Lelie (2013), and *Superdiversity in the Heart of Europe* by Dirk Geldof (2016).

In his short book *On Superdiversity* (actually an extended essay also translated into Dutch and Arabic), Ramadan (2011) mainly used superdiversity only as a point of departure philosophically to discuss diversity, "othering" and universalism. He posits that social, cultural, religious, and other modes of diversity offer both the opportunity and responsibility for individuals to consider their own "inner" diversity. "Thus," he (Ibid.: 19) says, "the super-diversity of our time requires an intimate way of dealing with our own beliefs, convictions and 'the other' – no diversity outside without a sense of diversity inside." For Ramadan, it follows that recognizing the complexity of others and our own make leads to the emergence of respect as a fundamental attitude and way of living.

Despite its title, Crul et al.'s (2013) book *Superdiversity* also only really uses the concept as a launchpad. Although there is some discussion of social and political dynamics in majority-minority cities, where the authors argue that "integration" or "assimilation" must take on entirely new meanings (also see Crul 2016), the book mainly concerns the views, experiences, and trajectories of the so-called second generation (the children born in Europe to first-generation migrants). Although interested in this particular category, they underline that it is impossible to think of the second generation as any kind of homogeneous group. Hence, the authors cite the superdiversity concept. The book's intent is to demonstrate how the future relies on "socially successful young people from this second generation [who]represent the most progressive forces within their own communities" (Ibid.: 11).

Superdiversity in the Heart of Europe by Geldof (2016) provides both a conceptual and empirical engagement with the concept in its full, multidimensional sense. Premised on the view that "The 21st century will be the age of superdiversity" (Ibid.: 16), Geldof focuses his book on developments in Belgium and the Netherlands. After tracing the complex diversification of these countries over the last decades – using what Grillo calls a 'superdiversity heavy' understanding, and importantly including patterns of transnationalism – Geldof ultimately interrogates questions of multiculturalism, interculturalism, and living together in increasingly diversifying societies. Among Geldof's main concerns is the fact that "reality is changing more quickly than our language"; subsequently, he asks, "How can we develop a language to conduct a meaningful dialogue about our common future?" (Ibid.: 18). His book provides a highly useful start.

The above literature review has looked across a variety of social science disciplines and the variety of ways superdiversity has been interpreted. Below, examining one discipline in particular, we can see how the concept has triggered meaningful new empirical studies and theoretical development.

Transforming a discipline: Sociolinguistic superdiversity

As briefly mentioned earlier, some of the most substantial calls for disciplinary rethinking around superdiversity have arisen within Sociolinguistics. Indeed, an entire field or approach of "sociolinguistic superdiversity" has emerged (Blommaert and Rampton 2011). Here, scholars are using superdiversity to pull together a number of existing, if not long-standing, approaches and insights within sociolinguistics.

An important tradition within Sociolinguistics (and Anthropological Linguistics) concerns processes and outcomes of so-called language contact and language change (Gumperz and Hymes 1972; Gumperz 1982). In keeping within this tradition in more recent years, Blommaert and Rampton (2011: 3) suggest, "there has been ongoing revision of fundamental ideas (a) about languages, (b) about language groups and speakers, and (c) about communication. ... [S]uperdiversity intensifies the relevance of these ideas." Given its attention to multidimensional characteristics and change, for many scholars superdiversity has provided a further shift from viewing language as a stable, bounded entity to something more open, mixed, and dynamic. It has encouraged language scholars to "focus on the very variable ways in which individual linguistic features with identifiable social and cultural associations get clustered together whenever people communicate" (Ibid.: 4). In keeping with this view, especially on modes of communicative mixing, David Parkin (2012: 83) writes of how "superdiversity produces 'affordances' and opportunities for semiotic crossovers which produce further diversity at an often bewildering pace, as seemingly befits the current global age."

Sociolinguistic superdiversity represents "a new theoretical approach to language in society, a new key in which Sociolinguistics can be played" (Blommaert 2015: 3). Instead of focusing on rather unsatisfactory notions of "languages," this approach focuses much attention on the notion of linguistic repertoires referring to "individuals' very variable (and often rather fragmentary) grasp of a plurality of differentially shared styles, registers and genres" (Ibid.). Sociolinguists turn more attention to communicative capacities within complex social environment, seeking to understand how people use, create, mix, and signal a variety of semiotic materials (Arnaut and Spotti 2014). These dynamics themselves contribute to complex environment be ever forming and constituting "super-diverse repertoires" (Blommaert and Backus 2013). Such repertoires are not just comprised of spoken vocabularies, grammars, genres and registers, but also gestures, postures, written and symbolic materials, and physical arrangements themselves.

The most comprehensive account of how the concept of superdiversity has impacted the discipline of Sociolinguistics is presented in *The Routledge Handbook of Language and Superdiversity* (Creese and Blackledge 2018a; also see Budach and de Saint-Georges 2017). In the *Handbook*, no less than 35 specialist chapters address myriad topics related to language and superdiversity, including: Sociolinguistics and social media, linguistic methodologies, digital language practices, heritage and communication, policy and planning, sports, employment, management and entrepreneurship, education, law and legal discourse. The *Handbook* editors, Angela Creese and Adrian Blackledge, describe the paradigm shift in their discipline, importantly noting its nuances given the ways in which "sociolinguistic superdiversity is a complex system subject to very different and separately developing forces, with multiple historicities and scales entering into uniquely situated communicative events" (Creese and Blackledge 2018b: xxviii). This historical and scalar approach is in line with what they wrote some ten years beforehand – namely, that:

> The ways in which people negotiate access to resources in increasingly diverse societies are changing in response to other developments, and we argue that the new diversity is not limited to "new" migrants who arrived in the last decade, but includes changing practices and norms in established migrant (and non-migrant) groups, as daughters and sons, grand-daughters and grand-sons, great-grand-daughters and great-grandsons of immigrants (and non-migrants) negotiate their place in their changing world. ... [W]e propose that looking at these phenomena through a sociolinguistic lens is key to a developed understanding of superdiverse societies.
>
> *Creese and Blackledge (2010: 550)*

The call is taken up by Karel Arnaut (2012: 11), who uses the concept of super-diversity as a platform to foster a "critical sociolinguistics of diversity" (CSD), an approach that first:

> must set off from super-diversity's transgressive moment, which consists of discarding the false certainties of multiculturalism and its endorsement of established differences and hierarchies. ... The second step consists in CSD embracing the radical unpredictability that comes with the melt-down of the diversity measurement system which super-diversity has provoked.

Accordingly, an array of sociolinguists (one conference on the sociolinguistics of superdiversity included 300 researchers) have pushed methodological and theoretical boundaries. The field and approach of sociolinguistic superdiversity has come to include such intriguing notions as: linguistic landscapes; languaging, polylanguaging and translanguaging; metrolingualism; digital superdiversity; multiple discursive practices; supervernacularization; multiple subject positions; sociolinguistic economies; and the polycentricity of semiotic resources (see, among others, Blommaert and Rampton 2011; Blommaert 2014; García and Wei 2014; Pennycook and Otsuji 2015; Rampton 2017; Creese and Blackledge 2018b).

Contributing to this field and approach, an abundance of books have ensued by sociolinguists, including: *Linguistic Superdiversity in Urban Areas* (Duarte and Gogolin 2013); *Ethnography, Superdiversity and Linguistic Landscapes* (Blommaert 2013a); *Language and Superdiversity* (Goebel 2015); *Language and Superdiversity* (Arnaut et al. 2015); *Linguistic Genocide or Superdiversity? New and Old Language Diversities* (Toivanen and Saarikivi 2016); *Diversity and Super-diversity: Sociocultural Linguistic Perspectives* (De Fina et al. 2017); and *Researching Language in Superdiverse Urban Contexts* (Mar-Molinero 2020).

Sociolinguistic superdiversity has been the basis of new work in several contexts such including studies of superdiversity, language and government authorities and asylum-seekers (Jacquemet 2011), schools (Creese and Blackledge 2010), and neighbourhoods (Blommaert 2014). It has also underscored groundbreaking sociolinguistic research on language and digital technologies. This includes the use of translation apps and Google translate, the incorporation of emojis and other symbols and digital signage. Jannis Andreoutsopoulos and Kaspar Juffermans (2014) discuss how such digital language practices in superdiverse settings extend the semiotic resources available for people to perform their identities and shape their social relationships. Similar projects examine superdiversity in relation to on- and offline communities (Stæhr 2014), forms of internet communication (Varis and Wang 2011), and practices of "buffalaxing" or the ways in which semiotic modes such as sounds, writing, and images are purposefully recombined (Leppänen and Häkkinen 2012). Stressing the implications of such work, Sirpa Leppänen and Ari Häkkinen propose that:

> besides functioning as a superdiverse social space, social media illustrate superdiversification also because in them language use, communication, dissemination of information, and mediation of cultural practices and products increasingly feature mobility, plurality, heterogeneity, and poly-centricity of semiotic resources and normativities through and with which participants express themselves and communicate with others.
>
> *Leppänen and Häkkinen (2012: 18)*

Thus in many unexpected ways, the concept of superdiversity has stimulated and generated a wealth of new thinking, research, and writing within one particular discipline, Sociolinguistics. An expanding abundance of literature demonstrates considerable implications for theory and methodology. However, as Michael Silverstein (2015) observes, both the emergence of superdiverse linguistic phenomena and their theorization bring practical challenges, especially to nation-state institutions:

> "[S]uperdiversity" presents multi-dimensional fluidity and excesses of language-ing (language behavior) which the institutional apparatuses of the state polity have been, as yet, effectively unprepared to countenance and assimilate into official practices. These excesses constitute realignment – or at least an audibility and visibility that can no longer be ignored – of how language communities intersect one with another within one or more pluri-lingual speech communities which the nation-state order is not yet prepared to embrace as its own.
>
> *Ibid.: 8*

While not seeing quite such levels of methodological transformation, another discipline to be challenged by the superdiversity concept has been History. Here, the debate may not be terribly widespread, but its grounds are significant.

The "newness" thing: History and superdiversity

Historian Josefien De Bock (2015) has observed how "the notion of superdiversity raises suspicion among historians" (Ibid. 583). Blommaert (2015: 2) paraphrases many within that discipline, who ask "Haven't we seen all of this before? And do we need superdiversity when so much it brings to the surface is a matter of recognition of patterns and processes already long present?" Or as Nancy Foner (2017: 49) bluntly asks, "What's new about super-diversity?"

These questions raise very similar issues to debates between historians and other social scientists regarding globalization (Bell 2003), transnationalism (Foner 1997), and migration and integration (Lucassen et al. 2006). When sociologists or anthropologists claim some societal development as "new," there are practically always historians who point to some seemingly same phenomena in the past. "Newness" claims are commonly contentious. Such debates are good, not just to probe "if" something is "new," but more importantly "how," "why/why not," and "so what"?

Addressing superdiversity, Foner (2017: 50) believes that "it is important to delve more deeply to understand parallels with the past, since there are more parallels than have been assumed. ... For a full understanding, I would argue, we need to look at both sides of the picture, analyzing the commonalities between past and present as well as the contrasts." Reflecting on 19th- to 20th-century migration to New York City, she admittedly chooses only one dimension of superdiversity, namely the proliferation of ethnic groups – noting that many scholars (as we have seen above) do indeed take only this interpretation of the concept. Not surprisingly, Foner shows how this period was comprised of a remarkable mixture of ethnicities – while noting that "today's greater ethnic diversity clearly matters" (Ibid.: 53). She also goes on to acknowledge that historical migration to the city did not come close to contemporary migration patterns in terms of the proliferation of legal statuses. Similarly, in a study of guestworker migration to Belgium, De Bock acknowledges that the complexities of recent migration-driven diversity undoubtedly differ in important ways from migration-driven diversity in the 1960s and 1970s. But, she stresses, comparison with a superdiversity lens shows that there are important similarities that bring insights into both the historical cases and current conditions.

Similarly, Grillo (2015: 7) points out, "Indeed, many cities, in many epochs, have been ethnically and culturally diverse, sometimes highly diverse. Super-Diversity Lite, if not everywhere, is certainly common. But is Super-Diversity Heavy peculiar to certain global cities under present conditions of globalisation and transnationalism?" Grillo's answer is a strong "yes." Moreover, he suggests that the superdiversity concept has arisen specifically because of the complex conditions of the present-day. But using it to look back into history can be revealing. This view is shared by Creese and Blackledge (2018b: xxv), who write:

> Looking at history through a superdiversity lens, and superdiversity through a historical lens, can inform understandings of past migrant populations and can help assess claims of contemporary exceptionalism, as historical examples provide insight into how current configurations of diversity are similar to, and different from, those in the past. Theoretically informed empirical work dealing with past migrations enables us to understand what exactly constitutes superdiversity, and to delineate what sets it apart from other instances of diversity, both today and in earlier periods.

In this way, Foner (2017) says, historians might be stimulated to undertake additional research and rethinking on diversities of the past. Blommaert (2015), indeed, writes that superdiversity should "provoke" historians to do so by offering them a unique orientation:

> What is truly new, therefore, is the paradigmatic perspective and not the "superdiverse" new objects. It is the perspective that enables us not just to analyze the messy contemporary stuff, but also to re-analyze and re-interpret more conventional and older data, now questioning the fundamental assumptions (almost inevitably language-ideological in character) previously used in analysis.)
>
> The fact, therefore, that there is only a small set of phenomena that can be called specifically 'superdiverse', does not reduce the usefulness of the theoretical intervention: recall that Quantum theory did not replace Newtonian physics, it just explained its exceptions, but in so doing it recast the foundations for an understanding of vastly more. It also did not need a new universe for that: the universe was exactly the same for Isaac Newton

and Niels Bohr; the understanding of the universe changed, not its existence. There is of course no reason to extend this analogy or take it too literally; but the comparison can show us the usefulness of new perspectives on old issues, how such perspectives can 'renew' the old issues, explain some of their previously inexplicable aspects, and so bring a very broad range of issues within their purview.

2015: 3

This is just the approach used in a detailed historical study of the ebbs and flows of Rotterdam's superdiversity since 1600 (van der Laar and van der Schoor 2019). The historians employ the concept and approach of superdiversity to investigate "a process of diversity on a local scale, stressing the important dimensions of ethnicity, gender, education, social status, generation or religion to explain processes of mobility or exclusion in a long-term perspective" (Ibid.: 22). In an example focused on linguistic change, Michael Silverstein (2015) describes pre-contact and post-contact dynamics in Northwest Coast North America as a context of superdiversity. He discusses the history of intersecting language communities and shifting social relations in order to interrogate whether increasing superdiversification has represented a mode of incremental or transformative change. And, while David Parkin (2012: 76) depicts the tremendous ethnic and linguistic diversity of pre-colonial and colonial Kenya and Uganda, he goes on to stress that:

> But it was hardly on the scale of modern superdiversity. For, by the latter, we understand the situation in late modern urban settings, and, with predictions that the majority of the world's population will be living in cities by about 2025, there clearly has been a qualitative shift. More research on older archives and records is needed to say more about this shift and to compare earlier with present periods.

Beyond importantly pointing to parallels between the past and the present as well as modes and dynamics of change, the approach advocated by many scholars is also to use historical expertise – especially highlighting "explanatory factors, including historical developments and the role of historically rooted social, political, and economic structures and institutions" (Foner 2017: 54) – to better understand continuities between the past and the present. As Grillo (2015: 12) puts it, "while cities such as London or New York are experiencing new 'super-diversities' this does not mean that 'old' diversities have simply disappeared." This is precisely the premise taken in a large European Research Council funded project on migration-driven diversification in Johannesburg, Singapore, and New York, resulting in a book entitled *Diversities Old and New* (Vertovec 2015b). Among other findings, the project demonstrated how one can only understand contemporary – and highly variable – conditions of superdiversity by research the ways that previous, historically and institutionally produced patterns of diversity still exist, are folded into, and continue to shape social and cultural processes surrounding more recent flows of immigration.

Historians still have much to contribute to the shaping of the superdiversity concept and approach. Hopefully, the concept will continue to offer something of value to them as well. In addition to the stimulation or provocation some have suggested for tasks of research and analysis, it has also been suggested that the concept is of much relevance to the teaching of history, too (Hawkey 2012).

Critiques of superdiversity

Not surprisingly or uninvitedly, given the number and breadth of interpretations of superdiversity, a number of scholars have been critical of the concept. Most of these criticisms are warranted and helpful in sharpening its meaning and use.

One of the foremost criticisms of superdiversity (or at least some readings of it) is that it does not give sufficient attention to race and racism. In referring to the original 2007 *Ethnic and Racial Studies* article on superdiversity, for instance, Les Back and Shamser Sinha (2016: 520), claim that "Vertovec's insouciant treatment racism works largely through omission. He includes just one short paragraph in his super-diversity essay on 'new patterns inequality and prejudice' and mentions the word 'racism' just once." For them, the fact that the article focused on a breadth of new configurations of migrant characteristics instead of race meant that it worked to "effectively erase close to 30 years of scholarship on the relationship between racism and urban multiculture" (Ibid.). A lack of centrality of a key variable does not mean erasure. Moreover, in the original superdiversity article, "No connection is made," they point out, "between the legacy of empire and racism, and the newer racist hierarchies that have emerged" (Ibid.: 521). Unpacking such a legacy goes far beyond the article's and concept's intent; in any case, a great many new migrants to Britain who are key to the emergence of superdiversity come from places that were never part of the British Empire (Filipinos, Algerians, Turks, Brazilians, Polish, etc.).

One way that race and racism were particularly addressed in that first key article on superdiversity was through underlining the significance of new forms of racialization and racism that arise with superdiversification. This is one important way that the concept can build on and enhance that long scholarship on race and racism. Grillo (2015: 12) believes that we need to take this further:

> I have encountered some researchers and policy makers who believe that the old diversities are the only ones there are. Many also continue to describe relations with those diversities through the traditional language of racism and racialisation, when in fact we lack an adequate vocabulary through which to depict, analyse and evaluate contemporary forms of 'othering' in the super-diverse city.

Umut Erel (2011: 705) makes a similar point in stating that "'super-diversity' requires an analysis of racism not in a dichotomous or top-down frame but as differentially positioning and constituting different groups and individuals".

At a roundtable seminar on race and superdiversity held at the University of Birmingham's Institute for Research into Superdiversity, Ipek Demir suggested that the superdiversity concept's lack of a strong direction on race "was a consequence of the genesis of the term, and in particular the fact that superdiversity does not stem from struggle or social movements (in contrast to analytical lenses such as race, class or gender)" (in Humphris 2015: 3). This is true: superdiversity was coined as a descriptive concept to address changing patterns of migration and their effects. New modes of racialization and racism – or Grillo's contemporary forms of "othering" or Erel's "differentially positioning and constituting different groups and individuals" – are among such significant effects. Attention to these will help us understand better "how racial hierarchies are re-formed, and how the ambivalence and allure of whiteness and class loss coexist in a 'super-diverse' place" (James 2014: 652).

It is certainly a fair point that much more can be done to strengthen and deepen the concept of superdiversity by way of greater recognition of processes of racialization and practices of institutional and everyday racism (cf. Rosbrook-Thompson 2018). Steve Garner (in press) helpfully describes the relationship between research on race/racism and superdiversity as "not either/or but both/and." Noting how, already, "Race inhabits accounts of superdiversity," he says "When I read much superdiversity literature, I see a multitude of connections into scholarship on race, lit up like scintillating maps of neural pathways, as the situations, experiences, and terminology evokes the movement and travel of ideas that are so bound up in one another."

In much the same way, Faten Khazaei (2018) advocates bringing superdiversity and intersectionality–which predominantly examines the combined effects of gender, race, and class – together in fruitful dialogue to achieve a better appreciation of how inequalities are produced and reproduced. The concepts and approaches are complementary, not competitive, she argues.

Also in the spirit of "both/and," Sofya Aptekar (2019: 54) reiterates the point that superdiversity is not just about differentiation of characteristics within the categories of race, but concerns myriad "other variables that intersect in ways that lead to unequal opportunities within ethnic groups as well as between them, including along dimensions of religion, age, gender, legal status, and class." However, she importantly points out, one:

> should not assume that the rise of super-diversity necessarily brings a decline in the role of the "old" categories of race, class, and gender. These categories may seem less reliable as signifiers of commonalities or differences in everyday encounters. However, they can continue to wield influence by shaping social organization of institutions, spaces, and communities.
>
> *Ibid.: 55*

This relates to a critique made by other scholars in their readings of superdiversity: namely, that modes and structures of power and inequality are insufficiently presented in the concept of superdiversity. Hence, Aptekar advocates, researchers should be sure to incorporate accounts and analyses of power, structural inequality, and hegemony into the ethnographic study of everyday superdiversity.

Aptekar's advice is certainly welcome. More can and should be done to understand better how the multidimensional diversification of variables described by superdiversity plays into, is shaped by, and often reinforces structures and practices of power and inequality. To a degree, this has already been addressed by Fran Meissner and me when we stressed that "conditions of superdiversity are inherently tied to power, politics and policy" (Meissner and Vertovec 2015: 552) and by "recognizing that conditions and processes surrounding superdiversity both produce, and are produced by, a range of differential power relations and modes of inequality" (Ibid.: 551). Fenneke Wekker (2019: 90) has indeed noted that "some scholars have employed super-diversity to emphasize the changing power balance in urban settings which have a growing and internally diversified migrant population" while Erel (2009: 10) uses superdiversity to point to "new hierarchies and power relations within the migrant group". Blommaert (2013b: 3) has taken this approach to power further by insisting that "we must realize that superdiversity has created unprecedented levels of polycentricity in social systems." In describing the superdiversity of Antwerp, he observes:

> There is not one single regime of power in my neighborhood, and no single group can be said to be in power everywhere and all of the time. There are times when shopkeepers and shoppers dominate the neighborhood, but of course, these times are never at night when shops are closed. The neighborhood is then dominated by several groups, some of which are rarely seen during the day. Power and control are dispersed over different groups, located in different sites and operating with different scopes and degrees of impact. Power, like the neighborhood, is complex and multiscalar.
>
> *Blommaert (2013a: 129)*

Another critique of the concept of superdiversity is based on presumptions concerning its basic premise. This is made by Finex Ndhlovu (2016) in a piece condemning the concept, yet one that curiously does not cite or draw upon any of the original superdiversity articles. His piece seems only based on a single, secondary reading of a few sociolinguists and the above-mentioned book by Ramadan (2011) that is not really about the superdiversity concept at all. He does not at all refer my original 2007 article. Further, despite the fact that Ndhlovu approvingly draws directly on various works of mine to critique the notion of multiculturalism, he groups multiculturalism and superdiversity together as representing "the tendency to homogenize cultural and social groups, and the uncritical embrace of elitist neoliberal conceptualizations of culture and identity" (2016: 28). He curiously does not seem aware that in addition to being a fellow critic of multiculturalism, I am also the originator of the superdiversity concept. Just how both accomplish this neoliberal thing (especially as superdiversity itself rose out of a critique of multiculturalism), in his piece, remains entirely unclear and unaddressed. Instead of such purported homogenization, Ndhlovu (Ibid.: 29) calls for alternative paradigms recognizing "the increasingly multi-formed, multidimensional and convoluted nature of migrant and diaspora identities that require us to rethink our understandings of cultural and identity politics." Perhaps because he cites no original superdiversity work, he does not take account of how the superdiversity concept and approach attempts to address exactly this point.

Ndhlovu deems the superdiversity concept to be wholly and hegemonically Euro-centric. To be sure, the concept arose out of a critique of models of multiculturalism mainly present in Britain, the Netherlands, USA, Canada, and Australia. The line of thinking concerning new migration patterns and changing, multidimensional variables, however, certainly needn't be limited to such contexts. Indeed, scholars worldwide have found value thinking through the superdiversity concept for very different contexts, as seen for instance in studies of Mexico (Acosta-García and Martínez-Ortiz 2015), South Africa (Madiba 2018), Dubai and Singapore (Kathiravelu in press), Malaysia (Chan 2020), Brazil (Liberali 2017), Indonesia (Goebel 2015), Turkey (Biehl 2015), and China (Varis and Wang 2011). Agnes Simic (2019) advocates a comparative view onto the how superdiversity shapes city spaces – and significantly, how people practically navigate superdiverse milieus – within cities of the global North and the global South, and by way of migration from cities of the global South to cities of the global North, and from cities of the global North to cities of the global South. Moreover, drawing on a study of female migrants from large Indian cities, Simic's approach is inherently transnational, pointing out how experiences of superdiversity in one context shape people's abilities to negotiate superdiversity in others.

> As bigger cities of the global South are growing in number and gaining weight on both local and global echelons, it is essential to consider them in more depth. However, this must be not only as 'end-station' places where superdiversity can be witnessed, either due to internal or international migration, but also as superdiverse places from which international migrants move to equally superdiverse locales, especially as a great number of international migrants have already lived in such superdiverse cities in their home (or another) country before moving to their (current) host country.
>
> *Ibid.: 184*

This kind of comparative and transnational approach (also see Heil 2020), especially linking contexts of global South and global North, promises social scientific advances of many kinds, not least to the concept of superdiversity.

Based on his reliance on secondary interpretation stemming from socio-linguistics, Ndhlovu's reading of superdiversity as a "post-modernist theory" is that, "the term superdiversity refers to the vastly increased range of resources – linguistic, religious cultural and technological – that characterize late modern societies. A key goal of superdiversity is the investigation into how and why diverse conceptualizations and understandings about these resources need to be recognized" (Ibid.: 33). I, for one, do not think that is what superdiversity refers to. So here we have – repeating at least one pathway that has occurred in the multiple trajectories of the concept – a criticism based on an interpretation of superdiversity.

In his article, Ndhlovu's main task is to promote a decolonialist approach to the study of diasporas and similar phenomena. He argues that "There is need for us to push for the recognition of alternative knowledges and alternative ways of conceptualizing cultural identities in order to both counter and complement dominant Euro-American epistemologies" (Ibid.: 37). Although Ndhlovu does not himself offer any such alternative ways, the overall call is certainly valid, important, and absolutely worth pursuing. However, his distortion of the concept provides a poor vehicle for this argument.

Willem Schinkel (2018) presents a kindred caricature of superdiversity. As part of an attack on the concept of "integration" – one with which, in most ways, I concur (Vertovec 2020) – and without really engaging with the superdiversity literature, Schinkel draws a simplistic rendering of the superdiversity concept as a kind of power tool of white elites that, somehow – again without clear elaboration – "constitutes the continuation of immigrant integration by other means" (Ibid.: 10). Meissner (2019) provides a robust response to Schinkel and his creation of a "straw figure" depiction of superdiversity – and for that matter, skewed and unfair description of all migration research.

Yet another harsh critique is mounted by Aneta Pavlenko (2018). She believes that the way superdiversity has been successfully taken up across disciplines and multiple ways demonstrates that the concept is just an exercise in sloganeering or branding, like an advertising campaign. Her argument superficially uses and conflates highly selective excerpts from across several disciplines and fields, and tars anyone who invokes the term with the same brush despite their very different conceptual takes on the term. Pavlenko is a linguist who acknowledges her lack of familiarity with migration studies. Nevertheless, in a yearning desire solely to colourfully criticize at whatever costs, she gives no intellectual credit to scholars who adopt the concept to explore and to try to understand real issues of social transformation, whether concerning modes of communication, social positionality, differential migration experiences, and emerging modes of living. Instead, she dismisses the use of superdiversity concept and approach as just a matter of career ladder climbing towards the "creation of a new academic hierarchy and new elite" (Ibid.: 2). It is a highly dubious conjecture, to say the least, that simply working with the superdiversity concept has been an important factor in advancing anyone's career or forging a new elite class of scholars. As we have seen over the preceding pages, a great number of scholars have found much value in the superdiversity concept – not for careerist reasons, but for the purposes of genuinely trying to understand significant social transformations occurring all around us on a range of scales.

Conclusion

Soon after its publication in 2007, the concept of superdiversity was being invoked in a range of public policy and media spheres. However, it is especially, and not surprisingly, in academia that the concept has been received and used extensively, not only across disciplines but also in a surprising number of ways. Sometimes fellow scholars have invoked the term in ways generally in line with its original purpose, sometimes in ways that are not, and sometimes in ways that are very interesting and, indeed, exciting.

In this chapter, I have arranged construed many of the uses of superdiversity in academic literature by way of seven types. These are, using superdiversity either as: (1) a marker of very much diversity (i.e., a way to say that diversification has boomed); (2) a context or backdrop to a study (i.e., a setting in which something particular is going on); (3) a description of more ethnicity (i.e., suggesting that through migration, we are seeing many more ethnic backgrounds within a society); (4) a call to move beyond ethnicity (i.e., a way to emphasize that social phenomena should be understood in intersectional ways); (5) a multidimensional reconfiguration (i.e., a way to consider the interplay of many factors and characteristics); (6) a methodological reassessment (i.e., a device for proposing new approaches within a discipline); (7) a way of addressing emergent social complexities (i.e., a springboard for considering significant shifts in social systems of different kinds); and (8) an approach to policy analysis (i.e., how complexity governance is addressed). Clearly, the concept of superdiversity has reflected, triggered, and been utilized for highly divergent academic interests.

I suggest that more than any other branch of social science, the concept has impacted sociolinguistics in the most far-reaching ways. For many years in that discipline, there had been apparent discontent among some scholars who had been trying to address certain open, mixed, and dynamic processes surrounding linguistic practices. Superdiversity was offered at the right juncture to stimulate significant disciplinary shifts.

In this chapter, too, I have addressed some of the issues that historians have had with the concept, as well as some of the critiques of superdiversity that have been made across different literatures. Many of these issues and critiques, it must be said, have often been focused on misinterpretations of superdiversity – or "Super-Diversity Lite" as Ralph Grillo (2015) has called such readings, since most simply refer to the limited phenomenon of more ethnicity. Some modes of criticism, especially concerning matters of power and race, have indeed been welcome contributions that will hopefully sharpen and extend the uses of super-diversity for social scientific analysis.

After coining the term some time ago, I have been especially interested in the ways superdiversity has "spoken to" a wide range of colleagues, the great majority of whom share many of the same concerns that I have. Over the years, as I have indicated in this chapter, the concept has travelled and morphed, and has been critiqued, misinterpreted, elaborated, and applied in a variety of ways. This exercise in reviewing the many meanings of super-diversity has been roughly akin to Raymond Williams' (1976) reflections on general, variable, and specialized uses of one or another "key term." Among other things, concerning single words or concepts that he examined, Williams was interested in "the explicit but often implicit connections which people were making, in what seemed to me, again and again, particular formations of meaning – ways not only of discussing but on another level of seeing many of our central experiences" (Ibid.: 15). This is what I believe has happened with "superdiversity": scholars have connected with and interpreted it within their empirical, disciplinary, and interest-focused formations of meaning. This has produced, just as Williams points out regarding other notions, "a shaping and reshaping in real circumstances and from profoundly different and important points of view" (Ibid.: 24).

As Fran Meissner (2015) has argued, the superdiversity concept emerged at a time when several older concepts seemed to have lost their explanatory power. It also arose at a time when certain patterns of diversification have been observably changing (see next chapter). Such patterns, which are also patterns of complex-ification, have been identified variously in a great many fields by researchers across disciplines. However, again as described by Ulrich Beck (2011: 53), *"we do not even have the language through which contemporary superdiversity in the world can be described, conceptualized, understood, explained and researched"* [italics in original]. Whether geographer, sociologist, political scientist, sociolinguist, or other kind of social science or humanities scholar, colleagues have been intently searching for concepts and descriptive accounts with which to describe processes and man-ifestations of diversification and complexification.

Cutting across the myriad meanings that have arisen since its emergence, Gloria Kirwan also detects certain common concerns:

> Essentially, superdiversity highlights the limpness of research which homoge-nises population datasets and fails to take account of the relevance of discernible differences in population characteristics and experiences. It rejects uncritical assumptions of conformity in research populations and the inherent strength of this framework is its commitment to identifying pattern distinctions within large populations. In this sense, superdiversity research is curiosity-driven, positioning it comfortably alongside the enquiring stance intrinsic to the sociological imagination as articulated by the Millsian tradition.
>
> *2022: 196*

As key tenets of a superdiversity orientation in the tradition of sociological inno-vation of C. Wright Mills, Kirwan suggests that the concept offers: a foundation of inquisitiveness; a focus on searching for groups-within-groups; the employ-ment of cutting edge data analytics; flexibility in managing sameness and differ-ence in a study cohort; concern to avoid conflation of distinct sub-groups; and a commitment to spotlighting diversification in a dataset. While she herself applies superdiversity in these ways to the study of mental illness, Kirwan suggests that "as a conceptual paradigm, superdiversity is currently underutilised in research on other important issues in society" (Ibid.: 203).

Angela Creese and Adrian Blackledge (2018b: xxiii) take such a cross-cutting view further, submitting that the superdiversity concept and approach "seeks to critique the ideological and structural apparatus of neoliberalism, to address inequality in all its forms, to situate its analysis historically, to be adaptable to different global contexts and temporal scales, and to have practical application to improve people's lives." These are bold claims which were never in my original intent, but in which I'm certainly happy that people have found, created, or interpreted such perspective and use.

By now, it is clear that there are many meanings of superdiversity. These have arisen by way of a widespread search for new concepts and language to describe changing, complexifying, social realities of various – albeit often related – kinds. In the first decades of this century, superdiversity has hap-pened to be a useful notion at the right time. Now it is being put to ever more uses as social transformations of diversification themselves continue apace. The concept has been specific enough to indicate something recognizable, but open enough to allow original perspectives. Antonio López Peláez and his colleagues (2022: 161) evaluate superdiversity in this way, too: "This concept, with all the semantic breath and defining ramifications that characterize it, has opened an interpretive door, and made possible an analytical framework that differs from the rest."

As scholars across disciplines and around the world have found, superdiversity points towards a variety of emergent social complexities. The next chapters take a closer look at current processes entailing and arising from these trends and pro-pose ways in which we might continue to better understand them.

References

Acosta-García, R. and E. Martínez-Ortiz 2015. "Mexico through a superdiversity lens: Already-existing diversity meets new immigration," *Ethnic and Racial Studies* 38(4): 636–49 https://doi.org/10.1080/01419870.2015.980289

Ambrosini, M. 2016. "Superdiversity, multiculturalism and local policies: A study on European cities," *Policy & Politics* 45(4): 585–603 https://doi.org/10.1332/0305573 16x14745534309609

Andreoutsopoulos, J. and K. Juffermans 2014. "Digital language practices in superdiver-sity: Introduction," *Discourse, Context, and Media* 4(5): 1–6 https://doi.org/10.1016/ j.dcm.2014.08.002

Antonsich, M. 2012. "Exploring the demands of assimilation among White ethnic majorities in Western Europe," *Journal of Ethnic and Migration Studies* 38(1): 59–76 https://doi.org/10.1080/1369183x.2012.640015

Aptekar, S. 2019 "Super-diversity as a methodological lens: Re-centring power and inequality," *Ethnic and Racial Studies* 42(1): 53–70 https://doi.org/10.1080/01419870.2017.1406124

Arnaut, K. 2012. "Super-diversity: Elements of an emerging perspective," *New Diversities* 14(2): 1–16

Arnaut, K., J. Blommaert, B. Rampton and M. Spotti 2015. *Language and Superdiversity*, London: Routledge https://doi.org/10.4324/9781315730240

Arnaut, K. and M. Spotti 2014. "Superdiversity discourse," *Working Papers in Urban Language & Literacies* 122: 1–11 https://doi.org/10.1002/9781118611463.wbielsi138

Aspinall, P. J. 2009. "The future of ethnicity classifications," *Journal of Ethnic and Migration Studies* 35(9): 1417–35 https://doi.org/10.1080/13691830903125901

Aspinall, P. J. 2011. "The utility and validity for public health of ethnicity categorization in the 1991, 2001 and 2011 British Censuses," *Public Health* 125(10): 680–6 https://doi.org/10.1016/j.puhe.2011.05.001

Aspinall, P. J. and F. Hashem 2011. "Responding to minority ethnic groups' language support needs in Britain," *Equality, Diversity and Inclusion* 30(2): 145–62

Aspinall, P. J. and M. Song 2013. "Is race a 'salient…' or 'dominant identity' in the early 21st century: The evidence of UK survey data on respondents' sense of who they are," *Social Science Research* 42(2): 547–61 https://doi.org/10.1016/j.ssresearch.2012.10.007

Back, L. and S. Sinha 2016. "Multicultural conviviality in the midst of racism's ruins," *Journal of Intercultural Studies* 37(5): 517–32 https://doi.org/10.1080/07256868.2016.1211625

Bailey, A. J. 2013. "Migration, recession and an emerging transnational biopolitics across Europe," *Geoforum* 44: 202–10

Bauböck, R. 2008. "Beyond culturalism and statism: Liberal responses to diversity," Eurosphere Online Working Paper No. 6: 1–34

Baycan, T. and P. Nijkamp 2012. "A socio-economic impact analysis of urban cultural diversity: Pathways and horizons," *Migration Impact Assessment*, P. Nijkamp et al. (eds.), Cheltenham: Edward Elgar, pp. 175–202 https://doi.org/10.4337/9780857934581.00013

Beck, U. 2011. "Multiculturalism or cosmopolitanism: How can we describe and understand the diversity of the world?" *Social Sciences in China* 32(4): 52–8 https://doi.org/10.1080/02529203.2011.625169

Bell, D. S. A. 2003. "History and globalization: Reflections on temporality," *International Affairs* 79(4): 801–14 https://doi.org/10.1111/1468-2346.00337

Berg, M. L. and N. Sigona 2013. "Ethnography, diversity and urban space," *Identities* 20(4): 347–60

Biehl, K. 2015. "Spatializing diversities, diversifying spaces: Housing experiences and home space perceptions in a migrant hub of Istanbul," *Ethnic and Racial Studies* 38(4): 596–607 https://doi.org/10.1080/01419870.2015.980293

Birmingham City Council 2012. Giving Hope, Changing Lives: Birmingham Social Inclusion Process. Green paper Birmingham City Council, Birmingham

Blommaert, J. 2013a. *Ethnography, Superdiversity and Linguistic Landscapes: Chronicles of Complexity*, Bristol: Multilingual Matters https://doi.org/10.21832/9781783090419

Blommaert, J. 2013b. "Citizenship, language and superdiversity: Towards complexity," *Tilburg Papers in Culture Studies 45*, Tilburg

Blommaert, J. 2014. "From mobility to complexity in sociolinguistic theory and method," Working Papers in Urban Language & Literacies 135, Kings College London,

Blommaert, J. 2015. "Superdiversity old and new," *Language & Communication*, 44(1): 82–89

Blommaert, J. and A. Backus 2013. "Superdiverse repertoires and the individual," in *Multilingualism and Multimodality*, I. De Saint-Georges and J. J. Weber (eds.), Rotterdam: Sense, pp. 11–32

Blommaert, J. and B. Rampton 2011. "Language and superdiversity," *Diversities*, 13(3): 1–21

Bobo, L. 2013. "A peek at America's super-diverse future," *The Root* 21 March

Bradby, H. 2012 "Race, ethnicity and health: The costs and benefits of conceptualising racism and ethnicity," *Social Science & Medicine* 76(6): 955–8

Bradby, H., G. Green, C. Davison and K. Krause 2017. "Is superdiversity a useful concept in European medical sociology?" *Frontiers in Sociology* 1(17): 1–18 https://doi.org/10.3389/fsoc.2016.00017

Budach, G. and I. de Saint-Georges 2017. "Superdiversity and language," in *The Routledge Handbook of Migration and Language*, S. Canagarajah (ed.), London: Routledge, pp. 63–78 https://doi.org/10.4324/9781315754512-4

Burdsey, D. 2013. "'The foreignness is still quite visible in this town': Multiculture, marginality and prejudice at the English seaside," *Patterns of Prejudice* 47(2): 95–116 https://doi.org/10.1080/0031322x.2013.773134

Busch, B. 2012. "The linguistic repertoire revisited," *Applied Linguistics* 33(5): 503–23 https://doi.org/10.1093/applin/ams056

Butcher, M. 2010. "Navigating 'New' Delhi: Moving between difference and belonging in a globalising city," *Journal of Intercultural Studies* 31(5): 507–24

Cardinal, A. 2022. "Superdiversity: An audience analysis praxis for enacting social justice in technical communication," *Technical Communication Quarterly* https://doi.org/10.1080/10572252.2022.2056637

Catney, G., N. Finney and L. Twigg 2011. "Diversity and the complexities of ethnic integration in the UK," *Journal of Intercultural Studies* 32(2): 107–114 https://doi.org/10.1080/07256868.2011.547171

Chan, R. S. K. (2020). "Aesthetics of super-diversity: The Cantonese ancestral clan building as a social integration platform," *Finisterra* 55(113): 45–62 https://doi.org/10.18055/Finis17553

Christensen, A. D. and S. Jensen 2011. "Roots and routes: Migration, belonging and everyday life," *Nordic Journal of Migration Research* 1(3): 146–55 https://doi.org/10.2478/v10202-011-0013-1

Cogo, A. 2012. "ELF and super-diversity: A case study of ELF multilingual practices from a business context," *Journal of English as a lingua franca* 1(2): 287–313

Coleman, D. A. and S. Dubuc 2010. "The fertility of ethnic minorities in the UK, 1960s–2006," *Population Studies* 64(1): 19–41

Colic-Peisker, V. and K. Farquharson 2011. "A new era in Australian multiculturalism? The need for critical interrogation," *Journal of Intercultural Studies* 32(6): 579–86 https://doi.org/10.1080/07256868.2011.618104

Cooney, M. 2009. "Ethnic conflict without ethnic groups: A study in pure sociology," *British Journal of Sociology* 60(3): 473–92 https://doi.org/10.1111/j.1468-4446.2009.01252.x

Crawley, H. 2010. "Moving beyond ethnicity: The socio-economic status and living conditions of immigrant children in the UK," *Child Indicators Research* 3(4): 547–70 https://doi.org/10.1007/s12187-010-9071-5

Creese, A. and A. Blackledge 2010. "Towards a sociolinguistics of superdiversity," *Zeitschrift für Erziehungswissenschaft* 13(4): 549–72 https://doi.org/10.1007/s11618-010-0159-y

Creese, A. and A. Blackledge (eds.) 2018a. *The Routledge Handbook of Language and Superdiversity*, London: Routledge https://doi.org/10.4324/9781315696010

Creese, A. and A. Blackledge 2018b. "Language and superdiversity: An interdisciplinary perspective," in *The Routledge Handbook of Language and Superdiversity*, A. Creese and A. Blackledge (eds.), London: Routledge, pp. xxi–xiv https://doi.org/10.4324/9781315696010

Crul, M. 2016. "Super-diversity vs. assimilation: How complex diversity in majority–minority cities challenges the assumptions of assimilation," *Journal of Ethnic and Migration Studies* 42(1): 54–68 https://doi.org/10.1080/1369183x.2015.1061425

Crul, M., J. Schneider and F. Lelie 2013. *Superdiversity: A New Perspective on Integration*, Amsterdam: VU University Press

Dahinden, J. 2009. "Are we all transnationals now? Network transnationalism and transnational subjectivity: The differing impacts of globalization on the inhabitants of a small Swiss city," *Ethnic and Racial Studies* 32(8): 1365–86

Datta, K., C. McIlwaine, J. Herbert, Y. Evans, J. May and J. Wills 2009. "Men on the move: Narratives of migration and work among low-paid migrant men in London," *Social & Cultural Geography* 10(8): 853–73

de Bock, J. 2015. "Not all the same after all? Superdiversity as a lens for the study of past migrations," *Ethnic and Racial Studies* 38(4): 583–95 https://doi.org/10.1080/0141987 0.2015.980290

De Fina, A., D. Ikizoglu and J. Wegner (eds.) 2017. *Diversity and Super-Diversity: Sociocultural Linguistic Perspectives*, Washington, D.C.: Georgetown University Press

Dhoest, A., M. Cola, M. Brusa and D. Lemish 2012. "Studying ethnic minorities' media uses: Comparative conceptual and methodological reflections," *Communication, Culture & Critique* 5(3): 372–91

Dhoest, A., K. Nikunen and M. Cola 2013. "Exploring media use among migrant families in Europe," *Observatorio* https://doi.org/10.7458/obs002013663

Dietz, G. 2013. "A doubly reflexive ethnographic methodology for the study of religious diversity in education," *British Journal of Religious Education* 35(1): 20–35 https://doi.org/10.1080/01416200.2011.614752

Drinkwater, S. 2010. "Immigration and the economy," *National Institute Economic Review* 213(1): R1–R4 https://doi.org/10.1177/0027950110380319

Duarte, J. and I. Gogolin (eds.) 2013. *Linguistic Superdiversity in Urban Areas: Research Approaches*, Amsterdam: John Benjamins https://doi.org/10.1075/hsld.2

Engbersen, G., E. Snel and J. de Boom 2010. "'A van full of Poles': Liquid migration from Central and Eastern Europe," in *A Continent Moving West?* R. Black et al. (eds.), Amsterdam: Amsterdam University Press, pp. 115–40 https://doi.org/10.1515/9789048510979-006

Erel, U. 2009. *Migrant Women Transforming Citizenship: Life Stories from Britain and Germany*, Farnham: Ashgate

Erel, U. 2011. "Reframing migrant mothers as citizens," *Citizenship Studies* 15(6–7): 695–709 https://doi.org/10.1080/13621025.2011.600076

Fanshawe, S. and D. Sriskandarajah 2010, *You Can't Put Me in a Box: Super-Diversity and the End of Identity Politics in Britain*, London: Institute for Public Policy Research

Fomina, J. 2006. "The failure of British multiculturalism: Lessons for Europe," *Polish Sociological Review* 156: 409–24

Foner, N. 1997. "What's new about transnationalism? New York immigrants today and at the turn of the century," *Diaspora* 6(3): 355–75 https://doi.org/10.3138/diaspora. 6.3.355

Foner, N. 2017. "What's new about super-diversity?" *Rosbrook* 36(4): 49–57

Francis, B., P. Burke and B. Read 2013. "The submergence and re-emergence of gender in undergraduate accounts of university experience," *Gender and Education* 26(1): 1–17 https://doi.org/10.1080/09540253.2013.860433

García, O. and L. Wei 2014. *Translanguaging: Language, Bilingualism and Education*, Basingstoke: Palgrave Macmillan https://doi.org/10.1057/9781137385765

Garner, S. In press. "'Not in a relationship': Superdiversity's anomalous disengagement from 'race'," in *The Oxford Handbook of Superdiversity*, F. Meissner, N. Sigona and S. Vertovec (eds.), Oxford: Oxford University Press

Gaye, N. 2011. *Super Diversity in Canada*, Ottawa: Policy Horizons Canada, Government of Canada

Geldof, D. 2016. *Superdiversity in the Heart of Europe: How Migration Changes Our Society*, The Hague: Acco

Geldof, D., M. Schrooten and S. Withaeckx 2017. "Transmigration: The rise of flexible migration strategies as part of superdiversity," *Policy & Politics* 45(4): 567–84 https://doi.org/10.1332/030557317x14972774011385

Goebel, Z. 2015. *Language and Superdiversity: Indonesians Knowledging at Home and Abroad*, Oxford: Oxford University Press https://doi.org/10.1093/acprof:oso/9780199795413. 001.0001

Gogolin, I. 2011. "The challenge of super diversity for education in Europe," *Education Inquiry* 2(2): 239–49 https://doi.org/10.3402/edui.v2i2.21976

Grillo, R. 2015. "Reflections on super-diversity by an urban anthropologist, or 'Super-diversity so what?'" Paper presented at the Academy of Urban Super-Diversity, Berlin

Gross, B. 2020. "Education for a common identity in times of superdiversity? The example of linguistic diversity and identity," *Pedagogia e Vita* 78: 124–34

Gumperz, J. J. 1982. *Discourse Strategies*, Cambridge: Cambridge University Press https://doi.org/10.1017/cbo9780511611834

Gumperz, J. J. and D. Hymes (eds.) 1972. *Directions in Sociolinguistics: The Ethnography of Communication*, London: Blackwell, pp. 35–71

Guo, S. 2010. "Migration and communities: Challenges and opportunities for lifelong learning," *International Journal of Lifelong Education* 29(4): 437–47 https://doi.org/ 10.1080/02601370.2010.488806

Hadj Abdou, L. and A. Geddes 2017. "Managing superdiversity? Examining the intercultural policy turn in Europe," *Policy & Politics* 45(4): 493–510 https://doi.org/ 10.1332/030557317x15016676607077

Hall, S. M. 2015. "Super-diverse street: A 'trans-ethnography' across migrant localities," *Ethnic and Racial Studies* 38(1): 22–37 https://doi.org/10.1080/01419870.2013. 858175

Hambye, P. and M. Richards 2012. "The paradoxical visions of multilingualism in education: The ideological dimension of discourses on multilingualism in Belgium and Canada," *International Journal of Multilingualism* 9(2): 165–88

Hampshire, J. 2013. "An emigrant nation without an emigrant policy: The curious case of Britain," in *Emigration Nations*, M. Collyer (ed.), London: Palgrave Macmillan, pp. 302–26

Hatziprokopiou, P. 2008. "Strangers as neighbors in the cosmopolis: New migrants in London, diversity, and place," in *Branding Cities. Cosmopolitanism, Parochialism and*

Social Change. S. Donald, E. Kofman and C. Kevin (eds.), New York: Routledge, pp. 14–27 https://doi.org/10.4324/9780203884294-7

Hawkey, K. 2012. "History and super diversity," *Education Sciences* 2(4): 165–79 https://doi.org/10.3390/educsci2040165

Heil, T. 2020. *Comparing Conviviality: Living with Difference in Casamance and Catalonia*, Basingstoke: Palgrave

Heugh, K. 2013. "Mobility, migration and sustainability: Re-figuring languages in diversity," *International Journal of the Sociology of Language* 222: 5–32

Hill, A. 2007. "The changing face of British cities by 2020," *The Observer* 23 December

Hiruy, K. and R. A. Hutton 2020. "Towards a re-imagination of the New African Diaspora in Australia," *African Diaspora* 12(1–2): 153–79 https://doi.org/10.1163/18725465-bja10010

Hogg, L. 2011. "Funds of knowledge: An investigation of coherence within the literature," *Teaching and Teacher Education* 27(3): 666–77

Hollingworth, S. and A. Mansaray 2012. *Language Diversity and Attainment in English Schools: A Scoping Study.* London: The Institute for Policy Studies in Education (IPSE), London Metropolitan University

Hollingworth, S. and K. Williams 2010 "Multicultural mixing or middle-class reproduction? The White middle classes in London comprehensive schools," *Space and Polity* 14(1): 47–64 https://doi.org/10.1080/13562571003737767

Humphris, R. 2015. "Race and superdiversity – what are the links?" Final Report, Institute for Research on Superdiversity [IRiS] Key Concepts roundtable series, University of Birmingham

Hüwelmeier, G. 2011. "Socialist cosmopolitanism meets global Pentecostalism: Charismatic Christianity among Vietnamese migrants after the fall of the Berlin Wall," *Ethnic and Racial Studies* 34(3): 436–53 https://doi.org/10.1080/01419870.2011.535547

Jacquemet, M. 2011. "Crosstalk 2.0: Asylum and communicative breakdowns," *Text & Talk* 31(4): 475–97 https://doi.org/10.1515/text.2011.023

James, M. 2014. "Whiteness and loss in outer East London: Tracing the collective memories of diaspora space," *Ethnic and Racial Studies* 37(4): 652–67 https://doi.org/10.1080/01419870.2013.808761

Jones, D. 2019. *Superdiverse Diaspora: Everyday Identifications of Tamil Migrants in Britain*, Basingstoke: Palgrave

Jørgensen, J. N. 2012. "Ideologies and norms in language and education policies in Europe and their relationship with everyday language behaviours," *Language, Culture and Curriculum* 25(1): 57–71 https://doi.org/10.1080/07908318.2011.653058

Juffermans, K. 2012. "Exaggerating difference: Representations of the Third World other in PI aid," *Intercultural Pragmatics* 9(1): 23–45 https://doi.org/10.1515/ip-2012-0002

Kandylis, G., T. Maloutas and J. Sayas 2012. "Immigration, inequality and diversity: Socio-ethnic hierarchy and spatial organization in Athens, Greece," *European Urban and Regional Studies* 19(3): 267–86 https://doi.org/10.1177/0969776412441109

Kathiravelu, L. In press. "Superdiversity from outside the mainstream: Conceptual productivity for empirical applications in highly regulated global cities," in *The Oxford Handbook of Superdiversity*, F. Meissner, N. Sigona and S. Vertovec (eds.), Oxford: Oxford University Press

Khazaei, F. 2018. "Grounds for dialogue: *Intersectionality and superdiversity*," *Tijdschrift voor Genderstudies* 21(1): 7–25 https://doi.org/10.5117/tvgn2018.1.khaz

Kirwan, G. 2022. "Superdiversity re-imagined: Applying superdiversity theory to research beyond migration studies," *Current Sociology* 70(2): 192–209 https://doi.org/10.1177/0011392120983346

Koch, G. 2009. "Intercultural communication and competence research through the lens of an anthropology of knowledge," *Forum Qualitative Sozialforschung* 10(1): Art. 15 https://doi.org/10.17169/fqs-10.1.1231

Kraus, P. A. 2012. "The politics of complex diversity: A European perspective," *Ethnicities* 12(1): 3–25

Leitão Ferreira, J. M. 2021. "Children's life in superdiversity contexts: Impacts on the construction of a children's citizenship – the Portuguese case," *Current Sociology* https://doi.org/10.1177/0011392120983340

Leone, M. 2012. "Hearing and belonging: On sounds, faiths, and laws," in *Transparency, Power and Control: Perspectives on Legal Communication*, V. K. Bhatia, C. A. Hafner, L. Miller and A. Wagner (eds.), Farnham: Ashgate, pp. 183–97

Leppänen, S. and A. Häkkinen 2012. "Buffalaxed superdiversity: Representations of the other on YouTube," *New Diversities* 14(2): 17–33

Li, G., J. Anderson, J. Hare and M. McTavish 2021. *Superdiversity and Teacher Education: Supporting Teachers in Working with Culturally, Linguistically and Racially Diverse Students, Families and Communities*, London: Routledge

Liberali, F. C. 2017. "Globalization, superdiversity, language learning and teacher education in Brazil," in *Initial English Language Teacher Education*, D. L. Banegas (ed.), London: Bloomsbury Academic, pp. 177–91

Lobo, M. 2010. "Interethnic understanding and belonging in suburban Melbourne," *Urban Policy and Research* 28(1): 85–99 https://doi.org/10.1080/08111140903325424

Longhi, S. 2013. "Impact of cultural diversity on wages, evidence from panel data," *Regional Science and Urban Economics* 43(5): 797–807 https://doi.org/10.1016/j.regsciurbeco.2013.07.004

López Peláez, A., M. V. Aguilar-Tablada, A. Erro-Garcés and R. M. Pérez-García 2022. "Superdiversity and social policies in a complex society: Social challenges in the 21st century," *Current Sociology* 70(2): 166–92 https://doi.org/10.1177/0011392120983344

Lucassen, L., D. Feldman and J. Oltmer (eds.) 2006. *Paths of Integration: Migrants in Western Europe (1880–2004)*, Amsterdam: Amsterdam University Press https://doi.org/10.1017/9789048504244

Madiba, M. 2018. "The multilingual university," in *The Routledge Handbook of Language and Superdiversity*, A. Creese and A. Blackledge (eds.), London: Routledge, pp. 504–17 https://doi.org/10.4324/9781315696010

Magazzini, T. 2017. "Making the most of super-diversity: Notes on the potential of a new approach," *Policy & Politics* 45(4): 527–45 https://doi.org/10.1332/030557317x14972819300753

Mar-Molinero, C. (ed.) 2020. *Researching Language in Superdiverse Urban Contexts: Exploring Methodological and Theoretical Concepts*, Bristol: Multilingual Matters https://doi.org/10.21832/9781788926478

Matejskova, T. 2013. "The unbearable closeness of the East: Embodied microeconomies of difference, belonging, and intersecting marginalities in postsocialist Berlin," *Urban Geography* 34(1): 30–5 https://doi.org/10.1080/02723638.2013.778630

Mavroudi, E. 2010. "Nationalism, the nation and migration: Searching for purity and diversity," *Space and Polity* 14(3): 219–33 https://doi.org/10.1080/13562576.2010.532951

McCabe, A., J. Phillimore and L. Mayblin 2010. "Below the radar: Activities and organisations in the third sector: a summary review of the literature," *Third Sector Research Centre Paper* 29, University of Birmingham

McDowell, L. 2013. *Working Lives: Gender, Migration and Employment in Britain, 1945–2007*, London: John Wiley & Sons https://doi.org/10.1002/9781118349229

Meissner, F. 2015. "Migration in migration-related diversity? The nexus between superdiversity and migration studies," *Ethnic and Racial Studies* 38(4): 556–67 https://doi.org/10.1080/01419870.2015.970209

Meissner, F. 2018. "Mainstreaming and superdiversity: Beyond more integration," in *Mainstreaming Integration Governance*, P. Scholten and I. van Breugel (eds.), Basingstoke: Palgrave, pp. 215–33

Meissner, F. 2019. "Of straw figures and multi-stakeholder monitoring – A response to Willem Schinkel," *Comparative Migration Studies* 7: 18 https://doi.org/10.1186/s40878-019-0121-y

Meissner, F. and S. Vertovec 2015. "Comparing super-diversity," *Ethnic and Racial Studies* 38(4): 541–55 https://doi.org/10.1080/01419870.2015.980295

Modood, T. 2008. "Is multiculturalism dead?" *Public Policy Research* 15(2): 84–8

Nathan, M. 2011. The Economics of Cultural Diversity: Lessons from British Cities, Doctoral dissertation, The London School of Economics and Political Science

Nathan, M. and N. Lee 2013. "Cultural diversity, innovation, and entrepreneurship: Firm-level evidence from London," *Economic Geography* 89(4): 367–94 https://doi.org/10.1111/ecge.12016

Ndhlovu, F. 2016. "A decolonial critique of diaspora identity theories and the notion of superdiversity," *Diaspora Studies* 9(1): 28–40 https://doi.org/10.1080/09739572.2015.1088612

Neal, S., K. Bennett, A. Cochrane and G. Mohan 2013. "Living multiculture: Understanding the new spatial and social relations of ethnicity and multiculture in England," *Environment and Planning C: Government and Policy* 31(2): 308–23 https://doi.org/10.1068/c11263r

Newall, D., J. Phillimore and H. Sharpe 2012. "Migration and maternity in the age of superdiversity," *Practising Midwife* 15(1): 20–3

Newton, J. and E. Kusmierczyk 2011. "Teaching second languages for the workplace," *Annual Review of Applied Linguistics* 31: 74–92 https://doi.org/10.1017/s0267190511000080

Ní Shé, É. and R. Joye 2018. "The health systems workforce in an era of globalised super-diversity: Exploring the global care chain landscape in Ireland" in *Work and Identity*, S. Werth and C. Bronlow (eds.), Cham: Palgrave Macmillan, pp. 101–16 https://doi.org/10.1007/978-3-319-73936-6_8

Nolan, M., D. M. MacRaild and N. Kirk 2010. "Transnational labour in the age of globalization," *Labour History Review* 75(1): 8–19 https://doi.org/10.1179/0961565 10x12568148663764

Oliviera, N. and B. Padilla 2017. "Integrating superdiversity in urban governance: The case of inner-city Lisbon," *Policy & Politics* 45(4): 605–22 https://doi.org/10.1332/030557317x14835601760639

Osipovič, D. 2010. Social Citizenship of Polish Migrants in London: Engagement and Non-Engagement with the British Welfare State, Doctoral thesis, University College London

Palaiologou, N. and D. Faas 2012. "How 'intercultural' is education in Greece? Insights from policymakers and educators," *Compare* 42(4): 563–84

Parker, S. G. and R. J. K Freathy 2011. "Context, complexity and contestation: Birmingham's Agreed Syllabuses for Religious Education since the 1970s," Journal of Beliefs and Values 32(2): 246–63

Parkin, D. 2012. "Concluding commentary," *New Diversities* 14(2): 73–85

Pavlenko, A. 2018. "Superdiversity and why it isn't: Reflections on terminological innovation and academic branding," in *Sloganization in Language Education Discourse*, B. Schmenk et al. (eds.), Bristol: Multilingual Matters, pp. 142–68 https://doi.org/10.21832/9781788921879-009

Pecoud, A. 2010. "What is ethnic in an ethnic economy?" *International Review of Sociology* 20(1): 59–76 https://doi.org/10.1080/03906700903525677

Pemberton, S. 2016. "Urban planning and the challenge of super-diversity," *Policy and Politics* 45(4): 623–41

Pennycook, A. and E. Otsuji 2015. *Metrolingualism: Language in the City*. London: Routledge https://doi.org/10.4324/9781315724225

Perrons, D., A. Plomien and M. Kilkey 2010. "Migration and uneven development within an enlarged European Union: Fathering, gender divisions and male migrant domestic services," *European Urban and Regional Studies* 17(2): 197–215

Phillimore, J. 2010. "Approaches to health provision in the age of super-diversity: Accessing the NHS in Britain's most diverse city," *Critical Social Policy* 31(1): 5–29 https://doi.org/10.1177/0261018310385437

Phillimore, J. 2013. "Housing, home and neighbourhood renewal in the era of superdiversity: Some lessons from the West Midlands," *Housing Studies* 28(5): 682–70 https://doi.org/10.1080/02673037.2013.758242

Phillimore, J. In press). "Social policy and superdiversity: Engaging with structure and agency," in *The Oxford Handbook of Superdiversity*, F. Meissner, N. Sigona and S. Vertovec (eds.), Oxford: Oxford University Press

Phillimore, J., N. Sigona and K. Tonkiss 2017. "Superdiversity, policy and governance in Europe," *Policy & Politics* 45(4): 487–91 https://doi.org/10.1332/0305573 17x15076320392001

Phillimore, J., N. Sigona and K. Tonkiss (eds.) 2020. *Superdiversity, Policy and Governance in Europe: Multi-Scalar Perspectives*, Bristol: Policy Press

Phillimore, J., J. Thornhill, M. Uwimana and Z. Latif. 2011. *Delivering in the Age of Superdiversity*, Birmingham: Department of Health

Phillips, D. 2007. "Ethnic and racial segregation: A critical perspective," *Geography Compass* 1(5): 1138–59

Piekut, A. and P. Rees 2011. "Living with Difference: Mapping Diversity in Leeds and Warsaw," Paper at International RC21 conference, Amsterdam

Poppleton, S., K. Hitchcock, K. Lymperopoulou, J. Simmons and R. Gillespie 2013. *Social and Public Service Impacts of International Migration at the Local Level*, London: The Home Office

Raco, M. and T. Taşan-Kok 2020. "A tale of two cities: Framing urban diversity as content curation in London and Toronto," *Cosmopolitan Civil Societies* 12(1): 43–66 https://doi.org/10.5130/ccs.v12.i1.6835

Ram, M., T. Jones, P. Edwards, A. Kiselinchev, L. Muchenje and K. Woldesenbet 2012. "Engaging with super-diversity: New migrant businesses and the research–policy nexus," *International Small Business Journal* 31(4): 337–56 https://doi.org/10.1177/0266242611429979

Ramadan, T. 2011. *On Superdiversity*, Berlin: Sternberg Press

Rampton, B. 2017. *Crossing: Language and Ethnicity among Adolescents*, London: Routledge, 3rd edn. https://doi.org/10.4324/9781315205915

Reid, C. and A. Sriprakash 2012. "The possibility of cosmopolitan learning: Reflecting on future directions for diversity teacher education in Australia," *Asia-Pacific Journal of Teacher Education* 40(1): 15–29

Richardson, K. and R. Fulton 2010. "Towards culturally competent advocacy: Meeting the needs of diverse communities," Better Health Briefing Paper 15, British Institute of Race Equality in Advocacy Services, Kidderminster

Rishbeth, C. 2016. Landscape Experience and Migration: Superdiversity and the Significance of Urban Public Open Space, PhD Thesis, University of Sheffield

Ros i Solé, C. 2013. "Cosmopolitan speakers and their cultural cartographies," *The Language Learning Journal* 41(3): 326–39 https://doi.org/10.1080/09571736.2013. 836349

Rosbrook-Thompson, J. 2018. "Understanding difference amid superdiversity: Space, 'race' and granular essentialisms at an inner-city football club," *Sociology* 52(4): 639–54 https://doi.org/10.1177/0038038516660039

Salway, S., R. Barley, P. Allmark, K. Gerrish, G. Higginbottom and G. Ellison 2011. *Ethnic Diversity and Inequality: Ethical and Scientific Rigour in Social Research*, York: Joseph Rowntree Foundation

Schinkel, W. 2018. "Against 'immigrant integration': For an end to neo-colonial knowledge production," *Comparative Migration Studies* 6(1): 1–17 https://doi.org/10.1186/ s40878-018-0095-1

Schiller, N. G. and A. Çağlar 2009. "Towards a comparative theory of locality in migration studies: Migrant incorporation and city scale," *Journal of Ethnic and Migration Studies* 35(2): 177–202 https://doi.org/10.1080/13691830802586179

Schiller, N. G., A. Çağlar and T. Guldbrandsen 2006. "Beyond the ethnic lens: Locality, globality, and born-again incorporation," *American Ethnologist* 33(4): 612–33 https:// doi.org/10.1525/ae.2006.33.4.612

Schmidt, G. 2012. "'Grounded' politics: Manifesting Muslim identity as a political factor and localized identity in Copenhagen," *Ethnicities* 12(5): 603–22 https://doi. org/10.1177/1468796811432839

Scholten, P. 2020. *Mainstreaming versus Alienation: A Complexity Approach to the Governance of Migration and Diversity*, Basingstoke: Palgrave https://doi.org/10.1007/978-3-030- 42238-7

Scholten, P. and I. van Breugel (eds.) 2018. *Mainstreaming Integration Governance: New Trends in Migrant Integration Policies in Europe*, Basingstoke: Palgrave https://doi.org/ 10.1007/978-3-319-59277-0

Silverstein, M. 2015. "How language communities intersect: Is 'superdiversity' an incremental or transformative condition?" *Language & Communication* 44: 7–18 https://doi. org/10.1016/j.langcom.2014.10.015

Simic, A. 2019. "The role of superdiverse home country cities in helping migrants negotiate life in superdiverse host country cities," *Geoforum* 107: 179–87 https://doi. org/10.1016/j.geoforum.2019.07.015

Song, M. 2009. "Is intermarriage a good indicator of integration?" *Journal of Ethnic and Migration Studies* 35(2): 331–48 https://doi.org/10.1080/13691830802586476

Stæhr, A. 2014. "The appropriation of transcultural flows among Copenhagen youth – The case of Illuminati," *Discourse, Context and Media* 4–5: 101–15 https://doi.org/ 10.1016/j.dcm.2014.03.001

Storey, D. 2011. "Football, place and migration: Foreign footballers in the FA Premier League," *Geography* 96(2): 86–94

Stubbs, S. 2008. "In place of drums and samosas: In a 'super diverse' Britain, the key to social cohesion is not a new British 'identity' but tackling poverty and inequality," *The Guardian* 13 May

Svenberg, K., C. Skott and M. Lepp 2011. "Ambiguous expectations and reduced confidence: Experience of Somali refugees encountering Swedish health care," *Journal of Refugee Studies* 24(4): 690–705 https://doi.org/10.1093/jrs/fer026

Syrett, S. and M. Lyons 2008. "Migration, new arrivals and local economies," *Local Economy* 22(4): 325–34 https://doi.org/10.1080/02690940701736710

Taylor-Gooby, P. and E. Waite 2014. "Toward a more pragmatic multiculturalism? How the UK policy community sees the future of ethnic diversity policies," *Governance* 27(2): 267–89 https://doi.org/10.1111/gove.12030

Toivanen, R. and J. Saarikivi (eds.) 2016. *Linguistic Genocide or Superdiversity? New and Old Language Diversities*, Bristol: Multilingual Matters https://doi.org/10.21832/9781783096060

Tremlett, A. 2014. "Making a difference without creating a difference: Super-diversity as a new direction for research on Roma minorities," *Ethnicities* 14(6): 830–48 https://doi.org/10.1177/1468796814542183

van Breugel, I. and P. Scholten 2017. "Mainstreaming in response to superdiversity? The governance of migration-related diversity in France, the UK and the Netherlands," *Policy & Politics* 45(4): 511–26 https://doi.org/10.1332/0305573 17x14849132401769

van der Laar, P. and A. van der Schoor 2019. "Rotterdam's superdiversity from a historical perspective (1600-1980)," in *Coming to Terms with Superdiversity*, P. Scholten et al. (eds.), Cham: Springer, pp. 21–55 https://doi.org/10.1007/978-3-319-96041-8_2

van Ewijk, A. R. 2011. "Diversity within police forces in Europe: A case for the comprehensive view," *Policing* 6(1): 76–92 https://doi.org/10.1093/police/par048

van Ewijk, H. 2018. *Complexity and Social Work*, London: Routledge https://doi.org/10.4324/9781315109275

Varis, P. and X. Wang 2011. "Superdiversity on the internet: A case from China," *Diversities* 13(2): 71–83

Vershinina, N., R. Barrett and M. Meyer 2009. Polish immigrants in Leicester: Forms of capital underpinning entrepreneurial activity, Leicester Business School Occasional Papers 86

Vertovec, S. 2006. "The emergence of super-diversity in Britain," ESRC Centre on Migration, Policy and Society Working Paper WP-06-25

Vertovec, S. 2007a. "Super-diversity and its implications", *Ethnic and Racial Studies* 30(6): 1024–54 https://doi.org/10.1080/01419870701599465

Vertovec, S. 2007b. "New complexities of cohesion in Britain," *A Thinkpiece for the Commission on Integration and Cohesion*, London: Communities and Local Government Publications

Vertovec, S. 2011. "The cultural politics of nation and migration," *Annual Review of Anthropology* 40: 241–56 https://doi.org/10.1146/annurev-anthro-081309-145837

Vertovec, S. 2015a. "Introduction: Formulating diversity studies," in *Routledge International Handbook of Diversity Studies*, S. Vertovec (ed.), London: Routledge, pp. 1–20

Vertovec, S. (ed.) 2015b. *Diversities Old and New: Migration and Socio-Spatial Patterns in New York, Singapore and Johannesburg*, Basingstoke: Palgrave https://doi.org/10.1057/9781137495488

Vertovec, S. 2020. "Considering the work of 'integration'," Max-Planck-Institute Working Paper 20-04, Göttingen

Walton-Roberts, M. W. 2011. "Immigration, the university and the welcoming second tier city," *Journal of International Migration and Integration* 12(4): 453–73

Wekker, F. 2019. "'We have to teach them diversity': On demographic transformations and lived reality in an Amsterdam working-class neighbourhood," *Ethnic and Racial Studies* 42(1): 89–104 https://doi.org/10.1080/01419870.2017.1406968

Williams, R. 1976. *Keywords: A Vocabulary of Culture and Society*, London: Fontana

Williams, C. and M. R. D. Johnson 2010. *Race and Ethnicity in a Welfare Society*, Maidenhead: Open University Press

Wimmer, A. 2009. "Herder's heritage and the boundary-making approach: Studying ethnicity in immigrant societies," *Sociological Theory* 27(3): 244–70 https://doi.org/ 10.1111/j.1467-9558.2009.01347.x

Yildiz, C. and A. Bartlett 2011. "Language, foreign nationality and ethnicity in an English prison: Implications for the quality of health and social research," *Journal of Medical Ethics* 37(10): 637–40 https://doi.org/10.1136/jme.2010.040931

4

DIVERSIFICATIONS

As presented in the previous chapter, several scholars with interest in the concept of superdiversity invoke it to portray a kind of state or condition of contemporary society. If superdiversity is indeed a state or condition, however, then it is one of ongoing change, one of process. As Fran Meissner and I (2015: 55) have proposed, we should be examining "diversity 'on the move'," a shift "from analyzing diversity to analyzing diversifications." Indeed, Ralph Grillo (2015: 5) urges, we should understand "super-diversity as a process rather than a state: 'super-diversification'."

Worldwide, multiple kinds of diversification are deeply transforming societies, economies, and polities. This chapter points to two key modes of diversification – migration-driven and demographic – that are linked and, each in themselves, comprise a variety of causalities, processes, dynamics, and outcomes.

Global migration diversifications

Migration-related diversifications are created and reproduced through mutually conditioning sets of changes. Such patterns of diversification entail and are modified by, among other things: evolving, numerous reasons for why people move; changing capacities, both enabling and restricting, for mobility across varying distances; evolving government policies, with ever-modified stipulations, concerning permanent, temporary, or circular migration schemes; increasing global competition for workers in a wide range of sectors (modified but not greatly stifled by the coronavirus pandemic), from technology specialists through care workers to construction labourers and farmhands; shifting age and gender profiles that are reflected in particular migration streams; a rise in global student migration; the enhancement of transnational social and economic practices, ever-enhanced by information and computer technologies sustaining the presence and ubiquity of

DOI: 10.4324/9780203503577-4

"digital diasporas"; new uses of sociotechnical systems and platforms in migration processes themselves; heightened security instruments to prevent migration together with augmented deportation measures; a seeming upsurge in both populist anti-immigration and white nationalist sentiments alongside sustained pro-migration, pro-refugee, pro-"diversity," and anti-racist public attitudes and civil society mobilizations; and a rise of "post-migration," "mixed" populations in a great many countries.

Over the past 30 years or so, global migration patterns have undergone a sea change. This transformation, Fran Meissner and I (2015: 542) point out:

> not only entail[s] the movement of people from more varied national, ethnic, linguistic and religious backgrounds, but also the ways in which the shifting patterns coincide with a worldwide diversification of movement flows through specific migration channels (such as work permit programmes, mobilities created by EU enlargement, ever-changing refugee and "mixed migration" flows, undocumented movements, student migration, family reunion, and so on); the changing compositions of various migration channels themselves entail ongoing differentiations of legal status (conditions, rights and restrictions), diverging patterns of gender and age, and variance in migrants' human capital (education, work skills and experience).

Within the interdisciplinary field that comprises migration studies, a range of theories address processes of migration (see, among others, Massey et al. 1998; King 2012; Brettell and Hollifield 2014; de Haas 2021). These include migration theories relating to: neo-classical economics, segmented labour markets, new economics, social networks, systems theory, cumulative causation, transition theory, world systems theory, transnationalism, and aspirations–capabilities. Each of these contributions to theory have significant (albeit sometimes seemingly limited) explanatory value and generally important things to say about migration phenomena. Perhaps, however, many of these theories are losing their broader explicatory appeal. This is not just due to mutable trends in social science, but to changing realities surrounding migration itself (see Bevelander 2020).

Already at the turn of this century in a critique of neo-classical theories that emphasize economic inequality as the main determinant of migration, Joaquín Arango (2000: 287) stressed that migration scholars must crucially take account of "the increasingly complex and different reality" surrounding international migration. He observes, "international migration has undergone deep changes. *Inter alia*, flows have become more global and heterogeneous in composition" (Ibid.). Following Arango's call, scholars of contemporary global migration are confronted with the task of discerning and describing emergent, ongoing, and multi-layered changes in processes, patterns, and impacts of migration as they manifest differentially in multiple sites around the world.

The United Nations/International Organization for Migration's (IOM) *World Migration Report 2020* (IOM 2020) indicates that in 2019, some 272 million people were residing in a country other than their country of birth (this is their broad definition of a migrant). The number comprises 3.5% of the world's population. This marks a sizable increase from 200 million global migrants (3.2% of world population) in 2010, 173 million (2.8% of world population) in 2000, and 153 million (2.9% of world population) in 1990. The numbers are huge, although the percentage of world population seems relatively small and in pace with the overall growth of the global populace. What these figures obscure, in any case, is the changing nature and motivations of the migrants themselves, their pathways, the conditions under which they move and the impacts of their movement for themselves, for the places and people they leave behind, and for the societies through which they pass and into which they move. The proportion of migrants in the global population has not changed greatly over the last 30 years, but their nature, origins, motivations, trajectories, and experiences have changed considerably.

In the latest, sixth edition of *The Age of Migration* (de Haas et al. 2020) – the closest thing we have to an internationally authoritative textbook on global migration – Stephen Castles, Mark Miller, and Hein de Haas stress the necessity of understanding migration processes and phenomena within broader trends surrounding globalization and social transformation. In addressing the gradual growth of global migration, they especially underline the different paces and qualities of international migration flows. For instance, recent increases in immigration into Western Europe, North America, and the Middle East have been fast and pronounced; a slower pace of growth rate for international migration is found in Africa, Eastern Europe, Asia, and Latin America. Around the world, however, there is a strong and rapid rise in long-distance, intercontinental migration flows. Further, the authors discern that "Throughout the world, while much migration remains regional, long-standing migratory patterns are persisting in new forms, while new movements are developing in response to economic, political and cultural change, and violent conflicts" (Ibid.: 9). They also describe far-reaching worldwide trends such as the emergence of new migration destinations, the proliferation of migration transitions (when emigration countries become immigration countries, including ones as varied as Poland, Spain, Morocco, Mexico, South Korea, and Turkey), and the feminization of labour migration. Across the world, immigrant skill levels have gone up while demands for low-skilled workers have been sustained (de Haas et al. 2019). Over the last decades, there have been considerable fluctuations in numbers of refugees, too, as disasters occur and conflicts arise and subside. As part of their global perspective, Castles, Miller, and de Haas also indicate that:

> While people have always moved, an increasing number of low- and middle-income countries have become integrated into global migration systems centered around old destinations in North America and Russia and more recent destinations in Western Europe, the Gulf and East Asia.

> This globalization of migration has confronted societies with unprecedented levels of diversity.
>
> *de Haas et al. (2020: 12)*

The globalization of migration sounds like a large, singular process. However, as this chapter demonstrates, the process is actually one of considerable complexification. Foremost among the constituent processes are a compounding of migration drivers, the proliferation of countries of origin, and the varying of legal statuses and perplexing of legal statuses.

Compounding migration drivers

Migration is never a matter of clear push and pull factors or unambiguous distinctions between voluntary versus forced migration. The reasons people leave their homelands today are inherently various. As Graeme Hugo described:

> Population mobility is probably best viewed as being arranged along a continuum ranging from totally voluntary migration, in which the choice and will of the migrants is the overwhelmingly decisive element encouraging people to move, to totally forced migration, where the migrants are faced with death if they remain in their present place of residence. The extremes in fact rarely occur, and most mobility is located along the continuum.
>
> *1996: 107*

Rather than just thinking that persecution leads to "refugees" and poverty leads to "economic migration," we must realize that migration always has multiple, interrelated causes or drivers or what are sometimes described as causal drivers (see Black et al. 2011). These include causal drivers that are:

* *political* (in which a state – riddled with corruption, oppression, and violence – fails to provide for a population, leading to poor governance, crime, conflict and state-sanctioned persecution, and/or repression);
* *social* (including family aspirations for betterment including physical safety, education, health, and well-being);
* *economic* (involving extensive inequalities, lack of opportunities limited access to food, goods and services, quests for better, more sustainable livelihoods);
* *demographic* (stemming from resource competition intensified by population growth and large numbers of young people); and
* *environmental* (from ecological degradation and catastrophe, changes to land and sea productivity, and other slow- and rapid-onset disasters especially and increasingly linked to climate change).

These causes perpetually trigger, influence, and intensify one another – hence the appropriateness of the notion "driver." Together they often prompt what

Alex Betts (2013) has importantly called "survival migration." "The five drivers rarely act in isolation," Richard Black and his colleagues (2011: S9) surmise, "and the interaction of the five drivers determines the details of movement. The nature of these interactions will influence the scale of movement, and movements at different scales – internal compared to international, for example – will be influenced by different interactions between drivers." These factors – together called driver configurations or complex driver environments – are further complicated by their respective and mutual temporality (slowness or suddenness), geography (local, region or global nature), and selectivity (affecting an entire population or specific group)(see Bijak and Czaika 2020; Czaika and Reinprecht 2020).

Moreover, importantly – and connected directly to the kinds of variables addressed by superdiversity – Black and colleagues point out that "The scale and direction of movement is linked to the personal circumstances of migrants, such as class, ethnicity, religion, language, education levels and connections with people in planned destinations, mitigated by the intervening effects of migration policies" (Black et al. 2011: S6). Different configurations of causal drivers may prompt migration by specific groups of individuals in specific places and periods (Garip 2012). So-called forced migration patterns and processes are inherently linked to compounded causes, too. Indeed, says Roger Zetter (2015: 21), due to ever more "complex and multicausal drivers, forced displacement can no longer be conceived as a discrete migratory process demarked by referee status, but part of an international migration continuum that also embraces authorized migration." Across such a continuum, shifting conditions and configurations prompting migration affect entire countries, leading to fluctuating national and regional patterns of movement.

Proliferating countries of origin

At the beginning of the twenty-first century, the IOM stressed that "Diversification of migration flows and stocks is the new watchword for the current dynamics" (IOM 2003: 4). More recent publications that examine the diversification of global migration flows – even those setting out to challenge the idea – tend to corroborate such diversification (see Benton 2013; Abel and Sander 2014; Czaika and de Haas 2014; de Haas et al. 2020). This diversification of migration, especially origin countries, is summarized in a UN Report:

> The scale and nature of international migration flows in developed countries, especially in Europe, has changed significantly since the 1970s. Between 1945 and 1973, all highly industrialized countries in Western Europe engaged in temporary labour recruitment which ended with the oil crisis of 1973-1974. This period was followed by new complex migration patterns accompanied by a rise in numbers of people migrating. International migration became increasingly global in nature, with more

countries becoming countries of origin, destination or transit. Former emigration countries changed to countries of immigration while family reunion and refugee and asylum-seeker movements added another dimension to the flows.

UN-DESA (2009: 7)

The diversification of countries of origin especially began to develop in the latter two decades of the twentieth century. "By the mid-1980s Europe had a population of foreign origin substantially different from that of ten years before" (OECD 2011: 9). In the 1990s, according to Hania Zlotnik, the then Director of the UN Population Division, "there has undeniably been a diversification of origins and destinations of international migrants in all regions of the world since 1965" (1998: 465). She noted how this trend intensified particularly since the 1980s, although with considerable differences in size, trends, and degrees of diversification among destination countries. Similarly, a group of World Bank analysts (Özden et al. 2011: 18–9) demonstrate that "Over the 1960-2000 period, the composition of world migration fundamentally changed" from a rather restricted body of migrant origin countries to a global array characterized by "greatly diversified migrant stocks." Further, as noted in a report by the Organization for Economic Co-operation and Development (OECD), into the 1990s:

Australia, Canada and the United States (and to a lesser degree also New Zealand), each an important node in a global migration system, continued to experience a changing geography of migration, with the balance of their intake swinging inexorably towards Asia and, especially in the case of the United States, towards Latin America. Diversification included new nationalities such as Sri Lankans, Vietnamese and Indonesians, many of whom were highly skilled.

A feature of migration in the 1990s was recognition of its increasing globalisation, as the numbers of countries involved in migration grew, helped by the opening of Central and Eastern Europe and by economic growth in Asian countries.

OECD (2011: 12)

Agencies including the World Bank, the UN Population Division and the IOM each highlighted the ongoing diversification of global migration, especially by way of migrants' countries of origin and channels of migration. Indeed, according to the latter,

The number of countries and nationalities concerned and directly involved in human mobility is rising steadily. None of the roughly 190 sovereign states in the international system is now beyond the reach of migration circuits. Indeed, they are all either countries of origin, transit of destination for migrants, and increasingly are all three simultaneously. Migration circuits span the globe like a spider's web, with complex ramifications and countless intersections. The current world map of migration is therefore multipolar.

IOM (2003: 4)

Through this process, today hardly a country in the world remains untouched by some migration flow from, through, and/or to it.

However, this has been and continues to be a highly uneven process globally. The diversification of origin countries is not a singular, evenly spread process. This is evident in a study by Mathias Czaika and Hein de Haas (2014) in which they examine changing patterns in volume, diversity, geographical scope, and general complexity of international migration between 1960 and 2000. Their study uses the United Nations Global Bilateral Migration Database composed of decennial censuses of migrant "stocks" (the accumulated number of people born in, or a national of, another country – as distinct from actual migrant "flows" or the number of people crossing borders). It is a sophisticated analysis of overall international migration patterns and change, albeit based on a rather limited and problematic data set. While initially setting out to challenge the view that there has been an increase in migration volume, diversity, spread, and complexity, Czaika and de Haas end up demonstrating that there has indeed been an increasing complexification in each of these dimensions – however, in each it is a skewed or asymmetrical process. Among their conclusions, Czaika and de Haas observe that:

While immigrant populations have become more diverse in new destination countries in Europe, this is not always the case elsewhere, such as the Americas and the Pacific, where immigrant populations have become less European but not necessarily more diverse in terms of diversity of origin countries. For instance, while immigration countries such as the U.S., Canada, Australia, and New Zealand used to attract Europeans, non-European immigration has been surging since the 1960s.

Ibid.: 314

With declining European emigration toward other countries, there has been major shift in global directionality of migration, with the transformation of Europe from a global source region of emigrants and settlers into a global migration magnet. This has led to an increased presence of phenotypically and culturally distinct immigrants in Europe as well as settler societies of European descent in North America and the Pacific. In other words, rather than an increased spread in terms of origin countries of migrants per se, the national and ethnic origin of immigrant populations has become increasingly non-European.

Ibid.

Overall, Czaika and de Haas show that there has been more migration from "an increasingly diverse array of origin countries" (Ibid.: 318) – although in many cases towards a more limited number of destination countries. In other words, the diversification of origin countries has been quite evident, but it has not been a process evenly distributed around the world. Some countries still receive more migrants – from a wider range of sources – than others.

The complex, uneven, and differentially distributed global pattern of diversification should indeed be understood as a fundamental feature of contemporary superdiversity. This perspective goes hand-in-hand with the latest views of de Haas et al. (2020: 9) who describe "the tendency for more and more countries to be significantly affected by international migration. Immigration counties tend to receive migrants from an increasingly diverse array of origin countries, so that most immigration countries have entrants from a broad spectrum of economic, social and cultural backgrounds." Again, the patterns are uneven. Two thirds of all international migrants live in just 20 countries, led by the USA, Germany, Saudi Arabia, Russia, and the UK (International Migrant Stock 2019; www. unmigration.org). It is an asymmetric global migration formation that is both constituted and perpetuated by asymmetric features of globalization, the world economic system, and its historical spread of inequalities (de Haas et al. 2019). This worldwide web of inequalities, reflected in the compounding of migration causal drivers and proliferation of migrant origin countries, is codified and perpetuated by systems of migration channels and legal statuses.

Perplexing legal statuses

Contributing to the broader process of superdiversification, migration categories and legal statuses have become more perplex, in the sense of processes that at once entail complicating, confounding, and hampering migration flows through bureaucracy and uncertainty. These processes were notably underway at the beginning of this century, when the IOM observed:

> For some years now, migration streams have become more diversified and complex. Receiving countries on all continents are encountering highly disparate population movements: students, women, migrants for family reunion purposes, highly qualified professionals, returning migrants, temporary workers, victims of trafficking, refugees, and undocumented persons (often emerging from one of the aforementioned categories). Migration is made even more complex through the various forms of settlement in the host country, i.e., temporary or definitive, seasonal or periodic, legal or clandestine.
>
> *IOM (2003: 16)*

Around this time, Eleonore Kofman (2002) also critically pointed to a diversification of migratory flows that were marked by an increasing heterogeneity of migrant statuses. The complexification of migration categories and statuses has continued through the present – indeed, it has intensified.

As we have discussed above, the reasons why people migrate are many. Yet, as Roger Zetter (2007: 178) suggests, "In the minds of policy makers and immigration officials it is necessary to fragment and make clear cut labels and categories of the often complex mix of reasons why people migrate and migrate between labels." This is not surprising, since a fundamental function of contemporary nation-states is to decide on who is allowed to enter its territory and under what conditions. The state's system of migrant classifications is a primary modus for doing so (Söderström et al. 2013), and borders are essentially where such classifications are made (Favell 2007). The multiple drivers and kinds of mobility they stimulate ultimately get filtered by state categories and policy regimes into what become known as types of migration. Today almost everywhere, and particularly in the rich world, there exist a basic set of classifications: temporary and permanent migrants, "economic" and "forced" migrants. These broad classes are themselves divided into further categories, the foremost including: workers (often deemed "skilled," "semi-skilled, or "low-skilled"), students, family members (for family formation or reunification), asylum-seekers and refugees, and undocumented or "illegal" migrants. Such general types themselves entail an enormous range of subtypes (see Salt 2005). Through these, a process of legal and conceptual sorting occurs for the explicit – mostly economic – purposes of individual nation-states, despite the fact that migrants themselves move across borders with very mixed means, attributes, and motivations (Van Hear et al. 2009).

The number of migrant categories and the administrative "tracks" they entail – whether concerning work, family reunification, asylum, education, retirement, or other – have been increasing and becoming more perplex. According to one international study, the number of entry tracks can be used to estimate the evolution of admission policy complexity (Beine et al. 2015). Along these lines, the migration law expert Elspeth Guild observes how:

> a number of states have developed the most amazingly complex categorizations of people according to their status as non-citizens. The example I always like to give to exemplify this is law is the list of residence permits notified by each EU Member State (other than Ireland and the UK which do not participate) under article 34 of the Schengen Borders Code as having the equivalence of a visa for entry into the common Schengen area.
>
> …each state has hundreds of different residence permits. What that means is the following. States only need different types of residence permits if the underlying rights which they evidence are different. These rights broadly speaking can be chopped into the following categories: length of time permitted for residence; type of economic activity permitted; other activities permitted (e.g. studies); access to benefits. So this means that EU

states cut and paste in an amazing number of different ways these facets of the lives of foreigners and document them with incredible detail in the form of multiple residence permits.

If you take the history of these Article 34 notifications, you will see that states mainly add more residence permits to the list and rarely take any off.

personal communication

States create migrant categories and classifications that determine immigration policies, laws, and rules. These function to sort or "filter" migrants by way of skills (education and occupations) and groups (including age cohorts, genders and familial relationships) as well as types of experience and countries of origin (see Anderson 2007). Indeed, Steffen Mau (2021) describes the arrangement of contemporary borders and admission regimes as a global "sorting machine."

The proliferation and complexification of migrant categories follows and shapes broad political strategies in a number of countries:

[P]ublic policy and practices prescribe and invent an increasing variety of new labels institutionalizing categories of semi-permanent transients. The proliferation of labels reveals the political agenda. Governments try to regulate, discriminate and differentiate the migratory impacts of socio-economic social transformation, representing them as viable labels in order to regulate entry.

Zetter (2007: 189)

Migrant categories and classifications are also used politically to attempt to engineer economic growth, ensure national cohesion, and manage security (Martin 2009). They are also part of an encompassing and ongoing endeavour to create, modify, or maintain particular narratives of the nation-state (Vertovec 2011).

Worldwide, as reflected in migration categories and statuses, migration policies have become ever more selective. "In other words, notwithstanding political rhetoric focusing on limiting the numbers of migrants coming in, the real aim of most migration policies seems to increase the ability of states to control *who* is allowed to immigrate" (de Haas et al. 2018: 353, emphasis in original). Such selection has been skewed towards the wealthy and the skilled, especially within particular regional groupings (de Haas et al. 2019). Restrictive measures have not necessarily brought down the number of migrants, but made many of them more vulnerable. Migrant selection criteria and categories, immigration policies, and admissions rules directly create the conditions under which immigrants live and work along with their legal rights, labour market outcomes, political incorporation, and social position (Sainsbury 2006; Ruhs and Martin 2008; Ruhs 2011).

Such conditions and measures allow or restrict people – in differentially ordered ways – to settle, build families, educate themselves and their children, gain employment, enter the housing market, make use of the health system, and engage in the system of political representation. While certain statuses are enabling, some statuses shut down or highly constrain these processes, effectively excluding people in a variety of ways from gaining a better foothold on life in the "host" country. At practically every stage and status concerning migrants and asylum-seekers, there are opportunities, restrictions, and consequences set by migration policies and institutional measures concerning:

- access to welfare, health, education, public services;
- permission and restrictions for work and the process, type, and focus of insertion into the labour market – including nature of employment contract, work conditions, and wages;
- nature of treatment by the criminal justice system;
- length and nature of residence;
- prospects of family reunification;
- nature of legal advice and support, including modes of appeal;
- forcible removal and deportation, or
- chances for permanent settlement and eventual possibility of gaining citizenship.

Celilia Menjívar (2006) further points out how legal statuses – even the grey area of "liminal legality" posed by undocumented status – can affect a breadth of phenomena including health risks, domestic violence, and identity. These contribute to the "legal violence" of immigration laws that govern the lives of immigrants:

> Designed to modify migratory practices and behaviors, these laws potentially violate individuals' human rights, make them suspect in the eyes of others, lead them to accept their self-depreciation as normal, and create conditions for immigrants to impose categories of domination on one another.
> ...In the case of immigrants in tenuous legal statuses, legal violence is rooted in the legal system that purports to protect the nation but, instead, produces spaces and the possibility for material, emotional, and psychological injurious actions that target an entire group of people with a particular set of shared social characteristics.
>
> *Menjívar and Abrego (2012: 1413–14)*

Migrant legal statuses parcel-out or limit rights and access to public resources in ways that inherently position people as closer-to/distant from the state. At the same time, they socially rank people (including high status skilled workers through low-status manual labourers to stigmatized asylum-seekers and "illegals"). For states, such a formal stratification continuum is a bureaucratic and institutional modus for the control of people, their mobility and their socio-economic positioning, public resources, political debate, and public opinion.

For migrants and asylum-seekers, the stages and statuses that comprise the stratification continuum have fundamental implications for individuals' earnings, health outcomes, housing, social network formation, locality, incorporation into neighbourhoods, and family dynamics.

Inspired particularly by the work of Lydia Morris (2002), the idea of a framework of migrant statuses as a social and legal stratification system was at the core – and, for me, remains as a defining feature – of the notion of superdiversity. Here the idea is that, in ways often unique to particular nation-states, not only are migrants generally stratified in a number of ways by legal statuses affecting their rights, but – due to the patterns of characteristics surrounding migrant flows – whole clusters of migrants (by way of combinations of nationality, ethnicity or race, gender, age, language and human capital) are socially positioned in a stratification system. Morris describes social and legal – or what she calls "civic" – stratification (after Lockwood 1996) as "the differential granting of rights by the state with respect to an expanding range of immigration statuses and the role of partial membership as a device in the management of migration" (2002: 103). This includes modes of surveillance, control, and policing. Civic stratification, she believes, "constitutes a complex ground of status diversity" (Morris 2004: 73). Already two decades ago, Eleonore Kofman has similarly pointed to "the increasing differentiation of migrant and refugee populations" and "the bewildering array of legislation regulating the entry, residence and employment status of this population" leading to "increasingly complex forms of differentiation and stratified rights" (2002: 1036). Inherently, such statuses, legal differentiations, and stratified rights are also intersectionally gendered, ethnicized, and racialized (Morris 2021).

Fran Meissner importantly builds on Morris's insights on legal status diversity, drawing attention to the "complexification of differentiations linked to a multiplicity of status tracks and consequently possible status trajectories" (2018b: 303). With regard to a range of specific migrant categories and the concomitant legal statuses they place on migrants, Meissner analyses what she calls "conditionalities of entry" and "parameters of presence." Both are crucial mediating factors producing social differentiation and stratification that mark conditions of superdiversity. Conditionalities of entry are the designated conditions that have to be met in order to make one eligible for a particular migration status track. Parameters of presence, according to Meissner, are requirements that must be met and maintained by a migrant once a particular legal status has been granted. "Thinking through the co-relevance of conditionalities of entry and parameters of presence points us to links between legal status differentiations and multi-dimensional configurations of superdiversity" (Ibid.: 293).

Migrant legal status has increasingly been singled out as a serious blockage to social mobility (Waters and Kasinitz 2021). This is the case not just formally and administratively, but cognitively as well. Here, Douglas Massey (2017) has described the immigration system, with its various categories and conditions, as a "critical agent" of stratification. The selective and stratifying processes at play in determining legal statuses also condition and propagate widespread stereotypes about groups and categories of people, which also serve to reproduce a range of social, economic, and political inequalities.

Such consequences have been variously evident and observed differentially. Some of the implications of legal status stratification or social policy within European societies are pointed out by Jenny Phillimore and her colleagues (2021: 13):

> The differentiation of rights and entitlements between migrants of differ-
> ent immigration statuses and lengths of residence is a relatively recent phe-
> nomenon. Many governments have attempted to restrict access to welfare
> including free healthcare, out of work benefits, social housing and child
> support. In doing so, they have inadvertently intensified superdiversifica-
> tion processes because access to social welfare resources can shape ways in
> which individuals are able to live.

The OECD pointed to other social impacts across worldwide member states. "One clear trend across the whole OECD in the past two decades," the OECD (2014: 45) notes, "has been the growing diversity of immigration. There is an increasingly wide cross-section of countries of origin, education levels, and migration categories (i.e., labour, family reunification, humanitarian, and free movement)." In its *International Migration Outlook 2014* report (OECD 2014), within a section entitled "The growing diversity of the immigrant population poses additional challenges," it is stated that:

> Over the past two decades, as immigration flows have become more diverse
> across the OECD, integration has become a greater challenge. That diver-
> sity applies not only to immigrants' countries of origin and destination, but
> to their education levels and the categories to which they belong – labour,
> free movement, family reunification, and humanitarian. Migration cate-
> gory is the single largest determinant of integration outcomes…
>
> *Ibid.: 37*

For these reasons, the OECD advocates: "As immigration flows grow more diverse in most countries, they must increasingly customise their integration policy instruments" (Ibid.: 106).

In thinking about and advocated the concept of superdiversity, one of my key purposes has been to underline and to better understand how differential, and often new, combinations of social and legal characteristics produce, mod-ify, or reinforce systems of stratification and inequality. Contemporary processes of migration-driven diversification have been at the core of the concept, and in light of these I've always seen systems of socio-economic stratification and inequality as being fundamentally conditioned by migration policies and legal frameworks. Indeed, in that original article I wrote: "In order to understand the nature and complexity of contemporary super-diversity, we must examine how

such a system of stratified rights and conditions created by immigration channels and legal statuses cross-cuts socio-cultural and socio-economic dimensions"
(Vertovec 2007: 1040). Fran Meissner and I (2015: 547) went on to stress the
point by saying:

> Differential migration channels (and the ways that these are variously com-
> prised of flows characterized by specific combinations of country of origin/
> ethnicity, gender and age) have been pivotal to the concept of superdiver-
> sity. Since migration channels and their respective legal conditions have a
> tremendous impact on the social, economic and political lives of migrants,
> these most clearly expose the fault lines of "community" thinking along
> ethnic lines alone. Appreciating these channels and statuses is necessary for
> understanding the combined workings of multidimensional patterns on
> outcomes of socio-economic inequality.

Legal classification systems sort people, award or retain rights, and channel
people into distinct social strata in terms of their national "desirability" (usually
by way of economic value). Such social stratification tends to reflect or manifest –
by government design or not – an individual's place of origin, race and ethnicity,
gender, age, and education level. In this way, processes surrounding the combination of numerous categories and their outcomes – to which the concept of
superdiversity draws attention – are intrinsically related to inequality.

Attesting to the differential ways migration drivers, processes, and nation-
state policies and categories combine very differently to create highly divergent
positions, possibilities, constraints, and outcomes, examples – rather stereotyp-
ical but nevertheless indicative – include the cases of: male and female students
from China, female nurses or domestic workers from the Philippines, families of
Syrian asylum-seekers, male construction workers from Bangladesh, high-tech
computer engineers from India, male and female farmworkers from Mexico,
male and female factory workers from Bulgaria, and unskilled males without
papers from a range of West African countries. Each of these examples represents a divergent set of multidimensional "sortings" of traits that have positioned
people very differently in various national hierarchies or stratification systems
(along with, moreover, very different temporalities based on the limited nature
of differing visa regimes; Mau 2021).

After a migrant arrives in a destination country already positioned in a system
of social stratification through combinations of legal classification and his or her
specific configuration of social characteristics, what happens next depends on a
series of influences. There is no uniform "integration" process (Vertovec 2020).
Rather, integration is a fuzzy concept referring to a broad span of sectors: labour
market, housing, language acquisition, education, legal administration, everyday
interactions, social services, and healthcare. One's ability to participate in each
of these sectors often itself depends on a combination of factors, including: legal
status, linguistic competence, age, gender, work skills, locality, social capital and

social networks, and education levels. Consequently, there are numerous possible pathways of "integration" that a migrant might follow, each depending on an intersection of multiple factors (cf. Meissner 2018a).

Further, each migrant embodies a complex array of identities, interests, practices, and social networks. It follows that a migrant newcomer can become an engaged participant in a new context … but not just in one way. For these reasons, we need to foster a kind of "complexity thinking" towards "integration" based on multidimensional and intersecting characteristics, non-groupist conceptualizations, non-linear trajectories of incorporation, diverse and overlapping networks and identities, complex modes of stratification, and multiple modes of belonging (this point is elaborated in Chapter 7). In considering complexity thinking about "integration," one should also bear in mind how these significant matters relate to phenomena and dynamics at a distance and across national borders.

Here I have in mind the relationship between superdiversity, stratification, diasporas, and transnationalism. Diasporas generally designate a social formation of people who purport to have a common origin or fundamental trait (usually ethnic, religious, national) that is dispersed across a region or around the world. There are many different types of diasporas, often reflecting specific histories of migration (Cohen 1997). Transnationalism refers to actual linkages and exchanges (social, economic, cultural, religious, and political) across distances and borders (Vertovec 2009), in this case among people who have migrated at some point in their collective history. Not all diasporas engage in sustained transnationalism, but all transnationalism among migrants takes place within diasporas. Migration-driven modes of diversification and conditions of superdiversity, as described in this chapter, have not only led to new social configurations but also to more complex diasporas and patterns of transnationalism (Cohen and Fischer 2018).

Often within the same country of origin, different causal drivers or distinctive combinations of them can lead to different processes of migration, including different people (by gender, age, family status, education, or skills). These lead to differing flows, trajectories, migration streams, and legal statuses, resulting in divergent socio-economic standing, gender patterns, family and age profiles, and geographies of settlement. In these ways, the social configurations of current day diasporas are very diverse. Further, given the specific socio-economic and legal conditions into which recent migrants have moved, some simply have more or less capacity and resources with which to engage in transnational activities than others – whether everyday FaceTime meetings with far-off family, running business activities in more than one place, participating in homeland party politics or religious activities, or – terribly important for many – remitting money.

Despite great disparities and differences within global diasporas and their discrepant abilities to engage in transnational practices, strong diasporic identities may nevertheless cut across social strata, inequalities, and legal statuses to bolster a consciousness of commonality. This in especially known to occur in times of heightened homeland need, such as in the aftermath of an earthquake.

Therefore, identifications and practices may ebb and flow or encounter variably "hot" and "cold" periods (Vertovec 1999). In these ways, changing patterns and practices surrounding diaspora and transnationalism can be seen as further modes of migration-driven diversification, adding to our conceptualization of superdiversity and its varied configurations.

Demographic diversifications

Angela Creese and Adrian Blackledge (2018b: xxiii) have rightly stressed that "To study superdiversity is to study not only new migrants but the mix of individuals in a place: 'old' and 'new' international migrants, native established populations, and resident minorities." This is indeed the approach that my colleagues and I took in the European Research Council project "Globaldivercities," which compared diversification dynamics in Singapore, Johannesburg, and New York (see https://www.mmg.mpg.de/366545/globaldivercities). Alongside four films and numerous journal publications, the project resulting in the book *Diversities Old and New* (Vertovec 2015a). In that project, our team followed an approach that takes into account discrete migrant traits and conditions, social relations and discourses of difference among diverse non-migrant populations, local racial and ethnic representations, and stark patterns of inequality that led to very different processes of diversification in each of those cities and specific neighbourhoods where we researched. We identified a number of common patterns that cross-cut our globe-spanning research sites, but also were able to observe how local histories, politics, social structures, and concepts made for stark differences between sites as well. Results underlined a point made throughout this book: context is crucial for the discrete shaping of diversification and development of superdiversity.

Evidence of demographic diversifications typically entails changes surrounding given categories within a population. Some stem from new migration flows, some from population dynamics among long-standing residents, and some from their combinations. Conventionally in much academic work alongside public debates, what are most often described as demographic diversifications are thought of in terms of enumerated changes to official, unidimensional categories of ethnicity and race (especially in the UK and USA, where often these concepts respectively presumed or considered to refer to culture and genetics are collapsed into the notion of "ethnoracial"), nationality or country of birth or citizenship (as in many European countries), or "migration background" (as described in Germany). These are among the kinds of categories that states use to enumerate, monitor, manage (and, especially in colonial settings, dominate), and develop policies targeting designated populations within their borders (see, among others, Cohn 1984; Nobles 2000; Kertzer and Arel 2002; Simon et al. 2015a). Each kind of official category has its history, purposes, and pitfalls. What is usually lost sight of, though, is the fact that such categories are socially and administratively constructed – yet they take on a kind of assumption of naturalness. "Official and scientific statistical categorisations *reflect* and *affect* the structural divisions of societies, as well as mainstream social representations. ... In this sense, censuses do more than reflect social realities; they also participate in the construction of these realities" (Simon et al. 2015b: 2, italics in original). This is the case even among academics who are supposed to remain critical of such constructs. Many scholars unfortunately lose sight of the fact that "researchers need to assume a false uniformity within broad ethnic or racial categories, a uniformity that is often induced by Census categories" (Hopkins 2009: 175). For instance, as described in the USA by Josh DeWind:

> An issue that has plagued immigration studies is that most of the social identity categories that are used analytically are also categories that are used or have their origin in usage by states to manage populations. Many studies are limited to such categories of state censuses, for example, to define racial and ethnic groups that often use more nuanced, overlapping, and contextually distinct categories ...
>
> Academics then have used state categories to frame studies of immigrant group incorporation and mobility, even if members of the groups define themselves as distinct on the basis of language, religion, class or the like. Measuring the "mobility" of Latinos, for example, compared to that of "Asians" is for many members of those groups meaningless, as these categories obscure significant differences between rich and poor, and educated and uneducated members of the groups. ... What is good for administration may not be good for explanation.
>
> *2009*

We saw in the previous chapter that despite considerable interest in the concept of superdiversity and its emphasis on multidimensional characteristics, it is hard to get beyond unidimensional understandings of demographic diversification based on singular categories such as race or nationality. As one team of scholars recently found:

> Our systematic literature review shows that while it is widely accepted that migration-related diversity is multidimensional and that a population with a migration background has diverse attributes and experiences beyond their ethnic, racial or country of origin differences, ethnic or racial diversity is still the starting point of almost a third of studies that examine migration-related diversity in urban context. Only a handful of studies make the effort to capture the complexity of a population's diversity by incorporating more than one aspect of demographic diversity.
>
> *Pisarevskaya et al. (2021)*

The problem is not entirely unknown to authorities. Already decades ago, Kenneth Prewitt (2002, 2005), the former Director of the US Census Bureau, reflected on challenges to conventional classification, counting, and policymaking in light of trends of burgeoning population diversification. Consequently, he observes, "classification is now a moving target" (2002: 17). Not least due to the rise of "diversity" discourse and various modes of so-called identity politics, there has emerged a widespread public trend towards expressing "who you are," reflected in multiple box-ticking or write-in self-identification of categories in many national censuses. Prewitt points out that such categories were not introduced for the purpose of redressing discrimination, but for the potential to assert social identity. "If this makes the classification less useful, or perhaps even useless, for race-sensitive policies," Prewitt (Ibid.) thinks, "that is the price to pay for the right to be recognized for what one is." In addition to a broader recognition of personalized social categories, "we might require a measurement system that reflects the dozens if not hundreds of different cultures, language groups, and nationalities represented in the fresh immigration stream" (Ibid.). Indeed through migration-driven diversification, Prewitt (2005: 13–4) notes that, "new immigrants add a complexity and uncertainty to ethno-racial classification and to the policies that flow from it." Precisely because of the "moving target" presented by diversification and the expectations to represent new groups, Prewitt foresees two possible outcomes: either a push towards measurement (like censuses) using ever more finely grained classifications, or system collapse – that is, the end of attempts to measure difference (also see Aspinall 2009, 2012, in press).

Urban diversities

Even with currently limited or widespread unidimensional approaches based on staid categories, it is apparent that on various scales from neighbourhoods to cities to nations, societies the world over have been growing more diverse for decades. Many places have indeed experienced accelerating rates of diversification in very recent times, especially major cities (Benton-Short et al. 2005). Demographic diversification is not just an urban phenomenon as often assumed, however; it is one entailing mid-sized cities, suburbs, small and rural towns, too (UN-DESA 2012). Diversification seems to be happening almost everywhere – but, just as with global migration, highly unevenly (Frey 2015; Mayes et al. 2021). Demographic diversification involves processes unfolding very differently, for different categories and at different paces, across localities, and on various scales. In many places in the global North, there is an observable increase of diverse neighbourhoods, including a *decline* in "White flight" (the exodus of people in the White racial category due to increasing presence of non-Whites) and a *growing* tendency for people to choose to live in diverse areas (Lee 2017). This trend may lead towards "the emergence of no-majority communities" (Farrell and Lee 2018) or more "global neighborhoods" (Zhang and Logan 2016) exhibiting diverse combinations of racial and ethnic groups. There are comparable trends in the global South, too (Kihato et al. 2010; Sharma 2018; Tirtosudarmo and Hadi 2018; Watson 2014; also see IOM 2015).

The unevenness of diversification within societies is important to underline. It is indeed – as we have noted above with reference to changing global migration flows – a significant aspect of superdiversity itself. As I have suggested concerning complex integration processes, urban diversification entails a variety of conditions that combine differently to produce distinctive outcomes. This is evident, for instance, in the differential growth of urban diversities. Asya Pisarevskaya, Peter Scholten, and Zeynep Kaşlı (2021) have conducted a study of 166 cities of various sizes in four countries: France, the Netherlands, Germany, and Italy. They emphasize the ways that varying factors – migration histories, local economies, municipal policies, housing stock, segregation dynamics, and multi-scalar insertion into larger political economies – have influenced the specific nature, degree, and type of migration-diversification that has ensued. In each city, they examined the volume of diversity (migrant share of total population), variety of diversity (number of origin countries – while acknowledging that this does not do justice to the multidimensionality stressed in the superdiversity concept), and spread of diversity (geographical distribution across an urban area). The team's cluster analysis led to a fivefold taxonomy of urban diversities, which they name and describe as:

- *superdiverse cities* (with an average of 16% migrant share of large populations averaging 1.3 million, 121 nationalities, above-average GDP, and low unemployment; this includes cities such as Amsterdam, Frankfurt, Rome, and Milan);
- *migrant minorities cities* (with a higher volume of 18% migrant share but somewhat less variety at 76 nationalities among smaller populations of some 270,000, with average GDP and unemployment rates; this includes Wuppertal, Konstanz, and Mulhouse);
- *new diversity cities* (average 11% migrant share from 76 nations, medium-sized populations of about 408,000 and average economic indicators within a strong industrial base; this includes places like Osnabruck, Eindhoven, Genoa, and Nimes);
- *low-migration cities* (only 7% migrant from 60 different national backgrounds in relatively small cities of 200,000, with below-average GDP, income and above-average unemployment; this includes Chemnitz and Dresden, Brest and Lille); and finally,
- *non-diverse cities* (with only 2% migrant share and 36 nationalities in medium-sized populations of 480,000 on average, with low GDP and high unemployment; examples here are Naples, Palermo, and Passau).

Although quite limited by the kinds and categories of data with which these researchers had to work, the study nevertheless underlines the ways that multiple conditions and traits combine to create distinctive patterns of diversification that both diverge and create similar outcomes. We can think of these kinds of outcomes relating to different diversification processes affecting neighbourhoods within cities, too (see Syrett and Sepulveda 2012). What remains to be done with this kind of study, however, is to examine the proportions and relations between the relatively "new" migrant diversities represented by recent migrations (say, of the last 20 years) and the longer resident, "old" diversities of previous migrant waves (for instance, of the 1960s and 1970s) alongside the populations with even longer or no migration histories. Such an approach would give a more comprehensive picture of diverging urban superdiversities.

In the USA, "rising diversity is a dominant demographic trend that appears to be spatially widespread, affecting virtually all segments of US society" (Lichter et al. 2017: 249). But here, also, diversification includes many processes, rates, local conditioning factors, and mixtures of old and new diversities. Considering diversification, diversity, and segregation as multiscalar phenomena, William Clark and his team (2015) undertook a sophisticated study of trends within Los Angeles (LA). While limited to data based on the simplest American racial classification scheme (White, Hispanic, Black, Asian), their cluster analysis of changing population configurations at the neighbourhood level in LA found exceedingly different mixtures of "homogeneous," "semi diverse," "diverse," and "very diverse" parts of the city. A key idea to emerge from the study is that of "dynamic diversity," referring to a kind of kaleidoscope of diversifications:

> The term dynamic diversity indicates that diversity is not in general a stable state but instead neighborhood populations are often in a state of transition. Sometimes change is toward increasing diversity, when the population shares of dominant ethno-racial groups are declining. Sometimes, when a larger ethno-racial group increases its share of the neighborhood population, change is in the direction from higher to lower diversity.
>
> *Ibid.: 1271*

Overall, Clark and his colleagues found "a clear trend toward decreasing homogeneity and increasing patterns of diversity" (Ibid.). Many parts of LA that were formerly predominantly Black or White areas have become more mixed with Hispanic and Asian populations. They conclude that: "There are decreasing areas of homogenous populations and a rapid increase in areas that are a mixture of all the racial and ethnic groups. Diversity and heterogeneity is the new structure of urban society in Los Angeles and will be in cities with large numbers of more than two ethnicities, certainly the situation now in most global cities" (Ibid.: 1279).

Laura Tach and her colleagues (2019) conducted a rather different kind of study of diversification trends across the USA. Drawing upon a superdiversity approach, they utilized a set of multidimensional variables to understand diversification, not just looking at ethnoracial variance but also economic indicators such as education, occupation, income, and housing along with social indicators including age, language, and nativity. Overall, they find that ethnoracial diversification is, not surprisingly, associated with social changes – but it is very weakly related to economic heterogeneity. This is because even if ethnoracial characteristics of a specific place are changing considerably, its economic traits (whether upper, middle or lower class) stay much the same. This is a function of both clustering and segregation within distinct local geographies. It appears that people predominantly arrange themselves into localities that reflect their social, and especially economic, characteristics. Despite widespread ethnoracial diversification, Tach et al. (Ibid.: 2196) observe that "there is clear evidence that the United States has become more segregated along economic lines." Also reflecting phenomena surrounding migration configurations described throughout this chapter, they describe how "processes of diversification may not unfold in the same fashion for all racial/ethnic groups given their distinct modes of incorporation and historical experiences of exclusion." Certain inequalities remain embedded and continuously reproduced, despite surrounding diversifications.

These findings concerning ongoing economic segregation relate to the matter, already flagged, that a key aspect of diversification processes is that fact that people with a range of social traits and markers move into areas that already comprise historically produced configurations of diversity and inequality. As I wrote in *Diversities Old and New*:

> Another important feature of urban diversification is that, since new migrants tend to inhabit those urban spaces which still play host to migrants from previous waves, new complexities are 'layered' on top of and positioned with regard to pre-existing patterns of diversity (including their socio-economic positions and geographical concentrations, social policies, daily interactions and physical environments that developed around such pre-existing patterns). How do prior conditions of diversity and practices of interaction affect the incorporation of new migrants who are characterized by significantly different traits?
>
> Differentially across cities and specific urban contexts within them, processes of diversification, conditions of super-diversity and the layered and positioned effects of 'old' and 'new' diversities have engendered changing patterns of prejudice, segregation, inequality and discord, as well as emergent practices of cooperation, civility, cosmopolitanism and conviviality. We still have much to learn about how, where, when and why such patterns and practices arise or transform.
>
> *Vertovec (2015b: 2)*

Age

In addition to variable, layered configurations, and geographies, processes of diversification also fundamentally entail differing configurations by way of age cohorts. Diversification looks very dissimilar, across various scales and geographies, depending on which age bracket one looks at. As William Frey (2021) observes in the USA (but with clear resonances elsewhere):

> the diversity profile of the U.S. population is rising rapidly. This is especially the case for the nation's younger population, which experienced the greatest white population losses. The statistics also imply that, as the white population ages and declines further, racial and ethnic diversity will be the hallmark demographic feature of America's younger generations, including Gen Z and those that follow.

This age-diversity distribution means that even if new immigration slows massively, ethnoracial diversity will continue to expand as current children grow up. In several societies, the population categorized as White is marked by rapid aging and declining numbers. Looking at ethnoracial categories from age 65+ through deciles down to under-18s and under-12s, each younger cohort is ever more ethnoracially diverse. In the older brackets, in many societies the elderly are now nevertheless more ethnoracially diverse too, with more foreign born, than they were in the past (Seltzer and Yahirun 2014). This has several implications for family and community life, not least in resources and practices concerning late life social and healthcare.

Despite the fact of older populations may be diversifying, "[Y]ounger age groups are experiencing the greatest rise in diversity" (Ibid.). As Daniel Lichter (2013: 361) puts it, "Diversity begins with children – from the 'bottom up'." On the one hand, some see that this age and generational profile will lead to a gradual breaking down of antagonism, discrimination, and racialized ill will across ethnic and racial boundaries, as children from various backgrounds play together, learn together, and grow up together into adulthood (Lee and Bean 2010). Opinion polls already demonstrate considerable inter-generational contrasts in attitudes towards diversity (Duffy 2021). This is surely due to localizing effects. Recent findings in the UK demonstrate how "a context of relatively high diversity in the country during an individual's formative years may ultimately produce more positive immigration attitudes later in life (though this may be dependent on inequality conditions)" (McLaren et al. 2021: 727). A major part of the context, too, is what we might call the discursive diversity sphere: that is, younger generations are growing up subject to a public space – especially including many varied kinds of media and images – inundated with strong messages about the values of diversity and recognizing difference (see Vertovec 2012).

However, in social structural terms, just as diversity can also be seen to begin with children, so can inequality. Today in the USA, again for example, there are large proportions of non-White children growing up in geographically segregated and economically dire conditions, especially marked by low income, bad housing, and poor education. This has direct bearing on future patterns of poverty and inequality. Referring to just one aspect of inequality, "Current racial and ethnic differences in educational attainment (and the quality of education) portend continuing inequality in the future," suggests Lichter (2013: 378), "especially as today's historically disadvantaged minority children assume adult roles."

"Mixedness"

In what some social scientists consider to be one of the most powerful modes of demographic diversification, the substantial growth in the number of people identifying across or between racial or ethnic categories is clearly underway. This is particularly evident, for instance, in the 2020 US Census. For instance, although it is the racial category evidently growing the slowest, the Black population of the USA is nevertheless increasingly showing a "diverse multitude of backgrounds" reflecting changes in intermarriage and international migration (Tamir 2021). More people are identifying as Black *and* something else (see below). Meanwhile, the inherently varied categories of so-called "Asians" (a category spanning origins from 20 countries; Gebeloff et al. 2021) and "Hispanics" (from 15 countries; Noe-Bustamante 2019) grew the most, that is by 29% and 20%, respectively.

In many places around the world, there is a significant population growth and diversification among people regularly deemed to be "mixed," "racially mixed," "multiracial," or "mixed heritage" (see Goldstein and Morning 2000; Liebler 2016; Song 2017). In various contexts and times, "mixedness" has referred to "Multiple identity markers – spoken languages, religious beliefs and practices, ethnic and racial affiliations, traditions and other cultural rituals, nationalities, etc." (Le Gall et al. 2021: 2). A substantial literature has developed around concepts and phenomena concerning mixed couples, families, and individuals. Countries that use categories of race and ethnicity have, over the last few decades, provided measures which attempt to provide more granularity in capturing such complex identification (cf. Aspinall 2009). This was the case for the US Census of 2020, which allowed people to tick many more boxes for "race" and "ethnicity" than ever before, as "officials tried to more accurately capture the profusion of complexity in American demographics" (Tavernise et al. 2021).

Subsequently, not only has the White population category declined for the first time in history, but "The United States grew significantly more diverse over the past decade, as the populations of people who identify as Hispanic and Asian surged and the number of people who said they were more than one race more than doubled" (Tavernise and Gebeloff 2021). Compared to ten years ago, some 25 million more people identify as belonging to two or more racial categories. "Mixed" people now comprise 10% of the American population. Further, "Multiracial people span all different combinations of races and ethnicities and make up the fastest-growing demographic in the country" (Tavernise et al. 2021). Rahsaan Maxwell similarly points to rising intermarriage rates in Europe and foresees that "The next generation of diverse Europeans will inhabit a world in which cultural mixtures are standard and historical nation-states are the starting points rather than the final definition of culture" (2016: 99).

Acknowledging "all the demographic diversity both between and within disparate multiracial populations" in a number of international contexts, Miri Song (2021: 1316–17) believes that "The growth and diversification of racially mixed people has necessitated not just a critical appraisal of existing racial taxonomies, but also a rethinking of contemporary racial projects" (also see Alba 2020; DaCosta 2020; Foster-Frau et al. 2021). Song's views are complemented by those of Gabrielle Varro (2022: xviii), who suggests, "Mixedness can also be seen as a microcosm in which to study the group boundaries between majority and minority and the social perception of the 'other' by members of the majority." The rapid rise of mixedness and its myriad forms, meanings, and dynamics manifests a vital way in which social categories are being remade and complexifying – a topic focused upon in Chapter 6.

Language

A further, significant set of diversifications are taking place in the realm of linguistic communication. This takes at least two forms: new languages introduced to a context through migration, and the expansion, mixing and innovation of linguistic phenomena in linguistically superdiverse places. In terms of the first type of linguistic change, the global diversification of migration flows over the last two or three decades has brought unprecedented variety to a great many places known to be key immigration hubs. In this way, we hear claims that there are now over 800 languages to be found in New York (https://www.worldatlas.com/articles/how-many-languages-are-spoken-in-nyc.html), over 300 languages in London (https://www.multilingualcapital.com/bilingualism-in-the-uk/languages-in-london/), over 250 languages in Sydney (https://www.smh.com.au/interactive/2014/sydney-languages/), and over 180 languages in Toronto (https://cubetoronto.com/toronto/how-many-languages-are-spoken-in-toronto-ontario/). Such developments have created highly interesting – and for service providers, challenging – superdiverse linguistic landscapes of spoken and written semiotics (Blommaert 2013). Such landscapes are not just relevant to cities, but especially to micro-environments of neighbourhoods, workplaces, schools, and sites of sport and leisure.

On the one hand, superdiverse linguistic landscapes present conditions in which immigrants may suffer. This is due to new or enhanced forms of linguistically based discrimination and racialized language ideologies. Meanwhile, immigrants and their linguistic differences are often the focus of restrictive narratives of the nation and contestations over the role of linguistic phenomena in public space. Such developments are not just to be found in New York, London, and the foremost immigrant destinations of the global North, but extensively across the global South as well. Examples of such developments and debates surrounding migrants and linguistic difference can be witnessed in locations as far afield as Johannesburg (Siziba and Hill 2018), Singapore (Rubdy and McKay 2013),

Buenos Aires (Monteagudo and Muniain 2020), Seoul (Park 2020), Cairo (Calvani 2003), and Delhi (Srinivas 2018).

On the other hand, superdiverse linguistic landscapes present myriad modes of contact and communication for their inhabitants. As we have reviewed in Chapter 3 by way of a range of exciting new theoretical and methodological approaches within Sociolinguistics, this kind of diversification has prompted and accelerated remarkable and dynamic linguistic practices. In what are described as aspects of linguistic superdiversity (see Blommaert and Rampton 2011; Arnaut 2012; Blommaert 2015; Creese and Blackledge 2018a), such practices are conceived and analysed via notions such as polylanguaging, translanguaging, metrolingualism, multiple discursive practices; supervernacularization and polycentricity of semiotic resources. And as we shall consider in Chapter 5, while dynamic new forms of crossover communications emerge, linguistic diversification and superdiversity often entail the hardening of linguistic categories and hierarchies, a backlash of linguistic anxieties and the manifestation of "linguaphobia."

Superdiversity can be seen as a condition and a set of processes. The combining of the multiple – intersecting, multiple categories or, in this case, interdependent and mutually conditioning multiple processes – is its central approach and message. This is also, as examined later in this book, at the core of thinking around social complexity, too.

Conclusion

Across various social scientific works, superdiversity has been described as a kind of condition brought about by significant social transformations. It has also been described as inherent to processes of social transformation themselves. This chapter has focused on the latter, examining influential aspects of diversification processes. It identifies two foremost processes of diversification, namely shifts in features of global migration and trends in demographic development, especially around categories or difference or so-called ethnoracial characteristics.

The concept of superdiversity, in the first instance, was created to address the effects of certain notable changes surrounding global migration flows since the 1990s. As described in the original 2007 *Ethnic and Racial Studies* article (Chapter 2 of this book), these changes entail new configurations of migrants' characteristics of country of origin, gender, age, migration channel, legal status, and more. In this chapter, we have looked at certain processes relevant or giving rise to the new configurations, commencing with the topic of migration causes or drivers. The most current view in the field of migration studies sees numerous drivers (economic, political, social, demographic, and environmental) at work, usually functioning together to influence migrants' decisions to move. Not only do such drivers work interdependently, but they also compound one another. For instance, environmental degradation impacts sustenance, food insecurity, and economic opportunities, which also effects political and social drivers of migration. Together such drivers shape migration patterns by way of conditioning which migrants move, when, how, and to where.

Among other consequences, the complex ways in which migration drivers effect and compound one another have also contributed to a global process whereby we have witnessed the profound proliferation of migrants' countries of origin. More people are now on the move from more places. Analysts have pointed out that this is not an even pattern globally, but one marked by variation. Migration-based diversification is not a uniform process, but one marked by greatly varying origins, numbers, movements, distances, directionality, destinations, timelines, and socio-economic characteristics. The uneven distribution of migrants by way of origins, together with the intersections of numerous other characteristics, is indeed a fundamental feature of how superdiversity is shaped. In this way, superdiversity looks very different from context to context around the world.

The differential features of superdiversity are also directly related to very differing systems of social stratification and inequality from place to place. Such systems are strongly determined by another major process described in this chapter, which is the growing perplexity of migration channels and accompanying legal statuses. Legal statuses are state categories for migrants extending or limiting their rights, living and working conditions, and prospects for settlement. Following the work of scholars such as Lydia Morris and Fran Meissner, we can see how migrant legal statuses reproduce modes of stratification and inequality. Such statuses and their conditions thereby have direct implications for so-called migrant integration processes. Legal statuses come to intersect with characteristics such as country of origin, age, and gender to differentially position distinct sets of migrants within societies. They should be seen as a key dimension in the multidimensional approach central to the concept of superdiversity.

Uneven and differential processes of diversification also underpin the shaping of discrepant urban diversities. There are multiple additional reasons for this, including the specificities of policy, history, geography, and multi-scalar economics. It is in cities that we can especially observe superdiverse dynamics when "new" diversities prompted by contemporary diversification processes interact with "old" patterns of difference and diversity. These kinds of interactions should be recognized as kaleidoscopic, ongoing states of transition, not some novel kinds of social stability. Moreover, we have discussed how patterns of urban economic stratification and segregation may still be reproduced while the local population is diversifying either through migration or demographic change.

Even without migration, many populations are diversifying demographically in terms of ethnoracial classifications (which of course are not unproblematic; see the next chapter). The size and distribution of non-White populations are expanding in what scholars have called "the diversity transition" (Alba and Foner 2015) or the "Diversity Explosion" (Frey 2015). This is especially to be seen, importantly, in age and diversity profiles. Diversification looks very different across age cohorts, with "bottom up" diversification accelerating as the youngest demographic cohorts show the highest diversity. Perhaps the most significant mode of demographic diversification, however, is the growth of what are often described as Mixed populations, or people who identify across or between racial or ethnic categories. The considerable increases in the number of people identifying with this category have led many national census agencies to alter their techniques for counting assorted kinds of mixedness. As discussed more at length in Chapter 6, the rise of mixedness is itself a meaningful feature of social complexification.

Finally, echoing major trends considered in Chapter 3, linguistic diversification was flagged as another substantial facet of superdiversity. Especially through migration, contact between people practicing different linguistic and communicative repertoires has prompted an array of fascinating concomitant processes currently being researched by sociolinguists and linguistic anthropologists. Linguistic diversification has also unfortunately prompted, in societies the world over, various kinds of backlashes, restrictive views of the nation, and new varieties of discrimination against migrants and their descendants.

In these ways, this chapter has emphasized certain processual aspects of superdiversity. As Meissner and I (2015) have emphasized, it is not only of critical importance to appreciate a multiplicity of processes simultaneously at work shaping social patterns and structures but also the differing and variable *speed, scale and spread* of processes. Some of the processes described in this chapter occur faster or slower in some places than in others, or they may sometimes stop and start (as we have seen with the covid pandemic). "[T]he geographic scale of diversification matters" (Tach et al. 2019: 2221), with some processes unfolding more at a neighbourhood or city scale than at national ones, giving rise to the differential urban diversities noted earlier. And some relevant processes are inconsistently spread – or occur more jointly, densely or thinly – from one region, country, or part of the city than in others; this is often due to general features of respective political economies or to specific policy frameworks.

All of these kinds of processual dynamics are at play by way of combining categories, characteristics, and statuses to shape a wide variety of outcomes, not least complex structures of inequality. Among other things, the concept of superdiversity and its emphasis on multidimensionality prompts observers to explore the several, confluent, and compound processes of diversification that together are shaping momentous forms of social transformation in societies the world over.

References

Abel, G. J. and N. Sander 2014. "Quantifying global international migration flows," *Science* 343(6178): 1520–22 https://doi.org/10.1126/science.1248676

Alba, R. 2020. *The Great Demographic Illusion: Majority, Minority, and the Expanding American Mainstream*, Princeton: Princeton University Press

Alba, R. and N. Foner 2015. *Strangers No More: Immigration and the Challenges of Integration in North America and Western Europe*, Princeton: Princeton University Press

Anderson, B. 2007. "Battles in time: The relation between global and labour mobilities," Policy and Society (COMPAS) *Working Paper* WP-07-55, Centre on Migration, Oxford

Arango, J. 2000. "Explaining migration: A critical view," *International Social Science Journal* 52(165): 283–96 https://doi.org/10.1111/1468-2451.00259

Arnaut, K. 2012. "Super-diversity: Elements of an emerging perspective," *New Diversities* 14(2): 1–16

Aspinall, P. J. 2009. "The future of ethnicity classifications," *Journal of Ethnic and Migration Studies* 35(9): 1417–35 https://doi.org/10.1080/13691830903125901

Aspinall, P. J. 2012. "Answer formats in British Census and survey ethnicity questions: Does open response better capture 'superdiversity'?" *Sociology* 46 (2): 354–64 https://doi.org/10.1177/0038038511419195

Aspinall, P. J. In press. "Capturing super-diversity in official data: How the decennial censuses in Britain are responding," in *The Oxford Handbook of Superdiversity*, F. Meissner, N. Sigona and S. Vertovec (eds.), Oxford: Oxford University Press

Beine, M., A. Boucher, B. Burgoon, M. Crock, J. Gest, M. Hiscox, P. McGovern, H. Rapoport, J. Schaper and E. Thielemann 2015. "Comparing immigration policies: An overview from the IMPALA database," *International Migration Review* 50(4): 827–63 https://doi.org/10.1111/imre.12169

Benton, M. 2013. "The changing face of international migration: Flows are increasingly fluid, diverse, and unconventional," *Migration Information Source*, www.migrationpolicy.org

Benton-Short, L., M. D. Price and S. Friedman 2005. "Globalization from below: The ranking of global immigrant cities," *International Journal of Urban and Regional Research* 29(4): 945–59 https://doi.org/10.1111/j.1468-2427.2005.00630.x

Betts, A. 2013. *Survival Migration: Failed Governance and the Crisis of Displacement*, Ithaca: Cornell University Press

Bevelander, P. (ed.) 2020. "Understanding International Migration in the 21st Century: Conceptual and Methodological Approaches," special issue, Comparative Migration Studies 8

Bijak, J. and M. Czaika 2020. "Assessing uncertain migration futures: A typology of the unknown," University of Southampton and Danube University Krems QuantMig Project Deliverable D1.1, Southampton/Krems

Black, R., W. N. Adger, N. W. Arnell, S. Dercon, A. Geddes and D. S. G. Thomas 2011. "The effect of environmental change on human migration," *Global Environmental Change* 215: S3–S11 https://doi.org/10.1016/j.gloenvcha.2011.10.001

Blommaert, J. 2013. *Ethnography, Superdiversity and Linguistic Landscapes: Chronicles of Complexity*, Bristol: Multilingual Matters https://doi.org/10.21832/9781783090419

Blommaert, J. 2015. "Superdiversity old and new," *Language & Communication* 44(1): 82–89

Blommaert, J. and B. Rampton 2011. "Language and superdiversity," *Diversities* 13(3): 1–21

Brettell, C. B. and J. F. Hollifield (eds.) 2014. *Migration Theory: Talking across Disciplines*, London: Routledge, 3rd edn. https://doi.org/10.4324/9781315814933

Calvani, D. 2003. Initial overview of the linguistic diversity of refugee communities in Cairo, American University in Cairo. Forced Migration and Refugee Studies Program (FMRS), Working Paper No. 4

Clark, W. A. V., E. Anderson, J. Östh and B. Malmberg 2015. "A multiscalar analysis of neighborhood composition in Los Angeles, 2000–2010: A location-based approach to segregation and diversity," *Annals of the Association of American Geographers* 105(6): 1260–84 https://doi.org/10.1080/00045608.2015.1072790

Cohen, R. 1997. *Global Diasporas: An Introduction*, London: University College London Press

Cohen, R. and C. Fischer (eds.) 2018. *Routledge Handbook of Diaspora Studies*, London: Routledge https://doi.org/10.4324/9781315209050

Cohn, B. S. 1984. "The census, social structure and objectification in South Asia in culture and history of India," *Folk* 26: 25–49

Creese, A. and A. Blackledge (eds.) 2018a. *The Routledge Handbook of Language and Superdiversity*, London: Routledge https://doi.org/10.4324/9781315696010

Creese, A. and A. Blackledge 2018b. "Language and superdiversity: An interdisciplinary perspective," in *The Routledge Handbook of Language and Superdiversity*, A. Creese and A. Blackledge (eds.), London: Routledge, pp. xxi–xiv https://doi.org/10.4324/9781315696010

Czaika, M. and H. de Haas 2014. "The globalization of migration: Has the world become more migratory?" *International Migration Review*, 48(2): 283–323 https://doi.org/10.1111/imre.12095

Czaika, M. and C. Reinprecht 2020. "Drivers of migration: A synthesis of knowledge," IMI Working Paper No. 163, Amsterdam

DaCosta, J. A. 2020. "Multiracial categorization, identity, and policy in (mixed) racial formations," *Annual Review of Sociology* 46: 335–53 https://doi.org/10.1146/annurev-soc-121919-054649

de Haas, H. 2021. "A theory of migration: The aspirations-capabilities framework," *Comparative Migration Studies* 9:8 https://doi.org/10.1186/s40878-020-00210-4

de Haas, H., S. Castles and M. J. Miller 2020. *The Age of Migration: International Movements in the Modern World*. London: Macmillan/Red Globe, 6th edn.

de Haas, H., M. Czaika, M. Flahaux, E. Mahendra, K. Natter, S. Vezzoli and M. Villares-Varela 2019. "International migration: Trends, determinants, and policy effects," *Population and Development Review* 45(4): 885–922 https://doi.org/10.1111/padr.12291

de Haas, H., K. Natter and S. Vezzoli 2018. "Growing restrictiveness or changing selection? The nature and evolution of migration policies," *International Migration Review* 52(2): 324–67 https://doi.org/10.1111/imre.12288

DeWind, J. 2009. Diversity Interview, Max-Planck-Institute for the Study of Religious and Ethnic Diversity, www.mmg.mpg.de/diversity-interviews/dewind

Duffy, B. 2021. *Generations: Does When You're Born Shape Who You Are?* London: Atlantic

Farrell, C. R. and B. A. Lee 2018. "No-majority communities: Racial diversity and change at the local level," *Urban Affairs Review* 54(5): 866–97 https://doi.org/10.1177/1078087416682320

Favell, A. 2007. "Rebooting migration theory: Interdisciplinarity, globality and transdisciplinarity in migration studies," in *Migration Theory*, C. Brettell and J. Hollifield (eds.), London: Routledge, pp. 259–82, 2nd edn. https://doi.org/10.4324/9780203950449

Foster-Frau, S., T. Mellnik and A. Blanco 2021. "'We're taking about a big, powerful phenomenon': Multiracial Americans drive change," *The Washington Post* 8 October

Frey, W. 2015. *Diversity Explosion: How New Racial Demographics Are Remaking America*, Washington, D. C.: Brookings Institution

Frey, W. 2021. "All recent US population growth comes from people of color, new census estimates show," www.brookings.edu/research

Garip, F. 2012. "Discovering diverse mechanisms of migration: The Mexico–US stream 1970–2000," *Population and Development Review* 38(3): 393–433 https://doi.org/10.1111/j.1728-4457.2012.00510.x

Gebeloff, R., D. Lu and M. Jordan 2021. "Inside the diverse and growing Asian population in the U.S.," *New York Times* 21 August

Goldstein, J. and A. Morning 2000. "The multiple-race population of the United States: Issues and estimates," *Proceedings of the National Academy of Sciences* 97(11): 6230–35 https://doi.org/10.1073/pnas.100086897

Grillo, R. 2015. "Reflections on super-diversity by an urban anthropologist, or 'superdiversity so what?'" Paper presented at the Academy of Urban Super-Diversity, Berlin

Hopkins, D. J. 2009. "The diversity discount: When increasing ethnic and racial diversity prevents tax increases," *The Journal of Politics* 71(1): 160–77 https://doi.org/10.1017/s0022381608090105

Hugo, G. 1996. "Environmental concerns and international migration," *International Migration Review* 30(1): 105–31 https://doi.org/10.1177/019791839603000110

IOM (International Organization for Migration) 2003. *World Migration Report 2003: Managing Migration*, Geneva: International Organization for Migration

IOM (International Organization for Migration) 2015. *World Migration Report 2015: Migrants and Cities*, Geneva: International Organization for Migration

IOM (International Organization for Migration) 2020. *World Migration Report 2020*, Geneva: International Organization for Migration

Kertzer, D. and D. Arel (eds.) 2002. *Census and Identity: The Politics of Race, Ethnicity, and Language in National Censuses*, Cambridge: Cambridge University Press

Kihato, C., M. Massoumi, B. A. Ruble, P. Subirós and A. M. Garland (eds.) 2010. *Urban Diversity: Space, Culture, and Inclusive Pluralism in Cities Worldwide*, Baltimore: Johns Hopkins University Press

King, R. 2012. "Theories and typologies of migration: An overview and a primer," *Willy Brandt Series of Working Papers in International Migration and Ethnic Relations* 3/12, Malmö

Kofman, E. 2002. "Contemporary European migrations, civic stratification and citizenship," *Political Geography* 21: 1035–54 https://doi.org/10.1016/s0962-6298(02)00085-9

Le Gall, J., C. Therrien and K. Geoffrion 2021. "Beyond borders: The everyday life of transnational mixed families," in *Mixed Families in a Transnational World*, J. Le Gall et al. (eds.), London: Routledge, pp. 1–24 https://doi.org/10.4324/9781003126263

Lee, J. and F. D. Bean 2010. *The Diversity Paradox: Immigration and the Color Line in 21st Century America*, New York: Russell Sage Foundation

Lee, K. O. 2017. "Temporal dynamics of racial segregation in the United States: An analysis of household residential mobility," *Journal of Urban Affairs* 39(1): 40–67 https://doi.org/10.1111/juaf.12293

Lichter, D. T. 2013. "Integration or fragmentation? Racial diversity and the American future," *Demography* 50: 359–91 https://doi.org/10.1007/s13524-013-0197-1

Lichter, D. T., D. Parisi and M. C. Taquino 2017. "Together but apart: Do US Whites live in racially diverse cities and neighborhoods?" *Population and Development Review* 43: 229–55 https://doi.org/10.1111/padr.12068

Liebler, C. 2016. "On the boundaries of race: Identification of mixed-race children in the United States 1960–2010," *Sociology of Race and Ethnicity* 2(4): 548–68 https://doi.org/10.1177/2332649216632546

Lockwood, D. 1996. "Civic integration and class formation," *British Journal of Sociology* 47(3): 531–50

Martin, P. 2009. "Demographic and economic Trends: Implications for international mobility," United Nations Development Programme *Human Development Reports*, Research Paper 2009/17, Nairobi

Massey, D. S. 2017. "Migration and categorical inequality," in *Immigration and Categorical Inequality*, E. Castañeda (ed.), New York: Routledge, pp. 26–43 https://doi.org/10.4324/9781315100371

Massey, D. S., J. Arango, G. Hugo, A. Kouaouci, A. Pellegrino and J. E. Taylor 1998. *Worlds in Motion: Understanding International Migration at the End of the Millennium*, Oxford: Clarendon

Mau, S. 2021. *Sortiermachinen: Die Neuerfindung der Grenze im 21. Jahrhundert*, Munich: C.H. Beck https://doi.org/10.17104/9783406775772

Maxwell, R. 2016. "Cultural diversity and its limits in Western Europe," *Current History* 115(779): 95–101. https://doi.org/10.1080/13562576.2010.532951

Mayes, B. R., A. Blanco, Z. Levitt and T. Melinik 2021. "America's demographics are changing. How has your county shifted?" *The Washington Post* 1 August

McLaren, L., A. Neundorf and I. Paterson 2021. "Diversity and perceptions of immigration: How the past influences the present," *Political Studies* 69(3): 725–47 https://doi. org/10.1177/0032321720922774

Meissner, F. 2018a. "Mainstreaming and superdiversity: Beyond more integration," in *Mainstreaming Integration Governance*, P. Scholten and I. van Breugel (eds.), Basingstoke: Palgrave, pp. 215–33

Meissner, F. 2018b. "Legal status diversity: Regulating to control and everyday contingencies," *Journal of Ethnic and Migration Studies* 44(2): 287–306 https://doi.org/ 10.1080/1369183x.2017.1341718

Meissner, F. and S. Vertovec 2015. "Comparing super-diversity," *Ethnic and Racial Studies* 38(4): 541–55 https://doi.org/10.1080/01419870.2015.980295

Menjívar, C. 2006. "Liminal legality: Salvadoran and Guatemalan immigrants' lives in the United States," *American Journal of Sociology* 111(4): 999–1037 https://doi.org/ 10.1086/499509

Menjívar, C. and L. J. Abrego 2012. "Immigration law and the lives of Central American immigrants," *American Journal of Sociology* 117(5): 1380–421 https://doi.org/10.1086/ 663575

Monteagudo, H. and F. R. Muniain 2020. "Language and migration. The sociolinguistic and glottopolitical dynamics of the Galician community in Buenos Aires from the nineteenth century to the present day," *Journal of Multilingual and Multicultural Development* 41(1): 97–107 https://doi.org/10.1080/01434632.2019.1621878

Morris, L. 2002. *Managing Migration: Civic Stratification and Rights*, London: Routledge https://doi.org/10.4324/9780203447499

Morris, L. 2004. "The control of rights: The rights of workers and asylum seekers under managed migration," Discussion Paper, Joint Council for the Welfare of Immigrants, London

Morris, L. 2021. *The Moral Economy of Welfare and Migration: Reconfiguring Rights in Austerity Britain*, Montreal: McGill-Queens University Press

Nobles, M. 2000. *Shades of Citizenship: Race and the Census in Modern Politics*, Stanford: Stanford University Press

Noe-Bustamante, L. 2019. "Key facts about U.S. Hispanics and their diverse heritage," Pew Research Centre https://www.pewresearch.org/fact-tank/2019/09/16/key-facts-about-u-s-hispanics/

OECD (Organization for Economic Co-operation and Development) 2011. *International Migration Outlook 2011*, Paris: OECD Publishing

OECD (Organization for Economic Co-operation and Development) 2014. *International Migration Outlook 2014*, Paris: OECD Publishing

Özden, Ç, C. Parsons, M. Schiff and T. L. Walmsley 2011 "Where on earth is everybody? The evolution of global bilateral migration 1960–2000," *The World Bank Economic Review* 25(1): 12–56 https://doi.org/10.1093/wber/lhr024

Park, M. Y. 2020. "'I want to learn Seoul speech!': Language ideologies and practices among rural marriage-migrants in South Korea," *International Journal of Bilingual Education and Bilingualism* 23(2): 227–40 https://doi.org/10.1080/13670050.2017. 1351419

Phillimore, J., H. Bradby, T. Brand, B. Padilla and S. Pemberton 2021. *Exploring Welfare Bricolage in Europe's Superdiverse Neighbourhoods*, London: Routledge https://doi.org/10.4324/9781003111504

Pisarevskaya, A., P. Scholten and Z. Kaşlı 2021. "Classifying the diversity of urban diversities: An inductive analysis of European cities," *Journal of International Migration and Integration* https://doi.org/10.1007/s12134-021-0081-z

Prewitt, K. 2002. "Does ethno-racial classification have a future in policymaking?" *Public Affairs Report* 44 (1): 1, 16–9

Prewitt, K. 2005. "Racial classification in America: Where do we go from here?" *Daedalus* 134 (1): 5–17 https://doi.org/10.1162/0011526053124370

Rubdy, R. and S. L. McKay 2013. "'Foreign workers' in Singapore: Conflicting discourses, language politics and the negotiation of immigrant identities," *International Journal of the Sociology of Language* 222: 157–85 https://doi.org/10.1515/ijsl-2013-0036

Ruhs, M. 2011. "Openness, skills and rights: An empirical analysis of labour immigration programmes in 46 high and middle income countries," Centre on Migration, Policy and Society (COMPAS) *Working Paper Series* WP-11-88, Oxford

Ruhs, M. and P. Martin 2008. "Numbers vs. rights: Trade-offs and guest worker programs," *International Migration Review* 42(1): 249–65

Sainsbury, D. 2006 "Immigrant's social rights in comparative perspective: Welfare regimes, forms of immigration and immigration policy regimes," *Journal of European Social Policy* 16(3): 229–44 https://doi.org/10.1177/0958928706065594

Salt, J. 2005. "Types of migration in Europe: Implications and policy concerns," Paper at European Population Conference, Strasbourg

Seltzer, J. A. and J. J. Yahirun 2014. "Diversity in old age: The elderly in changing economic and family contexts," in *Diversity and Disparities*, J. Logan (ed.), New York: Russell Sage Foundation, pp. 270–305

Sharma, S. 2018. "Superdiversity in Delhi: A historical understanding," in *The Routledge Handbook of the Governance of Migration and Diversity in Cities*, T. Caponio et al. (eds.), London: Routledge, pp. 275–85 https://doi.org/10.4324/9781351108478-27

Simon, P., V. Piché and A. A. Gagnon (eds.) 2015a. *Social Statistics and Ethnic Diversity: Cross-National Perspectives in Classifications and Identity Politics*, Cham: Springer https://doi.org/10.1007/978-3-319-20095-8

Simon, P., V. Piché and A. A. Gagnon 2015b. "The making of racial and ethnic categories: Official statistics reconsidered," in *Social Statistics and Ethnic Diversity: Cross-National Perspectives in Classifications and Identity Politics*, P. Simon et al. (eds.), Cham: Springer, pp. 1–14 https://doi.org/10.1007/978-3-319-20095-8_1

Siziba, G. and L. Hill 2018. "Language and the geopolitics of (dis)location: A study of Zimbabwean Shona and Ndebele speakers in Johannesburg," *Language in Society* 47(1): 115–39 https://doi.org/10.1017/s0047404517000793

Söderström, O., S. Randeria, D. Ruedin, G. D'Amato and F. Panese 2013. "Of mobilities and moorings: Critical perspectives," in *Critical Mobilities*, O. Söderström, S. Randeria, D. Ruedin, G. D'Amato and F. Panese (eds.), Lausanne: EPFL Press, pp. v–xxv

Song, M. 2017. "Generational change and how we conceptualize and measure multiracial people and 'mixture'," *Ethnic and Racial Studies* 40(13): 2333–39 https://doi.org/10.1080/01419870.2017.1344273

Song, M. 2021. "Who counts as multiracial?" *Ethnic and Racial Studies* 44(8): 1296–323 https://doi.org/10.1080/01419870.2020.1856905

Spellman, K. 2004. *Religion and Nation: Iranian Local and Transnational Networks in Britain*, Oxford: Berghahn

Srinivas, A. 2018. "Hindi's migrating footprint: How India's linguistic landscape is changing," *Hindustan Times* October 14

Syrett, S. and L. Sepulveda 2012. "Urban governance and economic development in the diverse city," *European Urban and Regional Studies* 19: 238–53 https://doi.org/10.1177/0969776411430287

Tach, L., B. Lee, M. Martin and L. Hannscott 2019. "Fragmentation or diversification? Ethnoracial change and the social and economic heterogeneity of places," *Demography* 56 (6): 2193–227 https://doi.org/10.1007/s13524-019-00835-w

Tamir, C. 2021. "The growing diversity of Black America," www.pewresearch.org

Tavernise, S. and R. Gebeloff 2021. "Census Shows Sharply Growing Numbers of Hispanic, Asian and Multiracial Americans," *New York Times* 12 August

Tavernise, S., T. Mzezewa and G. Heyward 2021. "Behind the surprising jump in multiracial Americans, several theories," *New York Times* 15 August

Tirtosudarmo, R. and A. Hadi 2018. "Jakarta, on the brink of being a divided city? Ethnicity, media and social transformation," in *The Routledge Handbook of the Governance of Migration and Diversity in Cities*, T. Caponio et al. (eds.), London: Routledge, pp. 301–12 https://doi.org/10.4324/9781351108478-30

UN-DESA (United Nations Department of Economics and Social Affairs) 2009. *International Migration Report 2009: A Global Assessment*, New York: UN-DESA

UN-DESA (United Nations Department of Economics and Social Affairs) 2012. *World Urbanization Prospects: The 2011 Revision*, New York: UN-DESA

Van Hear, N., R. Brubaker and T. Bessa 2009. "Managing mobility for human development: The growing salience of mixed migration," United Nations Development Program Human Development Research Paper 2009/20, Nairobi

Varro, G. 2022. "The overriding value of mixedness," in *Mixed Families in a Transnational World*, J. Le Gall et al. (eds.), London: Routledge, pp. xv–xxix

Vertovec, S. 1999. "Three meanings of 'diaspora', exemplified by South Asian religions," *Diaspora* 6(3): 277–300 https://doi.org/10.1353/dsp.1997.0010

Vertovec, S. 2007. "Super-diversity and its implications," *Ethnic and Racial Studies* 30(6): 1024–54 https://doi.org/10.1080/01419870701599465

Vertovec, S. 2009. *Transnationalism*. London: Routledge https://doi.org/10.4324/9780203927083

Vertovec, S. 2011. "The cultural politics of nation and migration," *Annual Review of Anthropology* 40: 241–56 https://doi.org/10.1146/annurev-anthro-081309-145837

Vertovec, S. 2012. "'Diversity' and the social imaginary," *Archives Européennes de Sociologie/European Journal of Sociology* 53(3): 287–312 https://doi.org/10.1017/s000397561200015x

Vertovec, S. (ed.) 2015a. *Diversities Old and New: Migration and Socio-Spatial Patterns in New York, Singapore and Johannesburg*, Basingstoke: Palgrave https://doi.org/10.1057/9781137495488

Vertovec, S. 2015b. "Introduction: Migration, cities, diversities 'old' and 'new'," in *Diversities Old and New*, S. Vertovec (ed.), Basingstoke: Palgrave, pp. 1–20 https://doi.org/10.1057/9781137495488_1

Vertovec, S. 2020. "Considering the work of 'integration'," Max-Planck-Institute *Working Paper 20-04*, Göttingen

Walby, S. 2009. *Globalization & Inequalities: Complexity and Contested Modernities*, London: Sage https://doi.org/10.4135/9781446269145

Waters, M. C. and P. Kasinitz 2021. "Race, legal status, and social mobility," *Daedalus* 150(2): 120–34 https://doi.org/10.1162/daed_a_01850

Watson, S. 2014. "Spaces of difference: Challenging urban divisions from the north to the south," in *The Routledge Handbook on Cities of the Global South*, S. Parnell and S. Oldfield (eds.), London: Routledge, pp. 407–17 https://doi.org/10.4324/9780203387832-46

Zetter, R. 2007. "More labels, fewer refugees: Remaking the refugee label in an era of globalization," *Journal of Refugee Studies* 20(2): 172–92 https://doi.org/10.1093/jrs/fem011

Zetter, R. 2015. "Protection in crisis: Forced migration and protection in a global era," Washington, D.C.: Migration Policy Institute

Zhang, W. and J. R. Logan 2016. "Global neighborhoods: Beyond the multi-ethnic metropolis," *Demography* 53: 193–53 https://doi.org/10.1007/s13524-016-0516-4

Zlotnik, H. 1998. "International migration 1965-96: An overview," *Population and Development Review* 24(3): 429–68 https://doi.org/10.2307/2808151

5
RESPONSES TO DIVERSIFICATION

Just as there are differing modes and dimensions of diversification – both migration-driven and demographic – there are many ways that people respond to these processes. Most often, people's responses to such social changes are oriented to a perceived diversification along a single dimension, namely ethnoracial characteristics. "Ethnoracial" entails a common conflation of notions surrounding ethnic and racial characteristics – the former usually presumed to be cultural and linguistic, the latter prevalently presumed to be biological. This chapter discusses some of these perceptions of and responses to ethnoracial diversification, factors stimulating them, and their variable outcomes.

It is difficult to address perceptions of and responses to ethnoracial diversification in a generalized manner. So many factors surrounding such perceptions and responses are highly contextualized. To start, clearly there are national differences in the ways that diversifications are perceived and responded to. To recognize this is not to reify the nation-state in a manner often criticized as methodological nationalism (Wimmer and Schiller 2002). It is, rather, to take realistic account of differences in perceptions and responses that are shaped significantly by respective, nationally specific public spheres comprised of: social and political histories (in some cases including colonialism), narratives and imaginaries of the nation, discrete geographies and demographies, the legacy of immigration and integration policies, patterns of social stratification, historically formed stereotypes and practices of racism or discrimination, and ongoing political discourses, media representations and public debates. Particular terms have very nationally specific connotations (such as "allochtoon and autochtoon" in the Netherlands, "Ausländer" in Germany, "Hispanic" in the USA, "preta" and "parda" in Brazil, and "coloured" in South Africa). Highly differential nation-state contexts matter to perceptions and responses to diversification (see Morning 2015).

DOI: 10.4324/9780203503577-5

The ways that national contexts shape such perceptions and responses are reflected in comparative studies. For example, the Global Attitudes Survey by the Pew Research Center (2016) regularly looks comparatively at attitudes concerning increasing diversity. The usual methodology is that 1,000 people in each of the surveyed countries are asked about their views in relation to matters of race, ethnicity, and nationality – and to diversity and diversification as phenomena in themselves. The results show considerable national differences on whether diversification is seen as good or bad for a country. For instance 63% of Greeks found that growing diversity made their country a worse place to live, as did 53% of Italians and 41% of Hungarians; only 22%, 24%, and 26% of Spaniards, French, and Swedes, respectively, thought this (Pew Research Center 2016; also see Pew Research Center 2021). Similarly varying results were found in a survey of 11 emerging economies (Pew Research Center 2020). The role of such factors as national imaginaries, representations, and political discourses is evident in countries such as Hungary, where comparatively low levels of ethnoracial diversity nevertheless trigger very negative attitudes towards diversification – largely because of the ways diversity is treated in the public sphere (Van Hootegem and Meuleman 2019).

Within countries as surveyed by Pew, attitudes to diversification also not surprisingly differ by political orientation. People identifying with parties on the right are more likely than those on the left to say that increasing diversity makes national life worse. These results, too, seem telling with regard to national conceptions and politics of diversification. They appear to show, too, that broad political orientations towards diversification vary nationally: for example, the German Right has more positive views towards diversification than the Greek Left.

In the Pew surveys and numerous others of its kind, commonalities rather than differences across national contexts are seen in views by education level. Everywhere, it appears, lower levels of education are associated with more negative attitudes towards diversification. In the UK, for example, "Education strongly predicts levels of both in-group attachment and out-group hostility in the white majority" (Sobolewska and Ford 2020: 9). Elsewhere, research findings suggest that "More educated respondents are significantly less racist and place greater value on cultural diversity than do their counterparts" (Hainmueller and Hiscox 2007: 399). This kind of finding is repeatedly born out in surveys on public opinion towards immigration (with implications for attitudes towards diversification): higher education is associated with more liberal attitudes towards immigration and support for immigrants. Apparently regardless of what one studies at university, whether Sociology, Engineering, Biology, or Business, higher education is associated with more liberal, or at least less intolerant, attitudes. Just why that is the case remains much debated and comparatively understudied (see Strabac 2011; Lancee and Sarrasin 2015; Finseraas et al. 2018). Causal mechanisms are unknown, but theories suggest that higher education leads to the development of cognitive skills that help people: process and understand information differently, question misinformation, foster more self-introspection perhaps facilitating empathy, or put people at ease about potential competition for resources like jobs.

In comparative studies, the process of ethnoracial diversification (in the Pew surveys, described as "an *increasing number* of different races, ethnic groups and nationalities") evidently produces quite varied, yet very often quite negative, responses. However, the idea of diversity itself (in the Pew surveys, described as "*having* people of many different backgrounds") is usually associated with much more positive evaluations (see Pew Research Center 2021). In the European Social Survey between 2002 and 2018, this paradox has been increasingly evident in several similar, regularly repeated questions on attitudes towards social differences (Ambrosini et al. 2019; Ramos et al. 2019; Van Hootegem and Meuleman 2019). The data shows that most people in many societies consistently declare themselves to be fairly comfortable with diversity, but less so with diversification. So what is it about diversification as a process that prompts negative reactions?

Public understandings of diversity and diversification

It would be overly simplistic to suggest merely that responses to diversification are often negative because the process triggers a widespread fear of change. For many, diversification means social change; often people don't like any kind of change to their social situation, and so it follows that many don't like the idea of diversification. Another permutation of this view on change concerns a negative reaction based on "nostalgic deprivation" or "the discrepancy between individuals' understandings of their current status and their perceptions about their past" (Gest et al. 2018: 1695). Such discrepancy is thought to prompt some people not just to respond negatively to ethnoracial diversification, which is viewed as a break from a less-diverse past, but even to undertake extreme action by joining the radical Right in order to try to halt the process. Fear of change and a sense of relative deprivation, compared to a real or imagined past, are surely important aspects of many responses to diversification. However, these are unlikely to offer full explanations of negative responses across all manners or variations of reactions to diversification, nor to all kinds, scales, speeds, and geographies of diversification. A range of theories and cases must be examined in order to gain a fuller understanding of the varieties of possible responses.

Prior to such an exercise, however, it is worth considering the fact that responses are inherently based on everyday perceptions, narratives, and interpretations of diversification. This includes – especially in this era of rampant misinformation – skewed facts or false depictions of diversification. Perceptions, narratives, and interpretations belong to a conceptual realm that we can call "public understandings of diversity and diversification." To understand people's responses to diversification, we should try to gain better insights into such public understandings.

By public, I think of a realm of shared if not dominant meanings, representations, discourses, and language continuously reproduced through a widely accessible set of media (akin to the ways in which Benedict Anderson [1983] describes print media and the formation of national, imagined communities). Of course, in many ways and especially in this age of fragmented media and social media, we should consider not understandings within *a* or *the* public but within and across multiple *publics* (Warner 2002). Each will have its own worldview and discursive particularities, but perhaps there are nevertheless some common conceptual frameworks.

Ideally such an inherently anthropological task entails examining how members of a public conceive of, and which narratives surround: the meaning of "diversity" and ideas surrounding what "diversification" actually entails; how people think "diversity" and "diversification" actually "work" (what causes or drives them and how they actually transform community life, public institutions, and political dynamics); and where "diversity" and "diversification" are spatially located (and how this maps onto other imagined social geographies, for instance involving crime and security, housing, economics, health, cultural practices, and collective moralities). Such an inquiry should give us better grasps on how ideas and narratives of "diversity" and "diversification" are shaped and influenced by discrete publics and diverse political discourses and imagery, and how such representations of diversity and diversification – as summary notions concerning the changing nature of social differences – shape both everyday encounters and larger social structural processes (see Vertovec 2021). Here, I can only suggest a few possible features of public understandings of these issues.

Categorizations

The various ways in which members of a public understand the heterogeneity of social differences in their neighbourhood, city, country, or the world involve, in a fundamental way, their modes of social categorization. Social categorization involves personally and socially constructed criteria by which individuals sort other individuals into various conceptual collectivities. They comprise the "classification systems through which individuals perceive and make sense of their environment" (Lamont et al. 2014: 574). As explained by Richard Jenkins:

> categorization is a routine and necessary contribution to how we make sense of, and impute predictability to, a complex human world of which our knowledge is always partial. The ability to identify unfamiliar individuals with reference to known categories allows us at least the illusion that we know what to expect of them.
>
> *2004: 82*

The discipline of Social Psychology is very largely devoted to understanding social categorization and its effects. Social categorization underpins the much-studied social psychological topics of in-/out-group formation, prejudice and stereotyping, intergroup relations, and implicit bias (see, e.g., Allport 1954; Brewer 1999, 2007; Dovidio and Gaertner 2010; Dixon and Levine 2012). Such categorizations are products of personal experience, received knowledge, and public discourse.

As noted in the previous chapter, state categories – especially those used in official censuses – have a direct role in reproducing certain, often nation-specific, social categories especially concerning race and ethnicity. Once more, we need to bear in mind that "Official and scientific statistical categorisations *reflect* and *affect* the structural divisions of societies, as well as mainstream social representations. ... In this sense, censuses do more than reflect social realities; they also participate in the construction of these realities" (Simon et al. 2015: 2, italics in original).

Social categories are arranged into schema ordering the social world, locally producing a kind of "lay demography" about the people around us (Bodenhausen et al. 2012). Applying such categories provides "ways – both institutionalized and informal – of recognizing identifying and classifying other people, of construing sameness and difference, and of 'coding' and making sense of their actions" (Brubaker 2009: 34). I would add, too, that categories create a "lay hierarchy" by way of which people assign aspects of social structure in terms of value and status, functioning to create and reproduce inequality. As Charles Tilly put it, "Categories matters. To the extent that routine social life endows them with readily available names, markers, intergroup practices, and internal connections, categories facilitate unequal treatment by both members and outsiders" (2005: 111).

Under conditions of diversification, newcomers are usually sorted quickly into existing schema. Social psychologists describe this process thusly:

> When initially encountering members of a novel group, an exemplar-based representation governs category judgments, but once enough experience with group members has occurred, a probabilistic, prototype-based representation appears to emerge. Regardless of which representational format one presupposes, people clearly do hold consequential beliefs about the features and characteristics that are associated with social groups. Categories are fundamentally represented in terms of descriptive features, but the representations consist of more than just a "laundry list" of characteristics that are individually correlated with category membership. Instead, these features are embedded within causal theories that do more than merely describe the category – they provide explanations for why the category is the way it is.
>
> *Bodenhausen et al. (2012: 320)*

Explanations for "why the category is the way it is" often entail normative, value-laded, and moralistic judgements about entire categories of people. First encounters give way to forms of "interaction-as-learned relationships" while newcomers eventually become "categorically known others" (Lofland 1998).

Relevant are the social categories, of course, held by white/non-migrant populations who are fundamental participants in superdiversity and social complexity (Alba and Duyvendak 2019). Yet one should not assume that categorization processes concerning newcomers are typically a matter of "native" Whites encountering new, immigrant non-Whites. A growing body of research examines the ways that long-established, post-migration ethnic minorities locally perceive and respond to immigrant newcomers from dissimilar origins. For instance, Susanne Wessendorf (2020) describes such processes in East London, where eastern European migrants have moved into superdiverse areas including large numbers of people with South Asian backgrounds; Orly Clergé (2019) unravels relations and perceptions between Black Americans, Jamaican, and Haitian immigrants on Long Island; Elaine Ho and Laavy Kathiravelu (2021) discuss views of recent migrants, categorization, and racialization by "co-ethnics" in Singapore. We must bear in mind, too, that immigrants themselves bring with them the definitions and meanings of social categories, such as race, in their places of origin "which interact with and become infused with those of their host country" (Davenport 2020: 225).

Such dynamics are directly related to the meeting of "old" and "new" diversities discussed in Chapter 4. In such settings, threat narratives and stereotypes abound, but so does empathy – as many long-standing residents relate their perceptions, categorizations, and social interactions towards newcomers to their own experiences of discrimination in early periods of arrival in the UK. Whether long-standing resident, old immigrant or new immigrant, we need to bear in mind that "classificatory struggles and negotiations [occur] between actors situated in a social field" (Wimmer 2008: 970). Everyone has their own positionality and experiences, as well as received concepts and narratives, which condition categorization processes.

Social categorization not only occurs through encountering others, but sometimes even through merely picturing them. Robert Miles (1989) described this as categorizing the "imagined other," for whom one only has a mental representation, as opposed to an "experienced other" with whom one has a direct observation or interaction. In these ways, anyone's lay demography of diversity and diversification includes a mixture of imagination, direct observation, and interpretations provided by others directly via social networks, through the media or from social media.

In practically any public understanding of diversity and diversification, a core feature of social categorization is the tendency towards what Rogers Brubaker has importantly described as *groupism*. This is "the tendency to take discrete, sharply differentiated, internally homogeneous and externally bounded groups as basic constituents of social life" (Brubaker 2002: 164). Consequently, groupism leads to "the tendency to represent the social and cultural world as a multichrome mosaic of monochrome ethnic, racial or cultural blocs" (Ibid.). It is common in many public understandings of diversity that society is considered to be comprised of groups that have clear boundaries, are homogeneous in values and practices, and bump up against and contest other, similarly conceived groups. To various degrees, groupism underpins what studies in terms of people's notions, feelings, and attitudes, as well as the sharpness of boundaries and the criteria of inclusion, concerning "in-groups" and "out-groups" (see Levine and Campbell 1972). Individuals perceive and behave towards others as members of their own social group or another different one, exercising what some believe to be a fundamental act of social cognition (Macrae and Bodenhausen 2001).

Groupism sits well with what Amartya Sen (2006: 20) has call the assumption of "singular affiliation." This refers to the belief that any and every person pre-eminently belongs to one category or collectivity only, "no more and no less." The assumption is widespread and popular not only with people across many publics, but especially among communitarian thinkers and political actors. Sen points out that

> The intricacies of plural groups and multiple loyalties [discussed at more length in Chapter 6 of this book] are obliterated by seeing each person as firmly embedded in exactly one affiliation, replacing the richness of leading an abundant human life with the formulaic narrowness of insisting that any person is "situated" in just one organic pack.
>
> *Ibid.*

I suggest, too, that much groupist and singular affiliation thinking is also inherently based on the idea of a fixed "pie" to be sliced and distributed (unequally) to purported groups – that is, the world is rife with *zero-sum groupism*. In this mode of understanding the diverse social world, one believes that if another group has acquired some kind of publically accessible resources – such as jobs, housing, government support, rights, or protective legislation – then, therefore, one's own group must have automatically suffered some (albeit perhaps not immediately discernable) proportionate disadvantage. This also underpins feelings of group-based unfairness, a sense that other groups are not "deserving" or have "cut in line" to gain resources (Hochschild 2018). Considering the social world to be comprised of bounded groups, along with viewing socio-economic or political resources as fixed, group win-or-lose elements, leads to a very conflictual, competition-based public understanding of diversity and diversification. It is in this sense, in the USA for instance, that Robert Reich has described the way "the white working class has been seduced by conservative Republicans and Trump cultists … into believing that what's good for Black and Latino people is bad for them, and that whites are, or should be, on the winning side of the social Darwinian contest" (2021).

Especially in a complex social environment, understandings of social categories and groupism may pertain to many criteria, however. In the "Diversity and Contact" project based at our Max Planck Institute (Schönwälder et al. 2016), a multidisciplinary team combined ethnographic research and a three wave panel study of 2,500 individuals to study everyday encounters and attitudes towards difference in 50 neighbourhoods across 16 German cities. When asked about "the people in your own neighbourhood" and whether and how they are "diverse," respondents distinguished a wide range of social characteristics. Those with differing national origins were described as "diverse" people in the neighbourhood, to be sure (just over half of respondents mentioned this) – but also people of differing ages, social classes, family forms, lifestyles, and beliefs. In everyday settings, "diversity" is potentially not only thought of as ethnoracial, but in terms of many social categories.

Nonetheless, it is known that across many everyday approaches to their social environments, people do tend to single out one category among many other possible ones (Prati et al. 2021). Ethnicity is a key lens through which a great many members of the public often consider social differences. Concepts of ethnicity combine groupism with *culturalism*, whereby:

> In this set of understandings, "culture" is: a kind of package (often talked of as migrants' "cultural baggage") of collective behavioural-moral-aesthetic traits and "customs", rather mysteriously transmitted between generations, best suited to particular geographical origins yet largely unaffected by history or a change of context, which instils a discrete quality into the feelings, values, practices, social relationships, predilections and intrinsic nature of all who "belong to (a particular) it".
>
> *Vertovec (1996: 51)*

While an anthropological view of culture underlines openness, change, and flexibility, this kind of folk culturalism considers culture as a set of closed, immutable differences passed on through lines of descent (also see Stolcke 1995; Baumann 1996, 1999).

Groupism and culturalism are also key elements of the social construction of "race," racial meanings, and everyday "race-making" (see, among others, Omi and Winant 1986; Lewis 2003; Saperstein et al. 2013). With "race," characteristics – especially phenotypes – are conceived to pertain to fundamental biological and physical (and therefore "natural") categories. Many people routinely attribute race by various, weighted characteristics of skin colour, ancestry, and sociocultural cues such as language (Schachter et al. 2021). Relatedly, social scientists describe processes of *racialization*, or the habit of attaching meaning to perceived cultural groups as quasi-biological entities (see, among others, Murji and Solomos 2005; Gans 2017; Hochman 2019). As described by Loïc Wacquant:

> [T]o racialize means to *naturalize*, to turn history into biology, cultural differences into dissimilarities of essence; to *eternalize*, to stipulate that those differences are enduring if not unchanging across time, past and present and future; and to *homogenize*, to perceive and picture all members of the racialized category as fundamentally alike as sharing a permanent essential quality that warrants differential treatment of its members in symbolic, social and physical space.
>
> *2022: 78, italics in original*

Racialization is often in play with reference to categories such as Muslims, Irish Travellers, or American Latinos. Racialized categories are marked by ambiguity, however. Ali Rattansi (2020: 65) points out how, in public imaginaries, "race" and racialized categories vary in the degree to which they contain mixes of biological and cultural notions of difference, superiority, and inferiority.

"Racism and racialization are *processes*, always 'works in progress', says Rattansi (Ibid.), "and liable to change and transformation from situation to situation, and during different historical periods" (italics in original).

Everyday categorizations of social, ethnic or racial groups are constantly reified, essentialized, and stereotyped. "Lay demographies" of social, racialized, and culturalized categories are also: imbued with assumptions about what gender means with regard to each category; stratified by way of notions concerning socio-economic and symbolic status and ranking; and spatialized such that such categories of difference build "mental maps" to create an envisioned landscape of diversity and diversification (including where one's own purported in-group sits within this imagined, stratified topography).

Such understandings are, moreover, variously framed, reproduced, and strengthened in public discourses and representations. To discuss these phenomena as matters of public understanding, social construction, mental imagery, and political discourse is not to dismiss them as unreal. To the contrary, "Racial idioms, ideologies, narratives, categories and systems of classification and racialized ways of seeing, thinking, talking and framing claims are real and consequential" (Brubaker 2002: 168). This holds correspondingly for other social categories beyond "race," too. Public understandings of diversity and diversification, themselves based on conceptual categories, are very palpable in the ways that they directly condition how people perceive their social world, develop their attitudes, and undertake their actions accordingly.

Conceptualizations

At this point, it is important to point out that, while public understandings and attitudes toward *diversity and diversification* are related to public understandings and attitudes towards *immigration*, they are not the same thing. But they certainly overlap and inform conceptualizations of each other.

There is by now a considerable body of literature on public opinion and immigration (see among others Rustenbach 2010; Vertovec 2011; Dražanová 2020; Kustov et al. 2021). The general public's views on immigration are shaped by a number of concerns, particularly: economic matters (conventionally a closed and limited labour market), cultural matters (particularly worries about the establishment of unassimilable minority cultural enclaves marked by radically different moralities, practices, and values, along with an assumed "watering down" or "undoing" of national culture), public welfare matters (largely concerning assumed burdens on schools, health services, and social welfare), and security matters (especially comprising anxieties about possible rises in criminality and terrorism).

These immigration-focused concerns certainly can relate to public understandings of diversity and diversification, since it is often believed that – through such varied economic, cultural, public welfare, and security matters – migration-driven diversification leads to a breakdown of national identity, economic dynamism, and social "cohesion." To counter these presumed processes of breakdown, nation-states widely engage in various debates, policies, and programmes to facilitate immigrant "integration" (itself a highly contested concept in contemporary migration studies: see, among others, Bertossi 2011; Meissner and Heil 2020; Vertovec 2020; Karimi and Wilkes 2021; Favell 2022).

It is the cultural dimension of attitudes towards immigration that overlaps most clearly with public understandings of diversity and diversification. It is often foremost in people's minds when considering immigration and its effects. This has been corroborated by Nobel Prize-winning economist David Card. Examining European Social Survey data across 20 countries, Card and his team discovered that only about 20% of people's attitudes towards immigration concern economic issues such as wage effects; 80% of attitudes concern cultural issues such as how people feel about living with others practicing a different language, religion, or culture (in Coy 2021; also see Van Hootegem and Meuleman 2019). In this way, immigration is largely conceived by many as a process fundamentally concerning the proliferation of (predominantly racialized) cultural differences.

As mentioned at the outset of this chapter, however, surveys show that most people are at ease, if not rather assenting, to the idea of diversity. For many people, diversity is often understood as a kind of "good mix" that culturally enriches, stimulates creativity, and adds "colour" to a society (cf. Byrne 2006). The idea of diversification, especially migration-driven diversification, however, can quickly lead to worries about a country or locality becoming "too diverse," thereby setting off a cascade of predicted negative effects. This aspect of public understanding concerns not the number of newcomers, but their multiplying differences. Such a prospect of diversification can arouse a deep sense of discomfort over anticipated social disorder (Foroutan 2019). In this aspect of public understanding, the positive, "good mix" notion of diversity is presumed to have a limit or at least a kind of balance.

"Too much" diversity was the core problem asserted in a notorious article by David Goodhart (2004). He argued that, while a certain amount of ethnic, racial and cultural difference poses no great hazard to a society, an ever-diversifying population will automatically lead to the erosion of collective norms and identities. This, in turn, will make people less willing to share resources, will breakdown mutual obligations to fellow citizens, and will overstretch public goodwill and notions of commonality. At the heart of this view is the presumption that people only really wish to share their taxes and collective goods with others like themselves. It follows, in this logic, that a process of persistently adding more people, with ever more kinds of social and cultural difference, will ultimately destroy the sense of solidarity that necessarily underpins welfare states.

For those familiar with the roots of Sociology, this kind of understanding of social solidarity is highly reminiscent of what Émile Durkheim called "mechanical solidarity" (2014 [1893]). With this concept, Durkheim proposed that in historically earlier or simpler, small-scale types of society, social cohesion is created and maintained by the homogeneity of individuals' values, traditions, and lifestyles. ("Mechanical" refers the interchangeability of parts that comprise a machine.) This he differentiated from "organic solidarity," which Durkheim thought to characterize the nature of social cohesion in large-scale, modern, industrial society. In this latter kind of solidarity, Durkheim claimed, cohesion arises through the interdependence of occupationally specialized individuals, importantly overseen by laws and institutions. ("Organic" refers to specific functions of organs that comprise a body.) In such public understandings of diversity and diversification, underpinned by interventions like Goodhart's, it is presumed that the only valid idea of solidarity is the kind Durkheim called "mechanical."

The relationship between ethnic diversity, solidarity, and social welfare has been a rigorously studied topic in the disciplines of Economics and Political Science. One way to address this relationship is to probe whether more diverse nation-states or localities actually spend less on welfare provisions: if so, there must be a reason – namely, that diversity must indeed be bad for social solidarity. An international overview of studies in this field shows no strong connection, and almost no causality, between ethnic diversity and social welfare spending (Stichnoth and Van der Straeten 2013). This was also clear in a detailed analysis of local spending in US cities over 50 years, following which Daniel Hopkins (2011: 69) concludes that "Ethnic and racial diversity does not consistently dampen the provision of public goods. Indeed, in recent years the impact of diversity has been inconsequential for most spending categories and positive for health."

Beyond actual spending patterns, however, a number of studies do show some evidence of negative effects of ethnic diversity and diversification on attitudes towards redistribution of public funds and resources. Still, the evidence is weak or mixed at best. A key reason for unclear results is that there are likely confounding factors at play. For instance, it might be that people in diversifying contexts are sceptical of public funding because of concurrent, broader patterns of economic decline, income stagnation, or labour market shrinkage. Under such conditions beyond diversification, people may become more sceptical of financial redistribution altogether. Also, diversifying areas tend to be areas of high churn, with lots of in- and out-movements. This leads to uncertainties and changing expectations about local social configurations – not least if people themselves are pondering whether to stay or go. Such flux and uncertainty are liable to make people less prone to support long-term investments in their locality through public funds. These kinds of dynamics are not accounted for in most studies of diversity and social welfare. Or perhaps endogeneity is a flaw in some research: it might be that places which spend more public funds just attract disproportionately White populations, and low-spending places end up with ever-more diverse populations. These are processes that occur even before people's attitudes towards diversity and public spending are shaped (Hopkins 2009).

Generally, the social science literature shows that diversity does not necessarily undercut public investments or reduce support for social welfare in diverse places, but it may in places that are becoming rapidly more diverse. A key factor surrounding this latter phenomenon – and one that should be borne in mind in relation to all of the rest of the responses to diversification described throughout this chapter – is the impact of political discourse. When changes in the proportion of racial and ethnic groups in an area are highly debated in the public sphere, especially in reified and adverse ways, it impacts strongly on people's attitudes towards diversification. Negative attitudes towards public spending (on diverse others) arise especially in such times and contexts in which notions of diversification-as-threat are constructed and reinforced by particular framings, representations, and rhetoric on racial and ethnic difference. These are constructed and manipulated by political actors and often reproduced in public media. As Erik Bleich, Irene Bloomraad, and Els de Graauw stress, "the relevance of framing and representation is clear: it is vital to understand how different groups are portrayed and the extent to which media representations affect public opinion, political mobilization and policy outcomes" (2015: 862). With regard to diversification, right-wing framings provide a sense of "politicized change" affecting social contexts that, in turn, instills negative responses to newcoming Others (Hopkins 2007).

Estimations

Goodhart' (2004) article promoted the idea that there is some kind of unspoken tipping point beyond which a level of tolerable diversity passes, through diversification processes, into an undesirable condition of "too much." An actual level was never described, nor was the reasoning as to why there should be such a demographic threshold. Nevertheless, the idea of a "too much" tipping point, a fatal "beyond-which" brink, often surely resonates in public understandings of diversity and diversification. Such resonance was evident in the lead-up to the UK Brexit referendum. On June 16, 2016, just days before the vote, the pro-Brexit UKIP (United Kingdom Independence Party) leader Nigel Farage launched a nationwide poster campaign. The now infamous campaign poster showed a photo of a very large queue of mostly non-White people, together with the slogan "Breaking point: the EU has failed us all. We must break free of the EU and take back control of our borders." The photo actually depicted people on the border between Croatia and Slovenia being escorted by police to a refugee camp. The image shows a long, curving line of people "producing a powerful impression of relentless human movement" (Faulkner et al. 2021: 202). UKIP's explicit intention was to misinform the public by giving the impression that masses were on their way to Britain. Moreover, the imposing "Breaking point" headline plainly poses a "too much," "beyond-which" brink, suggesting that its surpassing will lead to national disaster. Further, this poster connoted an impression of not just being swamped by sheer numbers, but also being overwhelmed by a wave of profound cultural difference. Being mainly comprised of adult male Syrian and Afghan asylum-seekers, most of the faces on the "Breaking point" poster also inherently imply (especially to the Islamophobic viewer) that they are Muslims. The image and "breaking point" message simultaneously suggest mass immigration overwhelming public resources and diversification diminishing Whiteness and imperilling Britishness (see Durrheim et al. 2018).

In these ways, public understandings of diversity and diversification can be manipulated by discourses of politicized change. Notions of a tipping point remain vague. The idea is usually not an identified cusp, fixed limit or known ratio, but a relative notion presumed to mark a condition between social order and chaos. Any population change that can be perceived or conveyed as too large or disproportional, too quick, too different, or seemingly endless can trigger negative attitudes due to inherent notions surrounding the presumed consequences of "too much" (Banulescu-Bogdan et al. 2021). Public attitudes can be manipulated by populist writers and politicians who portray any kind of diversification as exceeding an imagined tipping point.

But certainly size matters? What if a particular newcomer group is just considered too big? Yolande Pottie-Sherman and Rimal Wilkes (2017) undertook a meta-analysis of 55 studies concerning the relative sizes of immigrant groups and the degrees of negative responses to them. They found a considerable variety of findings across the studies, amounting to no clear causal link. Perhaps the central outcome of their meta-analysis was the consistent finding that "perceived rather than actual size had the largest and most consistent effect on prejudice" (Ibid.: 244). That is, if people *think* a particular group is very large – too large for a "good mix"? – negative attitudes might develop towards them.

However, one thing we do know about public understanding is that people regularly, and considerably, over-estimate the size and growth of migrant or minority groups (Sides and Citrin 2007; Duffy and Frere-Smith 2014; Hopkins et al. 2018). Indeed, the late Alberto Alesina and his colleagues confirmed this in a study of 24,000 survey respondents from six countries (France, Germany, Italy, Sweden, the UK, and the USA). "In all countries," they found, "respondents greatly overestimate the total number of immigrants, think immigrants are culturally and religiously more distant from them, and are economically weaker – less educated, more unemployed, and more reliant on and favored by government transfers – than is the case" (2021: 1). Their study underlines the fact that it is not only size that is frequently misapprehended, but other modes of social difference as well. Furthermore:

> The misperception about the size of the immigrant population is widespread among all groups of respondents, including left and right-wing ones. Respondents also systematically misperceive the composition of immigrants. They believe immigrants are more culturally distant from natives. For instance, they starkly overestimate the share of Muslim immigrants and underestimate the share of Christian immigrants. Misperceptions are pervasive also about the level of education and income of immigrants and about how much they rely on the receiving country's welfare state. Respondents who have the largest misperceptions are those with low levels

of education and who work in sectors with more immigrant workers, the non-college educated, women, and right-wing respondents. While left and right-wing respondents misperceive the share of immigrants to the same extent, they have very different views about the composition of immigrants and their contribution to the receiving country.

Ibid.: 3

Misperceptions about diversifications are largely fostered in, and gathered from, a public sphere, presenting a "world of misinformation." Alesina and his team highlight how "media coverage may not inflate misperceptions of the share of immigrants further, but may emphasize the perceived cultural diversity of immigrants" (Ibid.: 22). Additionally, they point to ways that anti-immigration parties have an incentive publically to manipulate information and foster stereotypes concerning cultural difference.

As Pottie-Sherman and Wilkes point out, it is the supposition of large, not actual, numbers that often prompt negative attitudes (for a variety of reasons described below). Negative attitudes are exacerbated by the related dynamic, identified by Alesina et al., that cultural distance of immigrant groups is also vastly misjudged. Often misperceptions of both size and cultural distance are purposefully manipulated. Providing members of the public with correct information on the actual (usually, much smaller-than-imagined) size of groups, however, has been shown to have little impact on the attitudes that have already formed by way of prior, "too large/too diverse" perceptions and narratives (Hopkins et al. 2018). Indeed, it may often be the case that such misperceptions are a consequence of negative attitudes, rather than the other way around.

Additionally, the more abstract the considered scale is beyond that of an individual's lived context, the greater the over-estimation of the size of any migrant or minority group. This is demonstrated in surveys showing that people often believe that immigration and diversification are problems on a national scale, but not problems affecting them where they live locally. "There is a clear perception gap between the importance of immigration as a national issue and the importance of immigration to individuals personally," note observers from the polling firm Ipsos-MORI (Duffy and Frere-Smith 2014: 88). For example, in the German federal state of Saxony, where the levels of foreign-born are miniscule compared to other parts of Germany, only 17% said that there is a local problem around diversification. Still, 58% of people said that nationally, diversification in Germany is putting the country in danger of being over-foreignized or *überfremdet* (Sachsen 2016). When abstracting from small-scale up to large-scale levels, people often envisage phenomena differently. Conversely, when people think something dreadful is looming out there on a larger scale and is on its way to their own local vicinity, anxieties arise. Once more, this local perspective of looming danger from a larger scale is agitated significantly when national level elites who politicize ethnic and racial change thereby provide distinct framings and rhetoric that are recapitulated on the local level.

A similar set of findings in Germany indicate that, among white German locals, an increase in the perceived ratio of the ethnic minority population – rather at odds with actual data – leads to feelings of group threat and strong exclusionary attitudes towards those considered foreigners broadly. "The higher the perceived size" the research team found, "the more pronounced are both the threat and anti-foreigner attitudes" (Semyonov et al. 2004: 681). As Thomas Pettigrew and his colleagues conclude, "Threat is perceptual; it involves what people think is the outgroup proportion and thus can be easily manipulated by political leaders and the mass media" (2010: 635; also see Wagner et al. 2006).

The readiness of some people to adopt right-wing interpretations of diversification is discussed in Eric Kaufmann's controversial book *Whiteshift* (2018). I certainly do not agree with many of his conclusions and prescriptions (especially the proposition that politicians should accept and even accommodate White grievances based on racial self-interests). What I do find interesting, however, is Kaufmann's research review in which he found that "The consensus of over 200 academic papers in the literature (an exhaustive sample of 2016) is that increases in diversity almost always produce elevated anti-immigration and far-right support" (Ibid.: 165). "Ethnic *change* is the irritant," Kaufmann stresses, "not levels of diversity" (Ibid.: 18). This is consistent with Hopkins' (2009: 175) assessment that "it is those communities that have undergone sudden demographic changes, not communities that have long been diverse, where diversity's effects are pronounced." We must bear in mind that responses to diversification are significantly matters of perception and discourse – and, therefore, liable to influence. We must not make the mistake of thinking that demographic conditions and changes themselves "make" people react in certain ways.

Framings

People differentially read and interpret social changes happening around them – or changes assumed to be about to occur. Attitudes and perceptions of immigrants and ethnoracial Others are not just drawn from known experiences and presumed threats, but from certain messages (including so-called "dog-whistles"), framings, narratives, and selective images that permeate the public sphere (Helbling 2014; Thorbjørnsrud 2015; Bos et al. 2016; Haynes et al. 2016). These are increasingly intensified and disseminated through social media (Ekman 2019; de Saint Laurent et al. 2020; Nortio et al. 2021). In diversifying places, derogatory or threatening discourses of political elites are drawn upon by locals (Hopkins 2009). Educational background, socio-economic circumstances, prior readings of history on various scales, and multiple self-identifications are all factors that combine in ways such that some individuals are more prone to certain messages, framings, narratives, and selective images than others (Matthes and Schmuck 2017).

In a multifaceted analysis of the European Social Survey since 2002, together with a large team of associates (Ambrosini et al. 2019), Arno Van Hootegem and

Bart Meuleman sought to find out how Europeans responded to the so-called "refugee crisis" of 2015. Their findings reveal that

> sudden inflows of asylum seekers do not necessarily or automatically set of a backlash of threat perceptions among the majority population. Instead, our results suggest that the political climate and media discourses on immigration and asylum might be more relevant, that the frame that political elites and media employ is what matters. Indeed, prior research shows that frames adopted by the media and political parties are important in shaping attitudes toward immigrants.
>
> *Van Hootegem and Meuleman (2019)*

The "great replacement theory" is one such framing or narrative concerning diversification. This rather unabashedly racist conspiracy narrative posits that migration and high birthrates among non-White people are purposefully being foisted upon Western societies in order to "replace" White people (see for instance Bowles 2019). The premise is not reserved to genetic or other racialized notions of diversification, but is often entangled with beliefs about cultural replacement too. For example, Björn Höcke, a German politician and leader of a far-right faction within the Alternative for Germany (AfD) party, has claimed that the "refugee invasion" is threatening Germans with "the death of their race" through "Africanization, orientalization and Islamization" (in Amann 2019). This now internationalized take on diversification not only seeks to stimulate a sense of discomfort, if not rage, over an alleged, politically engineered transposition (in the first instance, Whites losing jobs and votes to non-Whites), but also panic over an ultimate White "genocide." In addition, "great replacement theory" is meant to stimulate a strong sense of victimization, an affront that "someone is doing this to us – and they must be found out and stopped."

Also by way of matters of perception, frequently people's impressions of diversification processes are admixed with their interpretations of other concurrent social, cultural, and economic processes. The variety of backlash responses and narratives concerning diversification, for instance, is often mingled in people's minds with perceptions and reflections on other urban issues such as post-industrialization, gentrification, conflict, crime, housing shortages, and local power relations (see Jensen 2017). Together, these can confront people as a highly menacing basket of social environmental developments over which one has little control. These kinds of localized views of large, uncontrollable processes directly affecting one's living situation, often leading to anxieties around uncertainly, relate to how people might perceive others within such contexts of change. In experimental studies, David Sherman and his colleagues (2009) found that, under such conditions of uncertainty about shifting personal conditions and contexts, people accentuate markers of their in-group identity and feel more in-group entitativity (group tightness); at the same time, people project a heightened sense of polarization from out-groups. For some, ethnoracial diversification represents a condition of uncertainty – within this whole basket of contextual changes – leading to in-group bias, out-group stereotyping, mistrust, and even hatred of others who are perceived as highly different and socially distant.

Under conditions of diversification, a withdrawal into a tight in-group is otherwise described as "hunkering down" in Robert Putnam's (2007) well-known and much-disputed analysis of social reactions to diversity and diversification. In this study, Putnam purports to show that higher levels of diversity (based on the basic American racial classifications of White, Black, Asian, and Hispanic) lead to people withdrawing from social life and becoming generally less trustful. The most striking contention is that, according to Putnam, diversification correlates with people becoming less trustful not just of strangers and out-group members, but also of their own neighbours and in-group members. The ensuing presumption is that ethnoracial commonality facilitates social trust and cohesion, while ethnoracial heterogeneity dissipates it. (Due to such a presumption, Putnam has been accused of promulgating a Durkheimian "mechanical solidarity" view of social cohesion; see Portes and Vickstrom 2011.) In what he calls *constrict theory*, Putnam infers that diversification has negative social effects on everyone. Once we consider that "in-group and out-group attitudes need not be reciprocally related, but can vary independently," he says, "then we need to allow, logically at least, for the possibility that diversity might actually reduce *both* in-group *and* out-group solidarity – that is, both bonding [within group] *and* bridging [between group] social capital" (Ibid.: 144, italics in original).

Putnam's study has generated extensive debate and a vast literature – much of it questioning his data, methods, presumptions, and modes of analysis (useful overviews include Portes and Vickstrom 2011; Sturgis et al. 2011; van der Meer and Tolsma 2014) – as well as a huge number of related research projects (one recent meta-analysis of Putnam-stimulated works on ethnic diversity and social trust considers no less than 87 studies; Dinesen et al. 2020). Overall, the literature slightly leans towards the view that diversification does indeed reduce local levels of social trust (although social trust is a concept that includes many things). However, a major caveat in this Putnam-triggered research field on diversity-and-social trust concerns the concomitant, or even more powerful, effects of economic inequality, disadvantage, and deprivation. In keeping with the findings of a great many studies, James Laurence (2011: 70) stresses that, while "diversity has both positive and negative effects on social cohesion, we find that it is disadvantage which has the most detrimental impact, undermining both social capital and interethnic relations."

Beyond various public understandings and mixed social effects of diversification processes, it is clear that large segments of many populations respond to diversification – or even its prospect – negatively. Such negative responses may range from silent discontent to mild grumbling within one's own social circle, through hostile public behaviour to blatantly racist or xenophobic political action. What are some of the reasons for such negative responses?

Theories of negative response

In order to better understand negative responses to diversification (or better, to perceptions of diversification), one can turn initially to numerous, long-standing social science theories. One of the most relevant is *ethnic competition* theory, which holds that ethnic or racial groups that are large or growing, in proximity, and with relatively equal social-structural positions become antagonistic as they contend for scarce resources such as jobs, housing, schools, and state support (e.g., Gonzalez-Sobrino 2016). This is also sometimes discussed as the *conflict hypothesis* (e.g., Tajfel and Turner 1979), which maintains that animosity towards out-groups is heightened and tolerance is reduced under circumstances of growing out-group numbers.

Many approaches to negative responses are broadly subsumed within *group threat* theory. This entails a number of ways that members of an in-group develop negative attitudes towards out-groups when they believe that the latter pose a challenge to their well-being, whether in terms of resources, symbolic status, or distinctiveness (Riek et al. 2006). With regard to diversification, threat pertains as growing numbers of out-groups such as ethnic minorities lead to high levels of resentment, anger, and anxiety (Quillian 1995). This is because it is believed that the in-group will be overwhelmed (in terms of matters like housing, jobs, and votes) and that their economic position and social privileges will be reduced (Oliver and Wong 2003). A sense of anxiety arises as in-group members anticipate a diminishing of their own numerical preponderance, group status, political weight, or symbolic dominance (Major et al. 2016). Relatedly, those who consider their group's current, higher social and economic status to be wholly legitimate (based on their own set of norms, values and moralities) also tend to feel more threatened by diversification (Outten et al. 2018). Resulting feelings of threat regarding newcomers, moreover, may lead directly to increased support for conservative ideologies and support for anti-immigration policies (Craig et al. 2018a, 2018b). Further, members of dominant groups who believe that they normatively represent larger significant categories (such as Whites who consider themselves emblematic of their nation-state) may fear that increasing diversity threatens this claim to being nationally representative or "prototypical" (Danbold 2018).

In a powerful example, all of these factors surrounding group threat – especially, perceived diversification and the threat of loss of symbolic dominance and prototypicality – are touched on in Jennifer Richeson's views of contemporary American political dynamics. Drawing on the latest research in the field, she points to:

> very consistent and compelling evidence to suggest that some of what we have witnessed [in the January 2021 insurrection in Washington, D.C.] is a reflection of the angst, anger, and refusal to accept an "America" in which White (Christian) Americans are losing dominance, be it political, material, and/or cultural. And, I use the term dominance here, because it is not simply a loss of status. It is a loss of power. A more racially,

ethnically, religiously diverse US that is also a democracy requires White Americans to acquiesce to the interests and concerns of racial/ethnic and religious minorities.

[Trump] leaned into the underlying White nationalist sentiments that had been on the fringe in his campaign for the presidency and made his campaign about re-centering Whiteness as what it actually means to be American and, by implication, delegitimizing claims for greater racial equity, be it in policing or any other important domain of American life.

in Edsall (2021)

Space and place also often have much to do with negative responses to diversification, including reactionary politics. The "*halo effect*" represents a geographically oriented social scientific theory about right-wing beliefs linked to feelings of threat posed by diversity and diversification. "Halo" refers to a more ethnoracially homogeneous zone around or at the edge of a highly diverse area. If these halo zones are ones of high White concentration, anti-diversity attitudes within them may become increasingly prominent as an adjacent, diverse area increasingly diversifies (Bowyer 2008; Evans and Ivaldi 2020; Miller and Grubesic 2021). As Jens Rydgren and Patrick Ruth (2013: 718) describe the phenomenon, "xenophobia and immigration-negative attitudes are most common in areas close to neighbourhoods with a high proportion of immigrants, and not within such neighbourhoods; making such areas even more likely breeding grounds for radical right-wing populist mobilization." In this way, too, Kaufmann (2014) points to anti-immigrant sentiments and support for right-wing politics stemming from a threat of diversification not within one's own immediate locality, but in a nearby geographical area. "The presence of significant diversity in one's city or local authority," he surmises, "adds to threat perceptions because of the sense immigrants may soon introduce large-scale change into one's locale" (Ibid.: 272). Kaufmann summarizes the Halo effect as "the fact that opposition to immigration is greatest when immigrants are close, but not too close" (Ibid.). In a number of places across the USA, the halo effect seems to have played a role in recent Republican political mobilization (Miller and Grubesic 2021). The phenomenon is also consistent with social psychological findings about apprehensions of impending change that activate negative out-group prejudice (Hamilton and Bishop 1976).

Other context-specific, demographic-cum-geographical factors at play in shaping responses to diversification concern the impacts of *small but rapid diversification*. This phenomenon was considered by one of the early ethnic competition theorists, Susan Olzak (1992). She postulated that among a majority population, ethnic threat – in terms of both a sense of heightened competition and vulnerable in-group status – is more likely triggered by recent, albeit limited, increases in ethnic minority presence than by the stable presence of a large minority group or set of minority groups. That is, seemingly sudden changes in ethnic diversity, however small, are enough to trigger fear and dismay among a current majority.

This phenomenon appears to have been relevant during the American 2016 presidential election. Immediately prior to the election, a *Wall Street Journal* headline proclaimed: "Places Most Unsettled by Rapid Demographic Change Are Drawn to Donald Trump" (Adamy and Overberg 2016). In this *WSJ* article, the authors pointed out that "Small towns in the Midwest have diversified more quickly than almost any part of the U.S. since the start of an immigration wave at the beginning of this century. The resulting cultural changes appear to be moving the political needle." They conjectured that people in places that had diversified rapidly were more likely to vote for Trump. In the presidential primaries, "He took 73% of those [counties] where diversity at least doubled since 2000, and 80% of those [counties] where the diversity index rose at least 150%." Interestingly, they point to other important facts that are often overlooked in political analyses: "Unemployment is actually lower in rapidly diversifying counties than in the country on the whole, a sign that concerns over lost jobs are weighing less on voters in these areas. In counties where diversity at least doubled, unemployment averages 4.5%, compared with 4.9% nationally" (Ibid.).

Subsequently, a number of analyses now show that people from places that recently diversified rapidly have been drawn to Trump's side, from his initial election in 2016 through to the insurrection at the US Capitol building on 6 January 2021 (Pape 2021). Of course, there are manifold reasons why people have chosen to support Donald Trump, and responses to demographic change should not be considered as a sole cause (Hill et al. 2019). Nevertheless, as described by *New York Times* columnist Thomas B. Edsall (2017):

> Trump performed best in states and communities that were heavily white, but which had experienced relatively small increases in minority populations notably from immigrants. While small in absolute numbers, the rate of growth represented by these increases was often exceptionally high: For example, if the nonwhite share of the population grew from 2 to 6 percent, the rate of growth was 200 percent.

In addition to actually tallied demographic change, such support for Trump arose in areas where small but rapid diversification was not really substantial, but was perceived to be significant or described as dramatic and problematic by political elites. "I think it's more the unknown" admitted a Republican activist from Iowa concerning the reasons why her neighbours are uncomfortable with the prospect of increased diversity; "It's more a perceived problem than an actual problem" (in Keating and Karklis 2016). Addressing and boosting a mix of widespread racial resentments (mainly White worries about socio-economic competition with minorities) and anxieties surrounding the uncertainties of diversification, Trump's rhetoric and mode of framing proved successful "by reinforcing the boundaries drawn toward socially stigmatized groups" (Lamont et al. 2017: S173). The strategy found great appeal among large swathes of the American White working class (see Gest 2016).

Discomfort is not the only sentiment sometimes stimulated by small but rapid diversification. Again, as described earlier, feelings of in-group threat may lead to outright hostility toward out-groups. In this way, Kaufmann describes how "Rapid ethnic change, especially in places with limited experience of prior diversity, tends to be associated with radicalised White opinion and elevated far-right voting" (2014: 272). In the UK, Kaufmann shows that support for the far right British National Party (BNP) is strongest in electoral wards that were mainly populated by White British in 2001, but that experienced a fast increase in ethnic minority share (although still rather small relative to other parts of London) during the 2000s. In the Netherlands, Michael Savelkoul and colleagues (2017) similarly found that in areas with recent increases in ethnic minorities, there is a greater likelihood of voting for a popular, right-wing party. Once more, however, this might be largely a matter of certain perceptions of change, factual or not, relative to perceptions of one's own group. As H. Robert Outten and his colleagues (2012: 15) point out, "existing research has demonstrated that both actual increases in the relative size of the non-White population and Whites' perceptions of relative group size are related to appraisals of threat." In either case – that is, based on actual or imaginatively accentuated ethnoracial change – racist and right-wing politicians often capitalize on such perceptions to foment resentment, exacerbate antagonism, and generate votes.

Extending a point made earlier, diversification processes aren't stand-alone trends agitating many people. In a telling illustration, *The Economist* (2017) magazine conducted a study of what they called "migrantland." This refers to a broad collection of smaller towns in England that had experienced the largest and most rapid increases in new immigrant populations. "Migrantland" was exemplified in places like Boston on the east coast of Lincolnshire, where between 2005 and 2015 the immigrant population rose from around 1,000 to 16,000 or from 1 in 50 of the town's residents to 1 in 4. Across "migrantland," the study confirmed the link between places with significant increases in immigrants and the likelihood to vote Leave in the Brexit referendum. However, the *Economist* analysis also shows that across the same time span, these places had simultaneously suffered from a fall in wages (some due to competition with immigrants), a decline in manufacturing, the disappearance of public-sector jobs, and a sizable reduction of public services. Among residents of "migrantland," resentments of these trends – stoked and steered by targeted, xenophobic Brexit campaigns – focused on foreigners rather than on dire underlying conditions, the recent politics of austerity, or broader trends of regional socio-economic deprivation (also see Sobolewska and Ford 2020).

A final kind of negative response to diversification to which, I believe, not near enough attention is paid in broader literature (especially concerning the populist new right), concerns *linguistic anxieties*. In Social Psychology and Sociolinguistics, it is well established that many people, when hearing non-understood languages, or even being exposed to heavily accented or "broken" versions of their own language, react with adverse emotional responses. These include senses of awkwardness, impatience, frustration, irritation, and stress (see Cargile et al. 1994; Spencer-Rodgers and McGovern 2002; Blommaert et al. 2012). Many people find encounters with others who have heavy accents and/or limited linguistic competence in a majority language to be cognitively confusing, emotionally taxing, and generally unpleasant. They consider those people with limited linguistic competence to be untrustworthy, abnormal, and ignorant. Such reactions contribute to practices of marginalization, discrimination, exclusion, and stigmatization of linguistic (and again, often racialized) others.

Research has shown how linguistic phenomena are hierarchized in multilingual contexts. This includes not just a hierarchy of languages (with English, French, and German often given highest prestige over others, e.g., Spanish in the USA, Turkish in Germany, Urdu in Britain, or Arabic in France). There is also, contextually, a hierarchy of linguistic competences, repertoires, and registers, with what are perceived to be limited linguistic capacities generally castigated (Bresnahan et al. 2002; Rannut 2010; Lippi-Green 2011). Moreover, research on linguistic hierarchies is relevant to work in the field of linguistic discrimination, "linguaphobia," and linguistic prejudice. Again, this relates to individuals' uses of particular languages, levels of competence, and accents – especially if coming from a language origin lower on a presumed hierarchy. Work on deafness and sign-language conveys similar modes of linguistic discrimination (see Kusters et al. 2017).

Often, hostility towards growing linguistic superdiversity is expressed in very standardized or formulaic, if not politically received, statements (Musolff 2019). Such argumentation strategies or "topoi" castigating linguistic difference are regularly reproduced in right-leaning media (Wright and Brookes 2019). Examples of linguaphobia abound in the UK, where, once more, UKIP leader Nigel Farage has fuelled xenophobic sentiments by claiming that "in many parts of England you don't hear English spoken anymore." Following the Brexit furor and its heightened xenophobia in the Summer of 2016, this coincided with increased reports of people being harassed or attacked on public transport, in shops, or on the streets of British towns, for "not speaking English" (Cain 2018). In fact, at this time a man in Essex was "killed for speaking Polish" (Smith 2016). For many people, diversification means not just ethnic and racial change but an evolving linguistic chaos, communicative discomfort, and the erosion of national linguistic identity.

Given such widespread perspectives on increasing linguistic diversification and threat, Mary-Louise Pratt (2003) argued that myths and misconceptions about monolingualism and multilingualism have to be countered in order to build and sustain "a new public idea about language." In her view, a public with a developed understanding about language and actual, dynamic and crossover linguistic practices would recognize that a growing number of "linguistic others" are not potential enemies nor lesser members of society. People's views of language (and, for instance, its relation to national identity) can change. In the wake of increasing linguistic diversification, Fiona Copland and Joanna McPake (2021) draw on

Pratt to advocate such a new public idea of language (in their case, particularly in post-Brexit Britain). They see the need for a public programme providing information to counter stereotypes, questioning monolingual-centrism, and calling for widely acknowledging the reality and value of multilingualism in society. So, too, might the public understanding of diversity and diversification be subject of public programmes to counter negative responses. Such programmes might also draw on other modes of responses, outlined below, that are not negative.

Other responses

Representing a kind of counterbalance to theories of threat arising from diversification, a key body of work is broadly referred to as *contact theory*. This underlines the distinction between mere exposure to (or imagination of) diversity and diversification and actual instances and effects of social communication with conceived out-group members. Mere exposure to diversity has been defined as "being around and casually observing people of different ethnic backgrounds," whereas contact generally refers to "forms of social interaction, such as talking to people of a different ethnic background" (Dinesen and Sønderskov 2015: 553). Contact, moreover, is often discussed as something rather fleeting, entailing brief encounters or weak social ties, as distinct from intimate friendships and sustained social networks.

Based on the work of Gordon Allport (1954), contact theory posits that personal contact with out-group members can reduce prejudice towards that out-group. It is important to note that Allport's theory relies on certain conditions, including: an equivalent status of groups within the contact situation; common goals shared by those in contact; a sense of cooperation or at least lack of competition on the situation; and general support of wider authorities. Allport also acknowledged the continued role of inequalities in preventing positive outcomes of contact. There is a massive literature on contact theory, including copious social psychological studies variously testing its efficacy; there is also a substantial literature calling into question the benefits of contact theory (see review in Vertovec 2021). Overall, however, there is a considerable evidence clearly demonstrating that under suitable conditions, contact indeed "works" to reduce prejudice and improve interaction between people across various social boundaries (see especially Pettigrew and Tropp's [2006] meta-analysis of 515 contact studies). This includes insights into different types of contact (including indirect and imagined contact), when it functions, and how (e.g., Turner et al. 2007; Hewstone 2009, 2015; Christ et al. 2014). In assorted contexts and especially those undergoing diversification, contact between members of in-groups and out-groups can generate positive mutual responses in attitudes and social practices.

Threat-induced, hostile out-group attitudes versus contact-conditioned, positive out-group attitudes, however, do not simply pose themselves as exclusive, either-or responses to diversification (cf. Amin 2002). As the work of James Laurence importantly demonstrates, "both processes of threat and contact may be occurring with increasing diversity" (2014: 1328; also see Pettigrew et al. 2010). His analyses of the UK Citizenship Survey, for example, demonstrate that

> increasing community diversity does have a negative effect on inter-ethnic attitudes but only among individuals without inter-ethnic ties. Among those who do form ties, increasing diversity has no effect – that is, contact moderates the negative effect of community diversity. ...(A)s diversity in a community increases, both the threat and contact hypotheses are actually in operation".
>
> *Ibid.: 1332*

The effects of contact, of course, depend on actually having social interactions. In many social psychological studies, it is presumed that increasing diversity provides many more opportunities for positive contact – and that these will be taken up, leading to broad, positive effects. Research findings indicate that living in diverse residential areas is indeed associated with less prejudice via increased intergroup contact and reduced perceptions of out-group threat (Wagner et al. 2006; Pettigrew et al. 2010; Schlüter and Scheepers 2010; Schönwälder et al. 2016). Often drawing directly on contact theory, it is the strategy of many local government projects (especially under the banner of interculturalism) to create conditions for positive contact, in turn leading to better relations across neighbourhoods and cities (see, e.g., Zapata-Barrero 2017).

In the face of diversification, people may "hunker down" à la Putnam and avoid contact. Nevertheless, positive contacts do certainly happen and with no little frequency. However, these cannot be relied upon automatically. What's more, contact is of various kinds, and degrees of contact are often highly uneven among people in the same locality (Lichter et al. 2017). And, not surprisingly, some experiences of contact themselves might be regarded as negative rather than positive (Barlow et al. 2012; Graf et al. 2014; Hayward et al. 2017). This fact relates to what Ash Amin (2013: 5) calls a "darker aspect of everyday encounters of difference." Negative (possibly felt as undesirable, uncomfortable, aggressive or hostile) contact experiences can have a variety of implications, from more hunkering down and less willingness to interact, to enhanced prejudices and adversarial attitudes, to heightened, explicit forms of racist sentiment and behaviour. Negative contact may have political ramifications too, such as enhancing a fertile reception environment for racially divisive public discourse and a right-wing swing in voting. Relatedly, research has suggested that for many in newly diversified areas, negative experiences of contact with diverse immigrants directly led towards a greater tendency to vote Leave in the UK's Brexit referendum (Meleady et al. 2017).

As shown by numerous studies on diversity and cohesion, however, feelings of threat and the nature of everyday contacts are often directly related to socio-economic conditions and levels of disadvantage. The salience of differences is often augmented in contexts marked by scarce shared resources and a sense of group-based competition. Differential power relations among purported groups, often reflecting inequality, power imbalance, status stratification and geographic segregation, are clearly defining features of encounters and attitudes, too. Relative socio-economic status also has direct bearing on responses to the "halo effect" and those of small-but-rapid diversification. Research shows that if a diversifying area has poor socio-economic indicators, (White) people in an adjacent area that is either as deprived or better-off show more support for right-wing parties (Sümeghy 2021).

Economic segregation remains one of the most powerful social dividing lines: people tend to have little to do with others of differing socio-economic status (e.g., van Ham et al. 2018). Even in the same superdiverse neighbourhoods, many young white, relatively well-off gentrifiers – despite their "diversity-seeking" aspirations and pro-diversity attitudes – often have little actual contact with socio-economically as well as ethnoracially diverse others (Blokland and van Eijk 2010).

Within a shared socio-economic stratum, what happens through processes of diversification? A compelling case is made by Laurence (2014: 1344), whose analysis shows that

> In disadvantaged communities, increasing exposure to ethnic out-groups does foster negative out-group attitudes (i.e., evidence for the threat hypothesis). However, as diversity increases, individuals are more likely to possess inter-ethnic ties and individuals with inter-ethnic ties (in diverse, disadvantaged communities) appear to experience no negative effect.

However, again we mustn't limit ourselves to thinking that responses are either merely negative or positive – even, as Laurence suggests, knowing that negative experiences and attitudes can give way to positive ones. A variety of more nuanced modes of encounter, reactions, and outcomes of diversification need to be considered as well.

> [T]he nature of many if not most urban encounters – especially fleeting ones – is not either/or, positive or negative; they are often rather neutral, 'non-events'. This is largely due to city-dwellers' capacity for mutual indifference, described by urbanists since Simmel. Here, encounter traits are often unclear and certainly harder to describe, as they may be characterized by combinations of uncertainty or ambiguity, awkwardness or embarrassment, misunderstanding, anxiety, misgiving or mistrust – largely, perhaps, due to unclear social categories and unformed socio-spatial patterns. Such a grey range of the spectrum is especially likely under conditions of diversification, when people with new, rather undefined attributes arrive in urban settings.
>
> *Vertovec (2015: 256)*

Engaging in variable kinds of contact or even acting with fluctuating levels of indifference or "distanced co-existence" (Schönwälder et al. 2016: 231) may serve to shift attitudes towards out-groups. They do not necessarily break down notions and boundaries of social difference. In spite of contact and positive attitudes, people nevertheless tend to overlay a kind of categorical template of ethnoracial groups on their everyday community life and mental maps of their neighbourhoods. For instance, Talja Blokland (2003) describes how "realistic conflict" does certainly exist in diversifying urban neighbourhoods, often based on competition for explicit resources such as use of public spaces. People then frame "formulated threats in terms of 'we' and 'they' along ethnic lines and used these to organize difference and maintain their cohesion" (Ibid.: 19). This dynamic is well known and demonstrates threat theory. Yet Blokland also points to instances of "non-realistic conflict" in which there is no actual competition or threat in a neighbourhood, but still people often "apply prejudices to regain a comprehensive, understandable and manageable picture of the surrounding social milieu" (Ibid.: 20). That is, the received groupist, culturalist, and racialized understandings of diversity and diversification in a given context provide a kind of template that is regularly reproduced and reified, whether in a context of conflict or contact.

Even with such a template, social interactions and attitudes certainly needn't be undesirable or deleterious. We know that within changing, superdiverse contexts, a tremendous variety of social differences become the normal, uncontentious conditions of everyday life (Wessendorf 2014; Crul 2016; Schönwälder et al. 2016). This certainly does not mean that superdiversity signifies a "happy" social environment (as some critics have tried to paint the concept's purpose). To the contrary, studies that describe the normalcy of urban superdiversity also underline the ongoing presence of racism and other hostilities. The idea of normalcy stresses the point that superdiverse and diversifying contexts are the unquestioned and often uncontested backdrops of people's lives in which differences do not necessarily inhibit social life. In such contexts, both negative and positive interactions take place, with the latter tending to improve overall attitudes towards others, however defined. Sometimes, living within superdiversity means that the social boundaries of certain "groups" will be hardened; sometimes, the boundaries will be dissolved.

In keeping with my emphasis on the role of public representations of diversity and diversification, we should also be observant of the way that the issues are contextually framed. Thus in our Max Planck Institute's "Diversity and Contact" study mentioned earlier, we found that "In one neighbourhood, where its mixture is perceived as the core of its attractiveness, inhabitants state record frequencies of intergroup interaction and support for diversity. In another neighbourhood, narratives of decline go along with a distanced attitude to immigrants" (Schönwälder et al. 2016: 234).

Context-shaped attitudes can be projected towards prospects of future diversification, too. "How individuals respond to actual diversity," Maureen Craig and her colleagues (2018b: 211) write, "may shape how they respond to projected diversity. For instance, whites who already live in quite diverse environments may not feel particularly threatened by these projected demographic shifts and may actually push for more inclusive social policies." Such future orientations may combine with behavioural or value-based expectations, as well. In this way, Felix Danbold and Yuen Huo (2021) have found that members of dominant groups are surprisingly tolerant of both social change and intergroup difference in the present, so long as they expect some kind of future out-group assimilation, or cultural move in their own direction, in the future.

Throughout this chapter, the role of group categorization has been emphasized. Categorization is a natural human capacity – yet groupism, culturalism, and racialization are tendencies that may impact categorization dynamics to freeze social boundaries, stereotype purported group characteristics, and adversely affect social relations between members of ever-constructed and reproduced social categories. By way of trends acting to counter such outcomes, a major research finding on categorization and responses to diversification has been recently published in the prestigious *Proceedings of the National Academy of Sciences* by Xuechunzi Bai, Miguile Ramos, and Susan Fiske (2020). Reviewing longitudinal datasets of more than 12,000 people in 46 countries on six continents, they initially observed that in more homogeneous settings, people produce more differentiated stereotypes of out-groups. That is, the fewer the perceived groups in a setting, the clearer and more significant are views on their assumed differences. With increasing diversity, the characteristics of groups are actually perceived and represented to be more similar than different. These perceptions of commonality, in turn, serve to decrease prejudices and advance subjective feelings of well-being. In this way, Bai et al. found that

> Diversity, paradoxically, reduces perceived group differences… As actual diversity increases, with more exposure and experience, people may tone down previously exaggerated stereotypes, and start to realize latent and deep commonalities across groups, which eventually buffer against threat and yield more positive groups relations over time.
>
> *Ibid.: 12748*

They importantly conclude: "Perhaps human minds adapt to social diversity, by changing their symbolic maps of the array of social groups, perceiving overlaps, and preparing for positive future intergroup relations. People can adjust to diversity" (Ibid.: 12741). Still, the authors concede that such outcomes are not inevitable, not least since power dynamics remain at play and historically powerful groups are reluctant to lose their dominance. Hence, their conclusions are not blindly optimistic, but based on the recognition that superdiverse contexts remain challenged by segregation, inequality, group-based hostility, and conflict. Nevertheless, the findings of Bai, Ramos, and Fiske demonstrate that public understandings of diversity and diversification are malleable and seem to trend towards positive social categories, attitudes, and interactions.

Conclusion

Chapter 4 addressed a number of kinds of diversification that are currently underway in societies around the world. These include migration-related changes surrounding patterns of characteristics regarding global migrants and demographic shifts of ratios, especially by way of age and geography, regarding various population categories. This fifth chapter has included looks at some of the ways that people have responded to diversification (whether migrant-driven or demographic). Such responses have been founded on particular perceptions and attitudes. These perceptions and attitudes largely rest on public understandings of diversity and diversification, which themselves are based on highly contextualized processes of social categorization. Categories are conceptual, but their effects are actual, observable in patterns of interaction and measures of inequality.

Groupism, singular affiliation, culturalism, and racialization are tendencies in social categorization that often result in an intrinsic view of society as comprised of bounded and distinctly characterized groups, each competing with each other for limited resources. This coincides with an implicit assumption that only homogeneity can, should, or best provide social cohesion (akin to Durkheim's "mechanical solidarity"). Public understandings of diversity and diversification, and of social categories themselves, are not only shaped by personal experience and observation, but are also subject to influence by information, representations, and narratives present in various public spheres (especially mass media, political discourse, and social media). Several such public spheres include public misinformation and strategic political communication intended to prompt negative views and responses to diversification. Consequently, it is often perceptions of diversification, rather than actual numbers and features, which trigger negative responses. People who feel threatened by diversification, which may be for a variety of reasons, are more susceptible to misinformation and political manipulation.

There are many triggers and kinds of negative responses to processes of diversification. Most of these have to do with some sense of threat felt by members of a self-conceived in-group. Threat anxieties are based on assumptions that in-group members will be numerically overwhelmed in their locality. Often such feelings are based on some elusive notion of a tipping point between levels "good" and "too much" diversity. The idea of crossing such a threshold, albeit vague, sets off fears of a loss of group prestige, a competition for resources from jobs to public funds to the use of institutions, and the demise of commonality and sociocultural cohesion through a proliferation of cultural differences. Threat-based fears and anxieties are easily coupled with resentment, anger, and a feeling of victimhood – especially, again, if such feelings are generated, encouraged, manipulated, channelled, and reproduced through particular political discourses (many of which are xenophobic, racist, populist, and right-wing).

Misrepresentations notwithstanding, a broad set of literature engages Robert Putnam's (2007) study contending that diversification lowers levels of trust and social cohesion, both within and across groups. A strong qualification, if not contestation, of this theory arises from work showing that economic deprivation has a stronger or concomitant effect in diminishing trust and social cohesion. Further, a considerable amount of research demonstrates that, although negative responses indeed occur in diversifying settings, eventually these are replaced by more positive attitudes and behaviours following experiences of inter-group/category contact.

Responses to diversification are predominantly based on perceptions of diversification, themselves reflecting categorization, representation, and discourse. In Chapter 4, a variety of kinds and characteristics of diversification were described. Taken together, these comprise what we mean by superdiversity. Nevertheless, it is the singular dimension of "ethnoracial" that predominantly fixes the public understanding of diversification, shapes perceptions, and conditions attitudes. In keeping with one of the messages of this book, we must recognize that both conceptual (representations) and actual (social configurations and interactions) phenomena are becoming more multifaceted.

Bai et al. have importantly established that around the world, people can and do adapt to diversification by "changing their symbolic maps of the array of social groups, perceiving overlaps, and preparing for positive future intergroup relations" (Bai et al. 2020: 12741). In effect, public understandings of diversity and diversification can and do change. Is it possible to move beyond groupist, culturalist, racialized public understandings that focus almost solely on "ethnoracial" criteria, which are so easily manipulated by rightist political framing? Can social categories and representations of difference themselves be dismantled and reconstructed? How can people more widely come to discern, without threat, the increasingly complex features of diversity and diversification – indeed, superdiversity – emerging around us, and what might be the social effects of such conceptual change? All of these questions point to a recognition of new forms of social complexity.

References

Adamy, J. and P. Overberg 2016. "Places most unsettled by rapid demographic change are drawn to Donald Trump," *The Wall Street Journal* 1 November

Alba, R. and J. W. Duyvendak 2019. "What about the mainstream? Assimilation in super-diverse times," *Ethnic and Racial Studies* 42(1): 105–24 https://doi.org/10.1080/01419870.2017.1406127

Alesina, A., A. Miano and S. Stantcheva 2021. "Immigration and redistribution," unpublished paper, https://scholar.harvard.edu/files/stantcheva/files/alesina_miano_stantcheva_immigration.pdf

Allport, G. W. 1954. *The Nature of Prejudice*. Reading, MA: Addison-Wesley

Amann, M. 2019. "Kampf um Alles oder nix," *Der Spiegel* 6 September

Ambrosini, M., A. Van Hootegem, P. Bevelander, P. Daphi, E. Diels, T. Fouskas, A. Hellström, S. Hinger, A. Hondeghem, A. Kováts and A. Mazzola 2019. *The Refugee Reception Crisis: Polarized Opinions and Mobilizations*, Brussels: Éditions de l'Université de Bruxelles

Amin, A. 2002. "Ethnicity and the multicultural city: Living with diversity," *Environment and Planning A* 34: 959–80 https://doi.org/10.1068/a3537

Amin, A. 2013. "Land of strangers," *Identities* 20(1): 1–8 https://doi.org/10.1080/10702 89x.2012.732544

Anderson, B. 1983. *Imagined Communities: Reflections on the Origin and Spread of Nationalism*, London: Verso

Bai, X., M. R. Ramos and S. T. Fiske 2020. "As diversity increases, people paradoxically perceive social groups as more similar," *Proceedings of the National Academy of Sciences* 117(23): 12741–49 https://doi.org/10.1073/pnas.2000333117

Banulescu-Bogdan, N., H. Malka and S. Culbertson 2021. "How we talk about migration: The link between migration narratives, policy, and power," Washington, D. C.: Migration Policy Institute

Barlow, F. K., S. Paolini, A. Pederson, M. J. Hornsey, J. R. Radke, J. Harwood, M. Rubin and C. G. Sibley 2012. "The contact caveat: Negative contact predicts increased prejudice more than positive contact predicts reduced prejudice," *Personality and Social Psychology Bulletin* 38: 1629–43 https://doi.org/10.1177/0146167212457953

Baumann, G. 1996. *Contesting Culture: Discourses of Identity in Multi-Ethnic London*, Cambridge: Cambridge University Press

Baumann, G. 1999. *The Multicultural Riddle: Rethinking National, Ethnic and Religious Identities*, London: Routledge https://doi.org/10.4324/9780203906637

Bertossi, C. 2011. "National models of integration in Europe: A comparative and critical analysis," *American Behavioral Scientist* 55(12): 1561–80 https://doi.org/10.1177/0002764211409560

Bleich, E., I. Bloemraad and E. De Graauw 2015. "Migrants, minorities and the media: Information, representations and participation in the public sphere," *Journal of Ethnic and Migration Studies* 41(6): 857–73 https://doi.org/10.1080/1369183x.2014.1002197

Blokland, T. 2003. "Ethnic complexity: Routes to discriminatory repertoires in an inner-city neighbourhood," *Ethnic and Racial Studies* 26(1): 1–24 https://doi.org/10.1080/0141987002200025252

Blokland, T. and G. van Eijk 2010. "Do people who like diversity practice diversity in neighbourhood life? Neighbourhood use and the social networks of 'diversity-seekers' in a mixed neighbourhood in the Netherlands," *Journal of Ethnic and Migration Studies* 36(2): 313–32 https://doi.org/10.1080/13691830903387436

Blommaert, J., S. Leppänen, P. Pahta and T. Räisänen (eds.) 2012. *Dangerous Multilingualism: Northern Perspectives on Order, Purity and Normality*, New York: Palgrave Macmillan

Bodenhausen, G. V., S. K. Kang and D. Peery 2012. "Social categorization and the perception of social groups," in *The Sage Handbook of Social Cognition*, S. T. Fiske and C. N. Macrae (eds.), London: Sage, pp. 318–36 https://doi.org/10.4135/9781446247631.n16

Bos, L., S. Lecheler, M. Mewafi and R. Vliegenthart 2016. "It's the frame that matters: Immigrant integration and media framing effects in the Netherlands," *International Journal of Intercultural Relations* 55: 97–108 https://doi.org/10.1016/j.ijintrel.2016.10.002

Bowles, N. 2019. "'Replacement theory,' a racist, sexist doctrine, spreads in far-right circles," *New York Times* 8 May

Bowyer, B. 2008. "Local context and extreme right support in England: The British National Party in the 2002 and 2003 local elections," *Electoral Studies* 27(4): 611–20 https://doi.org/10.1016/j.electstud.2008.05.001

Bresnahan, M. J., R. Ohashi, R. Nebashi, W. Y. Liu and S. M. Shearman 2002. "Attitudinal and affective response toward accented English," *Language and Communication* 22: 171–85 https://doi.org/10.1016/s0271-5309(01)00025-8

Brewer, M. B. 1999. "The psychology of prejudice: Ingroup love and outgroup hate?" *Journal of Social Issues* 55(3):429–44 https://doi.org/10.1111/0022-4537.00126

Brewer, M. B. 2007. "The social psychology of intergroup relations: Social categorization, ingroup bias, and outgroup prejudice," in *Social Psychology*, A. W. Kruglanski and E. T. Higgins (eds.), New York: Guilford Press, pp. 695–715

Brubaker, R. 2002. "Ethnicity without groups," *Archives Européennes de Sociologie/European Journal of Sociology* 43(2): 163–89 https://doi.org/10.1017/s0003975602001066

Brubaker, R. 2009. "Ethnicity, race, and nationalism," *Annual Review of Sociology* 35: 21–42 https://doi.org/10.1146/annurev-soc-070308-115916

Byrne, B. 2006. "In search of a 'good mix': 'Race', class, gender and practices of mothering," *Sociology* 40(6): 1001–17 https://doi.org/10.1177/0038038506069841

Cain, S. 2018. "British 'linguaphobia' has deepened since Brexit vote, say experts," *The Guardian* 28 May

Cargile, A. C., H. Giles, E. B. Ryan and J. J. Bradac 1994. "Language attitudes as a social process: A conceptual model and new directions," *Language & Communication* 14(3): 211–36 https://doi.org/10.1016/0271-5309(94)90001-9

Christ, O., K. Schmid, S. Lolliot, H. Swart, D. Stolle, N. Tausch, A. Al Ramiah, U. Wagner, S. Vertovec and M. Hewstone 2014. "Contextual effect of positive intergroup contact on outgroup prejudice," *Proceedings of the National Academy of Sciences* 111(11): 3996–4000 https://doi.org/10.1073/pnas.1320901111

Clergé, O. 2019. *The New Noir: Race, Identity, and Diaspora in Black Suburbia*, Berkeley: University of California Press

Copland, F. and J. McPake 2021. "'Building a new public idea about language'? Multilingualism and language learning in post-Brexit UK," *Current Issues in Language Planning* https://doi.org/10.1080/14664208.2021.1939976

Coy, P. 2021. "What economists think about immigration doesn't really matter," *New York Times* 17 December

Craig, M. A., J. M. Rucker and J. A. Richeson 2018a. "The pitfalls and promise of increasing racial diversity: Threat, contact and race relations in the 21st century," *Current Directions in Psychological Science* 27(3): 188–93 https://doi.org/10.1177/0963721417727860

Craig, M. A., J. M. Rucker and J. A. Richeson 2018b. "Racial and political dynamics of an approaching 'majority-minority' United States," *Annals, American Academy of Political & Social Science* 677: 204–14 https://doi.org/10.1177/0002716218766269

Crul, M. 2016. "Super-diversity vs. assimilation: How complex diversity in majority–minority cities challenges the assumptions of assimilation," *Journal of Ethnic and Migration Studies* 42(1): 54–68 https://doi.org/10.1080/1369183x.2015.1061425

Danbold, F. 2018. Understanding Dominant Group Resistance to Social Change: The Role of Prototypicality Threat, PhD Thesis, University of California Los Angeles

Danbold, F. and Y. Huo 2021. "Welcome to be like us: Expectations of outgroup assimilation shape dominant group resistance to diversity," *Personality and Social Psychology Bulletin* https://doi.org/10.1177/01461672211004806

Davenport, L. 2020. "The fluidity of racial classifications," *Annual Review of Political Science* 23: 221–40 https://doi.org/10.1146/annurev-polisci-060418-042801

de Saint Laurent, C., V. Glaveanu and C. Chaudet 2020. "Malevolent creativity and social media: Creating anti-immigration communities on Twitter," *Creativity Research Journal* 32(1): 66–80 https://doi.org/10.1080/10400419.2020.1712164

Dinesen, P. T. and K. M. Sønderskov 2015. "Ethnic diversity and social trust: Evidence from the micro-context," *American Sociological Review* 80(3): 550–73 https://doi.org/10.1177/0003122445577989

Dinesen, P. T., M. Schaeffer and K. M. Søderskov 2020. "Ethnic diversity and social trust: A narrative and meta-analytic review," *Annual Review of Political Science* 23: 441–65 https://doi.org/10.1146/annurev-polisci-052918-020708

Dixon, J. and M. Levine (eds.) 2012. *Beyond Prejudice: Extending the Social Psychology of Conflict, Inequality and Social Change*, Cambridge: Cambridge University Press

Dovidio, J. F. and S. L. Gaertner 2010. "Intergroup bias," in *Handbook of Social Psychology*, S. T. Fiske et al. (eds.), Hoboken: Wiley, pp. 1084–121 https://doi.org/10.1002/9780470561119.socpsy002029

Dražanová, L. 2020. "What factors determine attitudes to immigration? A meta-analysis of political science research on immigration attitudes (2009–2019)," *Florence: EUI Working Paper RSCA 2020/85* https://doi.org/10.2139/ssrn.3739910

Duffy, B. and T. Frere-Smith 2014. *Perception and Reality: Public Attitudes to Immigration*, London: Ipsos MORI

Durkheim, É. 2014 (1893). *The Division of Labor in Society*, London: Simon and Schuster

Durrheim, K., M. Okuyan, M. S. Twali, E. García-Sánchez, A. Pereira, J. S. Portice, T. Gur, O. Wiener-Blotner and T. F. Keil 2018. "How racism discourse can mobilize right-wing populism: The construction of identity and alliance in reactions to UKIP's Brexit 'Breaking Point' campaign," *Journal of Community & Applied Social Psychology* 28: 385–405 https://doi.org/10.1002/casp.2347

The Economist 2017. "A portrait of Migrantland," The Economist 15 April

Edsall, T. B. 2017. "White-on-White voting," *New York Times* 16 November

Edsall, T. B. 2021. "White riot," *New York Times* 14 January

Ekman, M. 2019. "Anti-immigration and racist discourse in social media," *European Journal of Communication* 34(6): 606–18 https://doi.org/10.1177/0267323119886151

Evans, J. and G. Ivaldi 2020. "Contextual effects of immigrant presence on populist radical right support: Testing the "halo effect" on Front National voting in France," *Comparative Political Studies* 54(5): 823–54 https://doi.org/10.1177/0010414020957677

Faulkner, S., H. Guy and F. Vis 2021. "Right-wing populism, visual disinformation, and Brexit: From the UKIP 'Breaking Point' poster to the aftermath of the London Westminster bridge attack," in *The Routledge Companion to Media Disinformation and Populism*, H. Tumber and S. Waisbord (eds.), London: Routledge, pp. 198–208 https://doi.org/10.4324/9781003004431-22

Favell, A. 2022. *The Integration Nation: Immigration and Colonial Power in Liberal Democracies*, Cambridge: Polity

Finseraas, H., Ø. S. Skorge and M. Strøm 2018. "Does education affect immigration attitudes? Evidence from an education reform," *Electoral Studies* 55: 131–5 https://doi.org/10.1016/j.electstud.2018.06.009

Foroutan, N. 2019. *Die postmigrantische Gesellschaft: Ein Versprechen der pluralen Demokratie*, Bielefeld: Transcript https://doi.org/10.1515/9783839442630

Gans, H. J. 2017. "Racialization and racialization research," *Ethnic and Racial Studies* 40(3): 341–52 https://doi.org/10.1080/01419870.2017.1238497

Gest, J. 2016. *The New Minority: While Working Class Politics in an Age of Immigration and Inequality*, Oxford: Oxford University Press

Gest, J., T. Reny and J. Mayer 2018. "Roots of the radical right: Nostalgic deprivation in the United States and Britain," *Comparative Political Studies* 51(1): 1694–719 https://doi.org/10.1177/0010414017720705

Gonzalez-Sobrino, B. 2016. "The threat of the 'Other': Ethnic competition and racial interest," *Sociology Compass* 10(7): 592–602 https://doi.org/10.1111/soc4.12382

Goodhart, D. 2004. "Too diverse?" *Prospect* 95: 30–7

Graf, S., S. Paolini and M. Rubin 2014. "Negative intergroup contact is more influential, but positive intergroup contact is more common: Assessing contact prominence and contact prevalence in five Central European countries," *European Journal of Social Psychology* 44: 536–47 https://doi.org/10.1002/ejsp.2052

Hainmueller, J. and M. J. Hiscox 2007. "Educated preferences: Explaining attitudes toward immigration in Europe," *International Organization* 61(2): 399–442 https://doi.org/10.1017/s0020818307070142

Hamilton, D. L. and G. D. Bishop 1976. "Attitudinal and behavioral effects of initial integration of White suburban neighborhoods," *Journal of Social Issues* 32(2): 47–67 https://doi.org/10.1111/j.1540-4560.1976.tb02494.x

Haynes, C., J. L. Merolla and S. K. Ramakrishnan 2016. *Framing Immigrants: News Coverage, Public Opinion, and Policy*, New York: Russell Sage Foundation

Hayward, L. E., L. R. Tropp, M. J. Hornsey and K. Barlow 2017. "Towards a comprehensive understanding of intergroup contact: Descriptions and mediators of positive and negative contact among majority and minority groups," *Personality and Social Psychology Bulletin* 43: 347–64 https://doi.org/10.1177/0146167216685291

Helbling, M. 2014. "Framing immigration in Western Europe," *Journal of Ethnic and Migration Studies* 40(1): 21–41 https://doi.org/10.1080/1369183x.2013.830888

Hewstone, M. 2009. "Living apart, living together? The role of intergroup contact in social integration," *Proceedings of the British Academy* 162: 243–300 https://doi.org/10.5871/bacad/9780197264584.003.0009

Hewstone, M. 2015. "Consequences of diversity for social cohesion and prejudice: The missing dimension of intergroup contact," *Journal of Social Issues* 71(2): 417–38 https://doi.org/10.1111/josi.12120

Hill, S., D. J. Hopkins and G. A. Huber 2019. "Local demographic changes and US presidential voting, 2012 to 2016," *Proceedings of the National Academy of Sciences* 116(50): 25023–28 https://doi.org/10.1073/pnas.1909202116

Ho, E. L. and L. Kathiravelu 2021. "More than race: A comparative analysis of 'new' Indian and Chinese migration in Singapore, *Ethnic and Racial Studies* https://doi.org/10.1080/01419870.2021.1924391

Hochman, A. 2019. "Racialization: A defense of the concept," *Ethnic and Racial Studies* 42(8): 1245–62 https://doi.org/10.1080/01419870.2018.1527937

Hochschild, A. R. 2018. *Strangers in Their Own Land: Anger and Mourning on the American Right*, New York: The New Press.

Hopkins, D. J. 2007. "Threatening changes: Explaining where and when immigrants provoke local opposition," Paper presented at the annual meeting of the American Political Science Association

Hopkins, D. J. 2009. "The diversity discount: When increasing ethnic and racial diversity prevents tax increases," *The Journal of Politics* 71(1): 160–77 https://doi.org/10.1017/s0022381608090105

Hopkins, D. J. 2011. "The limited local impacts of ethnic and racial diversity," *American Politics Research* 39(2): 344–79 https://doi.org/10.1177/1532673x10370734

Hopkins, D. J., J. Sides and J. Citrin 2018. "The muted consequences of correct information about immigration," *The Journal of Politics* 81(1): 315–20 https://doi.org/10.1086/699914

Jenkins, R. 2004. *Social Identity*, London: Routledge, 2nd edn. https://doi.org/10.4324/9780203463352

Jensen, O. 2017. "Superdiversity in the post-industrial city: A comparative analysis of backlash narratives in six European neighbourhoods," *Policy & Politics* 45(4): 643–60 https://doi.org/10.1332/030557317x15046028381119

Karimi, A. and R. Wilkes 2021. "A methodological analysis of national models of integration: Time to think without the models?" *Journal of Ethnic and Migration Studies* https://doi.org/10.1080/1369183X.2021.1990748

Kaufmann, E. 2014. "'It's the demography, stupid': Ethnic change and opposition to immigration," *The Political Quarterly* 85(3): 267–76 https://doi.org/10.1111/1467-923x.12090

Kaufmann, E. 2018. *Whiteshift: Populism, Immigration and the Future of White Majorities,* London: Allen Lane

Keating, D. and L. Karklis 2016. "The increasingly diverse United States of America," *New York Times* 25 November

Kusters, A., D. O'Brien and M. De Meulder 2017. "Innovations in deaf studies: Critically mapping the field," in *Innovations in Deaf Studies,* A. Kusters, M. De Meulder and D. O'Brien (eds.), New York: Oxford University Press, pp. 7–52

Kustov, A., D. Laaker and C. Reller 2021. "The stability of immigration attitudes: Evidence and implications," *The Journal of Politics* 83(4): 1478–94 https://doi.org/10.1086/715061

Lamont, M., S. Beljean and M. Clair 2014. "What is missing? Cultural processes and causal pathways to inequality," *Socio-Economic Review* 12 (3): 573–608 https://doi.org/10.1093/ser/mwu011

Lamont, M., B. Y. Park and E. Ayala-Hurtado 2017. "Trump's electoral speeches and his appeal to the American white working class," *British Journal of Sociology* 68: S153–S180 https://doi.org/10.1111/1468-4446.12315

Lancee, B. and O. Sarrasin 2015. "Educated preferences or selection effects? A longitudinal analysis of the impact of educational attainment on attitudes towards immigrants," *European Sociological Review* 31(4): 490–501 https://doi.org/10.1093/esr/jcv008

Laurence, J. 2011. "The effect of ethnic diversity and community disadvantage on social cohesion: A multi-level analysis of social capital and interethnic relations in UK communities," *European Sociological Review* 27(1): 70–89 https://doi.org/10.1093/esr/jcp057

Laurence, J. 2014. "Reconciling the contact and threat hypotheses: Does ethnic diversity strengthen or weaken community inter-ethnic relations?" *Ethnic and Racial Studies* 37(8): 1328–49 https://doi.org/10.1080/01419870.2013.788727

Levine, R. A. and D. T. Campbell 1972. *Ethnocentrism: Theories of Conflict, Ethnic Attitudes, and Group Behavior,* New York: John Wiley & Sons

Lewis, A. E. 2003. "Everyday race-making: Navigating racial boundaries in schools," *American Behavioral Scientist* 47(3): 283–305 https://doi.org/10.1177/0002764203256188

Lichter, D. T., D. Parisi and M. C. Taquino 2017. "Together but apart: Do US Whites live in racially diverse cities and neighborhoods?" *Population and Development Review* 43: 229–55 https://doi.org/10.1111/padr.12068

Lippi-Green, R. 2011. *English with an Accent: Language, Ideology, and Discrimination in the United States,* London: Routledge https://doi.org/10.4324/9780203348802

Lofland, L. H. 1998. *The Public Realm: Exploring the City's Quintessential Social Territory,* New York: de Gruyter https://doi.org/10.4324/9781315134352

Macrae, C. N. and G. V. Bodenhausen 2001. "Social cognition: Categorical person perception," *British Journal of Psychology* 92(1): 239–55 https://doi.org/10.1348/000712601162059

Major, B., A. Blodorn and G. M. Blascovich 2016. "The threat of increasing diversity: Why many White Americans support Trump in the 2016 presidential election," *Group Processes & Intergroup Relations* 21(6): 931–40 https://doi.org/10.1177/1368430216677304

Matthes, J. and D. Schmuck 2017. "The effects of anti-immigrant right-wing populist ads on implicit and explicit attitudes: A moderated mediation model," *Communication Research* 44(4): 556–81 https://doi.org/10.1177/0093650215577859

Meissner, F. and T. Heil 2020. "Deromanticising integration: On the importance of convivial disintegration," *Migration Studies* https://doi.org/10.1093/migration/mnz056

Meleady, R., C. Seger and M. Vermue 2017. "Examining the role of positive and negative intergroup contact and anti-immigrant prejudice in Brexit," *British Journal of Social Psychology* 56(4): 799–808 https://doi.org/10.1111/bjso.12203

Miles, R. 1989. *Racism*, London: Routledge https://doi.org/10.4324/9780203633663

Miller, J. A. and T. H. Grubesic 2021. "A spatial exploration of the halo effect in the 2016 US presidential election," *Annals of the American Association of Geographers* 111(4): 1094–109 https://doi.org/10.1080/24694452.2020.1785271

Morning, A. 2015. "Ethnic classification in global perspective: A cross-national survey of the 2000 census round," in *Social Statistics and Ethnic Diversity*, P. Simon et al. (eds.), Cham: Springer, pp. 17–37 https://doi.org/10.1007/978-3-319-20095-8_2

Murji, K. and J. Solomos (eds.) 2005. *Racialization: Studies in Theory and Practice*, Oxford: Oxford University Press

Musolff, A. 2019. "Hostility towards immigrants' languages in Britain: A backlash against 'super-diversity'?" *Journal of Multilingual and Multicultural Development* 40(3): 257–66 https://doi.org/10.1080/01434632.2018.1520859

Nortio, E., M. Niska, T. A. Renvik and I. Jasinskaja-Lahti 2021. "'The nightmare of multiculturalism': Interpreting and deploying anti-immigration rhetoric in social media," *New Media & Society* 23(3): 438–56 https://doi.org/10.1177/1461444819899624

Oliver, E. J. and J. S. Wong 2003. "Racial context and inter-group prejudice in a multi-ethnic setting," *American Journal of Political Science* 47(4): 67–82 https://doi.org/10.1111/1540-5907.00040

Olzak, S. 1992. *The Dynamics of Ethnic Competition and Conflict*, Stanford: Stanford University Press

Omi, M. and H. Winant 1986. *Racial Formation in the United States: From the 1960s to the 1990s*, New York: Routledge

Outten, H. R., T. Lee, R. Costa-Lopes, M. T. Schmitt and J. Vala 2018. "Majority group members' negative reactions to future demographic shifts depend on the perceived legitimacy of their status: Findings from the United States and Portugal," *Frontiers in Psychology* 9, Article 79 https://doi.org/10.3389/fpsyg.2018.00079

Outten, H. R., M. T. Schmitt, D. A. Miller and A. L. Garcia 2012. "Feeling threatened about the future: Whites' emotional reactions to anticipated ethnic demographic changes," *Personality and Social Psychology Bulletin* 38(1): 14–25 https://doi.org/10.1177/0146167211418531

Pape, R. A. 2021. "What an analysis of 377 Americans arrested or charged in the Capitol insurrection tells us," *The Washington Post* 6 April

Pettigrew, T. F. and L. R. Tropp 2006. "A meta-analytic test of intergroup contact theory," *Journal of Personality and Social Psychology* 90(5): 751–83 https://doi.org/10.1037/0022-3514.90.5.751

Pettigrew, T. F., U. Wagner and O. Christ 2010. "Population ratios and prejudice: Modelling both contact and threat effects," *Journal of Ethnic and Migration Studies* 36: 635–50 https://doi.org/10.1080/1369183090351603

Pew Research Center 2016. "Europeans fear wave of refugees will mean more terrorism, fewer jobs," www.pewresearch.org

Pew Research Center 2020. "Attitudes toward diversity in 11 emerging economies," www.pewresearch.org

Pew Research Center 2021. "Diversity and division in advanced economies," www.
pewresearch.org

Portes, A. and E. Vickstrom 2011. "Diversity, social capital, and cohesion," *Annual Review of Sociology* 37: 461–79 https://doi.org/10.1146/annurev-soc-081309-150022

Pottie-Sherman, Y. and R. Wilkes 2017. "Does size really matter? On the relationship between immigrant group size and anti-immigrant prejudice," *International Migration Review* 51(1): 218–50 https://doi.org/10.1111/imre.12191

Prati, F., R. J. Crisp and M. Rubini 2021. "40 years of multiple social categorization: A tool for social inclusivity," *European Review of Social Psychology* 32(1): 47–87 https://doi.org/10.1080/10463283.2020.1830612

Pratt, M.-L. 2003. "Building a new public idea about language," *Profession* 2003: 110–19 https://doi.org/10.1632/074069503x85472

Putnam, R. 2007. "E pluribus unum: Diversity and community in the twenty-first century – the 2006 Johan Skytte Prize," *Scandinavian Political Studies* 30(2): 137–74 https://doi.org/10.1111/j.1467-9477.2007.00176.x

Quillian, L. 1995. "Prejudice as a response to perceived group threat: Population composition and anti-immigrant and racial prejudice in Europe," *American Sociological Review* 60: 586–611 https://doi.org/10.2307/2096296

Ramos, M. R., M. R. Bennett, D. S. Massey and M. Hewstone 2019. "Humans adapt to social diversity over time," *Proceedings of the National Academy of Sciences* 116(25): 12244–49 https://doi.org/10.1073/pnas.1818884116

Rannut, M. 2010. *Linguistic Human Rights: Overcoming Linguistic Discrimination*, Berlin: Walter de Gruyter

Rattansi, A. 2020. *Racism: A Very Short Introduction*, Oxford: Oxford University Press, 2nd edn. https://doi.org/10.1093/actrade/9780198834793.001.0001

Reich, R. 2021. "Texas freeze shows a chilling truth – how the rich use climate change to divide us," *The Guardian* 21 February

Riek, B. M., E. W. Mania and S. L. Gaertner 2006. "Intergroup threat and outgroup attitudes: A meta-analytic review," *Personality and Social Psychology Review* 10(4): 336–53 https://doi.org/10.1207/s15327957pspr1004_4a

Rustenbach, E. 2010. "Sources of negative attitudes toward immigrants in Europe: A multi-level analysis," *International Migration Review* 44(1): 53–77 https://doi.org/10.1111/j.1747-7379.2009.00798.x

Rydgren, J. and P. Ruth 2013. "Contextual explanations of radical right-wing support in Sweden: Socio-economic marginalization, group threat, and the halo effect," *Ethnic and Racial Studies* 36(4): 711–28 https://doi.org/10.1080/01419870.2011.623786

Sachsen (Saxony) 2016. *Sachsen-Monitor 2016*, www.staatsregierung.sachsen.de

Saperstein, A., A. M. Penner and R. Light 2013. "Racial formation in perspective: Connecting individuals, institutions, and power relations," *Annual Review of Sociology* 39: 359–78 https://doi.org/10.1146/annurev-soc-071312-145639

Savelkoul, M., J. Laméris and J. Tolsma 2017. "Neighbourhood ethnic composition and voting for the radical right in The Netherlands: The role of perceived neighbourhood threat and interethnic neighbourhood contact," *European Sociological Review* 33(2): 209–24 https://doi.org/10.1093/esr/jcw055

Schachter, A., R. D. Flores and N. Maghbouleh 2021. "Ancestry, color, or culture? How Whites racially classify others in the U.S.," *American Journal of Sociology* 126(5): 1220–63 https://doi.org/10.1086/714215

Schlüter, E. and P. Scheepers 2010. "The relationship between out-group size and anti-outgroup attitudes: A theoretical synthesis and empirical test of group threat and intergroup contact theory," *Social Science Research* 39: 285–95 https://doi.org/10.1016/j.ssresearch.2009.07.006

Schönwälder, S., S. Petermann, J. Hüttermann, S. Vertovec, M. Hewstone, D. Stolle, K. Schmid and T. Schmitt 2016. *Diversity and Contact: Immigration and Social Interaction in German Cities*, Basingstoke: Palgrave Macmillan https://doi.org/10.1057/978-1-137-58603-2

Semyonov, M., R. Rajman, A. Y. Tov and P. Schmidt 2004. "Population size, perceived threat and exclusion: A multiple indicators analysis of attitudes toward foreigners in Germany," *Social Science Research* 33(4): 681–701 https://doi.org/10.1016/j.ssresearch.2003.11.003

Sen, A. 2006. *Identity and Violence: The Illusion of Destiny*, London: Allen Lane

Sherman, D. K., M. A. Hogg and A. T. Maitner 2009. "Perceived polarization: Reconciling ingroup and intergroup perceptions under uncertainty," *Group Processes & Intergroup Relations* 12(1): 95–109 https://doi.org/10.1177/1368430208098779

Sides, J. and J. Citrin 2007. "European opinion about immigration: The role of identities, interests and information," *British Journal of Political Science* 37(3): 477–504 https://doi.org/10.1017/s0007123407000257

Simon, P., V. Piché and A. A. Gagnon 2015. "The making of racial and ethnic categories: Official statistics reconsidered," in *Social Statistics and Ethnic Diversity*, P. Simon et al. (eds.), Cham: Springer, pp. 1–14 https://doi.org/10.1007/978-3-319-20095-8_1

Smith, L. 2016. "'He was killed for speaking Polish': Brother's claim as man murdered in UK street in suspected race-hate attack," *The Mirror* 31 August

Sobolewska, M. and R. Ford 2020. *Brexitland: Identity, Diversity and the Reshaping of British Politics*, Cambridge: Cambridge University Press https://doi.org/10.1017/9781108562485

Spencer-Rodgers, J. and T. McGovern 2002. "Attitudes toward the culturally different: The role of intercultural communication barriers, affective responses, consensual stereotypes, and perceived threat," *International Journal of Intercultural Relations* 26: 609–31 https://doi.org/10.1016/s0147-1767(02)00038-x

Stichnoth, H. and K. Van der Straeten 2013. "Ethnic diversity, public spending, and individual support of the welfare state: A review of the empirical literature," *Journal of Economic Surveys* 27(2): 364–89 https://doi.org/10.1111/j.1467-6419.2011.00711.x

Stolcke, V. 1995. "Talking culture: New boundaries, new rhetorics of exclusion in Europe," *Current Anthropology* 36(1): 1–24 https://doi.org/10.1086/204339

Strabac, Z. 2011. "It is the eyes and not the size that matter: The real and the perceived size of immigrant populations and anti-immigrant prejudice in Western Europe," *European Societies*, 13(4): 559–82 https://doi.org/10.1080/14616696.2010.550631

Sturgis, P., I. Brunton-Smith, S. Read and N. Allum 2011. "Does ethnic diversity erode trust? Putnam's 'hunkering down' thesis reconsidered," *British Journal of Political Science* 41(1): 57–82 https://doi.org/10.1017/s0007123410000281

Sümeghy, D. 2021. "Halo effect of diversification and polarization, and the role of relative deprivation based on the 2018 Swedish parliamentary elections results," *Regional Statistics* 12(1) https://doi.org/10.15196/RS120106

Tajfel, H. and J. C. Turner 1979. "An integrative theory of intergroup conflict," in *The Social Psychology of Intergroup Relations*, W. G. Austin and S. Worchel (eds.), Monterey: Brooks/Cole Publishing Co, pp. 33–47

Thorbjørnsrud, K. 2015. "Framing irregular immigration in Western media," *American Behavioral Science* 59(7): 771–82 https://doi.org/10.1177/0002764215573255

Tilly, C. 2005. *Identities, Boundaries and Social Ties*, Boulder: Paradigm

Turner, R. N., R. J. Crisp and E. Lambert 2007. "Imagining intergroup contact can improve intergroup attitudes," *Group Processes & Intergroup Relations*, 10(4): 427–41 https://doi.org/10.1177/1368430207081533

van der Meer, T. and J. Tolsma 2014. "Ethnic diversity and its effects on social cohesion," *Annual Review of Sociology* 40: 459–78 https://doi.org/10.1146/annurev-soc-071913-043309

van Ham, M., T. Tammaru and J. J. Janssen 2018. "A multi-level model of vicious circles of socio-economic segregation," in *Divided Cities*, Paris: Organization for Economic Cooperation and Development (OECD), pp. 135–53 https://doi.org/10.1787/9789264300385-8-en

Van Hootegem, A. and B. Meuleman 2019. "Asylum seekers and immigrant threat: Is there a link? *The Conversation*, 15 October

Vertovec, S. 1996. "Multiculturalism, culturalism and public incorporation," *Ethnic and Racial Studies* 19(1): 49–69 https://doi.org/10.1080/01419870.1996.9993898

Vertovec, S. 2011. "The cultural politics of nation and migration," *Annual Review of Anthropology* 40: 241–56 https://doi.org/10.1146/annurev-anthro-081309-145837

Vertovec, S. 2015. "Conclusion," in *Diversities Old and New*, S. Vertovec (ed.), Basingstoke: Palgrave, pp. 247–58 https://doi.org/10.1057/9781137495488_14

Vertovec, S. 2020. "Considering the work of 'integration'," Max-Planck-Institute *Working Paper 20-04*, Göttingen

Vertovec, S. 2021. "The social organization of difference," *Ethnic and Racial Studies* 44(8): 1273–95 https://doi.org/10.1080/01419870.2021.1884733

Wacquant, L. 2022. "Resolving the trouble with 'race'," *New Left Review* 133/134: 67–88

Wagner, U., O. Christ, T. F. Pettigrew, J. Stellmacher and C. Wolf 2006. "Prejudice and minority proportion: Contact instead of threat effects," *Social Psychology Quarterly* 69: 380–90

Warner, M. 2002. "Publics and counterpublics," *Public Culture* 14(1): 49–90 https://doi.org/10.1177/019027250606900406

Wessendorf, S. 2014. *Commonplace Diversity: Social Relations in a Super-Diverse Context*. Basingstoke: Palgrave https://doi.org/10.1057/9781137033314

Wessendorf, S. 2020. "Ethnic minorities' reactions to newcomers in East London: Symbolic boundaries and convivial labor," *British Journal of Sociology* 71(2): 208–20 https://doi.org/10.1111/1468-4446.12729

Wimmer, A. 2008. "The making and unmaking of ethnic boundaries: A multilevel process theory," *American Journal of Sociology* 113(4): 970–1022 https://doi.org/10.1086/522803

Wimmer, A. and N. G. Schiller 2002. "Methodological nationalism and beyond: Nation–state building, migration and the social sciences," *Global Networks* 2(4): 301–34 https://doi.org/10.1111/1471-0374.00043

Wright, D. and G. Brookes 2019. "'This is England, speak English!': A corpus-assisted critical study of language ideologies in the right-leaning British press," *Critical Discourse Studies* 16(1): 56–83 https://doi.org/10.1080/17405904.2018.1511439

Zapata-Barrero, R. 2017. "Interculturalism in the post-multicultural debate: A defence," *Comparative Migration Studies* 5(1): 1–23 https://doi.org/10.1186/s40878-017-0057-z

6
SOCIAL COMPLEXITY

Ralph Grillo (2015: 2) has cogently contended that "super-diversity is a form of complexity." I wholly concur. The previous chapters have already invoked some ideas about complexity and how these relate to superdiversity. The original superdiversity article, reproduced in Chapter 2, notes that some of my initial thinking about the concept was inspired by ideas around cultural complexity. In Chapter 3, it was discerned that many academics' interests in superdiversity, spanning social science disciplines, have arisen through a widespread longing for new concepts, language, and approaches for researching and understanding contemporary forms of complexity and complex social transformations. Chapter 4 examined processes of diversification surrounding several social categories, arising especially through changing migration and demographic patterns. These have been described as an emergent processes of complexification affecting national and urban social configurations. And in Chapter 5, various responses to processes of diversification were discussed in light of shifting social perceptions, categorizations and attitudes that are especially prone to influence by political rhetoric, images, and discourses. The responses themselves both reflect a com-plexification of categories and an ever-more complex social and discursive field or set of publics. How do these all of these processes fit together? Why and how are such developments usefully described as "social complexity"?

The anthropology of social and cultural complexity

My exposition starts with reflections on my own discipline, Anthropology. With origins in the 19th century and expanding throughout much of the mid-20th century, the study of "complex societies" has represented an influential subfield of Anthropology (see for instance Eisenstadt 1961; Banton 1966; Kushner 1969). The topic concerns a historical, evolutionary view on the development of certain

DOI: 10.4324/9780203503577-6

types of society, with people described as "advancing" through stages such as bands, tribes, chiefdoms, and ultimately states. Common to most typologies and theories of complex societies are trait lists comprising integrated systems or sub-systems of social, economic, political, and religious components. Such lists often include assorted features of technology, architecture, occupational and craft specialization, irrigation and land use, surplus wealth, material culture, and warfare. The more traits that could be ticked off such a list, the more complex a society was deemed to be. Trait lists were used to compare societies, historically and in the present day, too. Some 50 years ago, for example, Robert Carneiro (1967) created a list of 205 different traits that he used purportedly to measure, compare, and rank the complexity of 100 societies. This kind of exercise has been much contested. Theorists have also debated how, or how much, features such as population size and spatial density affect the development of complex social systems. Overall, regardless of technological or material aspects, of most interest in this field of Anthropology have been patterns of social relationship that contribute to, or arise from, various kinds of economic, ecological, and cultural traits.

Thus at the heart of much anthropological thinking on "complex societies" have been matters of *social organization*, or regularities and structures of social relations, especially modes of social stratification and hierarchy entailing notions of status, rank, power, domination, and political arrangement (Barth 1972). Indeed it has been said that in this field, complexity is a general synonym for hierarchy (Graeber and Wengrow 2021: 515). That reading is perhaps too glib, not least since many scholars will contend that there is a lot more to it. For instance, not all social interactions are hierarchically stratified: there are forms of horizontal as well as vertical relations (consider occupations that are status equivalent; cf. Pool 2012). In any case, it is fair to say that across the anthropology of complex societies, the meaning of complexity has centred on the ways that societies, especially as they get larger and more role specialized, function socially and politically through differing kinds of social organization that entail the stratification of variously differentiated groups.

Research and theory on complex societies has largely gone out of fashion in contemporary Anthropology – perhaps because it inherently makes uncomfortable if not incorrect assumptions about purportedly simple(r) societies being less evolutionarily developed. It is especially uncomfortable because the depiction of such purportedly less advanced societies could be racialized. Particularly concerning the rise of large state systems, however, the study of "complex societies" is still in rather strong in Archeology (see for instance Smith 2011, 2021; Ross and Steadman 2017) where it is also substantially critiqued as well (see Yoffee 2005; Pauketat 2007; Graeber and Wengrow 2021).

Another kind of complexity – though never explicitly described as such – in the anthropological canon relates to what have been called "plural societies" (see, e.g., Benedict 1962; Smith 1965; Kuper and Smith 1969). Also centrally concerned with matters of social organization, studies in this now outdated field centrally focused on colonial and postcolonial societies comprised of population segments marked by their own respective social institutions (family forms, social networks, religion, language). This came to be associated with the study of ethnicity. Analysis of plural societies in this vein usually concerned issues of inter-ethnic resource competition and patterns of economic exchange, legal accommodation and differential rights, and modes of social and political incorporation.

The prominent Norwegian anthropologist Fredrik Barth was also interested in how people lived among a variety of seemingly discrete social and cultural spheres. While Barth had gained renown for his theorizing on varieties of social organization (see Eriksen 2015), especially his most famous contribution on the nature of ethnicity and ethnic boundaries (Barth 1969), his later writing explicitly considered the nature of social and cultural complexity (Barth 1989, 1993). In this work, he was less focused on social organization per se and more on the co-presence, confluence, and intermingling of meaning systems. His ethnographic example here was Bali, where Hindu, Muslim, Bala Aga (indigenous), modern Western, and sorcery-focused worldviews, social relations and cultural practices are to be found. In such contexts, Barth (1989: 130) wrote, "people participate in multiple, more or less discrepant, universes of discourse; they construct different, partial and simultaneous worlds in which they move; their cultural construction of reality springs not from one source and is not of one piece." This represented a shift from thinking about complexity solely in terms of technologies and social relations, to thinking about arrays of concepts and classifications. Barth conjectured that complex clusters, arrangements, and mixtures of meaning arise because meanings are fundamentally linked to each individual's discrete "constellation of experience" (Ibid.: 134). Importantly, he stressed that meanings are unevenly distributed in a population: actors are always socially positioned, and people construe their meanings of situations and events accordingly.

This is also the key message of Ulf Hannerz in his book *Cultural Complexity* (Hannerz 1992). Early on in this work, Hannerz recognizes that "The term 'complex' may in itself be about as intellectually attractive as the word 'messy'" (1992: 6). Nevertheless, he notes, "one of its virtues … is precisely its sober insistence that we should think twice before accepting any simple characterization of the cultures in question in terms of some single essence" (Ibid.). Echoing Max Weber and Clifford Geertz, Hannerz advocates an approach to the study of culture as: (1) a matter of ideas and modes of thought ("the entire array of concepts, propositions, values and the like which people within some social unit carry together, as well as their various ways of handling their ideas in characteristic modes of mental operation"; Ibid: 7), (2) forms through which meanings are externalized and made accessible (modes of public communication), and (3) their social distribution (how meanings are spread over a stratified population and imbue its social relationships). With Barth, Hannerz underlines the fact that an uneven distribution of meanings and other cultural elements within a population is related to the fact that actors are differentially positioned vis-à-vis each other. This latter perspective is elaborated throughout his book, in which Hannerz contemplates the contours and dynamics of what he calls the social organization of meaning.

> People, that is, manage meanings *from where they are* in the social structure. At any one time, the individual is surrounded by a flow of externally available, culturally shaped meaning which influences his ordering of experiences and intentions. Yet he is not merely a passive recipient of all sorts of available meaning, and he does not just contemplate it in the stillness of his mind. As soon as he has begun to form a conception of himself and the world, and of what is desirable and not desirable, he is actively involved in dealing practically, intellectually and emotionally with his particular situation. Thus, he will concern himself with meanings especially as they appear to relate to his own experiences and plans; to his involvements with other people, for one thing, and to his material needs and interest, for another. If need be, he may extend or modify the meanings available to him, activing improvisationally and innovatively "on the basis of" them rather than fully "in line with" them. His practical reason, that is, has a cultural foundation, but as he draws on extant meanings their forms may be made to vary and change.
>
> *Ibid.: 65, italics in original*

Hannerz refers to this social position-based process as the "perspectivation of meaning" which "implies less replication of uniformity, less extensive cultural sharing" (Ibid.: 66). Culture and society is thus subsequently seen as

> a network of perspectives, with a continuous production of overt cultural forms between them. In this manner, the perspectivation of meaning is a powerful engine in creating a diversity of culture within the complex society. Call the network a polyphony, as the perspectives are at the same time voices; term it a conversation, if it appears fairly low-key and consensual; refer to it all as a debate, if you wish to emphasize contestation; or describe it as a cacophony, if you find mostly disorder.
>
> *Ibid.*

While remaining based on features of social organization, in this perspective complexity is also seen to arise as a function of the production, innovation, distribution, expression, and reception of meanings within a socially differentiated population. Thomas Hylland Eriksen (2007) draws upon and extends Hannerz by similarly emphasizing the realm of meaning as a key feature of complexity, especially recognizing the ways identities and group belongings, criteria of inclusion and exclusion, and degrees of group incorporation can be constituted on considerably varying grounds or principles.

Key takeaways from this set of anthropological insights from the anthropology of cultural complexity represented by Barth, Hannerz, and Eriksen are that meaning and social organization not separate, but mutually constituted. However, meanings and perspectives are often a matter of social position, giving rise to uneven distributions of meaning that both condition and derive from social interactions.

Social science and complexity

Since before the turn of this century, the idea of complexity – as a particular set of approaches, concepts and language – has gained interest across many social sciences (see especially Byrne 1998; Thrift 1999; Urry 2003, 2005; Jörg 2011). Complexity represents both a scientific field and conceptual perspective, framework or mode of framing, rather than a unified body of theory (see Byrne and Callaghan 2013). Stemming largely from Physics, Mathematics, Biology, and other natural sciences, complexity science and its approach to complexity involve the investigation of systems of connection or assemblage, the arrangement of parts into and within some kind of whole. Further, a key premise is that systemic wholes, in turn, must be understood as more than the sum of their parts; the dynamic interaction and interdependence of their components create something that cannot be understood by analysing the components alone. Consequently, based on the fundamental idea that "more is different" (Philip Anderson, in Page 2015: 27), the idea holds that as the number of elements in a system increases or diversifies, so do the modes of interaction and interdependence – and, hence, the system's level of complexity. Another basic principle is that simple rules on a micro-level can produce complexity in a macro-system.

A number of social scientists have been attracted to complexity science, not least by way of a search for a language, approach, and possible methodology for achieving new understandings of social phenomena and processes. This is similar to the ways that, as we have seen in Chapter 3, social scientists have adopted superdiversity in a search for a language and perspective to describe their observations of social change. In this way, for example, sociologist David Byrne describes being attracted to complexity as an approach that provides "a new vocabulary and an overall view based on that vocabulary which could serve as a framework for understanding" (1998: 5). Some of the key vocabulary of complexity science includes: multiple causality, non-linearity, emergence, self-organization, tipping points and threshold phenomena, complex adaptive systems, feedback, instability, turbulence, chaos, and uncertainty.

As complexity was rapidly taken up as a key idea in numerous social science disciplines in the 1990s and 2000s, there appeared divergent takes or uses of its constituent concepts. Broadly, these have been grouped into what have been called "hard" and "soft" or "metaphorical" approaches to complexity (Cilliers and Preiser 2010). In some basic ways, these correlate to the difference between "the US style of social complexity which tends to see methods developed largely in physics and applied mathematics as automatically transferable to the social world (Santa Fe style) and a European tradition which has a much clearer relationship with philosophical arguments" (Byrne and Callaghan 2013: 9). Hard complexity in social science tends to entail methods such as computational social science, simulations, and agent-based modelling. These applications are applied to phenomena such as voting dynamics, traffic, riots, playgrounds, stock markets, and pandemics like COVID-19. Soft or metaphorical complexity is associated with more interpretive and conceptual work, including engagements with Philosophy (Cilliers 2007), postmodernism (Cilliers 2002), and assemblage theory (DeLanda 2019).

Bridging these varying takes and uses of complexity in the social sciences are common concerns and questions surrounding the nature of "complex systems [that] consist of situated, adaptive, diverse individuals whose interactions produce higher-order structures (self-organization) and functionalities (emergence)" (Page 2015: 22). How robust and durable are such systems, what patterns and structures form as components or agents change, and how do they become more complex over time? These concerns and questions also entail general complexity science interests in matters of equilibrium and randomness, the implications of interdependence, and the impacts of a diversity of components or agents (see Page 2010).

The concept of superdiversity is in line with many of these social scientific approaches to complexity (especially in the metaphorical sense). Increasing diversifications at various scales, especially arising from contemporary migration flows, add to conditions of complexity. This is, using some of the language of complexity science, due to: increasing numbers of actors (as migrant flows continue or rise), greater differentiation of their multiple characteristics (such as ethnicity, gender, age, legal status), and the growing interdependence of relationships between both the migrants' characteristics (leading to specific combinations of patterns of migration) and the characteristics of the new physical environments and social spaces in which they find themselves (the already diverse, usually urban contexts of immigration). Ensuing social dynamics and regularities of interaction arising from superdiversity can be described as emergent, self-organized, complex adaptive systems (including the mixed responses described in Chapter 5, often but not always shifting from threat and discrimination to contact and positive attitudes). Within such systems, the trajectories of social outcomes, however, are uncertain, unpredictable, and non-linear.

An additional social scientific take on complexity has been offered by the late Danilo Zolo, who described it as:

> the cognitive situation in which agents, whether they are individuals or social groups, find themselves. The relations which agents construct and project on their environment in the attempts at self-orientation – i.e. at arrangement, prediction, planning, manipulation – will be more or less complex according to circumstances. In the same way their actual connection with the environment will be more or less complex.
>
> *1992: 2–3*

That is, in addition to social dynamics and processes, Zolo adds a cognitive dimension to social scientific approaches to complexity. Drawing on Zolo, it must be recognized that people hold various mental constructs pertaining to the complexity of their environments and their relations to its components: this adds to the overall complexity of a social setting. As Scott Page (2015: 6) suggests, "Recall that in a complex system individuals are situated locally; they likely have distinct information and experiences. This diversity of situations begets diversity in how the agents interpret their worlds. Diversity therefore begets diversity." (Indeed, Page [2007] argues that such cognitive diversity is advantageous for better group problem-solving.) I see this perspective as akin to ideas about the confluence and complexity of meanings and social positions as described in the anthropology of Barth, Hannerz, and Eriksen.

Superdiversity is often considered to be about migrant populations and their changing, multidimensional but largely structural characteristics. To make more comprehensive the complexity-relevant qualities of superdiversity, we must also consider the multiple constellations of meaning that people have, negotiate, and reproduce *about* these changing, multidimensional characteristics. Among all people in such settings, their social positions inherently condition their individual sets of meaning.

Drawing on these literatures and vocabularies of complexity, the key point here is that social complexity should be considered as simultaneously encompassing the realms of social organization, meanings, and social relationships (see Vertovec 2021). Under conditions of superdiversity (considered as multiple causalities variously triggering increasing numbers, diversifications, and interdependencies), unpredictable non-linear processes of self-organization are set in train through which new patterns of social organization, meaning, and social relationship emerge.

Right now, we are living in a period of uncertainty as the interrelated complexities of configurations, representations, and encounters are in simultaneous flux. Conditions of contemporary superdiversity and social complexity entail not just an ongoing, if not increasing, set of diversifications (and variable responses to such processes), but also at the same time, the reworking and contestation of significant social categories and their meanings that imbue such configurations, representations, and encounters. We can observe this in: Black Lives Matter; trans activism and other claims for recognition, rights, and equality; ubiquitous attention to "diversity" – contributing to what is now a $8 billion "diversity industry" (Newkirk 2019) alongside a rise in publications and trainings on anti-racism; attention to Whiteness, White privilege, and White nationalism; "wokeness"; great strides in the representation of gays and lesbians alongside "don't say gay" politics; "cancel culture" and the "culture wars."

Along with the kinds of responses to diversification described in Chapter 5 and the shifting meanings of certain key categories described below, these are but a few prominent, public sphere manifestations of the changing significance of social categories and the shifting salience of "differences."

The salience of differences

Right now, multiple kinds of diversification and categorical reformulation are having transformative effects on societies, worldwide. Indeed in the 21st century, "The world is much more diverse on multiple dimensions and at many levels, typified by the salience of differences and their dynamic intersections" (Jones and Dovidio 2018: 45). The mutable and vacillating public salience of key categories of difference is a major component of contemporary social complexity, referring especially to the realm of meaning but with implications for social structures and interpersonal relations. A significant example is the escalating salience of race, in many countries across the globe, as a category (with respectively differential conceptualizations) recognized by way of its relation to social justice, public health, and inequality. This has been observed through: the prominence of notions of Blackness and a purported global raising of awareness of racial discrimination, especially in the wake of highly publicized police killings and the Black Lives Matter movement; notions of Whiteness, especially in terms of the White nationalist aspects of right-wing populism; and notions of Asianness, especially with respect to the explosion of anti-Asian prejudices attached to the COVID-19 pandemic. Aside from race, we have also seen noteworthy changes surrounding language to talk of disabled persons (Thomas 2015) and in the ways LGBTQ persons and relationships are represented on television (Albertson 2018).

The idea of social "difference" is, of course, based on the kinds of processes of social categorization discussed in the previous chapter. Identities or categories positively self-expressed as difference are often described as much by what they are *not* as by what they *are* (Woodward 1997). Those who invoke difference tend to do so by way of distinguishing, highlighting, mobilizing, and embellishing those traits and intersectionalities that make one different from some conventional, supposedly normative category (such as White, heterosexual, middle class, middle aged, male). Further, difference is understood to be the result of confluence of several social processes (West and Fenstermaker 1995) resulting in not just a matter of mere characteristics, but of inherent discrepancies in social experience, power, and social position (Barrett 1987).

Across the public sphere, social difference typically refers to classificatory rubrics of race and/or ethnicity, gender, religion, language, sexuality, disability, and age. Within each of these rubrics, a range of terms, markers, symbols, characteristics, and identities – some self-ascribed (as in-group criteria), some ascribed by others (as out-group criteria) – distinguish a typology of categories, definitions, or representations of designated sets of people (see Plaut 2010; Jones et al. 2014; Vertovec 2015). For a comprehensive understanding of how difference is shaped, defined, and contested, each category of difference should be examined in terms of its own meanings, intersections, constraints, and processes. It is important to avoid the tendency (especially in much diversity discourse and training) to treat all differences as the same in nature or consequence. Every category, criterion, or marker of difference (and their intersections) has a unique history of discrimination, with differential self- and other-ascribed meanings and discrete social, economic, and political outcomes (cf. Delgado and Stefancic 2017).

Fundamentally from a social scientific perspective, categories of social difference are socially, contextually, and historically constructed, while their boundaries and "contents" are continuously negotiated. The socially constructed nature of categories of difference by no means suggests that they should be dismissed as "unreal"; to the contrary, people invest their personal identities, networks, values, and emotions in such categories of difference. They are also the categories by way of which people are discriminated against, and therefore these also become sources of resistance and mobilization. Once more (rephrasing a point underscored in the previous chapter), while we fundamentally rely on categories of meaning to navigate our social worlds, it is particularly their *effects* that are very "real" indeed.

Salience can refer to the importance of, or degree of attention to, an issue in one's own mind and/or in the public sphere (including the extent of coverage in mainstream news outlets, social media and public debate, not least during election campaigns) (cf. Higgins 1996; Moniz and Wlezien 2020). The rise and fall of salience might also entail changing descriptions and narratives, as well as their respective weight. With regard to the salience of differences, this will also entail: the nature of the categories; their boundaries and their place in various narratives of history or current context; their rise, fall, redefinition, reoccurrence, and absence or prevalence in public sphere; and their role in social and political mobilizations by members of the categories themselves or by their antagonists.

The contemporary, shifting salience of difference should be considered as an essential factor of social complexity since it has many concomitant causes, processes, inflections, meanings, indicators, and consequences – some comparatively generalizable, some context-specific. In order to arrive at better understandings of current and future social complexity dynamics, there is a particular urgency to undertake social scientific work "scrutinizing social categories, processes of differentiation and outcomes in social, political, economic and geographical spheres. This includes the interrogation of presumptions and taken-for-granted categories, units, traits and variables of 'difference'" (Vertovec 2015: 10). To be sure, considerable advances have already been made in empirical research and social theory concerning this field. However, not least in current social and political conditions marked by robust contestation of social categories – as well as in a future to be overwhelmingly conditioned by complexities surrounding climate crisis, increased socio-economic and political stress, and increasing inequalities in its wake – there is a profound need at this moment to research, analyse, and theorize the malleability of social categories and their implications for social organization and interaction.

Today's changeable and fluctuating salience of difference derives from a significant, long-term cultural shift. The sustained trend is described by Pippa Norris and Ronald Inglehart, among other places, in their book, *Cultural Backlash* (2019). Reviewing an extensive set of surveys, Norris and Inglehart trace a revolution in cultural values in post-industrial societies, especially inter-generationally, over the past 50 years. This cultural shift can be characterized by a growing public ease with multi-ethnic environments, increasing secularism and a fading of religious identities and values in the public sphere, and the recognition of more fluid identities surrounding gender and sexuality. This trend has witnessed an "acceptance of gender and racial equality, and rights for the LGBTQI community. These sweeping changes have fostered growing tolerance of diverse lifestyles, religions, and cultures" (Ibid.).

More recently, however, Norris and Inglehart describe how such accumulated processes and outcomes of cultural transformation have come to a point where they trigger a conservative backlash, a defensive reaction to this strong and stable trend. The backlash is expressed in populism and authoritarian politics along with a pronounced voicing (especially in new right-wing media and across social media platforms) of contrary views and narratives concerning immigration and ethnic/racial diversity, religiosity versus secularism, sexuality, and gender. At the heart of all these developments – that is, the long-term liberal cultural shift and the more recent backlash against it – are categories of social difference. The social and political importance of "difference", that is, its salience, has grown and more recently surged due to both to the advocates of "difference" and the outspoken critics against them. Reactionary communication on right-wing social media networks, internet sites, and news organizations especially ensures that "difference" issues remain high on political agendas. Such saliences around social categories directly impact public understandings of diversity and diversification (as discussed in Chapter 5).

However, notions and categories of difference are not fixed, but continue to change. Across a number of key categories, we can witness modes and processes of change flowing in divergent directions with distinctive effects.

The multiplicity, mixing, making, and unmaking of social categories

Complexity in the realm of meaning has amplified as many basic categories of social difference have become central topics of public debate and have themselves expanded, proliferated, or merged. Categories have been, as it were, made, unmade, and mixed. As elaborated below, some examples include the following. Descriptions and conceptualizations of racial categories, in terms of characteristics and boundaries of belonging, have been reshaped worldwide by powerful events such as the death of George Floyd. In many societies, too, the number of people with mixed ethnic or racial heritage has grown tremendously; on many national censuses, one can tick more than one box for "ethnicity" or "race." Religious beliefs and practices are known to abound beyond the confines of established categories of religion. There are numerous new categories available for gender. Sexuality is now routinely referred to by the acronym LGBTQI (lesbian, gay, bi, trans, queer, and intersex), but there are many more classifications sometimes added to the list of possibilities. And within the rubric of language, not only do many places now comprise people speaking numerous languages (e.g., there are over 300 languages spoken in London schools) – bringing with it a massive upsurge in the number of bi- and multi-lingual people – but a range of linguistic features and practices are now observable that are difficult to classify as belonging to conventional language categories at all.

Beyond everyday modes of social categorization and state modes of classification (discussed in the Chapter 5), an important site in which categories are made and remade is the activity of social movements or so-called identity politics (see, among others, Alcoff and Mohanty 2006). In order to combat their subjugation or persecution, gain recognition, and otherwise struggle against inequalities, social category-based movements need to define who they are and what they want to change. "For standard identity politics supporters," Ange-Marie Hancock (2007: 65) writes, "a unitary category serves to bind people into a political group based on a uniform set of experiences." This often leads immediately to questions of reduction, reification, boundaries, positionality, and knowing exclusion of some who might regard themselves as group members. In acts of strategic essentialism (Spivak 1996), the process entails an oppressed group self-consciously and purposefully taking on certain stereotypes about itself in order to both underline their cause and disrupt or subvert structures of dominance. This is a key way that categories are made or remade, since the process derives from "a general dilemma of identity politics: Fixed identity categories are both the basis for oppression and the basis for political power" (Gamson 1995: 390).

Of course, the creation or maintenance of fixed social categories underpins the views of social realities, or worldviews, of many people. In their research on Brexit and British politics, Maria Sobolewska and Robert Ford discern a fundamental division in the UK between "identity conservatives" and "identity liberals," largely based on understandings of the nature of social categories. They suggest that

> The ethnocentric worldview of identity conservatives has two aspects: attachment to in-groups and hostility towards out-groups. They have clear ideas about who belongs to "us", and strong suspicions of groups deemed to fall outside the tribe. Conviction identity liberals see this worldview, and the political stances which flow from it, as morally wrong, and regard combatting ethnocentrism and the hostility to outsiders associated with it as a core political value. This conviction is reflected in a commitment to entrenching anti-prejudice social norms.
>
> *2020: 7*

The rise and fall of the salience of differences reflected in political debates and voting habits, Sobelewska and Ford assert, are largely based on the tensions surrounding these competing worldviews.

Over many years, Rogers Brubaker has importantly traced key developments concerning several, foremost social categories including race and ethnicity, nationalism, gender, religion, and language. Describing both the changing salience of difference and the malleability of categories, he (2016a: 416) observes that "As basic categorical frameworks have become the objects of self-conscious debate, critical scrutiny, strategic choice, and political claims-making, they have lost their self-evidence, naturalness, and taken-for-grantedness." At the same time as certain social forces attempt to stabilize and harden a number of social categories, Brubaker sees:

> A cumulative – and in recent years accelerating – destabilization of basic categorical frameworks has vastly enlarged the scope for choice and self-fashioning in the domain of sex, gender, and sexuality. And while nothing quite so dramatic has occurred in the domain of race and ethnicity, the complexification of the ethnoracial landscape, the increasing prevalence of ethnoracial intermarriage, and the challenges to prevailing systems of counting and categorizing by multiracial activists and others seeking official categorical recognition have combined to significantly enlarge the space for choice and self-fashioning in this domain too.
>
> *Ibid.: 434*

These are very current issues of public interest and scholarly attention, but there has been a rather long lead up to them in relevant social scientific inquiry. Particularly commencing in the 1990s, numerous scholars began voicing dissatisfaction with both linear assimilation and acculturation models in migration studies. Consequently, there arose various critiques of singular notions of group or cultural belonging. Subsequently, a range of concepts were introduced that variously sought to offer new, multiple perspectives, and category-transgressing understandings. Such concepts from this era include: intersectionality (Crenshaw 1991); segmented assimilation (Portes and Zhou 1993); ethnic options (Waters 1990); postethnic (Hollinger 1995); hyphenated identities (e.g., Verkuyten 2004); creolization (Hannerz 1987); hybridity (e.g., Werbner and Modood 1997); Third Space (Bhabha 1994); between two cultures (e.g., Watson 1997); biculturalism or dual identity (e.g., Yamada and Singelis 1999); multiculture (e.g., Gilroy 1993); bright versus blurred social boundaries (Alba 2005); anti-essentialism (e.g., Fraser and Ploux 2005); transnationalism (e.g., Schiller et al. 1992); diasporas (e.g., Cohen 1997); and cosmopolitanism (e.g., Vertovec and Cohen 2002). All of these are important forerunners, if not direct stimuli, of the concept of superdiversity.

Yet now, a couple of decades into the 21st century, it can be argued that we are experiencing ever-more "categorical flux" (Song 2021). Brubaker (2016b: 5) has described the current period as an "age of unsettled identities" in which "challenges to established categories have been spectacular." I prefer to frame our current condition in only slightly different terms, as an *age of contested categories of social difference*. This is due to the fact that not only are we seeing a multiplying and blurring of categories of social difference (not just self-ascriptions, as sometimes suggested by concepts of identity), but these processes have also precipitated variable modes of categorical backlash (as Norris and Inglehart describe). In other words, in many societies there has been an active push-back against category "unsettling," such that mainly conservative forces are now determined to define and lockdown the meaning of certain categories as well as halt the diversification of their respective societies.

The following sections give a few examples of how categories have been reshaped in recent times.

Race/ethnicity

Although scholars have long emphasized the socially constructed, historically and contextually contingent nature of the category of race, outside of academia "for some, race can only have consequence if it is a fixed construct" (Bobo 2018: 211). The desire for fixity is especially the position of many who are part of the backlash against the unsettling of difference. Yet it is clear that definitions and descriptions of what constitutes race can change across time and context, amounting to considerable fluidity of classifications within a single racial category. This is evident in Lauren Davenport's (2020) review of the meanings of race in which she regularly uses terms such as flexible, impermanent, unsettled, imprecise, and "more continuous and less strictly categorical" (Ibid.: 222). Many scholars now speak of racial fluidity, especially pertaining to changeable meanings surrounding the ways people are variably classified or identify themselves over time and across contexts, inconsistency in determining who belongs to given categories, and uncertainty concerning categorical boundaries (Telles and Paschel 2014). Such fluidity and inconsistency of attributes and boundaries has led social scientists such as Wendy Roth (2016) to emphasize the multidimensionality of race and racial identification.

To take one example, we can observe "various ways that people traditionally classified as 'Black' or of 'African descent' are actively transforming racial meanings" (Thomas and Clarke 2006: 2). Particularly as people who identify as Black share their experiences around the world, not only is the fluidity and multidimensionality of the category evident, but also the active processes of reconceptualizing Blackness. An example is provided by novelist Chimamanda Ngozi Adichie, who describes how, upon moving from Nigeria to the USA, she had to learn to be "Black" (Bady 2013). It is clear to her that variable meanings of Blackness have been differentially forged by history, context, and experiences of absorbing stereotypes.

> But then, there are different ways of being black, there are different blacks. I've come to very happily identify as black ... But my experience is different. My experience of blackness is different from African Americans, and for me it's still a learning process, because there are things that I can't inhabit. ... I wish there was a bit more understanding of the many blacks, and the many sorts of permutations of blackness.
>
> *Ibid.*

Such thinking about permutations, alongside fluidity and multidimensionality, also coincides with Marcelle Medford's (2019) consideration of "Black multiplicity." Medford describes this concept by way of examining the history of interactions between African Americans and Black immigrants from sub-Saharan Africa, the Caribbean, and Latin America. For her:

> Black multiplicities refers to the numerous analytical distinctions that separate Blacks. Black identities cannot be reduced to single demographic dimensions such as the Black middle class, the Black south, or Black immigrants. In other words, Black multiplicities does not simply mean Black diversity. We know that Black people, like any other racialized group of people, are incredibly diverse. But simply documenting the typologies of Blackness and the range of differences among Black people does not sufficiently capture the analytical interactions between various sociocultural and structural factors that produce Black multiplicities.
>
> … Because Black multiplicities, like intersectionality, is an analytical framework that explores the complexities of Blackness, it stands in contrast to monolithic constructions of Blackness. It goes beyond mere acknowledgements of Black diversity, which takes race as a master status and then subsequently incorporates considerations of gender, sexuality, ability, class, immigration status, and other variables. Multiplicities allow us to start with the assumption that a range of variables is already embedded within narratives of Blackness.
>
> *Ibid.: 3*

Medford's interest in the complexities of Blackness certainly contributes to the present chapter's concerns with social complexity entailing dynamics of meaning, social organization, and interaction. Similarly, a recognition of the "continuously negotiated and contested patterns of human social organization with often contextually variable meanings" leads Lawrence Bobo (2018: 214) to describe "race as a complex adaptive system."

The nonuniformity and changing patterns of racial categorizations that comprise the making and unmaking of "race" around "Blackness" are equally, if not more, relevant to pan-ethnic labels such as Asian, Latinx, MENA (Middle East and North African), Native American or First Peoples, Pasifika (peoples of Pacific islands), and BIPOC (Black, Indigenous and People of Color). These are already highly composite categories encompassing of other social categories, each with its own multiplicities and multidimensionality.

Further to the multiplicity of purportedly single racial categories, we can see the remarkable growth of "Mixed" populations and notions of "mixedness," described in Chapter 4, as phenomena representing processes of increasing categorical transgression (Song 2021). The evolution of mixedness is evident in not just increasing numbers of people describing themselves across various race and ethnic categories on national censuses, but in an expansion in the number of categories themselves. This is captured, for instance, in debates around changes in methods for obtaining such statistics (Aspinall in press). In this context reflecting the diversification of societies through migration, Peter Aspinall (2009: 1432) has shown how "evidence in national census programmes points to classifications on ethnicity and race becoming ever more complex." In many countries, official statistical offices grapple with the question of how to capture increasing diversity and people's growing self-awareness of multiplicity. Calls for complexifying ethnic statistics are made in order to be able to better trace and fine-tune data of disparities, areas of discrimination, and inequality. In places like the UK and USA where categories of race and ethnicity are counted, the need to understand contemporary trends in diversification has led to extra categories and the option for Census respondents to tick multiple boxes for race and ethnicity. In the USA, this has meant that at least 57 possible combinations of ethnic and racial categories are possible; in the UK, there are up to 80 possibilities of combination.

Despite a range of options offered, many people voice reluctance to choose between categorical affiliations:

> They insist instead, on their own composite identities presenting themselves in multiethnic or multiracial terms. Rather than subordinating one ancestry to another, many multiethnic individuals not only recognize and accept multiple ethnic ancestries but also either actively assert their multiplicity or construct a single and unique identity that recognizes the mixing that constitutes their perceived heritage.
>
> *Campbell and Hartmann (2007: 253)*

Many people now freely combine or experiment with social categories to identify themselves. "In today's presumably more accepting world, people with complex cultural and racial origins become more fluid and playful with what they call themselves" (Funderberg 2013). One example is Özlem Türeci – one of the founders of the COVID-19 vaccine company BioNTech – who describes herself as a "Prussian Turk" (Oltermann 2020). Another is Tiger Woods, who famously called himself "Cablinasian," an amalgam of Caucasian, Black, Indian, and Asian ("His father, Earl, was of African-American, Chinese and Native American descent. His mother, Kultida, is of Thai, Chinese and Dutch descent" [Younge 2010]). The profound growth of such a population segment and the unfixing, erosion or blending of categories that they represent, presages a more fluid image of new demographic realities that challenge conventional categories of social organization in societies around the world.

However, the autonomy of categorical identification is certainly not without challenge. In recent years, just as the fluidity and multiplicity of key social categories have been progressively recognized, they seemingly also reached hurdles if not limits. Most notably, such developments have surrounded notions of "transracial" (Brubaker 2016a, 2016b). The foremost case, in both public and academic debates, has been that of Rachel Dolezal, a woman who identifies as Black but whose inclusion in this category is contested by others. Based largely on Dolezal's story, philosopher Rebecca Tuval (2017) argued for the validity of the category "transracial," drawing parallels between notions of transracial and transgender by way of Dolezal and Caitlyn Jenner, a famous trans woman. Tuval proposed that people choosing to change racial categories should be accepted as a matter of personal choice, just like people choosing their own gender category. Tuval's article was immediately met by massive controversy, criticism, and personal attacks in both social media and academic forums, including if not especially among progressive writers, feminists, and critical Black scholars (see en.wikipedia.org/wiki/Hypatia_transracialism_controversy). Where Tuval saw symmetry between transracial and transgender, others underlined deep asymmetries having to do with lifelong experiences of prejudice, ancestry, positionality and power, collective harm, and forms of White privilege. While wholly recognizing the social construction and fluidity of categories, some scholars have even argued against too much openness and for more rigorous racial classification in order to track categorical, accumulated forms of inequality (Dembroff and Payton 2020). Such a view could be read perhaps as a form of strategic essentialism.

Brubaker provides a considered overview of the current state of affairs:

> Of course, essentialist understandings of race as a deep, authentic, and unalterable identity continue to be articulated in popular culture and scholarly work. They continue to inform the everyday understandings and practices of ordinary people. ... And needless to say, opportunities for choice, change, and unconventional performance enactment remain unequally distributed. ... Still, the declining authority of ancestry over racial and ethnic classification – a result of the increased salience of mixing and the greater awareness of the constructedness, artificiality, and elasticity of racial and ethnic categories – has substantially enlarged the space for choice, affiliation, and self-transformation.
>
> *2016b: 145–6*

Gender and sexuality

Gender has strongly developed as a field of academic study especially since the 1970s. There is now a massive literature surrounding the rubric. For many years, a foundational approach in the field was to regard "sex" as referring to biological difference and "gender" as a set of culturally based meanings and norms associated with sex. The rubric of *sexuality* concerns the ways "Individuals and groups give meaning to bodily sensations and feelings, make erotic acts into sexual identities, and create norms distinguishing between acceptable and unacceptable sexualities" (Seidman 2006: 3).

More recently, scholarly attention has also turned to an examination of fluid and multiple categories concerning gender and sexuality, another making and remaking that has triggered a backlash attempting to fix such categories. Indeed, research and theory is turning towards notions such as "custom gender" and other modes of personal self-making, aided by new media, technologies, and processes of commodification. Often based on earlier approaches, such as Judith Butler's (1990) views on the performativity and gender, Steven Seidman's (1997) work on "queering" or Harriet Bradley's (2007) ideas around "gendering" practices, there is an arguably new, rich ground of contemporary social difference categories and practices to investigate social scientifically. For example, Facebook has offered no less than 71 gender identities, or options for selecting one's gender/orientation on a Facebook profile. These include: pangender, Trans Female, Trans Male, Trans Person, Male to Female, Genderqueer, Agender, and Cisgender. In many places, LGBTQI has become a widespread categorical marker for Lesbian, Gay, Bisexual, Transsexual, Queer, and Intersex lives and identities. Sometimes up to 14 letters are added to the acronym to indicate other categories or simply a "+" symbol denoting further possible ascriptions of gender/sexuality difference.

The marker "trans" itself has profoundly transformative implications here, too. Once more as considered by Brubaker:

> The categories 'trans woman' and 'trans man' obviously make reference to the categories 'woman' and 'man'. Yet 'trans woman' is not intended or understood as implying equivalent to 'woman'; nor is it located between man and woman. It names a new position that transcends not simply the either-or, once-and-forever logic of the gender binary but also the prevailing one-dimensional bipolar framework through which we construct and imagine the space of gender possibilities. That is, the categories 'trans woman' and 'trans man' — and, even more clearly the category 'trans' itself — transcend not just the gender *binary* but the gender *continuum*.
>
> *2016b: 115, emphasis in original*

Recent political and public developments around this topic are widespread. Recognition of transgender categories is certainly rising. As described in the *Washington Post* following Joe Biden's electoral win, "the transgender community watched as the president-elect specifically mentioned them in his victory speech, the first U.S. president-elect in history to do so. [This marks] a symbolic shift from a presidential administration that has spent the past four years repeatedly erasing protections for transgender people — in health care, federal employment, federal prisons, homeless shelters and other housing services receiving federal funds" (Schmidt and Wax-Thibodeux 2020). It is also pointed out that in one national survey, more than 6 in 10 Americans said they have become more supportive towards transgender rights compared with five years ago, while more than 8 in 10 Americans are in favour of protections for LGBTQI+ people in jobs, public accommodations, and housing (Ibid.).

At the same time, there is considerable pushback from people who not only want to limit recognition of gays and lesbians and other non-normative sexualities, but who wish to reinforce binary conceptions of gender (e.g., Hesse 2022). Despite the fact that "A strong global movement has improved respect for the rights of lesbian, gay, bisexual and transgender (LGBT) people around the world," Human Rights Watch (2022) has found that 68 countries have national laws criminalizing same-sex relations between consenting adults; some 37 countries have laws that effectively criminalized trans people (Wareham 2020). Taking the USA as a prominent example, we witness various moves to limit classroom discussion of gender identity and sexual orientation in schools and to ban trans women from participating in sports. Thirty-three states have introduced more than 100 bills that aim to curb the rights of transgender people across the country (Krishnakumar 2021). Dan Cassino's (2022) research demonstrates how an emphasis on binary definitions of gender underpin and reinforce Republican identification in the USA and therefore votes:

> No wonder Republicans are targeting trans people: They embody the idea that sex is not fixed at birth, nor tied inexorably to biology, that gender and sex can be complicated, rather than dichotomous. Simply considering that possibility can threaten anyone who sees gender as divided neatly into male and female. This means attacking trans people is good politics for Republican politicians trying to secure their base. If the security of a firm, unchanging, binary view of gender is linked to identifying as a Republican, attacking any other gender identity can build support among their partisans.
>
> *Ibid.*

Religion

With regard to religious categories on both individual and collective levels, there are many unclearly defined religious affiliations, fuzzily bordered groups, and multiply affiliated people. Specialists observe that "religious diversity itself is changing in all these regards, becoming more complex, and relating in complex intersectionality with other categories of diversity" (Beyer and Beaman 2019).

For instance, it is reported that religious diversification in Brazil is mainly characterized by the expansion and differentiation of Pentecostal groups, rather than by the arrival of new religions. In fact, in many places it is internal diversification within religious traditions that exceed differences between traditions (Ibid.). Relevant phenomena contributing to the diversification of religion and the religious include the availability of a "religious marketplace" (Stark 2007) and trends towards a do-it-yourself, "patchwork quilt" of personalized spirituality, religious belief, and identity (Wuthnow 1998).

At the cutting edge of social scientific work on religion are attempts to identify new perspectives that can recognize, take account of, and analyse the social and political importance of new forms of being religious and new modes of religious belonging. Relatedly, research on religious diversity needs to take account of those substantial numbers of people – especially in modern Western societies – with "no religion" (indeed, this category is now the majority identification in Britain, for example). Therefore, observing religious categories these days concerns not just understanding a variety of longstanding religious traditions, but a plurality of modes and open-ended forms of religious belonging and ways of being religious.

Indeed, "the diversity of religious diversities is profuse and profound" (Bouma et al. 2022: 14), including "diversities of religious organization, religious identity profiles, religious history, religious policies, religious education, religion and sexuality, to say nothing of diversities of context, language, custom and forms of governance" (Ibid.:3). These kinds of developments have led scholars of religion to debate a variety of new concepts, including worldview complexity (Ibid.), multiple secularities (Wohlrab-Sahr and Burchardt 2012), and religious superdiversity (Burchardt and Becci 2016).

Contrary trends of firming and fixing religious boundaries and belongings often entail populist and identitarian groups pursing proselytism and efforts to strengthen and define religiously grounded civilizations (e.g., "Christendom" or the Ummah), orthodox identities, iconoclastic reactions, and fundamentalisms. Far more research is required today about processes of, and reactions to, religious diversification in contexts of religious nationalism (e.g., van der Veer 2021). These include formal and informal measures to avoid recognizing, or to limit, religious pluralism. Religious violence is of course a key issue in contexts of diversity as well, and there is much work still to be done about the ways in which religious symbols and ideologies are mobilized for violence (see Gorski and Türkmen-Dervişoğlu 2013).

Religion as a category of social difference remains a major dividing line in many societies. For instance, a recent Woolf Institute survey of 11,700 adults in England show that attitudes about religion drive negative perceptions of others more than ethnicity or nationality (Sherwood 2020). This is because religion is often perceived as a kind of a "red line" concerning values. The study also found that attitudes within minority faith communities were undergoing significant generational shifts, while intermarriage emerged as a key indicator of category attenuation.

Group self-consciousness and religious reification can be stimulated by the new presence of other religions, or when group members migrate from a largely mono-religious society (such as Pakistan) to a multi-religious one (such as the UK). The same can be said about contexts in which members of different traditions within a world religions meet (such as Polish and Mexican Catholics in the USA, or Indonesian and Moroccan Muslims in the Netherlands). In light of heightened self-consciousness and religious group mobilization, contexts of religious diversity often stimulate minorities to be more conscious of, and fight for, their recognition and civil rights as well as to participate more actively in politics. This, in turn, may stimulate the kind of strategic essentialism mentioned earlier.

Language

In Chapter 3, we looked at the ways sociolinguists and linguistic anthropologists have adopted a superdiversity perspective to reshape understandings of language from a stable, bounded entity to a more open, mixed, and dynamic set of communicative phenomena. Some of the most stimulating work in this field at present has to do with the ways that linguistic categories are being dynamically transgressed and transformed. This draws on and calls attention not just to the increasing complexity surrounding new and growing modes of co-presence of multiple languages and growing multilingualism of people in various contexts, but to their emergent and self-organized linguistic and communicative practices. Consequently, many scholars of language advocate a more open-ended view of language as cumulative repertoires – often gathered from various sources and entailing varying degrees of proficiency – comprising a plurality of differentially shared structures, lexicons, styles, registers, and genres.

In the words of Blommaert and Backus (2013: 14), the implications of the superdiversity concept and approach revolve around recognizing:

> (a) an increasing problematization of the notion of "language" in its tradi-
> tional sense – shared, bounded, characterized by deep stable structures; (b)
> an increasing focus on "language" as an emergent and dynamic pattern of
> practices in which semiotic resources are being used in a particular way –
> often captured by terms such as "languaging", "polylingualism" and so
> forth; (c) detaching such forms of "languaging" from established associa-
> tions with particular groups – such as "speech communities" or "cultures";
> (d) viewing such groups exclusively in terms of emerging patterns of semi-
> otic behavior with different degrees of stability – "speech communities"
> can be big and small, enduring as well as extremely ephemeral, since they
> emerge as soon as people establish in practice a pattern of shared indexical-
> ities; (e) and seeing people as moving through a multitude of such groups in
> "polycentric" social environments characterized by the presence and avail-
> ability of multiple (but often stratified) foci of normativity. ...The stability
> that characterized the established notions of language can no longer be
> maintained in light of the intense forms of mixing and blending occurring
> in superdiverse communication environments.

Sociolinguistics has long had in its toolkit important concepts to address modes of linguistic blending, such as pidgin and creole languages, "heteroglossia," code-switching, and language "crossing." In recent years and especially to address the emergent generation, creativity and profusion of new linguistic forms and practices in contexts of increasing linguistic complexity, a wealth of concepts and perspectives have been developed to understand the blending and blurring of linguistic categories. These include notions like: "metrolingualism," which pre-supposes that "multilingualism is not merely a plurality of languages but rather a creative space of language making, where rules and boundaries are crossed and changed" (Pennycook and Otsuji 2015: 16); "contemporary urban vernacu-lars," "codemeshing," and "flexible bilingualism." Of particular interest here is the notion of "translanguaging" (e.g., García and Wei 2014). This term entails recognizing how speakers employ a broad linguistic and semantic repertoire without regard for rules and boundaries. It leads away from categorizations of contained "languages" to a focus on how, within complex sociocultural environments, individuals use, create, mix, blend, and interpret semiotic materials. "Translanguaging differs from code-switching in that it refers not simply to a shift or a shuttle between two languages, but to the speakers' construction and use of original and complex interrelated discursive practices that cannot be easily assigned to one or another traditional definition of a language, but that make up the speakers' complete semiotic repertoire" (Creese and Blackledge 2018b: xxxiii). Such phenomena are evident in the *Rinkebysvenska* of Stockholm (Stroud 2004), *Kiezdeutsch* of Berlin (Heyd et al. 2019), and *Jafaican* or *Multicultural English* of London (Cheshire et al. 2011).

Public and state understandings of language and linguistic diversity are greatly out of tune with the latest understandings of sociolinguists and linguistic anthropologists. Categorical notions of fixed, bounded "languages" still prevail. Although many public agencies provide educational, health, electoral, state, and public information materials in many immigrant languages, there is always an assumption – indeed for many, a normative expectation – of linguistic assimilation and eventual, intergenerational replacement of an immigrant language with the "host" nation language. Immigrants are not only expected but also increasingly required to learn, speak, and conduct their affairs in the official national language(s). Citizenship and the passing of an integration course require a certain level of language acquisition. In recent years, governments have doubled down on language requirements for immigrants in a reflection of the assimilationist turn in policies (see Blackledge 2005). The most recent example is a contentious draft statement to EU home affairs ministers – championed by Emmanuel Macron (not coincidentally facing a political challenge from the far right) – declaring that migrants to Europe absolutely must learn the language of their new home countries (Boffey 2020). While in some ways this is not an unreasonable expectation (and most migrants themselves confirm that they wish to have a better grasp of the host society language), often the call, its measures and framing underscore an approach and public understanding of language that reproduces categorical fixity, boundedness, and othering, manifesting in intensified discrimination and social stratification. Migrants heard speaking their own languages, or engaging in hybrid or "translanguaging" repertoires, are often perceived as ignorant, "unintegrated," or unwilling to participate in wider society.

Another related area of interest concerning categorizations of linguistic difference concerns the ways that digital technologies and diasporic media have contributed to instances of "linguistic bricolage" such as translanguaging. Developments in technology have wrought "new, specialized modes of communication on digital platforms, involving new identity performance opportunities, as well as new norms for appropriate communicative behavior, and requiring new kinds of visual literacy-based semiotic work in new genres and registers" (Blommaert 2014: 8). This includes the use of translation apps and Google translate, the incorporation of emojis and other symbols and digital signage. Below, we look further into this significant field of digital, online social category construction.

Resonating concerns with complexity and change of categorical meanings, Alexandra Jaffe submits that "if we view superdiversity as an assemblage of tactics or stances, one of the things that it reasons to is the *tension between* conventional, essentializing, 'old' forms of linguistic and cultural authenticity and 'transactional' (situated 'emergent') forms of authentification and identification" (2016: 15, emphasis in original). This, she writes, entails a "construal of agency and the destabilization of certainties and orthodoxies regarding place, language and culture that is at the heart of a superdiverse stance" (Ibid.).

Intersectionality and complex inequality

This age of contested categories is one that is deeply – and, from society to society, differentially – transforming the social organization of difference. It has profound consequences for everyday life and social interaction, social stratification and inequality, rights, political representation, law and public policy and administration. Complexity-related changes in the meanings of social categories are not restricted to singular rubrics, but significantly entail their intersections.

Ever since the concept of intersectionality impacted upon the academic world, most prominently commencing with the work of Kimberlé Crenshaw (1991), scholars have debated and variously theorized the compound functioning of social categories. For many years, the bulk of a burgeoning literature was mostly concerned with the interplay of gender, race, and class (Lutz 2015). Yet two issues of relevance to our current discussion of complexity and social categories have been of concern to scholars of intersectionality.

One issue has to do with intersectionality and the stability and fluidity (or "fuzziness"; Hancock 2007) of social categories. How does the researcher undertake an assessment of intersectional dynamics and outcomes if the nature of the mutually conditioning categories themselves is in question? A solution may be to recognize both stability and fluidity: that is, to acknowledge that social categories are constructed and do change over time, but for periods, especially in social institutions, their meanings become "sedimented" to produce specific consequences (Walby et al. 2012). A related perspective is advocated by Leslie McCall (2005) to reconsider the ways categories are approached in order to understand "the complexity of intersectionality." In doing so, she identifies three distinct approaches. The first is anticategorical complexity, which is based on deconstructing categories (reflecting a view that "Social life is considered too irreducibly complex – overflowing with multiple and fluid determinations of both subjects and structures – to make fixed categories anything but simplifying social fictions that produce inequalities in the process of producing differences" (Ibid.: 1773). The second McCall titles intracategorical complexity, which has been perhaps one of the most conventional approaches by way of accepting given categories and probing their boundary-crossing or admixture. The third approach, actually favoured by McCall herself, is intercategorical complexity, which employs a method of only provisionally adopting fixed categories as a starting point in order to document their interrelations and relation to inequalities. Through this approach, McCall's mode of analysis arrives at "the complex outcome that no single dimension of overall inequality can adequately describe the full structure of multiple, intersecting, and conflicting dimensions of inequality" (Ibid.: 1791).

Another intersectionality issue of relevance to our theme has to do with diversification and the multiplication of categories. Here McCall (2005) has critiqued how intersectionality and other current sociological and feminist theories are "unable to fully grasp the current context of complex inequality" (2005: 1795), particularly "the complexity that arises when the subject of analysis expands to include multiple dimensions of social life and categories of analysis" (Ibid.: 1772). She calls for a renewed look at the construction, roles, interactions, and shifts of categories in order to gain a better understanding of how they produce complex inequalities (also see McCall 2001). Relatedly, Sylvia Walby draws directly on complexity theory to engage with concepts of and around intersectionality and complex social inequalities (see Walby 2007). Walby has pointed out that

> Traditional social theory addressed class inequality, but had difficulty when trying simultaneously to address gender, ethnicity, age, religion, nation, sexual orientation, and disability, and even greater difficulty in addressing their mutual constitution at points of intersection. Further, these social relations are more complex than class in that they involve not only inequality but also difference, thereby problematizing notions of a single standard against which to judge inequality.
>
> *2009: 2*

She argues that "it is this complicated combination of inequality and difference that the concept of 'complex inequalities' is intended to capture" (Ibid.: 18). Bringing our discussion fully around to social categories and the social organization of difference, Walby insists that the analysis of difference and complex social inequalities must be at the core of social theory.

In order to advance social theory, we must also be cognizant of the ways that the nature of the social itself is radically transforming. Already signalled by some of our brief look at ideas within current sociolinguistics, categories of difference and complex inequalities are far further complexified by the contemporary nexus of online/offline identities and practices.

Online/offline identities

The onset of social media, alongside other key technologies (especially the Internet, smartphones and GPS), has transformed the nature of the social – and with it, the nature of social categories and social complexity. People now have astoundingly multifaceted options and modes through which to (re)shape and embellish social categories and their meanings through their everyday – indeed, for many, fairly constant – engagements in social media practices, identities, forums, networks, and movements. With regard to the theme of this book, the importance of digital technologies, identities, and practices has been directly tied to the concept of superdiversity, for instance with regard to patterns of linguistic change (Andreoutsopoulos and Juffermans 2014), health behaviours (Samkange-Zeeb et al. 2020), and the study of migrant lifeworlds (Palmberger in press).

As the uses of the internet and social media initially generated and grew, many observers considered what the impact of the online "virtual" world and practices would be on those of the offline or "real" world. Now, social scientists who study the field tend to erase this binary distinction. The online and offline worlds are regarded as continuous and interpenetrated. "We inhabit the online-offline nexus," wrote Jan Blommaert and his team, "and while both zones have characteristics of their own, both have deeply influenced each other and must be seen as one sociocultural, economic and political habitat" (Blommaert et al. 2019: 1).

Akin to the ways that the telephone became an essential and ordinary part of social connection, for many individuals around the world, what comprises "the social" itself is increasingly enacted via a range, or "polymedia," of digital technologies and platforms (Madianou and Miller 2013). However, different kinds and dimensions of social relations tend to take place differentially across these polymedia. Research and theory point to a "scalable sociality" via digital technologies like social media (Miller et al. 2016). This refers to the fact that, through an array of online practices, individuals variously participate with greater or lesser privacy, with more or less intimacy, in smaller or larger groups. Central to the notion of scalable sociality, moreover, is the phenomenon that across these digital platforms, people manage facets or types of identities and degrees or kinds of self-presentation. Some of these have to do with social roles (e.g., daughter, co-worker, volunteer), some with social categories of difference (e.g., race/ethnicity, nationality, gender, sexuality, disability). Particularly because social media allows these identities and self-presentations to be scalable, people tend to develop a greater flexibility with regard to their online identity and their orientations to groups and categories (Ibid.).

Through digital technologies, sometimes one's identity or social category is ascribed by algorithmically configured data – possibly in racist and exclusionary ways (Benjamin 2019). Still, many see a profound power to create, curate, present, and perform a self, or selves, or aspects of each through social media and their myriad platforms and communities (Lupton 2014). Noting their capacity "to fragment the self into shifting, idealized presentations," Wayne Brekhus (2020: 125) describes how "Online platforms enhance the potential for selective self-presentation because their interfaces physically separate senders from receivers of information; they also allow actors to edit and revise this information easily, which gives them considerable control over their identity performances." This does not mean that we are witnessing a proliferation of fake or fabricated identities. Some online platforms, such as web forums and online gaming, indeed entail wholly anonymous if not largely invented identities. Other platforms, however, "become one of the chief locales for self-expression and the negotiation of identities and relationships" (Fuhse 2018: 90). For example, one study demonstrates how LGBTQI+ students importantly use social media to explore, conceal, protect, and express their identities (Talbot et al. 2020). Rather than exhibiting a fake identity, this research shows, social media thus can be seen as offering a kind of space where people might gain confidence in presenting significant facets of themselves.

Some users might present a range of personal identities or dimensions differently across social media platforms and social scales. Users of platforms like Facebook, however, may actually use this modality to pull together and display, rather than extend, their multiplicity. As Jan Fuhse explains:

> While the purely online identity construction of [web forums and gaming] is dissociated from offline worlds, social networking sites render full persons with their multiple entanglements visible. My work colleagues get to see my party pictures, and my sports friends have to deal with my political views, as expressed in posts, shares, likes and online discussion. In a way, social networking sites make for a fusion of our multiple social identities into a multi-faceted representation ...
>
> *2018: 91*

Twitter, too, involves what has been called "context collapse": rather than the opportunity to present multiple selves, the user is required to present a single, verifiable identity to an imagined audience – although some people nevertheless utilize numerous accounts, pseudonyms, and fake identities (Marwick and Boyd 2011).

The management of multiple identities or "shape shifting" (Davidson and Joinson 2021) across online/offline social worlds has led to a substantial augmentation of what Lee Rainie and Barry Wellman (2012) describe as "networked individualism." Particularly within the "new neighbourhood" of social media, "The hallmark of networked individualism is that people function more as connected individuals and less as embedded group members" (Ibid.: 12). Far more extensively than ever envisioned by Georg Simmel (1955/1922) in his writing on society as a web of affiliations (see below), people increasingly have a variety of partial memberships in multiple networks online. This can be understood as inherently multiplex individuals having many more sparsely dispersed, uniplex (single strand based on a single role or identity), weak tie relationships scaled across several social media platforms. Again underlining the nature of multiple identities online, Rainie and Wellman look at how:

> Moving among relationships and milieus, networked individuals can fashion their own complex identities depending on their passions, beliefs, lifestyles, professional associations, work interests, hobbies, or any number of

other personal characteristics. These relationships often depend on context, which provides networked individuals an opportunity to present different faces in different circumstances, especially online.

2012: 15

They discuss the idea of a networked self, "a single self that gets reconfigured in
different situations as people reach out, connect, and emphasize different aspects
of themselves" (Ibid.: 126). Although Rainie, Wellmann, and others are particularly interested in the online social media aspects of self and identity, these ideas
directly related to work in a significant branch of Social Psychology, namely
social identity complexity theory.

Social identity complexity

Identity – one of the vaguest but most written about social scientific concepts –
broadly refers to specific sets of group and individual understandings (Brubaker
and Cooper 2000; Jenkins 2004; Appiah 2018). Identity categories are continuously, contextually, and historically constructed and ascribed by both
self-definitions and definitions by others. Another way of explaining this dual
production is through "an interaction between assignment, what others say
we are, and assertion, who or what we claim to be" (Campbell and Hartmann
2007: 75). The social boundaries of identity categories, their social and political
claims, and the presumed characteristics or "cultural stuff" within them, are
subject to a range of social and political processes (see, among others, Barth 1969;
Lamont and Molnár 2002; Wimmer 2008).

As discussed in the previous chapter and above, public understandings of
identity categories are often posited around what Amartya Sen (2006) calls a
"singular affiliation," a reduction of many facets and categories to one. Moving
beyond such unidimensional interpretation, Sen notes how:

> In our normal lives, we see ourselves as members of a variety of groups –
> we belong to all of them. A person's citizenship, residence, geographic
> origin, gender, class, politics, profession, employment, food habits, sports
> interests, taste in music, social commitments, etc., make us members of a
> variety of groups. Each of these collectivities, to all of which this person
> simultaneously belongs, gives her a particular identity. None of them can
> be taken to be the person's only identity or singular membership category.
>
> *Ibid.: 4–5*

This endemic social condition is vividly described by author Zadie Smith:

> My trouble is I can't think of community in the singular. Doesn't
> everyone exist in a Venn diagram of overlapping allegiances and inter-
> ests? I'm a black person, also a woman, also a wife and mother, a Brit,

a European – for the moment – a Londoner, a New Yorker, a writer, a feminist, a second-generation Jamaican, a member of the African diaspora, a *Game of Thrones*-er, an academic, a comedy-nerd, a theory-dork, a hip-hop-head and so on.

I am delighted to be all these things and everyone, no matter where they are from – if they really think about it – will find themselves with a similar plurality of communities. At different moments, you'll feel the pull of certain commitments more strongly, especially if an aspect of your identity is particularly embattled.

2018

Generally referred to as a person's "multiple identities" (see Verkuyten 2014), such categories are often nested, intersectional, or hybrid. Individuals' multiple identities usually necessitate situational choices between sometime competing identities, often determined either by influential circumstances or purposeful intentions. In this way, multiple identities are directly related to the concept of "situational identity" (see review by Okamura 1981).

Throughout the course of everyday life, people purposefully or unconsciously switch or apply their multiple and situational identities as the situation demands or the opportunity arises. This is a rather banal observation, indeed a kind of truism. However, it is often not fully recognized that such identity-switching is often a kind of privilege, a recognition of being a full participant in, or even in control of, a given situation. But as described by journalist Gary Younge, many people do not always have the opportunity to choose and fashion their own identity categories:

> At any one time we have access to many identities, including race, sexuality, gender, nationality, class and religion. Far from being neutral, these identities are rooted in material conditions that confer power and privilege in relation to one another.
>
> These power relations, however, are not fixed. They are fluid in character, dynamic by nature and, therefore, complex in practice.
>
> The decisions as to which identities we assert, when we want to assert them and what we want to do with them are ours. But those decisions do not take place in a vacuum. They are shaped by circumstance and sharpened by crisis. We have a choice about which identities to give the floor to; but at specific moments they may also choose us.

2005

The situational restrictiveness that are sometimes imposed on some people, concerning some of their social categories, is especially acute concerning the kinds of legal statuses that serve to stratify migrants, discussed in Chapter 4. Such state-imposed categories are rarely open to any kind of fluidity and flexibility with regard to a range of public institutions, services, and largesse.

The opposite of what Younge calls a "vacuum" is what social scientists often refer to as the social field, an immediate environment of relations, power, meanings, and expectations. Within discrete contexts, choices of situational identity involve the afore-mentioned tension between identity assignment and assertion, taking place within the pressure fronts of a stratified social structures, representations, and interactions (Vertovec 2021). In assessing such tensions and the identity choices they bring about, relevant ideas to keep in mind include positionality, stigma, privilege, recognition, and voice.

Generally, people are aware that others have different group identities, that the nature of the groups varies (between, say, families, occupational groups, interest groups, and ethnic groups), and that perceptions of entitativity, or suppositions of variable group tightness, also diverge (Lickel et al. 2000). Social psychologists consider a number of fundamental interpretations that people normally engage to resolve the multiplicity of categorical differences between people (such as McGarty 2006; Schmid and Hewstone 2010; Gaertner and Dovidio 2014). These include distinguishing: a hierarchy of subordinate and encompassing categories (e.g., Berliner-German-European) or a dual identity model (e.g., simultaneously German *and* European). Nevertheless, individuals often struggle with dilemmas of how to recognize, resolve, or relate multiple identities. This includes not just orientations to others, but the potentially different ways they incorporate their multiple group memberships into their sense of self – and, crucially, what difference this might make to attitudes and behaviour towards others.

These concerns have given rise to the vital field of *multiple social categorization* (Crisp and Hewstone 2006, 2007; Prati et al. 2021) and *social identity complexity* theory (Miller et al. 2009; Brewer 2010; Schmid and Hewstone 2011). The field was ushered in through groundbreaking work by social psychologists Sonia Roccas and Marilynn Brewer (2002). With a focus on large social categories and symbolic communities, rather than on personal ties and roles such as within families, Roccas and Brewer highlight the ways that individuals recognize, represent, and interpret information about their own multiple identity categories. People share an in-group category on one dimension but belong to different categories in other dimensions. But this may not be reflected in an individual's self-representation, which may be a singular category or set that is regarded as mutually overlapping (e.g., Italian Catholic woman). The more an individual understands her multiple identities as distinct and non-overlapping, the higher her social identity complexity is said to be. As Roccas and Brewer explain:

> The actual complexity of multiple, partially overlapping group memberships may or may not be reflected in the individual's subjective representation of his or her multiple identities. For instance, a woman who is both White and Christian may think of her religious ingroup as composed primarily of White people, even though objectively there are many non-White Christians. Conversely, she may think of her racial ingroup as largely Christian, despite the fact that there are many Whites who embrace

other religions. By reducing the subjective inclusiveness of both ingroups to their overlapping memberships, the individual maintains a relatively simplified identity structure. When an individual acknowledges, and accepts, the nonoverlapping memberships of her multiple ingroups, her subjective identity structure is both more inclusive and more complex.

Ibid.: 89

That is, when individuals are subjectively embedded in simplified, singular affiliation, "us" versus "them" categories, they are said to have low social identity complexity; they see their in-group categories as highly similar and overlapping. The more self-aware they are of belonging to multiple, differentiated categories that do not necessary also contain other categorizations, they are regarding as having high social identity complexity; they see their in-group categories as far more distinct.

The implications of high social identity complexity are extremely significant. This is not only because social identity complexity relates to one's own self-concept, but it also bears on relationships between self and others. Extensive research has demonstrated that when people rely less on singular social categories and have greater awareness of their own complexity, the greater is the likelihood of developing positive attitudes towards others (Brewer and Pierce 2005; Crisp and Hewstone 2007; Miller et al. 2009; Schmid et al. 2009). Katharina Schmid and Miles Hewstone summarize the findings as such:

[W]hen individuals rely less on a single category the likelihood for the occurrence of intergroup discrimination is lower, while the likelihood for positive intergroup attitudes becomes greater. …If individuals are able to perceive their multiple ingroups in a less exclusive, but more differentiated and complex manner, they should also be able to recognize the complexity surrounding others' multiple category memberships. In short, individuals high in social identity complexity should be aware of the fact that others may be ingroup members on some dimensions, but outgroup members on others. This heightened cognitive complexity should then manifest itself in more positive intergroup perceptions and attitudes.

2011: 82–3

A growing realization of one's own self-categorizations leads to a growing awareness of others' multiple group categorizations, and this is shown to enhance positive attitudes. Conversely, too: positive social contact with others may stimulate more awareness of social identity complexity (Schmid et al. 2009; Schmid and Hewstone 2010). This latter finding has been extended to show that even exposure to socially diverse environments should increase, or at least provide opportunities for, awareness of one's own multiple, non-overlapping social categories and thereby stimulate higher social identity complexity (Schmid and Hewstone 2011; Prati et al. 2021).

As part of the Max Planck Institute's "Diversity and Contact" project, Katharina Schmid, Miles Hewstone, and Ananthi Al Ramiah analysed large-scale national surveys in Germany and the UK. They demonstrate that respondents living in more diverse neighbourhoods indeed show higher social identity complexity and exhibit less in-group bias and less social distance. Their findings "highlight that being exposed to diverse settings may influence how we think about ourselves, and the multiple social groups we belong to, in more complex, differentiated and inclusive terms, with positive consequences for intergroup relations" (Ibid.: 141). Similar results have been found in the USA as well (Miller et al. 2009). It also resonates with the work of Bai, Ramos, and Fiske, described in Chapter 5, which found that in contexts around the world, exposure to greater levels of social diversity actually breaks down stereotypes and prompts the rejection of singular categorical thinking, producing a more "multidimensional mental space" (2020: 12742)

Such analyses suggest far-reaching social consequences. Following a comprehensive review of "research [that] has consistently displayed the effectiveness of strategies that encourage a consideration of the complexity of others or oneself to reduce outgroup discrimination," Francesca Prati, Richard Crisp, Monica Rubini et al. sum up such potentials stemming from this field of Social Psychology:

> [I]n present day multicultural societies, where there are more opportunities for intercultural contact, a cognitive capability to go beyond simple social categorization is more adaptive in building new 'alliances' with members of different groups and promoting social integration. Research on multiple categorisation and social identity complexity has demonstrated that even if individuals are cognitively disposed to think categorically about social groups, they possess the computational ability to deal with social complexity and inconsistency in favour of more accurate evaluations of others and themselves. Even though this cognitive ability requires more cognitive resources than the use of heuristics, like other cognitive skills, it can be improved though practice.
>
> *2021: 56*

Contexts such as those posed by superdiversity and conditions for positive contact can be harnessed, moreover, for "improving the cognitive ability to handle complexity in different contexts" (Ibid.)

The positive effects of social identity complexity are not always automatic or guaranteed, however. For a start, some people have a high need, motivation, or vested interest in maintaining a status quo of simpler, singular (often groupist, culturalist, and racialized) single category representations of society (Roccas and Brewer 2002). Also, when people are treated like they are of but a single category, their chance for increasing their awareness of social identity complexity is greatly diminished. It has also been shown that given long-standing or exacerbated perceptions of group threat (as discussed in Chapter 5), individuals are less likely to consider their complex multiple categories and more likely to focus on the salience of a single identity category (Schmid and Hewstone 2011).

In a social world complexifying in the numerous ways described throughout this book, the value of widely fostering more complex understandings of social categories is clear. In the worlds of Marilynn Brewer:

> what we need now is more understanding of what institutional arrangements, social policies, and ideology promote complex rather than simple social identities. Pluralistic societies provide the potential for complex multiple identities but segregated living arrangements, discriminatory practices in legal, political, and economic arenas, and political power-mongering can all reduce the actualization of that potential.
>
> *2010: 28*

Once more we must bear in mind that not all people are equally free to reflect on their multiple categorical identities, especially when living in deprived social circumstances or subject to various forms of identity-based inequity or bigotry. While such forms of inequality and prejudice need to be tackled in and of themselves, measures to promote social identity complexity should be encouraged. "In this vein," Prati et al. (2021: 78) propose, "multiple and counter-stereotypic categorization interventions should increase the use of, reliance on and accessibility to increasingly complex ways of thinking about outgroup members to reduce discriminatory behaviours." With direct relevance to super-diversity and processes of diversification, and based on a range of research evidence, they hold that "something as simple as thinking about one's identity from multiple viewpoints may help to reduce rigid thinking, and this in turn increases open-mindedness in a society that is becoming increasingly diverse" (Ibid.: 77).

Conclusion

There have been numerous academic calls to consider complexity and engage in more "complexity thinking" about contemporary social phenomena (e.g., Urry 2003; Cilliers 2007; Stirling 2010; Cairney and Geyer 2017). This is especially important in light of the rise and development of contexts and permutations of superdiversity. With regard to such, Blommaert (2013) compellingly put his finger on the matter: "the problem is one of imagination: how do we imagine these new forms of complexity?"

In this chapter, I have presented a wide set of materials that, I believe, combine to characterize significant features of today's social complexity. Drawing on certain schools of Anthropology, I initially point to complexity as entailing changing forms of social organization. These have to do with patterns of social relations, stratification and inequalities, and power – often relating to entire social categories of people. Thus, the subsequent aspect of social complexity that I focus on has to do with the meanings comprising and surrounding social categories. This domain of meaning has two dimensions. The first dimension of meaning concerns the shifting, shared meanings of social categories – what I describe in terms of multiplicity, mixing, making, and unmaking (here, with regard to categories of race and ethnicity, gender and sexuality, religion, and language). These are often in constant negotiation – ever more intriguingly complicated by the nexus of online/offline self-presentations. The second dimension of meaning concerns the multiple social categories that pertain within every individual, their social identity complexity. Some people are more conscious of their own multiple, discrete identity categories; some people are more reliant on singular identity categories to classify themselves and others. Research has shown that individuals with high social identity complexity tend to have more positive attitudes towards people apparently different from themselves, largely through a concomitant ability to recognize the social identity complexity of others. This difference between individuals with high and low social identity complexity, and their discrepant perspectives and social relations that they give rise to, further contribute to complexity of social organization. Therefore, I stress that social complexity is something that runs across scales from *complexly organized societies* to *complexly organized sets of meaning* to *complexly organized selves* (cf. Brekhus 2020: 102).

Why describe these phenomena as social complexity? Like some other social scientists – and by way of addressing Blommaert's question of "how do we imagine these new forms of complexity?" – I choose to draw from complexity science metaphorically. The hard sciences of complexity mathematically and empirically examine and theorize effects when systems (and systems of systems) are subject to complexifying dynamics in terms of what happens with: more components, more differentiation, more relations and interdependencies, and greater uncertainties and emergent forms of organization arising from them. Superdiversity, I suggest, entails similar complexifying dynamics. That is, superdiversity also entails: more components (in terms of more people via migration or demographic change), more differentiation (changing social variables), more relations and interdependencies (new patterns of social variables themselves and interactions among people comprising them), and greater uncertainties and emergent forms of organization arising from them (new social and spatial arrangements, inequalities, social movements and political conflicts or compromises).

What is a major difference between conventional complexity theory in the natural sciences and social complexity under conditions of superdiversity? My answer is: human meanings. These include social categories, images, and representations, and varying understandings within diverse publics. As we have discussed, meanings about social categories (including self-identifications) are not only social constructed and subject to change, but they are derived, interpreted, and inhabited in relation to social positionality – which itself is not a singular fixture, but relational within settings, networks, and interactions.

This is what Hannerz (1992: 66) called the "perspectivation of meaning." It is a crucial dimension of social complexity itself, which both draws from and contributes to patterns of social organization (Vertovec 2021).

In his notable essay entitled "The uses of diversity," Clifford Geertz (1986) underscored his long-standing approach to culture-as-symbol-system by addressing the same kind of interactionist understanding of the relation between meanings, positionality, and social relations:

> Meaning, in the form of interpretable signs – sounds, images, feelings, artefacts, gestures – comes to exist only within language games, communities of discourse, intersubjective systems of reference, ways of worldmaking; … it arises within the frame of concrete social interaction in which something is something for a you and a me, and not in some secret grotto in the head; and … it is through and through historical, hammered out in the flow of events.
>
> *1986: 112–3*

The coming together of people enacting their differences facilitates, therefore, "not a convergence of views, but a mingling of them" leading to (akin to what social psychologists tell us) "the possibility of quite literally changing our minds" (Ibid.: 114). The history of each person, of all peoples, has been one of gradually changing minds in this manner. Such an open-ended, multiplex, or syncretic view of meaning, Geertz suggests, is an "enemy" to the propensity of "confining people to cultural planets" (Ibid.: 119). Such a propensity also entails what has been called, in this book, singular affiliation, groupism, culturalism, and racialization. Barth (1989: 124) conveys a perspective similar to Geertz on this matter when discussing the nature of living in societies characterized by complex cultural configurations and meaning systems. In these kinds of contexts – now ubiquitous, especially in cities around the world – Barth believes that living with social complexity involves "a multiplicity, inconsistency and contentiousness that deflects any critical attempt at characterization" (1989:124). Social complexity thus should be seen as both dynamic and uncertain.

By way of complexity concepts, what is emergent here in terms of self-organization within a complex adaptive system? Here Page instructs that "Adaptation can be at the level of the entities themselves, as is the case in a social system, or it can be at the population level… In social systems, both types of change occur" (2015: 25). Within the entity (individual), adaptation emerges as a reworking of multiple social categories and the relations linked to them; at the population level, I would suggest that emergence relates to the changing salience of difference (including both the rise in "diversity" and reactionary ethnocentrism), the malleability of social categories, and the patterning of multiple, intersecting inequalities (what McCall [2001] terms complex inequality).

Spanning both the individual and societal scales, another emergent property of social complexity is a massive multiplication of what Simmel (1955/1922) theorized as the modern "web of group-affiliations" (also see Broćić and Silver 2021). At the turn of the 19th/20th centuries, Simmel observed rapidly changing European urban society and noted how, increasingly, people were linked to numerous, diverse, and far-flung groups – from family and friends to occupational and interest groups. In modern societies, he noted, the individual comes "to stand at a point at which many groups intersect" (Simmel 1955/1922: 141). One's "web of group-affiliations" could eventually span "an infinite range of individualizing combinations" (Ibid.: 155). Moreover, no two people will have the exact set of intersecting networks or web of group affiliations. Such multiple and diverse connections, he believed, should create richer and more diversified personalities. At the same time, development of new networks and patterns of association should bring together people sharing specific interests together while they remain very dissimilar in other respects. While diverse connections and group-affiliations may create tensions and competing loyalties, overall these were seen as providing social stability (in ways similar to what anthropologists call the power of "cross-cutting ties" which tend to inhibit conflict and encourage reconciliation; see Kang 1976). "The main strength of Simmel's model," according to Mairo Diani (2000: 394), "lies probably in its capacity to recognize the dual nature of social memberships …: individuals differentiate their personality through multiple group memberships; at the same time, groups are distinctive in that they result from the convergence of specific individuals, but are also connected to each other by the fact of sharing some of their members." Contemporary conditions – particularly and powerfully enhanced by digital technologies and the time/space shrinkage they facilitate – have perpetuated possibilities for webs of group-affiliation to new heights. Now more than ever, society is "made out of a tangle of networked individuals who operate in specialized, fragmented, sparsely interconnected, and permeable networks" (Rainie and Wellman 2012: 21).

Superdiversity is a concept pertaining to a set of social conditions and processes giving rise to changing forms of social organization. These conditions also condition, arise from, and contribute to shifts in the meanings of multiple social categories and the social relations conditioned by them. Social categories of all kinds are now subject to tremendous flux – what I have described here as multiplicity, mixing, making, and unmaking. Such categories and relations have come to include an ostensibly seamless transition of online and offline modalities. Social complexity is a notion that addresses the relations between these elements across sociological scales in an assembly of codependent relationships and processes. Complexity thinking – an approach, a set of tools, and a vocabulary borrowed from natural sciences to conceptualize better these multiplicities of meaning and relationship – is not just of value for social understanding, but for ordinary individuals to gain a more coherent view of society and social change, a positive appreciation of others, and a fuller understanding of themselves.

References

Alba, R. 2005. "Bright vs. blurred boundaries: Second-generation assimilation and exclusion in France, Germany, and the United States," *Ethnic and Racial Studies* 28: 20–49 https://doi.org/10.1080/0141987042000280003

Albertson, C. 2018. *A Perfect Union? Television and the Winning of Same-Sex Marriage*, London: Routledge https://doi.org/10.4324/9781315207704

Alcoff, L. M. and S. P. Mohanty 2006. "Reconsidering identity politics: An introduction," in *Identity Politics Reconsidered*, L. M. Alcoff et al. (eds.), New York: Palgrave Macmillan, pp. 1–9 https://doi.org/10.1057/9781403983398_1

Andreoutsopoulos, J. and K. Juffermans 2014. "Digital language practices in super-diversity: Introduction," *Discourse, Context, and Media* 4(5): 1–6 https://doi.org/10.1016/j.dcm.2014.08.002

Appiah, K. A. 2018. *The Lies that Bind: Rethinking Identity*, London: Profile

Aspinall, P. J. 2009. "The future of ethnicity classifications," *Journal of Ethnic and Migration Studies* 35(9): 1417–35 https://doi.org/10.1080/13691830903125901

Aspinall, P. J. In press. "Capturing super-diversity in official data: How the decennial censuses in Britain are responding," in *The Oxford Handbook of Superdiversity*, F. Meissner, N. Sigona and S. Vertovec (eds.), Oxford: Oxford University Press

Bady, A. 2013. "The varieties of Blackness: An interview with Chimamanda Ngozi Adichie," *Boston Review* 10 July

Bai, X., M. R. Ramos and S. T. Fiske 2020. "As diversity increases, people paradoxically perceive social groups as more similar," *Proceedings of the National Academy of Sciences* 117(23): 12741–49 https://doi.org/10.1073/pnas.2000333117

Banton, M. (ed.) 1966. *The Social Anthropology of Complex Societies*, London: Tavistock

Barrett, M. 1987. "The concept of 'difference'," *Feminist Review* 26(1): 29–41 https://doi.org/10.1057/fr.1987.18

Barth, F. 1969. "Introduction," in *Ethnic Groups and Boundaries*, F. Barth (ed.), Oslo: Universitetsforlaget, pp. 9–38

Barth, F. 1972. "Analytical dimensions in the comparison of social organizations," *American Anthropologist* 74(1–2): 207–20 https://doi.org/10.1525/aa.1972.74.1-2.02a01720

Barth, F. 1989. "The analysis of culture in complex societies," *Ethnos* 54: 120–42 https://doi.org/10.1080/00141844.1989.9981389

Barth, F. 1993. *Balinese Worlds*, Chicago: University of Chicago Press

Benedict, B. 1962. "Stratification in plural societies," *American Anthropologist* 64(6): 1235–46 https://doi.org/10.1525/aa.1962.64.6.02a00070

Benjamin, R. 2019. *Race after Technology: Abolitionist Tools for the New Jim Crow*, Cambridge: Polity

Beyer, P. and L. G. Beaman 2019. "Dimensions of diversity: Toward a more complex conceptualization," *Religions* 10(10) https://doi.org/10.3390/rel10100559

Bhabha, H. 1994. *The Location of Culture*, Abingdon: Routledge

Blackledge, A. 2005. *Discourse and Power in a Multilingual World*, Amsterdam: John Benjamins Publishing

Blommaert, J. 2013. "Citizenship, language and superdiversity: Towards complexity," Tilburg Papers in Culture Studies 45, Tilburg

Blommaert, J. 2014. "From mobility to complexity in sociolinguistic theory and method," Kings College London Working Papers in Urban Language & Literacies 135

Blommaert, J. and A. Backus 2013. "Superdiverse repertoires and the individual," in *Multilingualism and Multimodality*, I. De Saint-Georges and J. J. Weber (eds.), Rotterdam: Sense, pp. 11–32

Blommaert, J., Y. Lu and K. Li 2019. "From the self to the selfie," Tilburg Papers in Culture Studies 222, Tilburg

Bobo, L. D. 2018. "Race as a complex adaptive system," *Du Bois Review* 15(2): 211–15 https://doi.org/10.1017/s1742058x19000043

Boffey, D. 2020. "EU draft declaration sets out stricter rules on migrant integration," *The Guardian* 9 November

Bouma, G., A. Halafoff and G. Barton 2022. "Worldview complexity: The challenge of intersecting diversities for conceptualising diversity," *Social Compass* https://doi.org/10.1177/00377686221079685

Bradley, H. 2007. *Gender*, Cambridge: Polity

Brekhus, W. H. 2020. *The Sociology of Identity: Authenticity, Multidimensionality, and Mobility*, New York: John Wiley & Sons

Brewer, M. B. 2010. "Social identity complexity and acceptance of diversity," in *The Psychology of Social and Cultural Diversity*, R. J. Crisp (ed.), Oxford: Wiley-Blackwell, pp. 11–33

Brewer, M. B. and K. P. Pierce 2005. "Social identity complexity and outgroup tolerance," *Personality and Social Psychology Bulletin* 31: 428–37 https://doi.org/10.1177/0146167204271710

Broćić, M. and D. Silver 2021. "The influence of Simmel on American Sociology since 1975," *Annual Review of Sociology* 47: 87–108 https://doi.org/10.1146/annurev-soc-090320-033647

Brubaker, R. 2016a. "The Dolezal affair: Race, gender, and the micropolitics of identity," *Ethnic and Racial Studies* 39(3): 414–48 https://doi.org/10.1080/01419870.2015.1084430

Brubaker, R. 2016b. *Trans: Gender and Race in an Age of Unsettled Identities*, Princeton: Princeton University Press

Brubaker, R. and F. Cooper 2000. "Beyond 'identity'," *Theory and Society* 29(1): 1–47 https://doi.org/10.1023/a:1007068714468

Burchardt, M. and I. Becci 2016. "Religion and superdiversity: An introduction," *New Diversities* 18(1): 1–7

Butler, J. 1990. *Gender Trouble: Feminism and the Subversion of Identity*, London: Routledge

Byrne, D. 1998. *Complexity Theory and the Social Sciences: An Introduction*, London: Routledge

Byrne, D. and G. Callaghan 2013. *Complexity Theory and the Social Sciences: The State of the Art*, London: Routledge

Cairney, P. and R. Geyer 2017. "A critical discussion of complexity theory: How does 'complexity thinking' improve our understanding of politics and policymaking?" *Complexity, Governance and Networks* 3(2): 1–11 https://doi.org/10.20377/cgn-56

Campbell, S. and D. Hartmann 2007. *Ethnicity and Race: Making Identities in a Changing World*, Thousand Oaks: Pine Forge

Carneiro, R. L. 1967. "On the relationship between size of population and complexity of social organization," *Southwestern Journal of Anthropology* 23(3): 234–43 https://doi.org/10.1086/soutjanth.23.3.3629251

Cassino, D. 2022. "Why are Republicans so focused on restricting trans lives?" The Monkey Cage, *Washington Post* 21 March

Cheshire, J., P. Kerswill, S. Fox and E. Torgersen 2011. "Contact, the feature pool and the speech community: The emergence of Multicultural London English," *Journal of Sociolinguistics* 15(2): 151–96 https://doi.org/10.1111/j.1467-9841.2011.00478.x

Cilliers, P. (ed.) 2007. *Thinking Complexity*, Mansfield: ISCE Publishing

Cilliers, P. 2002. *Complexity and Postmodernism: Understanding Complex Systems*, London: Routledge

Cilliers, P. and R. Preiser 2010. "Why difference," in *Complexity, Difference and Identity*, P. Cilliers and R. Preiser (eds.), Dordrecht: Spring, pp. v–ix

Cohen, R. 1997. *Global Diasporas: An Introduction*, London: University College London Press

Creese, A. and A. Blackledge 2018b. "Language and superdiversity: An interdisciplinary perspective," in *The Routledge Handbook of Language and Superdiversity*, A. Creese and A. Blackledge (eds.), London: Routledge, pp. xxi–xiv https://doi.org/10.4324/9781315696010

Crenshaw, K. 1991. "Mapping the margins: Identity politics, intersectionality, and violence against women," *Stanford Law Review* 43(6): 1241–99 https://doi.org/10.2307/1229039

Crisp, R. J. and M. Hewstone (eds.) 2006. *Multiple Social Categorization: Processes, Models and Applications*, London: Psychology Press

Crisp, R. J. and M. Hewstone 2007. "Multiple social categorization," *Advances in Experimental Social Psychology* 39: 163–254 https://doi.org/10.1016/s0065-2601(06)39004-1

Davenport, L. 2020. "The fluidity of racial classifications," *Annual Review of Political Science* 23: 221–40 https://doi.org/10.1146/annurev-polisci-060418-042801

Davidson, B. I. and A. N. Joinson 2021. "Shape shifting across social media," *Social Media + Society* 7(1): 1–11 https://doi.org/10.1177/2056305121990632

DeLanda, M. 2019. *A New Philosophy of Society: Assemblage Theory and Social Complexity*, London: Bloomsbury https://doi.org/10.5040/9781350096769

Delgado, R. and J. Stefancic 2017. *Critical Race Theory: An Introduction*, New York: New York University Press, 3rd edn. https://doi.org/10.2307/j.ctt1ggjjn3

Dembroff, R. and D. Payton 2020. "Why we shouldn't compare transracial to transgender identity," *Boston Review* 18 November

Diani, M. 2000. "Simmel to Rokkan and beyond: Towards a network theory of (new) social movements," *European Journal of Social Theory* 3(4): 387–406 https://doi.org/10.1177/13684310022224868

Eisenstadt, S. N. 1961. "Anthropological studies of complex societies," *Current Anthropology* 2(3): 201–22 https://doi.org/10.1086/200188

Eriksen, T. H. 2007. "Complexity in social and cultural integration: Some analytical dimensions," *Ethnic and Racial Studies* 30(6): 1055–69 https://doi.org/10.1080/01419870701599481

Eriksen, T. H. 2015. *Fredrik Barth: An Intellectual Biography*, London: Pluto Press

Fraser, N. and M. Ploux 2005. "Multiculturalism, anti-essentialism, and radical democracy," *Cahiers du Genre* 39(2): 27–50 https://doi.org/10.3917/cdge.039.0027

Fuhse, J. A. 2018. "New media and socio-cultural formations," *Cybernetics & Human Knowing* 25(4): 73–96

Funderberg, L. 2013. "The changing face of America,' *National Geographic* October

Gaertner, S. L. and J. F. Dovidio 2014. *Reducing Intergroup Bias: The Common Ingroup Identity Model*, Philadelphia: Psychology Press

Gamson, J. 1995. "Must identity movements self-destruct? A queer dilemma," *Social Problems* 42(3): 390–407 https://doi.org/10.1525/sp.1995.42.3.03x0104z

García, O. and L. Wei 2014. *Translanguaging: Language, Bilingualism and Education*, Basingstoke: Palgrave Macmillan https://doi.org/10.1057/9781137385765

Geertz, C. 1986. "The uses of diversity," *Michigan Quarterly Review* 25(1): 105–23

Gilroy, P. 1993. *The Black Atlantic: Modernity and Double Consciousness*, Cambridge, MA: Harvard University Press

Gorski, P. S. and G. Türkmen-Dervişoğlu 2013. "Religion, nationalism, and violence: An integrated approach," *Annual Review of Sociology* 39: 193–210 https://doi.org/10.1146/annurev-soc-071312-145641

Graeber, D. and D. Wengrow 2021.*The Dawn of Everything: A New History of Humanity*, New York: Farrar, Straus and Giroux

Grillo, R. 2015. "Reflections on super-diversity by an urban anthropologist, or 'superdiversity so what?'" Paper presented at the Academy of Urban Super-Diversity, Berlin

Hancock, A. M. 2007. "When multiplication doesn't equal quick addition: Examining intersectionality as a research paradigm," *Perspectives on Politics* 5(1): 63–79 https://doi.org/10.1017/s1537592707070065

Hannerz, U. 1987. "The world in creolization," *Africa* 57(4): 546–59 https://doi.org/10.2307/1159899

Hannerz, U. 1992. *Cultural Complexity: Studies in the Social Organization of Meaning*, New York: Columbia University Press

Hesse, M. 2022. "Republicans thought defining a 'woman' is easy. Then they tried," *Washington Post* 6 April

Heyd, T., F. von Mengden and B. Schneider (eds.) 2019. *The Sociolinguistic Economy of Berlin: Cosmopolitan Perspectives on Language, Diversity and Social Space*, Boston: Walter de Gruyter https://doi.org/10.1515/9781501508103

Higgins, E. T. 1996. "Knowledge activation: Accessibility, applicability, and salience," in *Social Psychology: Handbook of Basic Principles*, E. T. Higgins (ed.), New York: Guildford Press, pp. 133–68

Hollinger, D. 1995. *Postethnic America: Beyond Multiculturalism*, New York: Basic Books

Human Rights Watch 2022. "#OUTLAWED: The love that dare not speak its name," http://internap.hrw.org/features/features/lgbt_laws/

Jaffe, A. 2016. "What kinds of diversity are super? Hidden diversities and mobilities on a Mediterranean island," *Language & Communication* 51: 5–16 https://doi.org/10.1016/j.langcom.2016.06.005

Jenkins, R. 2004. *Social Identity*, London: Routledge, 2nd edn. https://doi.org/10.4324/9780203463352

Jones, J. M. and J. F. Dovidio 2018. "Change, challenge, and prospects for a diversity paradigm in social psychology," *Social Issues and Policy Review* 12(1): 7–56 https://doi.org/10.1111/sipr.12039

Jones, J. M., J. F. Dovidio and D. L. Vietze. 2014. *The Psychology of Diversity: Beyond Prejudice and Racism*, Oxford: Wiley Blackwell

Jörg, T. 2011. *New Thinking in Complexity for the Social Sciences and Humanities*, Dordrecht: Springer https://doi.org/10.1007/978-94-007-1303-1

Kang, G. E. 1976. "Conflicting loyalties theory: A cross-cultural test," *Ethnology* 15(2): 201–10 https://doi.org/10.2307/3773330

Krishnakumar, P. 2021. "This record-breaking year for anti-transgender legislation would affect minors the most," *edition.cnn.com* 15 April

Kuper, L. and M. G. Smith (eds.) 1969. *Pluralism in Africa*, Berkeley: University of California Press

Kushner, G. 1969. "The anthropology of complex societies," *Biennial Review of Anthropology* 6: 80–131

Lamont, M. and V. Molnár 2002. "The study of boundaries in the social sciences," *Annual Review of Sociology* 28: 167–95 https://doi.org/10.1146/annurev.soc.28.110601.141107

Lickel, B., D. L. Hamilton, G. Wieczorkowska, A. Lewis, S. J. Sherman and A. N. Uhles 2000. "Varieties of groups and the perception of group entitativity," *Journal of Personality and Social Psychology* 78(2): 223–46 https://doi.org/10.1037/0022-3514.78.2.223

Lupton, D. 2014. *Digital Sociology*, London: Routledge https://doi.org/10.4324/9781315776880

Lutz, H. 2015. "Intersectionality: Assembling and disassembling the roads," in *Routledge International Handbook of Diversity Studies*, S. Vertovec (ed.), London: Routledge, pp. 363–70 https://doi.org/10.4324/9781315747224

Madianou, M. and D. Miller 2013. "Polymedia: Towards a new theory of digital media in interpersonal communication," *International Journal of Cultural Studies* 16(2): 169–87 https://doi.org/10.1177/1367877912452486

Marwick, A. E. and D. Boyd 2011. "I tweet honestly, I tweet passionately: Twitter users, context collapse, and the imagined audience," *New Media & Society* 13(1): 114–33 https://doi.org/10.1177/1461444810365313

McCall, L. 2001. *Complex Inequality: Gender, Class and Race in the New Economy*, London: Routledge https://doi.org/10.4324/9780203902455

McCall, L. 2005. "The complexity of intersectionality," *Signs* 30(3): 1771–800 https://doi.org/10.1086/426800

McGarty, C. 2006. "Hierarchies and minority groups: The roles of salience, overlap, and background knowledge in selecting meaningful social categorizations from multiple alternatives," in *Multiple Social Categorization*, R. J. Crisp and M. Hewstone (eds.), Hove: Psychology Press, pp. 25–49

Medford, M. M. 2019. "Racialization and Black multiplicity: Generative paradigms for understanding Black immigrants," *Sociology Compass* 13(7) https://doi.org/10.1111/soc4.12717

Miller, D., J. Sinanan, X. Wang, T. McDonald, N. Haynes, E. Costa, J. Spyer, S. Venkatraman and R. Nicolescu 2016. *How the World Changed Social Media*, London: UCL Press

Miller, K. P., M. Brewer and N. L. Arbuckle 2009. "Social identity complexity: Its correlates and antecedents," *Group Processes and Intergroup Relations* 12: 79–94

Moniz, P. and C. Wlezien 2020. "Issue salience and political decisions," in *Oxford Research Encyclopedia of Politics*, W. R. Thompson (ed.), Oxford: Oxford University Press, https://doi.org/10.1093/acrefore/9780190228637.013.1361

Newkirk, P. 2019. "Diversity has become a booming business: So where are the results?" *Time* 10 October

Norris, P. and R. Inglehart 2019. *Cultural Backlash: Trump, Brexit, and Authoritarian Populism*, Cambridge: Cambridge University Press.

Okamura, J. Y. 1981. "Situational ethnicity," *Ethnic and Racial Studies* 4(4): 452–65 https://doi.org/10.1080/01419870.1981.9993351

Oltermann, P. 2020. "Uğur Şahin and Özlem Türeci: German 'dream team' behind vaccine," *The Guardian* 10 November

Page, S. E. 2007. *The Difference: How the Power of Diversity Creates Better Groups, Firms, Schools, and Societies*, Princeton: Princeton University Press

Page, S. E. 2010. *Diversity and Complexity*, Princeton: Princeton University Press

Page, S. E. 2015. "What sociologists should know about complexity," *Annual Review of Sociology* 41: 21–41 https://doi.org/10.1146/annurev-soc-073014-112230

Palmberger, M. In press. "Migrants and new media: Digital ethnography, transnationalism and superdiversity," in *The Oxford Handbook of Superdiversity*, F. Meissner, N. Sigona and S. Vertovec (eds.), Oxford: Oxford University Press

Pauketat, T. R. 2007. *Chiefdoms and Other Archaeological Delusions*, Lanham, MD: Altamira

Pennycook, A. and E. Otsuji 2015. *Metrolingualism: Language in the City*, London: Routledge https://doi.org/10.4324/9781315724225

Plaut, V. C. 2010. "Diversity science: How and why difference makes a difference," *Psychological Inquiry* 21: 77–99 https://doi.org/10.1080/10478401003676501

Pool, C. A. 2012. "The formation of complex societies in Mesoamerica," in *The Oxford Handbook of Mesoamerican Archeology*, D. L. Nichols and C.A. Pool (eds.), Oxford: Oxford University Press, pp. 169–87 https://doi.org/10.1093/oxfordhb/9780195390933.013.0012

Portes, A. and M. Zhou 1993. "The new second generation: Segmented assimilation and its variants," *The Annals of the American Academy of Political and Social Science* 530(1): 74–96 https://doi.org/10.1177/0002716293530001006

Prati, F., R. J. Crisp and M. Rubini 2021. "40 years of multiple social categorization: A tool for social inclusivity," *European Review of Social Psychology* 32(1): 47–87 https://doi.org/10.1080/10463283.2020.1830612

Rainie, H. and B. Wellman 2012. *Networked: The New Social Operating System*, Cambridge, MA: MIT Press https://doi.org/10.7551/mitpress/8358.001.0001

Roccas, S. and M. B. Brewer 2002. "Social identity complexity," *Personality and Social Psychology Review* 6(2): 88–106 https://doi.org/10.1207/s15327957pspr0602_01

Ross, J. C. and S. R. Steadman 2017. *Ancient Complex Societies*, London: Routledge https://doi.org/10.4324/9781315305639

Roth, W. D. 2016. "The multiple dimensions of race," *Ethnic and Racial Studies* 39(8): 1310–38 https://doi.org/10.1080/01419870.2016.1140793

Samkange-Zeeb, F., L. Borisova, B. Padilla, H. Bradby, J. Phillimore, H. Zeeb and T. Brand 2020. "Superdiversity, migration and use of internet-based health information–results of a cross-sectional survey conducted in 4 European countries," *BMC Public Health*, 20(1): 1–12 https://doi.org/10.1186/s12889-020-09329-6

Schiller, N. G., L. Basch and C. Blanc-Szanton 1992. "Transnationalism: A new analytic framework for understanding migration," *Annals of the New York Academy of Sciences* 645(1): 1–24 https://doi.org/10.1111/j.1749-6632.1992.tb33484.x

Schmid, K. and M. Hewstone 2010. "Combined effects of intergroup contact and multiple categorization: Consequences for intergroup attitudes in diverse social contexts," in *The Psychology of Social and Cultural Diversity*, R. J. Crisp (ed.), Oxford: Wiley-Blackwell, pp. 299–321 https://doi.org/10.1002/9781444325447.ch13

Schmid, K. and M. Hewstone 2011. "Social identity complexity: Theoretical implications for the social psychology of intergroup relations," in *Social Cognition, Social Identity, and Intergroup Relations*, R. Kramer et al. (eds.), Philadelphia: Psychology Press, pp. 77–102

Schmid, K., M. Hewstone, N. Tausch, E. Cairns and J. Hughes 2009. "Antecedents and consequences of social identity complexity: Intergroup contact, distinctiveness threat, and outgroup attitudes," *Personality and Social Psychology Bulletin* 35(8): 1085–98 https://doi.org/10.1177/0146167209337037

Schmidt, S. and E. Wax-Thibodeux 2020. "How a Biden presidency could advance transgender rights — and lead to backlash," *Washington Post* 17 November

Seidman, S. 1997. *Difference Troubles: Queering Social Theory and Sexual Politics*, Cambridge: Cambridge University Press https://doi.org/10.1017/cbo9780511557910

Seidman, S. 2006. "Theoretical perspectives," in *Handbook of the New Sexuality Studies*, S. Seidman et al. (eds.), London: Routledge, pp. 3–13

Sen, A. 2006. *Identity and Violence: The Illusion of Destiny*, London: Allen Lane

Sherwood, H. 2020. "Religious intolerance is 'bigger cause of prejudice than race,' says report," *The Observer* 15 November

Simmel, G. 1955 (1922). *Conflict and the Web of Group Affiliations*, New York: The Free Press

Smith, M. E. (ed.) 2011. *The Comparative Archaeology of Complex Societies*, Cambridge: Cambridge University Press https://doi.org/10.1017/cbo9781139022712

Smith, M. G. 1965. *The Plural Society in the British West Indies*, Berkeley: University of California Press

Smith, M. L. 2021. "The process of complex societies: Dynamic models beyond site-size hierarchies," *World Archaeology* 53(1):122–36 https://doi.org/10.1080/00438243.2021.1965015

Smith, Z. 2018. "I have a very messy and chaotic mind," *The Guardian* 21 January

Sobolewska, M. and R. Ford 2020. *Brexitland: Identity, Diversity and the Reshaping of British Politics*, Cambridge: Cambridge University Press https://doi.org/10.1017/9781108562485

Song, M. 2021. "Who counts as multiracial?" *Ethnic and Racial Studies* 44(8): 1296–323 https://doi.org/10.1080/01419870.2020.1856905

Spivak, G. 1996. "Subaltern studies: Deconstructing historiography?" in *The Spivak Reader*, D. Landry and G. MacLean (eds.), London: Routledge, pp. 203–37

Stark, R. 2007. *Sociology*, Belmont: Wadsworth

Stirling, A. 2010. "Keep it complex," *Nature* 468(7327): 1029–31 https://doi.org/10.1038/4681029a

Stroud, C. 2004. "Rinkeby Swedish and semilingualism in language ideological debates: A Bourdieuean perspective," *Journal of Sociolinguistics* 8: 163–230 https://doi.org/10.1111/j.1467-9841.2004.00258

Talbot, C. V., A. Talbot, D. J. Roe and P. Briggs 2020. "The management of LGBTQ+ identities on social media: A student perspective," *New Media & Society* https://doi.org/10.1177/1461444820981009

Telles, E. and T. Paschel 2014. "Who is black, white, or mixed race? How skin color, status, and nation shape racial classification in Latin America," *American Journal of Sociology* 120(3): 864–907 https://doi.org/10.1086/679252

Thomas, C. 2015. "Disability and diversity," in *Routledge International Handbook of Diversity Studies*, S. Vertovec (ed.), London: Routledge, pp. 43–51 https://doi.org/10.4324/9781315747224

Thomas, D. A. and K. M. Clarke 2006. "Introduction: Globalization and the transformations of race," in *Globalization and Race*, K. M. Clarke and D. A. Thomas (eds.), Durham, NC: Duke University Press, pp. 1–34 https://doi.org/10.1515/9780822387596-002

Thrift, N. 1999. "The place of complexity," *Theory, Culture & Society* 16(3): 31–69 https://doi.org/10.1177/02632769922050610

Tuval, R. 2017. "In defense of transracialism," *Hypatia* 32(2): 26–78 https://doi.org/10.1111/hypa.12327

Urry, J. 2003. *Global Complexity*. Cambridge: Polity

Urry, J. 2005. "The complexity turn," *Theory, Culture & Society* 22(5): 1–14 https://doi.org/10.1177/0263276405057188

van der Veer, P. 2021. "Minority rights and Hindu nationalism in India," *Asian Journal of Law and Society* 8(1): 44–55 https://doi.org/10.1017/als.2020.51

Verkuyten, M. 2004. *The Social Psychology of Ethnic Identity*, London: Psychology Press https://doi.org/10.4324/9780203338704

Verkuyten, M. 2014. *Identity and Cultural Diversity: What Social Psychology Can Teach Us*, London: Routledge https://doi.org/10.4324/9780203710142

Vertovec, S. 2015. "Introduction: Formulating diversity studies," in *Routledge International Handbook of Diversity Studies*, S. Vertovec (ed.), London and New York: Routledge, pp. 1–20 https://doi.org/10.4324/9781315747224

Vertovec, S. 2021. "The social organization of difference," *Ethnic and Racial Studies* 44(8): 1273–95 https://doi.org/10.1080/01419870.2021.1884733

Vertovec, S. and R. Cohen 2002. "Introduction: Conceiving cosmopolitanism," in *Conceiving Cosmopolitanism*, S. Vertovec and R. Cohen (eds.), Oxford: Oxford University Press, pp. 1–22

Walby, S. 2007. "Complexity theory, systems theory, and multiple intersecting social inequalities," *Philosophy of the Social Sciences* 37(4): 449–70 https://doi.org/10.1177/0048393107307663

Walby, S. 2009. *Globalization & Inequalities: Complexity and Contested Modernities*, London: Sage https://doi.org/10.4135/9781446269145

Walby, S., J. Armstrong and S. Strid 2012. "Intersectionality: Multiple inequalities in social theory," *Sociology* 46(2): 224–40 https://doi.org/10.1177/0038038511416164

Wareham, J. 2020. "New report shows where it's illegal to be transgender in 2020," *Forbes* 30 September

Waters, M. C. 1990. *Ethnic Options: Choosing Identities in America*, Berkeley: University of California Press

Watson, L. (Ed.) 1997. *Between Two Cultures: Migrants and Minorities in Britain*, Oxford: Blackwell

Werbner, P. and T. Modood (eds.) 1997. *Debating Cultural Hybridity: Multi-Cultural Identities and the Politics of Anti-Racism*, London: Zed

West, C. and S. Fenstermaker 1995. "Doing difference," *Gender & Society* 9(1): 8–37 https://doi.org/10.1177/089124395009001002

Wimmer, A. 2008. "The making and unmaking of ethnic boundaries: A multilevel process theory," *American Journal of Sociology* 113(4): 970–1022 https://doi.org/10.1086/522803

Wohlrab-Sahr, M. and M. Burchardt 2012. "Multiple secularities: Toward a cultural sociology of secular modernities," *Comparative Sociology* 11(6): 875–909 https://doi.org/10.1163/15691330-12341249

Woodward, K. (ed.) 1997. *Identity and Difference*, London: Sage

Wuthnow, R. 1998. *After Heaven: Spirituality in America since the 1950s*, Berkeley: University of California Press https://doi.org/10.1525/9780520924444

Yamada, A. M. and T. M. Singelis 1999. "Biculturalism and self-construal," *International Journal of Intercultural Relations* 23(5): 697–709 https://doi.org/10.1016/s0147-1767(99)00016-4

Yoffee, N. 2005. *Myths of the Archaic State: Evolution of the Earliest Cities, States, and Civilizations*, Cambridge: Cambridge University Press https://doi.org/10.1017/cbo9780511489662

Younge, G. 2005. "We can choose our identity, but sometimes it also chooses us," *The Guardian* 21 January

Younge, G. 2010. "Tiger Woods: Black, white, other," *The Guardian* 29 May

Zolo, D. 1992. *Democracy and Complexity: A Realist Approach*, Pittsburgh: Penn State Press

7

CONCLUSION

Superdiversity refers both to a process of simultaneous migration-driven diversification across various social and legal characteristics and to the social configurations arising from such a process. The introduction of this concept in 2007 appealed across the social sciences to scholars who variously adopted it to describe facets of diversification and interrelated social transformations beyond migration-related ones, intersecting multivariate characteristics resulting from such processes, their implications for other areas of social development, and their challenges for specific social science methodologies themselves. For a great many social scientists, superdiversity has provided a way to talk about certain kinds, modes, or sites of complexification in which new, multifaceted, interwoven, and interdependent assemblages of social phenomena are manifesting.

For these reasons, in this book I have considered superdiversity through: the ways and reasons why academics have been variously attracted to the concept; the modes by which diversification processes continue to develop; the kinds of responses to superdiversity and diversification that often arise within certain publics and the makeup of the social categories involved in such responses; and relevant frameworks for thinking about superdiversity and social complexity, drawing on certain approaches, perspectives, and vocabulary from complexity theory in the natural sciences. The complexity approach that I have highlighted includes concerns with: the playing out of multiple causes, processes, and outcomes in migration; subsequent non-linear or unpredictable developments in politics, economies, and societies; and the emergence of new forms of organization on different levels (here, the scales of social organization, shared social categories, and individual identities). To approach and describe such matters as complexity should not obfuscate them, however. "Complexity does not imply that there are no patterns and that no regularities can be discerned" (Castles et al. 2014: 52). Indeed, across a substantial and ever-growing literature invoking superdiversity,

DOI: 10.4324/9780203503577-7

complex new patterns of social, cultural religious, and linguistic phenomena are being described in widespread places around the world. These global processes and outcomes vary substantially. As I have suggested, "the layered and positioned effects of 'old' and 'new' diversities have engendered changing patterns of prejudice, segregation, inequality and discord, as well as emergent patterns of cooperation, civility, cosmopolitanism and conviviality" (Vertovec 2015b: 2).

Concerning all of these facets of social complexity in superdiversity – multiple causes, processes and outcomes in migration, unpredictable developments in politics, economies, and societies, and the emergence of new forms of organization – context matters. Aspects of context that shape superdiversity processes and conditions include: state policies and official classifications; political debates (especially involving racisms and xenophobias); historical narratives of the nation and its others; modes, sites, and sources of power; notions of personhood and subjectivity; and the ongoing evolution of social categories underpinning group identities and individual performance practices. Although its causal, intermediate and consequent processes are many, diversification is globally prevalent. Subsequent social, economic, political, and cultural patterns emerge and shift in light of context-specific phenomena. Superdiversity plays out differently, either challenging, shifting or reproducing social structures and inequalities, in different places, times, and tempos.

Dynamics of superdiversity and concomitant social complexity, especially tied to migration, are sure to continue into the future. As discussed in Chapter 4, this is due to an array of multiple, overlapping, interdependent, and mutually conditioning processes affecting which, when, how, and to where people move. Due to such a mix of influences, great discrepancy and uncertainty will continue to characterize how migration and diversification processes transpire around the world on varying scales. These entail highly contextualized phenomena surrounding social, economic, political, demographic, and environmental drivers. The latter is especially acute, as climate change is bound to impact profoundly the other sets of migration drivers. Adverse social and economic consequences of climate change will trigger significant political turmoil and differentially affect population groups and social categories. However, such causes, processes, and outcomes affecting potential migration and diversification futures are inherently uncertain in both the short- and long-term, locally and globally (see Bijak and Czaika 2020). People the world over will need to migrate to survive. At the same time, in the rapidly ageing societies of the developed industrial world, acute labour shortages will necessitate the ongoing need for, and adjustments of, migration policies and management. These, I believe, will significantly entail the proliferation of new or refurbished temporary and circular migration schemes – quite likely akin to those already at play in Singapore, "especially in terms of 'ensured transiency', physically controlled containment, limitations on interaction with locals, and if need be, modalities for simple and quick expulsion" (Vertovec 2020b). While serving the needs of employers, such schemes are bound to exacerbate discrimination and the exploitation of migrants. We can anticipate both the ongoing diversification of societies worldwide through migration, but also the continued embedding of group-based inequalities not least through restrictive state policies and legal status specifications.

Ongoing diversification and the unsettled superdiversity it brings will also occasion an array of public responses. Described in Chapter 5, responses are often negative, based on common understandings of group categories comprised of groupist, singular affiliation, culturalist, and racialized conceptualizations. Such understandings sit squarely with threat narratives, zero-sum beliefs, "too much diversity" anxieties, and forms of linguaphobia that are contrived, stoked, and manoeuvred by political actors. Negative attitudes if not hostilities, along with embedded and concomitant social stratifications, are intensified by such public understandings. However, a considerable amount of research demonstrates that more positive responses to diversification and superdiversity are possible if not likely to emerge, too. People are able to adapt their perceptions and attitudes towards difference and diversity. These tend towards the positive particularly when conditions of "contact" are right, and even when individuals are merely exposed to a wide range of social categories. It is clear that negative narratives and framings in the public sphere pose great obstacles for the development of positive interactions, relations, outlooks, and attitudes surrounding social differences.

In Chapter 6, the notion of social complexity was explored to offer a further approach to understanding superdiversity and diversification. The chapter proposes three different kinds or layers of complexity that rest upon and influence each other. These are complexities in social organization, complexities in meanings of social categories, and complexities in self-identities. Cumulatively, these layers affect social structures of stratification, everyday practices, and interactions (Vertovec 2021). Complexities in social organization represent a classic subject in much Anthropology of the 20th century. This field, now largely out of fashion, concerns an evolutionary take on social structures and the way that phenomena such as status and power stratify people – often based on the idea of various groups – into social hierarchies. The anthropologists Barth, Hannerz, and Eriksen have been key figures emphasizing how social organization also conditions cultural meanings, their positionalities, and their minglings. These insights lead us to consider complexities in meanings between and within social categories. Here, it has been emphasized that social categories not only help people classify and orient themselves to the world, but that they carry considerable power in shaping interactions and social structures.

Social categories are regularly works-in-progress. This is now more evident than ever, as several key social categories such as race, gender, sexuality, religion, and language can be seen as fluid and in flux. Finally, complexities in self-identities are brought to the fore in discussion of multiple, situated personal identities. Work around Social Identity Complexity theory shows that people often have very different self-awareness of their categorical belongings. Some have more cognizance, some less regarding the distinctiveness of the social categories to which they identify. It has been established through extensive research that fostering higher social identity complexity, or self-awareness of distinct multiple belongings, can lead to more positive attitudes towards others. Complexities in social category meanings and complexities in self-identities are anathema to people – especially manipulative politicians – who wish to keep social categories simple and fixed, usually in terms of what we have discussed as singular affiliation, groupism, culturalism, racialization, and linguistic boundedness. Simple categories support rigid social structures and hierarchies; complex categories challenge and might serve to break down such rigid social structures and hierarchies.

Migration-driven diversification involves each type or level of social complexity, creating ever more complex modes of superdiversity. People arriving in a country with differential, multidimensional sets of intersecting characteristics and categories are initially slotted or sorted into particular, often spatially manifested positions in social stratification systems. Sometimes their characteristics challenge such systems; sometimes the system powerfully dominates (as with undocumented migrants). The effects of migration on complexifying social categories are significant, too. As seen by Mihaela Vieru, "Large-scale multiple migration also means increased diversity, multiple identities, overlapping societal memberships, geographically spread-out diaspora communities, and rich human and social capital" (2017: 1). Stephen Castles, Hein de Haas, and Mark Miller also importantly point out that

> Immigrants may be able to make a special contribution to the development of new forms of identity. It has always been part of the migrant condition to develop multiple identities, which are linked to the cultures both of the country of origin and of the destination ...
>
> Immigrants are not unique in this; multiple identities are becoming a widespread characteristic of contemporary societies. But it is above all migrants who are compelled by their situation to have multilayered socio-cultural identities, which are constantly in a state of transition and renegotiation. ... Despite current conflicts about the effects of ethnic diversity on national cultures and identity, immigration does offer perspectives for change. New principles of identity may emerge, which may be neither exclusionary nor discriminatory ...
>
> *2014: 330*

In these ways and more, migration-driven diversification and resultant forms of superdiversity present a kaleidoscopic social complexity spanning scales and levels of analysis. Each realm of social complexity discussed here – namely social structure, social categories and meanings, and individual self-identifications – have their own multiple causes, processes, and outcomes. Nevertheless, they are fundamentally linked to each other. As modes of complexity, too, they are subject to uncertainty and emergence: within each, we cannot predict how the parts and their arrangements will play out to affect the whole. We do know, as mentioned, that negative public interventions in media and political discourse concerning difference and diversity can and do serve to shape negative assessments of social processes, harden adverse categorizations, damage social relations, and limit more comprehensive understandings of selves and others. Can alternative public interventions concerning difference and diversity work in the other direction?

Superdiversity, social complexity, and public initiatives

"The coming question of the Twenty-first Century," Stuart Hall (1993: 359) famously and tellingly foresaw, is how to fashion "the capacity to live with difference." Following the discussions in this book, I would argue that "the capacity to live with difference" might best be grounded in a capability and competence in understanding social categories and their non-essentialist, flexible, multiple, and overlapping qualities. "How to fashion" this is a key question. Just as Mary-Louise Pratt (2003) called for "a new public idea about language" (see Chapter 5), we might do well to advocate a *new public understanding of diversity and diversification*. The following section offers some ideas for what and how this might develop.

One kind of new public understanding has already been in play for some years now. The notion of "diversity" has become embedded in the public sphere across an astounding number of sites (see Vertovec 2015a). "'Diversity' is the focus of a wide-ranging corpus of discourses, institutional structures, policies and practices in business, public sector agencies, the military, universities and professions. … the current period is pervaded with discourses about diversity" (Vertovec 2012: 287). This is not just a phenomenon in societies of the global North, but gradually in the South as well. "Diversity" in this sense entails a public and corporate language, activities, and institutional structures based on a normative, yet ambiguous, polysemic, and banal notion of recognizing and valuing social difference. Furthermore, within pronounced notions of "diversity," there often remains an unresolved question of just who is considered different or diverse vis-à-vis whom. Despite the vagueness of the "diversity" idea and its highly differing approaches, goals and orientations of policies, programmes and institutional arrangements, however, the discourse has nevertheless wrought cumulative social impacts. Indeed, I (2012) suggest that persistent and ubiquitous "diversity" discourse has transformed the *social imaginary*, in Charles Taylor's sense of "the ways that people imagine their social existence, how they fit together with others, how things go on between them and their fellows, the expectations that are normally met, and the deeper normative notions and images that underlie these expectations" (2007: 23). Of course, "diversity" discourse does not necessarily and automatically sensitize everyone – and indeed, as we have discussed in this book, there are discourses, narratives, and political agendas that strongly push-back against "diversity" as a widely accepted, good thing.

Arguably, too, much "diversity" discourse may serve to promulgate understandings of social categories in terms of singular affiliation, groupism, culturalism, racialization, and linguistic boundedness. I propose that in today's diversifying, superdiverse environments, the task before us is to move from an awareness of the "diversity" of seemingly bounded groups to an awareness of the complexity of social identities. It is in this sense that I urge a new public understanding of diversity and diversification. This would fit with the vision of Bhikhu Parekh, who has long advocated creating a public space in which diverse and often excluded people are able "to interact, enrich the existing culture and create a new consensual culture in which they recognise reflections of their own identity" (in Parekh and Bhabha 1989: 27). Parekh has also compellingly described the multiple nature of social identities in ways that directly resonate with notions flagged throughout this book, such as the perspectivization of meanings, individuals' webs of affiliations, and the importance of cross-cutting ties:

> The importance of plural social identities in individual and social life can hardly be exaggerated. Since every social identity represents a particular way of looking at the world, plural identities mean plural perspectives each supplementing the insights and correcting the limitations of others, and collectively they all create the possibility of a broader and more nuanced and differentiated view of the world. Identities do not co-exist passively: their interaction pluralizes each of them, and discourages their essentialization and reification. Since every social identity links us to a particular group of people, makes us part of its historical narrative, and gives our lives a meaning and depth, the plurality of them offers us multiple belonging, loyalties and sources of meaning, and enable us to construct several overlapping narratives of our lives. We are able to appreciate that society and humankind in general can be classified on several different axes, and that those falling out of view or appearing hostile from the perspective of one identity might be partners or friends from another. This helps us to grasp and cope with the inescapable complexity of human life and to avoid taking a simplistic view of it.
>
> *2008: 23–4*

This vision must be tempered with the acknowledgement that many people do not acknowledge, experience, or value the plurality of identities. Not only is there widespread incidence of what social psychologists call low social identity complexity (Chapter 6), but the conditions of diversification and superdiversity can instil feelings of dislocation that often turn people *towards* simplicity, essentialism, and singular affiliation as a kind of coping strategy (McLennan 1995: 90). Here, too, Parekh has valuable insights:

> The opposite happens when a single identity becomes dominant. Individuals then see themselves, their society and the world from a single perspective, and not only fail to notice several aspects of them, but take a highly skewed and distorted view of those they do. They divide humankind along a single axis, see individuals and groups as friends or foes, and ignore their commonalities and overlapping ties. … [T]hey become obsessive about it, cling

to it desperately, and worry constantly lest its dilution or disappearance should destabilize their lives and deprive them of all meaning. They guard it fiercely against external threats and purge it of "alien" internal elements, taking an excessively simplistic and ultimately unsustainable view of it.

2008: 24

Polarized polymedia exacerbate this tendency, both cognitively and socially. Accordingly, people sort themselves into closed, like-minded, categorically homogeneous social networks both online and offline (Tokita et al. 2021). Such attitudinal clustering is directly linked with social and attitudinal fragmentation leading to democratic dysfunction and social injustice. It seems evident, especially given processes of diversification and conditions of superdiversity, that a continued dominance of essentialist meanings around social categories poses a range of negative consequences to society across all scales.

Instead, more positive and just outcomes could ensue by realizing that "the potential for intergroup conflict may be reduced in societies that are more complex and differentiated along multiple dimensions that are not perfectly correlated, rather than being split along one central, typically ethnic or religious, fault line" (Hewstone et al. 2007: 108). In other words, diversification and conditions of superdiversity can be publically identified and addressed in ways to reduce "the potential for polarizing loyalties along any single group distinction," thereby increasing "'tolerance for outgroups in general" (Ibid.). The ambition is idealistic, but wholly worth pursuing. And as Scott Page has suggested:

> Building that shining city on the hill in which our variety of interests, political beliefs, economic frameworks, and cultural identities cross-cut and overlap to produce a vibrant, innovative, sustainable, and tolerant society will require a nuanced knowledge of how to construct interventions that self-reinforce.

in Baldassarri and Page (2021: 5)

Such interventions towards a new public understanding of diversity and diversification should entail ways of encouraging greater awareness of the multiplicities and cross-cutting features of social categories and instilling certain modes of complexity thinking (especially an awareness of multiple causes, processes and outcomes) pertaining to social life. What might such interventions look like? Some ideas are sketched below in the areas of public policy and governance, political representation, and public campaigns.

Policy

In the UK, former municipal Chief Executive Ted Cantle has observed the unconstructive if not deleterious effects of public policies based on simplistic, fixed social categories (especially ethnicity). In addition to leading towards unfair or misguided policies, such categories in policies and practice tend to reinforce biased views in public understanding (cf. Phillimore in press). Hence:

> The support for simple homogeneous identities through categorisation, funding and representation must be curtailed and reflected with more heterogeneous and multifaceted forms. This will mean an acceptance that much of our existing, simplistic and "groupist" forms of identity will have to change, along with the way in which they are instrumentalised through public policy.
>
> *Cantle (2016: 154)*

Attempting to address overlapping and flexible categories is part of the broader challenge in policy and governance surrounding social complexity and complexification processes. This is the key topic engaged by Peter Scholten (2020) in his book *Mainstreaming versus Alienation*, subtitled *A Complexity Approach to the Governance of Migration and Diversity*. Particularly in light of the impacts of migration and superdiversity, Scholten examines how (especially urban) policymakers currently do and should confront social complexity. The problems span a range of policy fields, from housing through education, employment, social welfare, health, and planning. Regardless of the field, Scholten demonstrates how policies often "derail" when complexity is ignored, denied, not sufficiently taken into account, or not coped with. They fall short, miss their targets, or possibly even have unintended negative consequences. One of the biggest problems is a belief in "one-size-fits-all" models when dealing with very different kinds and categories of migrants, for instance. These will obviously not work efficiently given the growing variation of needs, overlapping characteristics, and differing social positions comprising superdiversity linked to multiple social categories simultaneously in play. There are also serious policy dilemmas caused by friction between different levels of government and their crossed understandings of social phenomena, assumptions about groups, the effects of labelling and reification via official statistical categories, and the overestimation of the effects of group-targeted government intervention. Instead, in order to better address superdiversity and other modes of social complexity, Scholten calls for more flexibility, reflexivity, and openness for change within policymaking. Indeed, he underlines the need for mainstreaming and rather constant monitoring, updating, and recalibration of policies and institutions across government in the face of emergent and "unforeseeable and uncontrollable dynamics of migration and diversity" (Ibid.: 5). Scholten's recommendations fit well alongside other, complexity-based approaches to policy making such as that of Andy Stirling (2010, 2016), who advocates that policy decision-making processes must remain plural and conditional in light of the inherent uncertainty of complex systems (also see Geyer and Rihani 2012; Klijn and Koppenjan 2014).

Scholten wishes to foster a complexity governance perspective that should underlay the structural process of mainstreaming matters of migration and superdiversity across departments and scales of government, public institutions, and society more broadly. It is in the nature of contemporary migration and diversification processes that they should not be approached as stand-alone topics that can be merely "fixed" or engineered by the state. Instead, they require an open, adaptable, responsive, and joined-up mode of policymaking that cuts across generic policy sectors. "Precisely because of the complexity of superdiversity, there is no one way, no 'great model', for policies on superdiversity" (Scholten in press).

Within the public sector, there have been similar calls to recognize the prevalence and local shape of superdiversity – that is, an awareness of migrants' multi-dimensional characteristics that differentially position them to others, to the state and to institutions. In Chapter 3 of this book, we saw how superdiversity has been brought squarely into the field of policy and governance, and that scholars and policymakers from a wide variety of public service domains have called for such recognition. Again, this includes recommendations to incorporate superdiversity into policy areas such as education (e.g., Guo 2010; Gogolin 2011; Gross 2020; Li et al. 2021), housing (Walters 2015), medical sociology (Bradby et al. 2017), healthcare (Phillimore 2010), nursing (Culley 2014) and the training of health workers (Ní Shé and Joye 2018), mental illness (Kirwan 2022), entrepreneurship (Sepulveda et al. 2011), child protection services (Leitão Ferreira 2021), technical communication (Cardinal 2022), and social work (van Ewijk 2018). Most of these particularly call for a shift away from a reified, single group-by-group approach to service delivery. Such a "tick box" approach to public service delivery was seriously criticized in a report by Britain's Institute for Public Policy Research (Fanshawe and Sriskandarajah 2010). After a substantial review of local practices, expert interviews and a variety of focus group meetings, the report concluded that:

> One of the biggest challenges of all is to how to design policy interventions that can take into account the complexity but be manageable enough to be put into practice. After all, one of the most appealing features of the tick-box approach is that it presents a relatively easy way for over-worked, under-paid officials to check how well they are doing on equalities. Our key message is that we need to devise new interventions that do not simply apply out dated or irrelevant categorisations and assume all those people who tick certain boxes have the same characteristics or need the same approach. Drawing on wider discussions about public service delivery, we need a flexible, individualized approach to meet individual needs. If we can personalize public services, then we can personalize our approach to equality.
>
> *Ibid.: 32–3*

As Jenny Phillimore (in press) discerns across many social policy fields, current provisions are inadequate because groupist methodologies fail to attend for the level of complexity associated with superdiversity. She recommends that better services could be shaped by always considering the intersection of clients' characteristics and the role of legal status in shaping their access to services.

Together with a pan-European research team, Phillimore has examined the challenges of social policy formation and delivery in an assortment of superdiverse contexts. "The complexity of populations, particularly in arrival zones and other intensely superdiverse areas," they observe, "frequently defy attempts at monitoring, mapping or classifying. Moreover, the interaction between different variables of difference shapes individuals' experiences and can result in social problems that are extremely complex" (Phillimore et al. 2021: 13–4). The team calls for a "superdiverse critical social policy" framework that would:

> account for the intersection of all variables that affect individuals' access to welfare. These may include sexuality, (dis)ability, migration status, age, education level, transnational connections, life stage, employment and more. Analysis would need to be multidimensional, focusing upon the intersections of multiple variables and the ways that they help us to account for the differences that make a difference to individuals and groups' access to, and outcomes from, social welfare. Such an analysis would help to identify the shortcomings of the welfare state and to begin to think about how it might be re-imagined in an era of superdiversity.
>
> *Ibid.: 40–1*

The British city of Birmingham, for one, has endeavoured to mainstream superdiversity and a complex approach to social categories into its policies and practices. In 2012 they published an official green paper on social inclusion entitled *Giving Hope, Changing Lives: Making Birmingham an Inclusive City* (Birmingham City Council 2012). One of the seven commitments that the City Council laid out, alongside supporting families and children out of poverty and empowering people to shape their neighbourhood, is to "embrace super-diversity." This entails a full recognition of the fact that there are now no less than 187 nationalities in the city, intersecting with tremendous status differences and needs, and presenting policymakers and politics with the task of rethinking the way they undertake governance. Consequently, "What is needed is a step change in the way that city leaders and citizens connect and communicate, the way plans for the city are shaped and the way that services are provided" (Ibid.: 30).

"Immigrant integration" is one key policy field in which, from international to national to municipal scales, policy approaches are often misguided and unsuccessful because of highly limited conceptions of the people and processes involved (see especially Favell 2022). One-size-fits-all models are rampant. Here, Scholten discerns that "A key concept such as 'integration' has not only been coproduced in close relationship with states seeking to control interethnic relations, it also reproduces state-centric ideas on societal integration that defy the complexification of migration and diversity" (2020: 197). In a telling way, this has been recognized by the Organization for Economic Co-operation and Development (OECD). To repeat this statement from Chapter 4, the OECD's *International Migration Outlook 2014* report includes a section entitled

"The growing diversity of the immigrant population poses additional challenges," in which it is stated that:

> Over the past two decades, as immigration flows have become more diverse across the OECD, integration has become a greater challenge. That diversity applies not only to immigrants' countries of origin and destination, but to their education levels and the categories to which they belong – labour, free movement, family reunification, and humanitarian. Migration category is the single largest determinant of integration outcomes...
>
> *Ibid.: 37*

Consequently, "As immigration flows grow more diverse in most countries, they must increasingly customise their integration policy instruments" (Ibid.: 106).

As discussed in Chapter 4, by way of a confluence of factors such as migration drivers, channels, and legal statuses, migrants usually arrive in a new destination already positioned in a system of sociocultural, economic, and political stratification. Further, migrants themselves engage a complex array of identities, interests, practices, and social networks. Within these complex arrays, a migrant newcomer can become an engaged participant in a new context … but not through a linear, unitary process, into a singular, national sociocultural entity – as much "integration" policy and debate imagines (Favell 2022). It is very difficult to dismantle "integration thinking" in the public sphere (Vertovec 2020a). Through better engagement with public debate, however, as social scientists we might be able to nudge policymakers into recognizing that, yes, a newcomer can become an engaged participant in a new context … but not just in one unilinear way. Ideally such nudging should be in the direction of fostering, instead, a kind of "complexity thinking" that is able to consider the presence of newcomers – indeed, all manners of "difference" – in terms of multidimensional and intersecting characteristics, non-groupist understandings, non-linear trajectories, diverse and overlapping networks and identities, complex modes of stratification and power differentials, and multiple modes of belonging.

This approach is advocated by Kelly McKowen and John Borneman (2020), among others, who encourage the view that to better understand and facilitate so-called "integration" processes, we need to emphasize firstly that social processes should be understood as uneven, fluctuating, intersubjective, and multiscalar. Secondly, identity categories should be appreciated as multiple, nested, and situational. This includes acknowledging affiliations within a local city and neighbourhood, associations, workplaces, religious congregations, and transnational affiliations in ways that decentre the nation-state. Such a conceptualization reflects an attempt to deflect a groupist understanding (while recognizing that the general people categorize in these terms of affiliations much of the time). Thirdly, belonging should be a notion open to understandings of the ways that newcomers bring meanings, goods, practices, and habits into their own performative repertoire, as co-productions refashioned together with long-standing residents.

This kind of call is certainly not new – indeed, it is evident in certain policy shifts concerning immigrants that were already identified by Rogers Brubaker back in 2001. This includes "a shift from thinking in *homogeneous* units to thinking in terms of *heterogeneous* units," "a general openness to cultural diversity," and "a shift from a *holistic* approach … to a *disaggregated* approach that discards the notion of assimilation as a single process, considers multiple reference populations, and envisions distinct processes occurring in different domains" (Brubaker 2001: 543–4, emphasis in original). In Germany, by way of example, such shifts have been evident in the emergence of policies and government approaches recognizing modes of incorporation with conscious reference to the diversity of immigrants – a policy framework described by Karen Schönwälder and Phil Triandafilopoulos (2016) as "the new differentialism." Such a view of immigrants and receiving contexts is also taken by a wide range of scholars invoking superdiversity as a device for describing new complexities of immigrant characteristics, social formations, identities and belongings, and patterns of incorporation (see Meissner and Vertovec 2015; Vertovec 2019; Meissner and Heil 2020). To be sure, it is known that many people among the general public already exercise such capacity for complex thinking about migration and diversity (Schönwälder et al. 2016). Instead of reproducing an "integration" narrative based on an idea of fixed groups proceeding along an imagined singular course of becoming part of a unitary national society, it would be far more realistic and just for policy and governance to be based on recognizing complex immigrants undertaking manifold paths to differentially incorporating into complex societies.

Representation

The need to acknowledge multiple and non-essentialist understandings of groups is not only, or even foremost, an issue concerning immigrants. It is significant for all members of today's complex societies by way of political representation, social justice, and the amelioration of structural inequality. This view was inherent to the political philosophy of Iris Marion Young. In place of the traditional political structures which aim to create a homogeneous public, she saw the need for a participatory democracy based on the idea of a "heterogeneous public." "Instead of a fictional contract," Young (1990: 116) wrote, "we require participatory structures in which actual people, with their geographical, ethnic, gender and occupational differences, assert their perspectives on social issues within institutions that encourage the representation of their distinct voices." Yet Young did not wish for the reification of simplistic "group" differentiated representation since she appreciated that all persons have multiple group identifications and affiliations. Young wrote:

> Oppression has often been perpetrated by a conceptualization of group difference in terms of unalterable essential natures that determine what group members deserve or are capable of, and that exclude groups so

entirely from one another that they have no similarities or overlapping attributes. To assert that it is possible to have social group difference without oppression, it is necessary to conceptualize groups in a much more relational and fluid fashion

Ibid.: 47

This view of group differentiation as multiple, cross-cutting, fluid, and shifting implies another critique of the model of the autonomous, unified self. In complex, highly differentiated societies like our own, all persons have multiple group identifications. The culture, perspective, and relations of privilege and oppression of these various groups, moreover, may not cohere. Thus individual persons, as constituted partly by their group affinities and relations, cannot be unified, themselves are heterogeneous and not necessarily constant.

Ibid.: 48

In these ways, and with regard to a variety of interests that an individual may harbour, "group differences cut across individual lives in a multiplicity of ways that can entail privilege and oppression for the same person in different respects" (Ibid.: 42).

It is evident, however, that certain categories of people are the sustained subjects of discrimination and inequality-based groups, or collections of people considered to share a category. Therefore, Young advocated that categorical groups should be recognized, but in terms of the structural inequalities they bear, not their assumed shared, substantive quality. She stressed that purported groups based on social categories possess no essential attributes, no common nature. People within a category may, or course, variously share aspects of affinities and social relations, social practices, similar experiences, shared histories, mutual social status, overlapping self-identities. Sometimes, too, they establish formally organized associations to support the development of a named group based on many of these mutual descriptions. Group categories indeed become reified in public discourse and activity, at times by many of their members. Yet these elements do not qualify as, nor need to be based upon, common essential attributes. The keys to groupness are facets of categorical identification based on social relations and social status, not some substantive, ontologically given attribute or catalogue of traits. "[W]hat makes a group a group is less some set of attributes its members share than the relations in which they stand to others" (Young 2000: 90).

Young's social or affinity-based understanding of groups as relational rather than substantial also underlines the fact that categorical group borders are not hard or fixed. Like many authors cited in Chapter 6, Young stressed that people inhabit multiple group-differentiated identities with much overlap and undecided borders:

The most important criticism of the idea of an essential group identity that members share, however, concerns its apparent denial of differentiation within and across groups. Everyone relates to a plurality of social groups; every social group has other social groups cutting across it. The group "men" is differentiated by class, race, religion, age, and so on; the group "Muslim" differentiated by gender, nationality, and so on.

Young (2000: 88)

Cross-cutting, partial identities characterize the social worlds of most people. Therefore, purported groups are inherently marked by their internal diversity. Within any group, people share some features and do not share others. Reviewing the work of Young, Adam Tebble explains: "This becomes clearer when it is realised that their internal diversity is itself dynamic; that is, cultural groups are themselves internally diverse in continually new ways – often because of interaction with other groups – and it is this fact that causes the group to constantly change its character" (2002: 271). The changing character of group categories is a significant dimension of what I have been describing as social complexity. For political representation and a general understanding of social categories, it is important to describe group-based discrimination, while recognizing "the ever-unfolding character of groups, without presupposing at any stage either their ontological stasis or internal homogeneity" (Ibid.: 272). As Tebble is quick to underline, however, it is difficult to achieve this balance.

One crucial way of moving toward this kind of democratic representation is to create a public or civic culture that inherently recognizes such open and overlapping social categories. In his call for a politics of "living identity through difference," Stuart Hall based the shift to such a political culture on establishing that "all of us are composed of multiple social identities, not one. That we are all complexly constructed through different categories, of different antagonisms, and these may have the effect of locating us socially in multiple positions of marginality and subordination, but which do not operate on us in exactly the same way" (1991: 57). Indeed, Hall concludes, a politics which is able to address people through multiple identities "is the only political game that the locals have left" (Ibid.: 59).

This kind of call is also at the heart of David Hollinger's (1995) notion of the "postethnic." For Hollinger:

> A postethnic perspective recognizes that most individuals live in many circles simultaneously and that the actual living of any individual life entails a shifting division of labor between the several "we's" of which the individual is a part. How much weight at what particular moments is assigned to the fact that one is Pennsylvania Dutch or Navajo relative to the weight assigned to the fact that one is also an American, a lawyer, a woman, a Republican, a Baptist, and a resident of Minneapolis?
> ... [T]he willingness of the postethnic to treat ethnic identity as a question rather than as a given also helps to distinguish the postethnic from the

unreconstructed ethnocentrist for whom ethnic identity is a more settled proposition, often entailing the accepted of ostensibly primordial ties.

Ibid.: 106–7

Within a postethnic perspective, according to Hollinger, one is cognizant of the value of group affiliations, but posed to resist a rigidification of social categories. Akin to certain approaches to the concept of cosmopolitanism and multiple subjectivity, the individual political subject is understood as member of a number of different categories simultaneously, navigating and mediating plural loyalties and interests (see Vertovec and Cohen 2002).

This does not negate, overlook, downplay, or deny people's identification with groups. As in Leslie McCall's (2005) concept of "intercategorical complexity," it advocates the provisional acceptance of categories in order to take full account of group-based inequalities. The approach acknowledges that categorical group-belonging is indeed psychologically, socially, and emotionally important to many people, but also that it is categorical group identification by others that serves to create, maintain, and reproduce inequalities. Yet in this perspective, identity and affiliation is not reduced to understandings of categorical groups that are unidimensional, preset, bounded, and unchanging. Individuals may well identify with a significant social category and derive a sense of belonging from it … but that is not all of a person. Public understanding needs to be nudged toward an ever present awareness of *category-plus* – that is, that individuals may be considered to be part of and identify with a social group, but they are more than that category, and the category is more than just them – more complex, more changing, and more varied. This kind of awareness is key to breaking down understandings of social categories based on singular affiliation, groupism, culturalism, racialization. It is also an understanding that fosters and extends high degrees of social identity complexity which, as presented in Chapter 6, has been demonstrated to carry a range of positive effects on attitudes and social interactions.

One, somewhat simple way to instil an awareness of category-plus is memorably suggested by Mari Matsuda:

> The way I try to understand the interconnection of all forms of subordination is through a method I call "ask the other question." When I see something that looks racist, I ask, "Where is the patriarchy in this?" When I see something that looks sexist, I ask, "Where is the heterosexism in this?" When I see something that looks homophobic, I ask, "Where are the class interests in this?" Working in coalition forces us to look for both the obvious and non-obvious relationships of domination, helping us to realize that no form of subordination ever stands alone.
>
> *1991: 1189*

Such a method significantly helps one resist simplifications by regularly and routinely asking what combination or alternative sets of categories or factors or processes might be in play concerning a specific situation, trend, or outcome. It is a kind of exercise in complex thinking that should lead to enhanced comprehension of political representation in contexts of superdiversity and social complexity – and even greater self-awareness along the lines of social identity complexity. Promoting such ordinary thought manoeuvres among and across publics should be part of the task of creating a robust civic culture in which multiple affiliations are represented.

Campaigns

Perhaps a greater awareness of the open, fluid, and porously bounded nature of social categories and multiple affiliations could be fostered by some kinds of public information campaigns (PICs). PICs generally refer to widely available communications typically aiming to shape beliefs, attitudes, social norms, and actual behaviours in (at least a segment of) the mass public (Weiss and Tschirhart 1994). Public health campaigns are probably the most familiar example of this genre. Through particular presentations of issues and solutions, PICs work through ideas, information, powerful images, argument, the heightening of attention, the arousal of emotion, and the invoking of values or moral obligations. Their goal is to change underlying knowledge, perceptions, interpretations, behaviour, and preferences.

PICs comprise messaging in broadcast media, outdoor advertising, print media, and social media posts. Evidence shows that media exposure works differently in different circumstances, on different media, for different people (Abroms and Maibach 2008; Jeong and Bae 2018). Regardless of media, it seems that conversations between two or more people, face to face, on the telephone or online, regarding a PIC topic have the most significant effects on knowledge, intention, and behaviour. Rather than just passively observing a PIC message, "when people are exposed to a media message of a public campaign, they will be more likely to talk with someone else about the campaign topic, and as a result of this interpersonal communication (rather than of direct exposure to media) increase their awareness, knowledge, attitude, intention, and behavior promoted in the campaign" (Solovei and van den Putte 2020: 597–8). So the ideal is: have a public campaign … and try to get people to talk about it.

Campaigners already well know that simply providing information about a topic is not enough to affect attitudes and behaviour. Similarly, "myth-busting" is often not only of limited effect, but it may backfire and increase the phenomenon address. Instead, many public campaigns also try to affect how the public thinks about an issue by changing the way that it is framed. To do this best, Heaven Crawley recommends, is to make sure "to have an understanding of the reasons why people think and behave in the way that they do" (2009: 4).

Some of these reasons are indicated by Natalia Banulescu-Bogdan (2022), who considers many of the ways that governments, advocate groups, and non-government organizations have created information campaigns to counter negative narratives about migrants. "In recent years, dozens if not hundreds of messaging campaigns have been launched to tackle xenophobia and present a more positive view of migration," she says. "These messages often attempt to promote solidarity, boost compassion, and/or elevate the contributions of newcomers" (Ibid.: 23). Information campaigns that seek to change people's minds may fall flat or backfire, meet with resistance, or actually serve to entrench xenophobic or racist views. Why might that be the case? Banulescu-Bogdan indicates four main challenges to changing public attitudes and shifting prevailing narratives. First, social media facilitates the ways that people can control their information environment, cherry-pick news and views, and reproduce echo chambers. It is easy to block out PICs. Second, existing beliefs and viewpoints are very difficult to change, as people can easily dismiss, discount, or ignore counter views. Third, people often consider new or alternative information that challenges their beliefs as exceptions to what they know, if not misinformation. And fourth, many beliefs and viewpoints are grounded in social identities (recalling the discussion of threat narratives in Chapter 5 of this book), which may also entail values, morals, and norms: information alone is highly unlikely to shift these. In times of great uncertainty when people are fearful of their own conditions, messages attempting to spark empathy or compassion for others may not be openly received. Further, Banulescu-Bogdan adds, campaigners should reflect on the danger of heightening group threat or grievance (and, I would add, groupist understanding) by inadvertently spotlighting categorical differences and hardening social boundaries.

While likely not avoiding all of these pitfalls, perhaps PICs designed to create a new public understanding of diversification and diversity can be different from those seeking to focus on instilling more positive attitudes towards migrants or specific social categories. That is, with an emphasis on the fluidity, flexibility, and multiplicity of everyone's social categories, all who see such campaigns might be prompted to reflect on how such messaging touches their own positions and identities. This might, hopefully, stimulate some heightening of social identity complexity amongst a span of the population. A few examples suggest what such broad messaging campaigns, rather ones than targeted on compassion for migrants, might draw from.

Many years ago, I conducted research on a set of relevant public campaigns or interventions in Berlin (Vertovec 1996). These were the years immediately after *die Wende*, the period of transformation following the fall of the Berlin Wall, when the city and country were subject of profound public reflections on their collective identities. I looked at initiatives by three institutions in Berlin, each explicitly intended to bring about a *Mentalitätsveränderung*, or conceptual reshaping concerning identities and ways of living together. These each differentially entailed attempts to deconstruct inflexible ideas of "Germanness" and to foster a sense of *Weltoffenheit*, literally "world-openness" meaning liberal-mindedness or cosmopolitanism. One initiative by a state agency was a billboard campaign, *Was ist Deutsch?* ("what is German?"), undertaken throughout the city at busstops and underground stations. With hundreds of often rhyming short questions, slang, in-jokes, and stereotypes (translated examples include: Sauerkraut? Love of home [*Heimat*]? Volkswagen? A Holiday house in Spain? Bureaucracy? Hitler salute? Cleaning?), the posters provocatively toyed with and joked about national identity. Another initiative was a "workshop of cultures" set up in a former brewery, which offered and curated a space for meeting others and creating new forms of cross-cutting expression. This facilitated exhibitions and conferences, neighbourhood projects, training (in skills such as photography and filmmaking), and a cafe. The third initiative was a radio station with eclectic mixes of world music, multilingual programming and disc jockeys with foreign accents. "We speak with an accent" was indeed one of the station's promotional slogans, meant to indicate the city's multiplicity or hybridity. The station pursued a strategy to provide good music and to "change something in the head of listeners" while not "pointing fingers," as one of its directors said (Ibid.: 392). The three initiates represent very different experiments, I would say, in publically promoting a shift from fixed social categories.

Some years later in 2010, the German Federal Anti-discrimination Office (Antidiskriminierungsstelle des Bundes) launched a comparable poster campaign. With the theme *Vielfalt statt Einfalt – Gemeinsam für Gleichbehandlung* ("Diversity instead of monotony/simplemindedness – together for equal treatment"), a variety posters concerning ethnicity, sexuality, age, religion, gender, and (dis) abledness were presented with slogans and photos of ordinary people. The campaign's purpose was to support a change of awareness, or *Bewusstseinswandel*, towards a discrimination-free culture in Germany (ADS 2010: 10). In order to gain attention and prompt new thinking and discussion, the meanings of the poster messages were intended "only to become clear at second glance" (*deren Botschaft sich erst auf den zweiten Blick erschließt*; Ibid.: 14). For example, one photo of a middle-aged woman in a headscarf was accompanied with the quotation "Discrimination? A born Turk, Muslim, headscarf-wearer, and woman. Any questions?" (*Diskriminierung? Gebürtige Türkin, Muslimin, Kopftuchträgerin and Frau... Noch Fragen?*). The posters were disseminated through an internet portal, in newsletters, brochures, and other publications, by visits to associations, universities, and schools (presentations were made at 1,500 schools), on billboards in public places including 4,000 at train stations and airports in 128 cities around the country, and over a million free postcards at cinemas, bars, and restaurants. Sometime later, the campaign was evaluated with a representative sample of citizens, 18% of whom recalled its messaging. This was followed by another, similar campaign by the federal office called *Kein Mensch passt in eine Schublade!* ("No one belongs in a drawer!"). Six different posters, each once more, respectively, devoted to a key category of social difference, showed a library-style card cabinet with drawers variously marked Turk, Russian, Roma or blind, learning challenged, deaf. These campaigns were highly innovative endeavours in trying to break down widespread understandings of social categories, stimulate discussions, and break about less discriminatory perspectives.

Another, highly effective public campaign strategy is through the use of personal stories (Crawley 2009), especially ones that allow an audience to come to their own conclusions (Banulescu-Bogdan 2022). A good example of a broadcast personal story of category multiplicity came not through a strategic public initiative, but by an independent, individual endeavour. "Before you call the cops" is a short video made and posted by actor and activist Tyler Merritt in 2018. Impact was initially modest, but the video gained notice and went viral on Twitter in May 2020 immediately after the death of George Floyd and the notorious incident of a White woman (named Amy Cooper) who made a 911 call about being threatened by a Black man (actually, a bird watcher) in Central Park. "Before you call the cops" has tallied hundreds of thousands of views on YouTube and was shown on the nationally televised talk show, Jimmy Kimmel Live. The YouTube video of that Kimmel screening has gained over three million views. The majority of comments to that video overwhelmingly show that viewers were emotionally moved.

In Merritt's video, he – a soft-spoken, somber, middle-aged Black man with a greying, short beard, and dreadlocks – speaks directly to camera in a dark studio for the entire 3 minutes, 10-second duration. "Before you call the cops, I just want you to know," he says, "the first thing that I did when I woke up this morning was yell at my alarm clock." He goes on to mention that: his parents were from the South but he was raised in Las Vegas and "that city still has my heart'; "I hate spiders. I'm a vegetarian – I'm not proud about it. I've done goat yoga – I'm really not proud about that"; he knows every word from the NWA's "Straight Outta Compton" album as well as from the musical "Oklahoma"; he doesn't like bananas, he's a Christian and teaches at a Sunday School; he's often asked if he's a Muslim – "I'm OK with that"; he doesn't hate Trump but prays for him; he has a multiracial family and his father is a veteran who taught him how to say "Yes, sir" and "yes, ma'am" to everyone he meets; he loves basketball and also hockey; he's never been to jail or owned a gun; "I hate that anyone at all might possibly be afraid of me"; "I'm a proud man … I'm a proud Black man"; "Does any of this really matter? No. I just wanted you to get to know me better … before you call the cops."

The viral uptake of the video in one way speaks for itself. It certainly was very widely shared and likely got people talking. A negative response to "Before you call the cops" was published in *New York Times Magazine* by author Thomas Chatterton Williams (2020). While acknowledging the power of counterintuitive reversal, Williams was critical that "the specific and acutely racialized fashion in which Merritt makes the case for his full-spectrum humanity is nonetheless rooted in a narrowing shorthand of hobbies, fears and tastes stereotypically understood to be not 'black.' 'Before You Call the Cops' is humanizing but only if mankind's default face remains white." He suggests that Merritt is addressing a White audience with pleas for White acceptance of Black humanity. "That all Americans might be worthy of the presumption of a total humanity, one that isn't ultimately classed or raced — that would be a truly radical vision." The *New York Times Magazine* online comments to Williams' critique tended to vehemently disagree. Several of these are worth examining since they demonstrate a pervasive desire to move beyond fixed social categories:

> Who defines Blackness anyway? Is there some type of monolithic intrinsic Blackness or Black culture? Are there boxes to check? No goat yoga or bird watching? Black dancers, once excluded, are helping reshape ballet

aesthetic. Isn't that a good thing? These young people in the streets. They seem comfortable in their skins and with each other. I think they are a refutation of many theories of race and community.

lin

Attempting to cross the divides of race or class with commonality has always felt forced to me. It is when people share their uniqueness that I feel most startled out of my prejudices or assumptions of class or race. I vote for permission to be weird, to share a non sequitur thought, a personal memory, to be exactly who you are, and not an emissary. In that sense the Tyler Merritt video spoke to me: I am white, allergic to yoga, I wake without an alarm, and I am a lapsed vegetarian. ...The combination of similarity and difference is what I crave: the freedom to be inconsistent, interesting, undogmatic, in other words simply human.

lj

But if it's binary all the time –"blacks" and "whites", then aren't we perpetuating the problem and overgeneralized labels? We can speak of age, gender, color, nationality, ability, etc. Many people have stories of oppression, and if we reduce problems to "white" culture that is just as ignorant – as if we are all the same! No more than "blacks". And what is blackness? Who defines that? How is this black man's story not "black" enough?

Michelle

most reader criticism could have been resolved with inclusion one more word in the title: 'perceived' whiteness, ie, We Need to Stop Measuring Black Lives by Their Perceived Whiteness. That one word clarifies the author's point that the issue is about how black people are perceived by whites. That is, that black people often have to go out of their way to show how similar they are to white people, and to somehow erase or smother their innate differences (those which are heavily scrutinized by many white people). Then, and only then, do their lives all of a sudden matter.

J

As a black person, I get tired of reading that "[Something] is so white" when X is something I do all the time and I know other black people who engage in the same activity. Activities of the middle class or simply anything not done by inner city, low-income blacks are often automatically tagged "white." Black people who enjoy these things are often mocked as "acting white" by blacks and whites.

Lifelong Reader

Whatever their grounds for doing so, ultimately they don't feel safe at first contact. But they can move past it, and Merritt is giving them reasons to. Real reasons, not visions. Usefully, these reasons are not rooted in an identity that insists on being exclusive—blackness—but still demanding. Instead, he defines an identity that is diffused over broad categories that come closer to a "universal" humanity. They don't exclude blackness, but they don't fixate on it either.

Mike in MA

Clearly, the public messaging represented by "Before you call the cops" got people talking and possibly raised awareness about categories and shifted some perspectives. Perhaps it might even stimulate some sense of social identity complexity.

In these ways, public campaigns or interventions can foster complexity thinking along the lines we have discussed in this book. Thomas Hylland Eriksen advocates the notion of "complexity as a way of seeing" (2015: 373). "If complexity is assumed from the outset," he says, "complex descriptions necessarily follow, rather than monocausal explanations or simplistic generalizations" (Ibid.). If institutions, agencies, and significant sectors of the media develop better practices for presenting and probing complex issues, it will mark an important step towards stimulating the public themselves to consider more comprehensively, and to ask more probing questions around, the phenomena we describe in this book as superdiversity and social complexity (Vertovec 2017).

This is not asking people to master complexity theory. The general public can be considered as already self-equipped with the conceptual and narrative tools to make their own, more wide-ranging assessments. With perhaps a little nudging, everyone should be able to recognize, seek out and themselves reason-through multi-factor information and interwoven processes. After all, multiple causes, processes, and outcomes aren't just matters in advanced Sociology. As described in Jason Mittell's (2015) book, *Complex TV*, every contemporary mini-series like "Game of Thrones" or "Breaking Bad" is inherently based on these. If mass audiences can follow an intricate mini-series with multi-threaded, intersecting storylines, and a variety of multidimensional characters, they already are equipped to draw connections between a range of facts and processes concerning migration, diversification, and everyday social categories, too.

Conclusion

Superdiversity is a concept calling attention to new patterns of social configuration surrounding migration-driven diversification. It points to the need to recognize, in social science and public policy, the changing intersections of multiple categories – most notably nationality, race/ethnicity, gender, age, legal status, religion, and language. The particular and highly variable ways in which these combine – in the course of migration, resettlement, and transnational practices – play a significant role in conditioning people social and spatial positions, opportunities and constraints, and multiple pathways of incorporation in societies and their social structures. Indeed, shifting patterns of superdiversity bear direct relation to social structures, especially modes of stratification. Most often, particular combinations of categories serve to position people dissimilarly in quite specific sites within hierarchical formations that have been called complex inequalities (McCall 2001; Walby 2007, 2009). Indeed, because several processes related to superdiversity are in play at various stages and scales with uncertain, emergent consequences, it makes some sense to consider these dynamics in terms of concepts concerning complexity.

This book has re-examined, recapitulated, and updated many views on the concept of superdiversity. It has also advocated that migration-driven superdiversity should be seen as part of general, broader complexification trends involving demography alongside certain dynamics regarding group-based and individual categories. The conceptual framework connecting these topics is based on the inherent, mutually conditioning relationship between social organization and multiple, intersecting social categories. Structures of social organization, especially systems of social, economic, spatial, and political stratification, are built upon social categories; social categories encapsulate and often reproduced social organization (cf. Vertovec 2021). The construction of, and narratives around, social categories is also what lies at the heart of most responses to processes of migration-driven diversification and changing saliencies around social difference. All of these phenomena are currently undergoing unprecedented complexification in terms of more elements (particularly newcomers), more variables, and new arrangements of interrelation and interdependence between the elements and variables. Moreover, the categories themselves are ever more complex in their combinations and reformulations. The reassessments entailed by changing categorical definition and salience affect individual understandings of one's own multiple categorical belonging, too. Together, the dynamics on each one of these levels – social organization, shared social categories, and individual identities – comprises what has been described here as social complexity.

Simplistic and reductionist views of social categories stand in the way of more comprehensive understandings of not only migration, but a range of issues affecting contemporary society in practically every society on Earth. They are the basis of much discrimination, hostility, conflict, and inequality. This is because social categories are all too often conceived of in terms of what we have discussed as singular affiliation, groupism, culturalism, racialization, and linguistic boundedness. These framings lead to a range of negative responses to processes of diversification and complexification, especially notions of threat to one's own professed categorical group. More widespread thinking about open and multiple social categories not only will bring benefits to social scientific theory and comprehension, but to wider, non-academic public views of groups and categorical identities. Amartya Sen has written that "The hope of harmony in the contemporary world lies to a great extent in a clearer understanding of the pluralities of human identity, and in the appreciation that they cut across each other and work against a sharp separation along one single hardened line of impenetrable division" (2006: xiv).

Drawing on the accumulated examination of superdiversity and social complexity developed in earlier chapters, this final chapter has roughly sketched some ideas for promoting a new public understanding of diversity and diversification based on the recognition of multiple categories and a general line of complexity thinking. Such an undertaking would importantly seek to prompt more ongoing consideration of the nature and work of multiple casual factors and ensuing processes, less simplistic categorization, and more awareness of complexities in many areas of social life. In keeping with this approach, I have suggested (largely following Peter Scholten and Jenny Phillimore) that in the policy and public sector there should be less singular targeting of groups, an abandonment of unilinear interpretations of processes such as "integration," and more openness and flexibility in responding to social changes and accepting uncertainty. Next, inspired by Iris Marion Young, a multiple category approach to political identities was advocated. A central feature of such an approach is not to deny the existence of groups, but to recognize that groups are important to see as the basis for many forms of discrimination. Yet is important to consider that groups are fundamentally based on positions deriving from social relations and stratification, not from fixed, unchanging, essential attributes. Along with this view is an emphasis on multiple social identities within groups. Along with the ideas of Stuart Hall, David Holllinger, and Leslie McCall, these insights support an approach to building a politics based less on groupism and more on the exercise of multiple identities and interests that accompany them. We need a complexity-based approach to categories that emphasizes category-plus. Self-identified groups are discernibly important to people, but they should not serve as the be-all and end-all of political subjectivity. There is always more, always a -*plus*, to categorical identifications. Constantly asking Mari Matsuda's "other question" is a useful way or remaining cognizant of this fact. A final component considered for developing a new public understanding of diversification and diversity, I submit, is through innovative Public Information Campaigns (PICs). In order to avoid many of the drawbacks of such campaigns, social complexity-related PICs should not endeavour to get people to like each other more, but to be more aware of the fluidity, flexibility, and multiplicity of everyone's social categories, including one's own. Such interventions might cultivate a heightened sense social identity complexity which, as social psychologists have shown (Chapter 6), potentially has far-reaching valuable effects on attitudes, social relations, and broader perspectives on society and social complexity. In an overarching sense, then, such PICs might help inculcate Thomas Hylland Eriksen's idea of "complexity as a way of seeing."

Directly and purposefully hindering any attempts to shift public understandings of complexity, superdiversity and multiple social categories are politicized framings, selective images, agitated discourses and threat narratives that seek to entrench worldviews based on singular affiliation, groupism, culturalism, racialization, and linguistic boundedness. These abound in right-wing broadcasting, social media, and populist politics. Because practically everyone is aware in some way of their multiple identities, even at rather low levels of social identity complexity, these can be illuminated and leveraged by PICs and other public debates to raise awareness of social complexity in ways that are non-threatening but self-evident. In this way, too, people might come to realize webs of affiliation linking others thought to be forever in a socially distant group. Boundary-crossing social contact is another phenomenon proven to have beneficial effects on social attitudes, and people may well be more prone to engage in contact if they can come to know and accept their actual or potential cross-cutting ties.

Tackling negative public rhetoric alone is insufficient for bringing about improved attitudes and social relations in contexts of superdiversity and social complexity. Social stratification and inequality are not only entrenched and reproduced by negative and simplistic categorizations, but may underpin them. That is, for instance: threat narratives are often successful because some people are already subject to precarious socio-economic conditions. It may not be hard to convince them, by way of zero-sum groupism, that the presence of some monolithic categorical other will inherently make things worse for themselves. In such cases, it is not surprising if antagonistic attitudes, hostile interactions, and reactionary political mobilization are bound to result. Skillfully crafted PICs for social complexity will need to take such situations strategically into account. In the first instance, notions of overlapping multiplicity and cross-cutting networks can weaken if not devastate viewpoints built on zero-sum perceptions.

Pervasive complexity thinking about superdiversity and social categories will not inherently or automatically bring about a diversity utopia (of collective het-erophilia, the broad valuation, or indeed sacralization of difference; Taguieff 2001: 26–7), but such a perspective might diminish the possibilities for diversity dystopias (largely based on heterophobia, or negative evaluations of all difference; Ibid.: 20–1). Inequality – in terms of social status, economic resources, symbolic representation, and political voice – remains both the key and the outcome concerning future developments. Migration, superdiversity, and social complexity are all fundamentally shaped and conditioned by prevailing inequalities. The dynamics within each of these conjoined topics can either manifest, shift, or altogether challenge inequalities. As demographic diversification continues apace, the durability of categorical inequalities (Tilly 1998; Massey 2007; Castañeda 2017) might productively be assuaged in part by more complex perceptions of said categories. As considered earlier in this book, global migration-driven diversification and resultant forms of superdiversity are set to continue, but increasingly affected by modes and patterns entangled with climate change. Unless numerous policies on scales from international to national and municipal are rethought by way of the categories they address (or create), future superdiversities will likely be marked by new as well as engrained modes of complex inequality.

As the wonderful Michael Palin (2003) has observed, "Contrary to what the politicians and religious leaders would like us to believe, the world won't be made safer by creating barriers between people. ... Armageddon is not around the corner. This is only what the people of violence want us to believe. The complexity and diversity of the world is the hope for the future." This should indeed be our desired orientation. However, it can only be achieved, particularly in ways that might mitigate new or entrenched inequalities, through fair modes of and opportunities for migration and a greater awareness of the multiplicities of social categories, superdiversity, and social complexity.

References

Abroms, L. C. and E. W. Maibach 2008. "The effectiveness of mass communication to change public behaviour," *Annual Review of Public Health* 29: 219–34 https://doi.org/10.1146/annurev.publhealth.29.020907.090824

ADS (Antidiskriminierungsstelle des Bundes) 2010. *Bericht über Schwerpunkte und Arbeit der Antidiskriminierungsstelle des Bundes*, Berlin: Antidiskriminierungsstelle des Bundes

Baldassarri, D. and S. E. Page 2021. "The emergence and perils of polarization," *Proceedings of the National Academy of Sciences* 118(50) https://doi.org/10.1073/pnas.2116863118

Banulescu-Bogdan, N. 2022. "From fear to solidarity: The difficulty in shifting public narratives about refugees," Migration Policy Institute Reports, Washington D. C.

Bijak, J. and M. Czaika 2020. "Assessing uncertain migration futures: A typology of the unknown," University of Southampton and Danube University Krems QuantMig Project Deliverable D1.1, Southampton/Krems

Birmingham City Council 2012. *Giving Hope, Changing Lives: Birmingham Social Inclusion Process*. Green paper Birmingham City Council, Birmingham

Bradby, H., G. Green, C. Davison and K. Krause 2017. "Is superdiversity a useful concept in European medical sociology?" *Frontiers in Sociology* 1(17): 1–18 https://doi.org/10.3389/fsoc.2016.00017

Brubaker, R. 2001. "The return of assimilation? Changing perspectives on immigration and its sequels in France, Germany, and the United States," *Ethnic and Racial Studies* 24(4): 531–48 https://doi.org/10.1080/01419870120049770

Cantle, T. 2016. "The case for interculturalism, plural identities and cohesion," in *Multiculturalism and Interculturalism*, N. Meer et al. (eds.), Edinburgh: Edinburgh University Press, pp.133–57

Cardinal, A. 2022. "Superdiversity: An audience analysis praxis for enacting social justice in technical communication," *Technical Communication Quarterly* https://doi.org/10.1080/10572252.2022.2056637

Castañeda, E. (Ed.) 2017. *Immigration and Categorical Inequality: Migration to the City and the Birth of Race and Ethnicity*, New York: Routledge https://doi.org/10.4324/9781315100371

Castles, S., H. de Haas and M. Miller 2014. *The Age of Migration: International Population Movements in the Modern World*, New York: The Guildford Press, 5th edn.

Crawley, H. 2009. *Understanding and Changing Public Attitudes: A Review of Existing Evidence from Public Information and Communication Campaigns*, Swansea: Centre for Migration Policy Research

Culley, L. 2014. "Nursing and super-diversity," *Journal of Research in Nursing* 19(6): 453–55 https://doi.org/10.1177/1744987114548755

Eriksen, T. H. 2015. "Cultural complexity," in *Routledge International Handbook of Diversity Studies*, S. Vertovec (ed.), London and New York: Routledge, pp. 371–8 https://doi.org/10.4324/9781315747224

Fanshawe, S. and D. Sriskandarajah 2010. *You Can't Put Me in a Box: Super-Diversity and the End of Identity Politics in Britain*, London: Institute for Public Policy Research

Favell, A. 2022. *The Integration Nation: Immigration and Colonial Power in Liberal Democracies*, Cambridge: Polity

Geyer, R. and S. Rihani 2012. *Complexity and Public Policy: A New Approach to 21st Century Politics, Policy and Society*, London: Routledge https://doi.org/10.4324/9780203856925

Gogolin, I. 2011. "The challenge of super diversity for education in Europe," *Education Inquiry* 2(2): 239–49 https://doi.org/10.3402/edui.v2i2.21976

Gross, B. 2020. "Education for a common identity in times of superdiversity? The example of linguistic diversity and identity," *Pedagogia e Vita* 78: 124–34

Guo, S. 2010. "Migration and communities: Challenges and opportunities for lifelong learning," *International Journal of Lifelong Education* 29(4): 437–47 https://doi.org/10.1080/02601370.2010.488806

Hall, S. 1991. "Old and new identities, old and new ethnicities," in *Culture, Globalization and the World-System*, A. D. King (ed.), Basingstoke: Macmillan, pp. 41–68 https://doi.org/10.1007/978-1-349-11902-8_3

Hall, S. 1993. "Culture, community, nation," *Cultural Studies* 7(3): 349–63 https://doi.org/10.1080/09502389300490251

Hewstone, M., N. Tausch, J. Hughes and E. Cairns 2007. "Identity, ethnic diversity and community cohesion," in *Identity, Ethnic Diversity and Community Cohesion*, M. Wetherall et al. (eds.), Los Angeles: Sage, pp. 102–12 https://doi.org/10.4135/9781446216071.n9

Hollinger, D. 1995. *Postethnic America: Beyond Multiculturalism*, New York: Basic Books

Jeong, M. and R. E. Bae 2018. "The effect of campaign-generated interpersonal communication on campaign-targeted health outcomes: A meta-analysis," *Health Communication* 33(8): 988–1003 https://doi.org/10.1080/10410236.2017.1331184

Kirwan, G. 2022. "Superdiversity re-imagined: Applying superdiversity theory to research beyond migration studies," *Current Sociology* 70(2): 192–209 https://doi.org/10.1177/0011392120983346

Klijn, E. H. and J. F. Koppenjan 2014. "Complexity in governance network theory," *Complexity, Governance & Networks* 1(1): 61–70 https://doi.org/10.7564/14-cgn8

Leitão Ferreira, J. M. 2021. "Children's life in superdiversity contexts: Impacts on the construction of a children's citizenship – The Portuguese case," *Current Sociology* https://doi.org/10.1177/0011392120983340

Li, G., J. Anderson, J. Hare and M. McTavish 2021. *Superdiversity and Teacher Education: Supporting Teachers in Working with Culturally, Linguistically and Racially Diverse Students, Families and Communities*, London: Routledge https://doi.org/10.4324/9781003038887

Massey, D. S. 2007. *Categorically Unequal: The American Stratification System*, New York: Russell Sage

Matsuda, M. J. 1991. "Beside my sister, facing the enemy: Legal theory out of coalition," *Stanford Law Review* 43(6): 1183–92 https://doi.org/10.2307/1229035

McCall, L. 2001. *Complex Inequality: Gender, Class and Race in the New Economy*, London: Routledge https://doi.org/10.4324/9780203902455

McCall, L. 2005. "The complexity of intersectionality," *Signs* 30(3): 1771–800 https://doi.org/10.1086/426800

McKowen, K. and J. Borneman 2020. "Digesting difference: Migrants, refugees, and incorporation in Europe," in *Digesting Difference*, K. McKowen and J. Borneman (eds.), Cham: Palgrave Macmillan, pp. 1–27 https://doi.org/10.1007/978-3-030-49598-5_1

McLennan, G. 1995. *Pluralism*, Buckingham: Open University Press

Meissner, F. and T. Heil 2020. "Deromanticising integration: On the importance of convivial disintegration," *Migration Studies* https://doi.org/10.1093/migration/mnz056

Meissner, F. and S. Vertovec 2015. "Comparing super-diversity," *Ethnic and Racial Studies* 38(4): 541–55 https://doi.org/10.1080/01419870.2015.980295

Mittell, J. 2015. *Complex TV: The Poetics of Contemporary Television Storytelling*, New York: New York University Press

Ní Shé, É. and R. Joye 2018. "The health systems workforce in an era of globalised super-diversity: Exploring the global care chain landscape in Ireland," in *Work and Identity*, S. Werth and C. Bronlow (eds.), Cham: Palgrave Macmillan, pp. 101–16 https://doi.org/10.1007/978-3-319-73936-6_8

OECD (Organization for Economic Co-operation and Development) 2014. *International Migration Outlook 2014*, Paris: OECD Publishing

Palin, M. 2003. "Letter from London," Palin's Travels 18 September http://palinstravels.co.uk/static-51?topic=1752&forum=12

Parekh, B. 2008. *A New Politics of Identity: Political Principles for an Interdependent World*, Basingstoke: Macmillan

Parekh, B. and H. Bhabha 1989. "Identities on parade," *Marxism Today*, June, pp. 24–9

Phillimore, J. 2010. "Approaches to health provision in the age of super-diversity: Accessing the NHS in Britain's most diverse city," *Critical Social Policy* 31(1): 5–29 https://doi.org/10.1177/0261018310385437

Phillimore, J. In press. "Social policy and superdiversity: Engaging with structure and agency," in *The Oxford Handbook of Superdiversity*, F. Meissner, N. Sigona and S. Vertovec (eds.), Oxford: Oxford University Press

Phillimore, J., H. Bradby, T. Brand, B. Padilla and S. Pemberton 2021. *Exploring Welfare Bricolage in Europe's Superdiverse Neighbourhoods*, London: Routledge https://doi.org/10.4324/9781003111504

Pratt, M.-L. 2003. "Building a new public idea about language," *Profession* 2003: 110–9 https://doi.org/10.1632/074069503x85472

Scholten, P. 2020. *Mainstreaming versus Alienation: A Complexity Approach to the Governance of Migration and Diversity*, Basingstoke: Palgrave Macmillan https://doi.org/10.1007/978-3-030-42238-7

Scholten, P. In press. "The governance of superdiversity: A complexity perspective," in *The Oxford Handbook of Superdiversity*, F. Meissner, N. Sigona and S. Vertovec (eds.), Oxford: Oxford: Oxford University Press

Schönwälder, S., S. Petermann, J. Hüttermann, S. Vertovec, M. Hewstone, D. Stolle, K. Schmid and T. Schmitt 2016. *Diversity and Contact: Immigration and Social Interaction in German Cities*, Basingstoke: Palgrave Macmillan https://doi.org/10.1057/978-1-137-58603-2

Schönwälder, K. and T. Triandafilopoulos 2016. "The new differentialism: Responses to immigrant diversity in Germany," *German Politics* 25(3): 366–80 https://doi.org/10.1080/09644008.2016.1194397

Sen, A. 2006. *Identity and Violence: The Illusion of Destiny*, London: Allen Lane

Sepulveda, L., S. Syrett and F. Lyon 2011. "Population superdiversity and new migrant enterprise: The case of London," *Entrepreneurship & Regional Development* 23(7–8): 469–97 https://doi.org/10.1080/08985620903420211

Solovei, A. and B. van den Putte 2020. "The effects of five public information campaigns: The role of interpersonal communication," *Communications* 45(s1): 586–602 https://doi.org/10.1515/commun-2020-2089

Stirling, A. 2010. "Keep it complex," *Nature* 468(7327): 1029–31 https://doi.org/10.1038/4681029a

Stirling, A. 2016. "Knowing doing governing: Realizing heterodyne democracies," in *Knowing Governance*, J. P. Voß and R. Freeman (eds.), London: Palgrave Macmillan, pp. 259–89

Taguieff, P.-A. 2001. *The Force of Prejudice: On Racism and Its Doubles*, Minneapolis, MN: University of Minnesota Press

Taylor, C. 2007. *Modern Social Imaginaries*, Durham, NC: Duke University Press

Tebble, A. J. 2002. "What is the politics of difference?" *Political Theory* 30(2): 259–81 https://doi.org/10.1177/0090591702030002004

Tilly, C. 1998. *Durable Inequality*, Berkeley, CA: University California Press

Tokita, C. K., A. M. Guess and C. E. Tarnita 2021. "Polarized information ecosystems can reorganize social networks via information cascades," *Proceedings of the National Academy of Sciences* 118(50): 1–9, https://doi.org/10.1073/pnas.2102147118

van Ewijk, H. 2018. *Complexity and Social Work*, London: Routledge https://doi.org/10.4324/9781315109275

Vertovec, S. 1996. "Berlin Multikulti: Germany, 'foreigners' and 'world-openness'," *Journal of Ethnic and Migration Studies* 22(3): 381–99 https://doi.org/10.1080/1369183x.1996.9976546

Vertovec, S. 2012. "'Diversity' and the social imaginary," *Archives Européennes de Sociologie/ European Journal of Sociology* 53(3): 287–312 https://doi.org/10.1017/s000397561200015x

Vertovec, S. 2015a. "Introduction: Formulating diversity studies," in *Routledge International Handbook of Diversity Studies*, S. Vertovec (ed.), London and New York: Routledge, pp. 1–20 https://doi.org/10.4324/9781315747224

Vertovec, S. 2015b. "Introduction: Migration, cities, diversities 'old' and 'new'," in *Diversities Old and New*, S. Vertovec (ed.), Basingstoke: Palgrave Macmillan, pp. 1–20 https://doi.org/10.1057/9781137495488_1

Vertovec, S. 2017. "Mooring, migration milieus and complex explanation," *Ethnic and Racial Studies* 40(9): 1574–81 https://doi.org/10.1080/01419870.2017.1308534

Vertovec, S. 2019. "Talking around super-diversity," *Ethnic and Racial Studies* 42: 125–39 https://doi.org/10.1080/01419870.2017.1406128

Vertovec, S. 2020a. "Afterword: "The work of 'integration'," in *Digesting Difference*, K. McKowen and J. Borneman (eds.), Cham: Palgrave Macmillan, pp. 251–66 https://doi.org/10.1007/978-3-030-49598-5_12

Vertovec, S. 2020b. "Low-skilled migrants after Covid19: Singapore futures?" COMPAS Coronavirus and Mobility Forum blog, https://www.compas.ox.ac.uk/2020/low-skilled-migrants-after-covid-19-singapore-futures/

Vertovec, S. 2021. "The social organization of difference," *Ethnic and Racial Studies* 44(8): 1273–95 https://doi.org/10.1080/01419870.2021.1884733

Vertovec, S. and R. Cohen 2002. "Introduction: Conceiving cosmopolitanism," in *Conceiving Cosmopolitanism*, S. Vertovec and R. Cohen (eds.), Oxford: Oxford University Press, pp. 1–22

Vieru, M. 2017. "Integration in host societies and development: Adapting policy approaches to the new mobility," World Bank, *KNOMAD Policy Brief* 7, Washington, D. C.

Walby, S. 2007. "Complexity theory, systems theory, and multiple intersecting social inequalities," *Philosophy of the Social Sciences* 37(4): 449–70 https://doi.org/10.1177/0048393107307663

Walby, S. 2009. *Globalization & Inequalities: Complexity and Contested Modernities*, London: Sage https://doi.org/10.4135/9781446269145

Walters, G. 2015. "The challenges of superdiversity for social housing," Institute for Research into Superdiversity (IRiS) Working Paper Series No. 5, Birmingham

Weiss, J. A. and M. Tschirhart 1994. "Public information campaigns as policy instruments," *Journal of Policy Analysis and Management* 13(1): 82–119 https://doi.org/10.2307/3325092

Williams, T. C. 2020. "We need to stop measuring Black lives by their Whiteness," *The New York Times Magazine* 18 June

Young, I. M. 1990. *Justice and the Politics of Difference*, Princeton: Princeton University Press

Young, I. M. 2000. *Inclusion and Democracy*, Oxford: Oxford University Press

INDEX

Note: *Italicised* and **bold** page numbers refer to figures and tables, respectively.